D1600952

THE STORY

OF OUR LIVES

THE STORY OF OUR LIVES

OF OUR LIVES

An Epic Quest for
the Soul of Our Tradition

An in-depth elucidation of "The Lost Princess"
A Tale by Rebbe Nachman of Breslov

YAAKOV KLEIN

A PROJECT OF THE

LOST
PRINCESS
INITIATIVE

LPITorah.org

Typesetting: Eden Chachamtzedek

DISTRIBUTED BY:
Feldheim Publishers
POB 43163 / Jerusalem, Israel
208 Airport Executive Park
Nanuet, NY 10954
www.feldheim.com

DISTRIBUTED IN EUROPE BY:
Lehmanns
+44-0-191-430-0333
info@lehmanns.co.uk
www.lehmanns.co.uk

DISTRIBUTED IN AUSTRALIA BY:
Golds World of Judaica
+613 95278775
info@golds.com.au
www.golds.com.au

Printed in Israel

For

Shmuel Shmelke

May the lessons in this book serve as
eternal guideposts along your journey
to the Lost Princess of connection.

Hold fast to the tzaddikim,
their teachings will illuminate your path.

With boundless love, and
a prayer that I may one day
merit to deserve the
title you granted me.

Abba

Dedicated to our children,

Emma, Sam, Jordan, Laura, and Julia

You are the light of our lives.

Our blessing to you is that you should always see success in whatever you seek to accomplish, and that your quest for the Lost Princess of inspired living be a fruitful and meaningful one.

May the awesome merit of
Rebbe Nachman ben Feiga
and the light of his Torah revelations
stand by you always, and may Hashem
continue to shower His love, light, and kindness
upon you for many happy, healthy,
and fulfilling years to come.

Yoni and Allison Bellows

Dedicated to the exalted memory of two giants
of spirit whose legacy lives on in the flaming souls
of those who have been inspired by their example of
what it means to love Hashem, to love the Torah,
and to love the Jewish nation:

Rebbe Yeshayah *zy"a*
ben **Reb Moshe Steiner** of Kerestir

רבי **ישעיה** בן רבי **משה שטיינר**

ג׳ באייר תרפ״ה

Rebbe Kalonymus Kalman *Hy"d*
ben **Reb Elimelech Shapira** of Piaseczna

רבי **קלונימוס קלמיש** בן רבי **אלימלך שפירא**

ה׳ בחשוון תש״ד

Reb Shaye'le taught the world how
to love every Jew with all of our heart and soul.

The Piaseczner taught the world how to hold
on to faith in the midst of the void.

These teachings, saturated with the deepest
mesiras nefesh, will hold us up until Mashiach arrives.

May our children, Shimon, Miriam, and Elimelech,
walk in the footesteps of these angels among men.

Yitzchok Menachem & Gitty Haas

ADVANCE PRAISE FOR
THE STORY OF OUR LIVES

(Quotes presented in the order received)

The Story of Our Lives is bursting with inspiration, depth, and practical guidance. In this important work, R' Yaakov Klein delves deeply into the teachings of the *tzaddikim* and derives core principles to illuminate the path of the spiritual seeker.

RABBI DOV BER COHEN
EDUCATOR AND AUTHOR OF "MASTERING LIFE:
A UNIQUE GUIDEBOOK TO JEWISH ENLIGHTENMENT"

Reb Yaakov has written a beautiful, deep, and soulful book. A book filled with *ga'aguim* (yearnings) for *deveikus* which inspires readers to delve deeper in their *avodas Hashem.*

RABBI DOV BER PINSON

I am impressed by the special outpouring of your heart toward Breslover Chassidus. Your words uplift and delight. They are sourced in the tradition of the *mashpi'im*, yet one can easily sense the *"Anochi"* of *Ana nafshi kesavis yehavis* — "I have written my soul down and given it to you"; the "path to the side," in the language of the story's imagery...

RABBI BEZALEL NAOR
AUTHOR, LECTURER, AND FOUNDER OF OROT INC.

We are told that the tzaddikim of past paved the way for us. We are told they thought about each person's struggle and hardship in this world. When learning the heartfelt work of my dear *chaver* R' Yaakov Klein, one is able to sense the unimaginable care, love and concern Rebbe Nachman *ztz"l* had for each and every one of us. This work provides all the lost princesses of the world a tangible formula to be able to detect home once again. *Ashrei Ha'am Shekacha Lo!*

RABBI SHLOMO KATZ
WORLD RENOWNED MUSICIAN, MASHPIA.
AUTHOR OF "THE SOUL OF JERUSALEM,"
"REBBE NACHMAN'S SOUL," AND MANY OTHER WORKS.

LETTER OF RECOMMENDATION
"THE STORY OF OUR LIVES"

The great Chassidic leaders were called by the Hebrew title *"Admor."* This is generally rendered as "Master." Truly, Rebbe Nachman of Breslov was a great charismatic leader — a great Master. His impact was so powerful that still today, more than two hundred years since his passing, tens of thousands of adherents revere his memory. This is not due simply to his personality alone, as, for more than two hundred years, people haven't had the ability to meet him personally. Rather, he was the Master of Jewish lore, the Master of the inner light. His remarkable works *Likutei Moharan* and *Sefer HaMiddos* attest to this.

Another facet of Rebbe Nachman's genius was his treatment of parables. The *Midrash Shir HaShirim* (1:8) teaches, "Do not underestimate the value of parables. They are similar to the handles of a heavy crate. By lifting the handles, you thereby have control of the whole crate."

R' Yaakov Klein has done a great service by unraveling the first of Rebbe Nachman's parables. Part of this great feat is his drawing upon parallels from the teachings of other great Torah giants. We are indebted to him for rendering these great treasures to the English-reading public. These vast stores of wisdom will be to the benefit of all. From these springs, many will imbibe wisdom.

Signed,

Rabbi Moshe Zuriel
AUTHOR OF OTZROT RAV KOOK
AND LEKET PIRUSHEI AGGADDA
FORMER MASHGIACH OF YESHIVAT SHA'ALVIM

בס"ד

Rav Judah Mischel
Mashpiah

אור לי"א טבת תש"פ

With **The Story of Our Lives**, R' Yaakov Klein יי׳ has revealed a new and exciting pathway toward understanding the thought and teachings of Rabbeinu, Rebbe Nachman of Breslov זיע״א, prayerfully interpreting the מעשה מאבידת בת מלך, The Lost Princess, unlocking so much of its beauty, meaning and depth. In this incredible commentary, filled with heartful insight and creativity, R' Yaakov has *"turned Torah into Tefillah"*, transforming lofty and abstract content into a work of deep and personal contact.

Reb Nosson of Breslov זיע׳ qualifies the analysis and frames our study of Rebbe Nachman's stories in his 'Second Introduction' to *Sipurei Ma'asios*:

"הָרוֹצֶה לְהִסְתַּכֵּל בְּאֵלוּ הַמַּעֲשִׂיוֹת בְּעַיִן הָאֱמֶת לַאֲמִתּוֹ לְהָבִין וּלְהַשְׂכִּיל בָּהֶם לִמְצֹא בָהֶם דְּבָרִים נִפְלָאִים וְנוֹרָאִים, וְאִם אָמְנָם אִי אַפְשָׁר לָבוֹא עַד תְּכוּנָתָם לְהָבִין כָּל קִשּׁוּר הַמַּעֲשֶׂה מֵרֹאשָׁהּ לְסוֹפָהּ עִם כָּל זֶה יָבִין מְעַט מְזְעֵיר מֵהֶם וְיֶעֱרַב לְנַפְשׁוֹ מְאֹד"

"One can learn these stories with an attempt to understand them in truth, plumb their depths and discover wonderous, awesome concepts...Admittedly, though it may be impossible to grasp the full meaning of these stories from beginning to end, nonetheless, even just a small amount of understanding is very sweet for the soul..."

R' Yaakov's masterpiece is indeed *"very sweet for the soul"* and brings us that much closer, personally and collectively, to reuniting the *Bas Melech*, the soul of the Jewish Nation with The King, our Father in Heaven. An erudite *peirush* filled with positivity and optimism, R' Yaakov's teachings give voice to our spiritual yearning.

This wonderful *sefer* illuminates and encourages, strengthens and lifts-up our searching generation, so ready for the Return of the Lost Princess.

So may it be, and may we merit to continue to experience and share in the complete Redemption, speedily in our days.

בכבוד וידידות,
judah mischel

מוצאי עשרה בטבת תש"פ
יומא דהלולא של מוהרנ"ת זי"ע
בין צרעה ובין אשתאול

אַל־תִּשְׂמְחִי אֹיַבְתִּי לִי
כִּי נָפַלְתִּי קָמְתִּי
כִּי־אֵשֵׁב בַּחֹשֶׁךְ
ה' אוֹר לִי

Do not rejoice over me, my enemy.
For though I have fallen, I will yet rise,
and though I sit in darkness,
Hashem is a light for me.

MICHAH 7:8

אִלּוּלֵי שֶׁיָּשַׁבְתִּי בַּחֹשֶׁךְ
לֹא הָיָה אוֹר לִי

Had I not sat in darkness,
it would not have been light for me.

MIDRASH TEHILLIM 5:1

CONTENTS

PART I

DUSK

CHAPTER 1

Searching for the Fire of Youth *21*

CHAPTER 2

Our Tale Begins *35*

PART III

DAWN

APPENDICES

FOREWORD

IN YOUR HANDS, you hold a storybook. More accurately, you hold a remarkable book about our story — yours and mine.

Allow me to begin with a story.

Before the Baal Shem Tov passed away, he appointed his closest disciples to serve as his personal messengers to the world. Each would use his distinct talent as a means of carrying forth the light and fire of their master. One disciple, Reb Yaakov, was disappointed to have been designated as the Rebbe's official storyteller. He would travel from town to town, from village to village, sharing his memories of the Rebbe. Although he felt that he had more to offer, he embarked on his life's mission with simple faith and surrender. Wherever he would go, he would tell stories of the Baal Shem Tov and would be rewarded with a few rubles for his efforts.

Once, he received an invitation from a wealthy Jew in Vitebsk to spend a Shabbos as a "scholar-in-residence," sharing tales and recollections of the tzaddik. He was promised a considerable "honorarium" in return. Reb Yaakov was welcomed with great excitement and anticipation. However, much to his dismay, he simply could not remember a single story. Throughout the entire Shabbos the crowds continually returned home disappointed. Ashamed, Reb Yaakov was preparing to leave after Shabbos when suddenly he remembered a long-forgotten tale which he hurriedly shared with his host.

"Once, many years ago, the Baal Shem Tov took me along with a number of chassidim to a distant town on the night of

December 25 when the local villagers gathered together for the holiday celebration. It was dangerous for any Jew to be seen that night, but the Baal Shem Tov instructed me to go and tell the bishop that Reb Yisrael ben Reb Eliezer would like to speak with him. Somehow, I made my way to the podium where the bishop was about to address the crowd and told the bishop that the Baal Shem Tov wanted to speak with him. The priest turned pale and began to tremble. He asked me if he could come back a bit later. When I returned to the Baal Shem Tov, he told me that the bishop must come immediately. I relayed this message, and the bishop excused himself and went with me to the Rebbe. The bishop and the Baal Shem Tov spent a few hours talking together, after which the bishop emerged dressed as a Jew. After that, he mysteriously disappeared."

As he listened to this tale, Reb Yaakov's host began to cry. He looked directly at Reb Yaakov and asked him, "Don't you recognize me? I am the bishop!"

The host told Reb Yaakov, "I am a Jew, born to a long line of illustrious *talmidei chachamim*. But over time I left Yiddishkeit, converted, and eventually became a bishop. That night, the Baal Shem Tov brought me back and sent me to spend years in *galus* in order to repair the damage done over my 'years away.' When I asked the Baal Shem Tov, 'How long will I have to wander? When will I know that I'm finally forgiven?' he gave me a sign. He told me that if someone were to come and tell me my story, then I would know that my time had come, and that my *teshuvah* was complete. When I first saw you, I was overjoyed. I remembered you. When I saw that you couldn't recall the story, I davened with all my heart until Hashem opened your heart to remember."

Now, my friends, you are holding *The Lost Princess* in your hands. Around forty-five years ago, a *yeshivah bachur* from Queens was invited by the *shamash* of his shul to search through some bags of *shaimos* and see if there was anything he wished to salvage. That day I found an old Yiddish version of *The Lost Princess*. I had heard many times, "Yes, Rebbe Nachman was a great tzaddik, but his teachings are not for everyone." Despite that, or perhaps because of it, I ventured ahead and read the tale. I was completely mesmerized. I, too, began to cry: How did Rebbe Nachman know? Who could have told him my story 150 years before I was born?

In 1806, shortly before his illness, Rebbe Nachman started telling the stories, the *Sippurei Maasios*.

> I tried to bring you back to Hashem, through my talks and Torah teachings, but they haven't worked. So now I must tell you stories...

The first of his stories is *The Lost Princess*.

> My lessons are like entering a palace with many entrances, halls, and chambers. All are of awesome beauty, with story upon story, each which is its own unique style. No sooner do you enter a room, fascinated by the novelty of the design, that you notice an opening leading to another room. And all of the rooms are linked in this way, with hidden entrances in every room, leading to another story and another room. Everything is linked and bound to everything else with profound wisdom and beauty.

Here enters our guide, a beautiful young man with profound wisdom way beyond his years, R' Yaakov Shalom Klein. Rebbe Nachman once told Reb Nosson, "I am a beautiful tree with many wondrous branches." I truly believe that Yaakov Shalom is one of those wondrous branches who has been blessed not only with the "pen of an expert scribe" (*Tehillim* 45:2), but the unique ability to unveil the burning relevance of *The Lost Princess*, to help us find our way through the rooms and hidden entrances leading to the Lost Princess within ourselves. This book is not merely a commentary on Rebbe Nachman's famous tale. It is a practical manual that can and must be disseminated and used to wake up our generation.

I recently had the pleasure of meeting with a very distinguished group of *mechanchim* and *mechanchos*, all of whom expressed the great challenges they were experiencing in their effort to reach their students, to inspire and share with them their own love of Yiddishkeit. I told them of a young woman I know who recently took a teaching position in a girl's high school. These tenth graders seemed completely disinterested and unimpressed with the fine curriculum that was being thrown their way. Many of their teachers had already written them off as potential "OTD" (off the *derech*) candidates who were impossible to motivate and lacked any interest in Yiddishkeit. This "rookie" handed each girl a copy of *The Lost Princess* and the girls have been studying it for the past six months. A literal revolution has taken place in their davening and overall attitude towards Hashem. They are expressing the simple joy of having the privilege to join the viceroy along his journey to find the missing princess, the soul, the faith and happiness that we are all looking for. In short, for the first time in their lives, someone is telling them their own story. Having heard their own "once upon a time" they are excited to revisit Chumash and Rashi, Halacha and Navi. *The Story of Our Lives* is not meant in any way to substitute, *chas v'shalom*, for a regular regimen of Torah study. It simply has the remarkable ability to open up our minds and hearts to receive that which is rightfully ours. It is a primer, an exquisite entrance into the great palace of *Toras Hashem*.

Yaakov Shalom has poured his soul into this *sefer*. You'll feel that as you move along the path paved for us long ago by the great master Rebbe Nachman of Breslov who began his tale with the unforgettable words: "Along the way, I told a story..."

Rav Moshe Weinberger

PREFACE

I will not die, for I shall live, and I shall tell the stories of God.

Tehillim 118:17

God created man because He loves stories. The whole world is God telling a story. The deepest depths of closeness to God is when you can tell Him your story.

– Reb Shlomo Carlebach

The Essence of Chassidus, the Core of Life

IT IS WITH overwhelming gratitude to the Master of the world Who has allowed me to taste from the unique wine of Rebbe Nachman of Breslov's teachings that I present this book to you, my dear reader.

The Lost Princess, the timeless tale this volume is devoted to exploring, has long been seen as a roadmap of the spiritual journey and a guide to weathering the storms that seek to blow out the dancing flame of our Jewishness. Pertinent to Jewish spiritual life throughout the ages, the tale has become more and more relevant in the two centuries since it was first told to a handful of marginalized chassidim in a small Ukrainian village. Seen through the lens of the modern era with all of its wonder and challenge, it becomes clear that *The Lost Princess* is the story of our generation, a nation of broken hearts yearning for home, of searching Jews yet moved by the wailing of the *neshamah* echoing from behind the barricades to search for the quintessence of being. The spiritual darkness Rebbe Nachman saw when he spoke of a great heresy that would descend upon the world was our darkness. Indeed, it was this very darkness Rebbe Nachman intended to dispel by igniting a glorious torch of faith, clarity, and radical encouragement that would burn until the coming of Mashiach. My effort in this book, a commentary on *The Lost Princess*, has been to put a magnifying glass to Rebbe Nachman's fire still flickering defiantly in the cold, dark night so that our holy nation might draw near and further benefit from its warmth and illumination.

The tale of *The Lost Princess* may be seen as sitting at the centermost core of Chassidic theology in general and Rebbe Nachman of Breslov's universe in particular. Spanning only about two-and-a-half pages of Hebrew text, this short story somehow manages to encompass the primary messages the tzaddikim so valiantly attempted to convey in the thousands of pages of their *sefarim hakedoshim*. In the simplest, starkest terms, Rebbe Nachman's tale seems to accomplish the impossible, lucidly and succinctly portraying the universal experience of the spiritual seeker and providing an intimate overview of his treacherous journey with all its ups and downs, triumphs and failures, developments and descents. A work of fictional artistry and a revelation of other-worldly brilliance, *The Lost Princess* is a masterpiece of timeless truth whose themes echo across the generations in ever-resounding tones, bringing joy, guidance, and encouragement to the hearts of all those who are fortunate enough to hear it.

Seldom does a single parable — in its limited scope — encompass all of life, retaining relevance to all of its various ages and stages. The story explicated in this volume is a rare example of such a work, overflowing with universal wisdom necessary for each and every step along our glorious journey. As our title suggests, the tale of *The Lost Princess* is "the story of our lives." Accommodating all life-circumstances within its broad framework, *The Lost Princess* treats the many-faceted nature of the human experience, retaining ultimate relevance to every Jew regardless of age, stage, background, or spiritual level. A manual for our entire existence, this book is one to keep at our side throughout the entirety of our brief and treacherous foray on planet earth. Its illuminating lessons retain their sweetness for all eternity.

On a personal note, this work holds special meaning to me and is particularly dear to my heart. The story of *The Lost Princess* has been a part of my life for as long as I can remember. As a child, this magical tale accompanied me at countless bedtimes as I drifted off to sleep. Later, I read the illustrated children's version again and again, ever enchanted by the twists and turns in the plot and the wondrous events the pictures portrayed. As I grew a bit older, I put away the illustrated edition and began to study the Hebrew version in the *sefer Sippurei Maasios*. When I grew older still, it suddenly dawned on me that the story of *The Lost Princess* is a mirror image of my own; the illustrations accompanying my worn text of this glorious tale, the events of my very own life. The amount of times I have dipped my battered bucket into the life-giving waters of this story over the years to lift my sights, regain my sense of direction, and find the strength necessary to carry on searching for the ethereal essence of meaning is simply incalculable. The tale of *The Lost Princess* has been a constant companion, like a dear old friend; always there for me, through thick and thin — a rock and a shoulder to lean on.

As I put the final touches on this book, I burst into tears. Their suddenness surprised me, but not their appearance, as the enormity of the lessons this story conveys and the manner in which its messages cut to the very core of life is genuinely overwhelming. It is my hope that, by means of the elucidation offered in this work, you will be able to discern your own story from behind the veil of Rebbe Nachman's words, just as I did mine. Writing this book has been an absolutely transformative experience. It is my fervent hope that you will find reading it to be the same.

Waking Up the World

"THE WORLD TELLS stories to put people to sleep. I tell stories to wake people up." With these iconic words, uttered just four years before his untimely passing, Rebbe Nachman of Breslov (1772– 1810) introduced the final puzzle piece of his glorious path to *avodas Hashem*: *Sippurei Maasios*, thirteen wondrous original tales. While storytelling had always been a major part of the Chassidic tradition, Rebbe Nachman's tales make up a genre of their own. Adventurous themes, endearing characters, epic twists, and lucid wisdom packed into stories within stories within stories, Rebbe Nachman's tales were a far cry from the parables and miraculous accounts relayed by the other Chassidic giants. Even in secular circles, *Sippurei Maasios* is appreciated as a work of world-class literature and studied in universities worldwide. Pinchas Sadeh, a secular Israeli poet and renowned literary critic, once said, "I have come to the conclusion that it is possible that Rabbi Nachman is not only perhaps the greatest writer in modern Hebrew literature, but one of the greatest creative writers in the history of world literature." *Sippurei Maasios* is extremely imaginative, an enchanted maze that draws the reader into a strange world of warriors, beggars, demons, merchants, princesses, pirates, and emperors — a world with different parameters in which time is inconsequential, space a figment of the imagination, and where anything can happen to anyone.

In the words of a great Jewish writer:

> His tales? Each contains many others. Imagine a series of concentric circles whose fixed centers are buried in man's innermost being: the I inside the I, conscience becomes silence and peace, memory inside memory. And all are inhabited by princes and sages. By haunted creatures seeing one another, one in another. By survivors of calamities, refugees, fugitives, messengers and innocent children, orphans and beggars endlessly roaming the world only to meet again in a cave or in

a palace, reunited and fulfilled in ways that go beyond the experience they have gone through or have been subjected to, perhaps unwittingly. Following them, we plunge into the supernatural and yet the word miracle is never pronounced. For in the Breslover's universe, everything is miraculous, even the most common event. On his lips, the most deprived, most primitive of men are endowed with powers; his objects have the gift of song, just as his forests, his trees, his animals and his morning breezes all have the gift of laughter.[1]

But beyond the veneer of a good read or even a privileged glimpse into the awesome imagination of a tzaddik turned master-storyteller, *Sippurei Maasios*, like all of the diverse literature Rebbe Nachman produced in his short lifetime, is a *revelation*, a novel method of serving Hashem in the final generation before Mashiach's arrival.

In his magnum opus, *Likutei Moharan*, Rebbe Nachman teaches that the mystical secrets of our holy Torah have the power to heal Jewish souls who have been stricken with the most horrible spiritual maladies. However, just like a doctor must administer medication using a method that will not harm the patient, the tzaddik must clothe his remedy, the blindingly radiant secrets of Torah, in what appear to be simple, entertaining stories. Imperceptibly woven into the fabric of the plot, the deepest secrets of creation are able to ride along with the garment of the story, entering the Jewish heart and stirring it to greater levels of spiritual engagement.[2]

In *Likutei Moharan* 60, a glorious lesson which, taught shortly after the tale of *The Lost Princess* was told, is widely seen as an introduction to *Sippurei Maasios* in general and an explanation of this story in particular,[3] the Rebbe teaches that it is possible for

---

1. *Souls on Fire*, p. 180

2. *Likutei Moharan* 164. See also *Kedushas Levi, Devarim*, "Dabeir."

3. See Appendix D, where the bond between this lesson and our story is explored.

a Jew to fall into such a deep spiritual slumber that none of the seventy approaches to the Torah can succeed in waking him. When a person falls into this spiritual and emotional state of numbness, apathy, and despair of ever growing close to the Master of the world, there is only one thing that can shake him from his slumber: *Sippurei Maasios M'Shanim Kadmoniyos*, Tales from Ancient Days. These stories are referred to as "ancient" because they derive from the exalted level of *"Atik Yomin,"*[4] the supernal realm of Divine mercy from which the entirety of Torah derives.[5] Crafted by the tzaddikim with the most delicate and careful intention, these lofty tales contain the power necessary to waken the Jewish soul from her sleep and motivate even the lowliest sinner to return to our loving Father in heaven. *The Lost Princess*, the first of these exalted tales from ancient times to be revealed by Rebbe Nachman, is a story that has the unique power to shake the world from its stupor and fill our lives with a flood of joy, clarity, and Divine mercy.

Because of the frighteningly exalted source from which these stories derive, even the tiniest details of the plot are of absolute consequence; entire worlds depend on each and every one.[6] Secrets, impenetrable secrets that may be disclosed only by way of a great many garments are the threads that make up the tapestry of *Sippurei Maasios*. Rebbe Nachman referred to these stories as a last-ditch effort to transform and elevate the consciousness of his followers.[7] As such, these thirteen tales represent perhaps the most accessible doorway into the tzaddik's universe. Everybody likes a good story, and, with modest effort, it is possible to perceive moral and spiritual guidance from between the lines of each. However, as one proceeds from section to section, the gnawing

---

4. See *Daniel* 7:9.
5. See *Idra Rabba, Zohar* 3:136b.
6. See *Chayei Moharan* 60–61.
7. See Reb Nosson's first introduction to *Sippurei Maasios*.

feeling that one has failed to scratch even the surface of the depth, meaning, and mystery behind each and every letter grows stronger and stronger. "These are not simple stories," Reb Nosson warns in his introduction to *Sippurei Maasios*. Not simple at all.

The Purpose of This Book

A GREAT JEWISH thinker once wrote, "You can affect a person only if you reach his inner life, the level where every human being is insecure and feels his incompleteness, the level of awareness that lies beyond articulation."[8] This book is an attempt to contact and engage that facet of the human personality we each share in common, the inner child locked away behind the barriers of our sophistication who yearns for the redemption that will allow his great gifts to once more illuminate our lives. I have striven to write this book in an open and vulnerable manner, pouring my soul into the words so they might qualify as *"devarim hayotzim min haleiv nichnasim el haleiv"* — words that exit the heart which are able to enter the heart.[9] Although this work certainly holds academic value in its exploration and interpretation of the tale, it is far from a theoretical study. Rather, the commentary should be approached with the expectation of spiritual awakening, as an entranceway into the literary *mikvah* of this purifying tale. Studying this book in a dry, intellectual manner as nothing more than a novel path toward metaphoric clarification in a piece of classical literature is sure to render the true treasures of *The Lost Princess* inaccessible to the reader.

The primary purpose of this book, then, a work more concerned with sensitivity of heart than cogency of mind, is to

---

8. *You Are My Witnesses*, p. 80.
9. *Sfas Emes, Shoftim* 7:3.

xxxii THE STORY OF OUR LIVES

uplift, encourage, inspire, guide, and lend penetrating clarity to the pursuit of true joy and peace of mind for which we so desperately yearn. Speaking to the universal inner child within in an attempt to make his presence known, this book is intended for every Jew regardless of age, background, or current stage in life. The key in allowing the story's natural impact to be felt is to attempt to discover our own journey between the lines of the tale and commentary and strive to apply the lessons in a manner that is relevant to our immediate spiritual situation. There is much wisdom and truth in the words of author, thinker, and activist Elie Wiesel:

> It is as though Rebbe Nachman wanted people to understand that it is more important for man to halt and consider the mystery of his own life than that of the world's origins. Danger and evil are not in the walk toward death but in the digression. Man advances toward more than one goal, lives on more than one level, loves and despairs in more than one way for more than one reason. Yet he does not know whether his deeds fall into a main or secondary pattern or if his awareness is blessing or curse. The human condition gains in impact at the very moment it breaks apart. Every fragment contains the whole, every fissure bears witness that man is at once the most fragile and the most tenacious of all creatures. Rebbe Nachman is more concerned with man than with mankind. Because he reacts more directly to the individual. His relationship with earth and heaven is filled with as many secrets as are contained by heaven and earth. Rebbe Nachman tightens the episodic events and lets the canvas flutter because he prefers the moments to years, the infinitely small to the infinitely large, the jolts of a life to a lifetime without surprises.[10]

---

10. *Souls on Fire*, p. 182.

I conclude with a prayer:

Master of the world, in gifting the final era with the exalted soul of Rebbe Nachman of Breslov *zy"a* and the glorious teachings with which You filled his mighty heart, You sent us a redemptive *ruach* — a remedy before the terrible afflictions of our time. May the awesome barriers preventing the fullest expression of this tzaddik's eternal light continue to falter and may his graceful words of wisdom and truth persist in awakening the hearts of a slumbering generation toward true closeness with You in thought, feeling, and action. May we merit to apply the lessons of this awesome story to our lives in a proper and healthy way, embarking on the individual and communal search for the Lost Princess with a spirit of abiding hope, unshaking conviction, and holy stubbornness that can enable us to overcome any obstacle. In the merit of Rebbe Nachman ben Feiga and all of the other angels among men whose teachings fill this work, may we merit to dance with great joy in the presence of *Kudsha Brich Hu u'Shechintei* atop the golden mountain of Your dwelling place, in the courtyard of the third Beis HaMikdash, speedily, and in our days. Let it be soon! Let it be today!

Yaakov Klein
Elul 5780
Jerusalem

ABOUT THIS BOOK

1. In researching for this book, I sought interpretations of *The Lost Princess* that are practical, relevant, and relatable to our generation's struggles. It must be clearly stated that this book claims neither to present the "true" interpretation of this story nor to reveal its mystical secrets. To attempt such a feat would be foolish as well as dangerous. Rather, my primary intention in this work is to derive inspiration, guidance, and psychospiritual insight from the tale for the sake of *avodas Hashem*, an undertaking approved by Reb Nosson in his second introduction to *Sippurei Maasios*:

   > See and focus upon every detail of this story and you will understand wondrous hints and awesome inspiration regarding how much one needs to strengthen himself in searching and seeking *avodas Hashem*, as the verse states "And seek out My Face, constantly."[1]

   In the pursuit of inspirational interpretation, permission is granted for each individual to search within the stories and attempt to discover lessons that are meaningful to him. This is further demonstrated in a letter Reb Nosson wrote to his son regarding an interpretation of *The Lost Princess* he had received. Although Reb Nosson takes issue with this particular interpretation, he stresses that he derived great pleasure from the fact that a Jew invested time and energy into interpreting

---

1. *Tehillim* 105:4.

the story and that this interpretation also contains some truth, because Rebbe Nachman's words encompass many different meanings.[2]

2. There are many different paths taken by the Breslover *mashpi'im* to elucidate this story. Most notable among them is Reb Nosson's interpretation presented in the second introduction to *Sippurei Maasios*, where he reads the tale as referring to the story of the Jewish nation as a whole and their general task of lifting up the *Shechinah* from her exile. In this book, I have taken a more particularized route, seeing the story as embodying the personal journey of each individual Jew.

3. One of the primary goals of this book is to present a seamless and unified interpretation that runs through the entire tale from beginning to end. In many of the existing works devoted to interpreting the tales, the symbolism of the characters and objects is always shifting — at one point a symbol may hint to one idea while at another point it hints to a second. In addition, there are often multiple interpretations presented for a single symbol. This makes it difficult to follow the flow of the story and can cause the reader to lose sight of the bigger picture. Therefore, in this book, I have gathered elements from interpretations presented in many earlier works on *Sippurei Maasios* and attempted to identify a general theme and system of symbolization that would remain consistent throughout the entire length of the story.

4. The primary source upon which this path toward interpreting *The Lost Princess* is based is the interpretation of Rav Nissin Dovid Kivak *shlita*, as presented in the weekly "*Aleh L'Terufah*" publication, years 2017–2018. In addition, the writings of Reb Nosson of Nemirov, Rav Levi Yitzchak

---

2. See *Alim L'Terufah* 2.

Bender (*Levias Chen*), Reb Avraham ben R' Nachman (*Koch-vei Ohr/Pirush al Hamaasios*), The Tcheriner Rav (*Kedushas Shabbos/Zimras Ha'aretz*), R' Yitzchak Meir Barlev (*Sefer Orach Mishor*), Rav Shalom Arush (*The Garden of Yearning*), R' Adin Steinsaltz (*The Tales of Rabbi Nachman of Bratslav*), R' Aryeh Kaplan (*Rebbe Nachman's Stories*), R' Erez Moshe Doron (*Wings*), Dr. Yakov Shammai Azriel (*The Quest for the Lost Princess*) and the recorded *shiurim* of my rebbi, Rav Moshe Weinberger *shlita*, have served as primary sources of insight into this remarkable tale. For the sake of brevity and uniformity, I have used a more general term "the Breslover *mashpi'im*," to refer to these sources throughout the book. In addition, this book features many *chiddushim* that Hashem has granted me in His overwhelming kindness.

5. In its original form, *The Lost Princess* is not divided into separate sections. However, for the purpose of organizational coherence, this book contains three parts; *Dusk*, *Night*, and *Dawn*, each of which marks a major stage in the story. In addition, a new chapter marks each new development in the tale. There are twenty-one chapters in all, the numerical value of the Divine Name "*Ekyeh*," which is the Name associated with *teshuvah*.[3]

6. At the end of each chapter, the primary points of encouragement and guidance are presented succinctly in a section entitled "Life Lessons." These concise formulations contain some of the most fundamental elements of Rebbe Nachman's spiritual path to *avodas Hashem*. The sixty-six "Life Lessons" are collected and presented in Appendix C.

7. In other appendices to this work, the reader will find a section including deeper allusions to the tale from diverse areas

---

3. See *Likutei Moharan* 6.

of Torah thought, a study of a few major themes explored in the commentary, a survey of connections between *Likutei Moharan* 60 and our tale, a foundational introduction to some basic ideas in Kabbalistic thought, and a relevant essay from R' Hillel Zeitlin.

8. *The Lost Princess* is a tale of *teshuvah* and spiritual recovery. Therefore, in the commentary, I have drawn heavily upon the teachings of four masters of *teshuvah*: Rav Avraham Yitzchak HaKohen Kook (1865–1935), Reb Tzadok HaKohen of Lublin (1823–1900), his rebbe, Rebbe Mordechai Yosef Leiner of Ishbitz (1801–1854), and Rebbe Nachman of Breslov — extraordinary tzaddikim whose Torah revelations share many similarities, primarily their awesome relevance to our unique generation. I have also drawn from the teachings of R' Hillel Zeitlin *Hy"d*, a unique and enigmatic individual whose own spiritual journey and extensive, remarkable writings embody many of the ideals discussed in this work.

9. In many ways, this book is an extension of my previous work, *Sunlight of Redemption: An Illuminated Path toward Inner Freedom*. The discerning reader will recognize many parallels to the *Yaakov/Eisav paradigm* discussed in *Sunlight of Redemption* which is further broadened and developed in the present work. It is no surprise that the opening teachings in two of Rebbe Nachman's major works, *Likutei Moharan* and *Sippurei Maasios*, share a deep and abiding bond.

10. It must be clearly stated that while any benefit gained from this special work is in the sole merit of the great tzaddikim whose teachings fill its pages, any error must be attributed to myself alone. With awe and trembling, I humbly beg forgiveness from the great masters whose words I have quoted and attempted to explain, if I have erred in that explanation or have not understood them properly.

ACKNOWLEDGMENTS

THE FINAL STAGE in the writing of a book is the acknowledgments, a section where the author expresses gratitude to all those who assisted, directly and indirectly, in the composition of the work. I can't speak for other authors, but for me, the acknowledgments is always the most difficult part of writing my books. I sit before a blank screen, fingers hovering over the keypad for what feels like an eternity, unable to begin. How is one to decide who to thank, and who to leave unmentioned? How is one to constrict boundless appreciation into the limited vessels of letters and words? If this task is always difficult, it is even more so when it comes to the acknowledgments of the present work, *The Story of Our Lives*. As the story of my life expressed in words and a literary portrait of my soul's deepest message to the world, I feel a need to thank *everyone*: the contributors to this project as well as the detractors, both friends and strangers, acquaintances of the past as well as the future — those I have not yet met. No matter how I approach this task, I begin with the awareness that I have already fallen short. I will say too little. I will mistakenly leave people out. But if I have learned one thing throughout the course of researching and writing this book, it is that a Jew must never allow the specter of failure from preventing him from giving it his best shot; perfection is never an ultimate goal. And so, in the spirit of giving it my all, please allow my heart to sing a song of thanks and appreciation to all those who have carried me along this journey.

Poschim b'chvod achsanya, the Host of the world, the Master of existence: What I want to express is beyond words. It rises above from the depths of my heart: a song, a prayer, a whisper of love. For the sunshine and the rainy days, for the laughter and the tears. For the mighty Hand that spans the realms of infinity and reaches into this finite world to grasp my own. I am never alone. Thank You for giving me the privilege of being a *frum* Jew in the final generations before Mashiach arrives. May I live up to Your belief in me.

To my special parents: Your belief in me and conviction that I can accomplish anything I set my mind to have carried me to wonderful places. My very being pulses with your passion for teaching, guiding, and bringing the awareness of Hashem and the beauty of His Torah to our holy nation. My joy over the completion of this book is, by right, your joy. Tatty, thank you for opening so many doors for me into the wondrous universe of the Breslover chassidim. It is clear to me that your *tefillos* by the *tziyon* of the tzaddik over the years directly influenced my journey to Rebbe Nachman, resulting in this book and in the founding of the Lost Princess Initiative. Thank you for everything!

To my special in-laws: Although we live half a world away, having been able to witness the way you open your hearts and home to whoever is in need of friendship, warmth, and community has served as a tremendous example to us. We are so privileged to be the beneficiaries of your love and support, founded in your largesse of spirit, openness, and good-natured character. Thank you for everything!

I would like to express my gratitude to Dov and Amy Snow of "The Chicago Jewish Home" for gifting a novice writer with a weekly column in your wonderful publication. That series of articles on *The Lost Princess* formed the skeletal foundation of the present work. The world will now reap the fruits of the seed of faith, trust, and opportunity you planted. Thank you!

My friend Ari Sasson made available to me Rav Nissin Dovid

Kivak's writings on *The Lost Princess*, an invaluable resource from which many of the primary themes in this commentary are drawn. Thank you!

I would like to express my gratitude to *yedid nafshi*, Yitzchok Haas, for his generous support of this project. Yitzchak, it has been an absolute privilege getting to know you and learn from you. Your sweetness, *tzidkus*, and staunch dedication to making the teachings of the tzaddikim available to our generation is incredible to watch. Thank you so much for your friendship, your trust, and your excitement about my work. Your support means the world to me. It is such an honor for this work to bear your family name. I hope you take just as much pleasure holding this *sefer* as I will, because it is not my *sefer*. It's ours.

I would like to express my gratitude to *yedid nafshi*, Yoni Bellows for his generous support of this project. Yoni, from the moment I met you late one Friday afternoon over some sushi, Chassidus, and *niggunim*, I knew this would be a long and abiding friendship. I have learned so much from you over the years, your passion for *ruchniyus* and thirst for *divrei Elokim Chaim* is so incredibly inspiring to me. Our relationship, founded upon the teachings we have shared, is one I cherish deeply. Thank you for your support of this project. Your belief in me allows me to believe in myself, to continue trying to share the light of Chassidus with *am Yisrael*. May the merit of the tzaddikim and all the learning and exploration fostered by the Lost Princess Principles Course stand by you and your beautiful family, and may we share in many *simchos* together in the years to come.

To all of those who lent their support for this project: Dan Feinstein, Moishe Gottesman, Moishe Weider, Gil Bashe, the Vogel family, Zev Alexander, Devorah First and family — this book could never have happened without your passion and generosity. Thank you for partnering with me to help make this dream a reality!

To the Wisdom Tribe team, Yaakov, Yoel, and Aviva — thank

you for your guidance, your wonderful design, and your tenacity in working through the difficult conditions of the Corona Era. Your artistic creations have lent the most wonderful vessels for the brilliant light LPI is sharing with the world. Thank you!

To Rav Moshe Tzuriel and Rav Judah Mischel — thank you so much for your beautiful *haskamos* to this *sefer*!

To all those who took the time out of their busy schedules to review the manuscript and put their impressions into writing: Rabbi Bezalel Naor, Rabbi Avi Fishoff, Rabbi Dov Ber Pinson, Chaya Rivka Zwolinski, Rabbi Yehoshua Gerzi, Dr. David Lieberman, Rabbi Reuven Boshnack, Dr. Henry Abramson, Gedale Fenster, Rav Joey Rosenfeld, Rabbi Dov Ber Cohen, Rav Shlomo Katz, and Menachem Poznanski, Rav Leibish Hundert — thank you! Your support means the world to me!

To Rav Shlomo Katz, Rav Joey Rosenfeld, Rav Binyomin Weinrib, and Rav Dovid'l Weinberg — thank you for being my friends, role models, and rabbeim guiding me along this often lonely "*shvil min hatzad*." Being able to share this adventure with each of you is one of the greatest privileges of my life.

To *yedidei nafshi*, Akiva Zneimer, Judah Klein, Simcha Levin, Ahron David Hershman, Akiva Bruck, Menachem Portnoy, Levi Newman, Shragi Russel, R' Binyomin Kaufman, Yehuda Honikman, Kovi Fleishman, Yonatan Attias (and the many others I am undoubtably forgetting at the moment), thank you for your friendship, your caring, your sharing, and support. I cherish each and every one of you. May we continue to grow closer to each other and, together, to the Master of the world in the years and decades to come.

To Aryeh Blumstein, Yaakov Josephy and the #TYH *chevrah*, it is such an honor to be a part of the incredible movement toward a positive and God-conscious Yiddishkeit you have created. *Ashrecha*! *Ashreinu*!

To Rav Leibish, Reb Pesachya, and the *chevrah* at Yeshivat Shaarei Shalom, the moments spent learning, dancing, sharing, singing, and exploring together in our *beis midrash* will remain forever etched deep in my heart. Thank you for creating such a warm, open, and illuminated space for spiritual growth and *kirvas Elokim.*

To Michael Benmelech and the *chevrah* at The Lighthouse Project, thank you for all the incredible work you do to illuminate the darkness of social media with our holy Torah and for granting me a platform to spread the teachings of Rebbe Nachman to thirsty souls all over the world. May you see continued *hatzlachah* in your *avodas hakodesh*!

To the ever-growing LPI family, thank you for the excitement, the engagement, the sharing, and the unending support you have shown for our vision. It is you who will carry the shining messages we are exploring to a world in desperate need of light, clarity, and comfort. Here's to many years of exploration, elevation, closeness, and shared passion for a shift of consciousness that will prepare our generation for the final redemption — we are only just beginning!

To my students at Yeshivat Mevaseret Tzion: So many of the ideas in this book were developed in our *vaadim, farbrengens,* and late-night conversations. The excitement, passion, and sincerity that shines forth from your expansive hearts and inquisitive minds has allowed us to delve deeply into some of the most important concepts in our holy tradition. It has been the gift of a lifetime to be able to explore these life-changing ideas together with you. A special thank you to Rav Isaacson and Rav Burg for believing in me and granting me the space to share the teachings that changed my life with exalted souls that ended up doing more of the same. As I expressed many times in the past, your yeshivah is a true *kiddush Hashem,* a paradigm of openness, honesty, and true spiritual striving. Thank you for the opportunity to be a part of it.

Thank you to all those (there are too many of you to list by name, but you know who you are) who looked over parts of the manuscript and lent their invaluable advice.

Thank you to my brother-in-law and *chavrusa*, Yitzchak Rapoport, for everything. It has been such a gift to live up the block from your beautiful family, to delve into the Torah's depth each morning, and to follow your lead along this journey called life. Thank you!

To Rabbi Zucker, R' Daniel Green, and the Kehillah Kedosha Ramat Eshkol family, there are no words to express my gratitude for the *makom Torah* and *Tefillah* that the Rav and the *chevrah* have created. Thank you for elevating my Shabbosim and gifting me with a place to experience *tefillah* as the *hishtapchus haleiv v'hanefesh* it is intended to be.

Thank you to Jerry Latinik and the holy *chevrah* of Dagan, Efrat, for the love, the *niggunim*, the support, and the glorious opportunity to delve into the teachings of Chassidus with some of the most special *neshamos* I have ever met. You guys are unbelievable, and the flames of holiness you are stoking, founded on the Geulah Values you share, will with time become a mighty torch of Torah, *avodah*, and *gemillus chassadim* filled with the greatest soul and devotion. You are truly a community of Jews searching for the Lost Princess of feeling and connection. And it has been an honor and a privilege to be a part of it. Jerry, you are a powerhouse of *chessed, ruach*, and *simchah*. Watching you invest your all into Just One Chessed and all of your amazing projects has been a true inspiration to me. May you continue to see *nachas* from Moshe, Ben and the rest of your amazing family. Here's to many more years of learning, davening, and serving Hashem together!

To the "Kisvei Breslov Chaburah" — you are the proof that technology can, with the proper guidelines, be elevated to dizzying heights. Thank you for filling my daily life with insight, beauty, and the electrifying energy unique to Mashiach's foot soldiers. *Chazak*!

To my *rabbeim*, Rav Binyomin Feldman, Rav Leibish Hundert, Rav Yehoshua Gerzi, and Rav Shmuel Zucker, thank you for all of the insight, guidance, and direction you have brought into my life. Each and every one of you has had a tremendous impact on me, and I cherish the relationships we share. Thank you!

Rebbe, Rav Weinberger, there are absolutely no words to describe how grateful I am for everything you do for me. Thank you for your love, your support, your insight, your guidance, and your belief in me that far transcends my own and holds me up when the going gets tough. Thank you for your most beautiful Foreword. Thank you for making yourself available to me, to serve as a role model and mentor for me on this path of being *mechazeik* our generation with the wellsprings of the tzaddikim from which we have merited to drink. I daven that I should merit to continue to learn from you for many happy, and healthy years filled with *nachas, yishuv hadaas,* and *kol tuv b'ruchniyus u've-gashmiyus* during which Rebbe will be continuing to teach, lead, and elevate our generation, Thank you for everything!

To the *hanhalos* of the esteemed bastions of Torah and *avodah,* Torat Shraga, Ashreinu, Lev HaTorah, Darche Noam, and Yeshivas Matisyahu, thank you for allowing me to share Torah and *neginah d'Kedushah* with the *neshamos* in your care! I look forward to many more sessions of elevation and yearning in the years to come!

Thank you to Mrs. Chana Devorah Sklar for your superb and professional editing. You managed to amend the *"guf"* of the text while leaving the *"neshamah"* wholly intact. Thank you for another job well done.

Thank you to Mrs. Eden Chachamtzedek, for your beautiful and elegant typesetting.

Thank you to my sister Rivky for far more than her expert proofreading.

Acharon achronah chaviv, to my wonderful wife, Shira. As I was researching for this *sefer* and found that the tzaddik had first recounted *The Lost Princess* on 11 Av, 1806, my heart skipped a beat. "Wait a minute," I thought. "11 Av, that date sounds familiar!" And then I remembered — 11 Av is the day we stood under the *chuppah* and began this incredible journey together. How fascinating that on the same exact date Rebbe Nachman first told his story about the search for the Lost Princess, I found mine — 211 years later. Shira, *ein milim*, there are no words that can possibly convey the appreciation I feel toward you. For your unwavering support, staunch friendship, and gentle guidance, for the incredible partnership we share in our nurturing care of Shmuel Shmelke, for the sense of utter completion you bring to a very incomplete soul, thank you.

THE STORY OF THE

LOST
PRINCESS

A Tale by Rebbe Nachman of Breslov

The Rebbe spoke up and said, "While on a journey, I told a story. Whoever heard it had a thought of repentance. This is the story."

There was once a king who had six sons and one daughter. The daughter was very precious in his eyes and he loved her very much. He took very great delight in her.

On one occasion, when the king was together with her on a certain day, he grew angry with her and threw the following words from his mouth: "May the no-good one take you." That night she went to her room, and in the morning, no one knew where she went.

Her father was very pained and he went here and there looking for her. The viceroy stood up, for he saw the king's pain. He requested a servant, a horse, and money for expenses, and he went to search for her. He searched for a very long time until he found her. (Now we will tell of how he searched until he found her.)

The viceroy traveled here and there for a long time through deserts, fields, and forests. He searched for her for a very long time. Finally, while traveling through the desert, he saw a path to the side, and thought it over. "Since I have traveled for so long in the desert and I cannot find her, let me follow this path. Perhaps it will bring me to an inhabited area." And he walked for a very long time.

After some time, he saw a castle. Many soldiers stood around it. The castle was very beautiful and neat and the troops were very orderly. The viceroy was afraid that the soldiers would not let him enter. But he thought it over and

עָנָה וְאָמַר: בַּדֶּרֶךְ סִפַּרְתִּי מַעֲשֶׂה, שֶׁכָּל מִי שֶׁהָיָה שׁוֹמְעָה הָיָה לוֹ
הִרְהוּר תְּשׁוּבָה. וְזוֹ הִיא:

מַעֲשֶׂה בְּמֶלֶךְ אֶחָד, שֶׁהָיוּ לוֹ שִׁשָּׁה בָנִים וּבַת אֶחָת. וְאוֹתָה
הַבַּת הָיְתָה חֲשׁוּבָה בְּעֵינָיו מְאֹד, וְהָיָה מְחַבְּבָהּ בְּיוֹתֵר, וְהָיָה
מִשְׁתַּעֲשֵׁעַ עִמָּהּ מְאֹד.

פַּעַם אַחַת הָיָה מִתְוַעֵד עִמָּהּ בְּיַחַד בְּאֵיזֶה יוֹם, וְנַעֲשָׂה
בְּרֹגֶז עָלֶיהָ, וְנִזְרְקָה מִפִּיו דִּבּוּר: שֶׁהַלֹּא טוֹב יִקַּח אוֹתָךְ.
בַּלַּיְלָה הָלְכָה לְחַדְרָהּ, וּבַבֹּקֶר לֹא יָדְעוּ הֵיכָן הִיא.

וְהָיָה אָבִיהָ מִצְטַעֵר מְאֹד, וְהָלַךְ לְבַקְּשָׁהּ אָנֶה וָאָנָה. עָמַד
הַשֵּׁנִי לַמַּלְכוּת, מֵחֲמַת שֶׁרָאָה שֶׁהַמֶּלֶךְ מִצְטַעֵר מְאֹד, וּבִקֵּשׁ
שֶׁיִּתְּנוּ לוֹ מְשָׁרֵת וְסוּס וּמָעוֹת עַל הוֹצָאוֹת, וְהָלַךְ לְבַקְּשָׁהּ.
וְהָיָה מְבַקְשָׁהּ מְאֹד, זְמַן מְרֻבֶּה מְאֹד עַד שֶׁמְּצָאָהּ. [עַתָּה
מְסַפֵּר אֵיךְ בִּקְּשָׁהּ עַד שֶׁמְּצָאָהּ.]

וְהָיָה הוֹלֵךְ אָנֶה וָאָנָה זְמַן רַב, וּבַמִּדְבָּרִיּוֹת וּבַשָּׂדוֹת
וּבַיְעָרִים וְהָיָה מְבַקְשָׁהּ זְמַן רַב מְאֹד, וְהָיָה הוֹלֵךְ בַּמִּדְבָּר,
וְרָאָה שְׁבִיל אֶחָד מִן הַצַּד, וְהָיָה מְיַשֵּׁב עַצְמוֹ: בַּאֲשֶׁר שֶׁאֲנִי
הוֹלֵךְ כָּל כָּךְ זְמַן רַב בַּמִּדְבָּר וְאֵינִי יָכוֹל לִמְצָאָהּ אֵלֵךְ בַּשְּׁבִיל
הַזֶּה, אוּלַי אָבוֹא לְמָקוֹם יִשּׁוּב. וְהָיָה הוֹלֵךְ זְמַן רַב.

אַחַר כָּךְ רָאָה מִבְצָר, וְכַמָּה חֲיָלוֹת הָיוּ עוֹמְדִים שָׁם סְבִיבוֹ,
וְהַמִּבְצָר הָיָה נָאֶה וּמְתֻקָּן וּמְסֻדָּר מְאֹד עִם הַחֲיָלוֹת. וְהָיָה
מִתְיָרֵא מִפְּנֵי הַחֲיָלוֹת, פֶּן לֹא יַנִּיחוּהוּ לִכְנֹס. וְהָיָה מְיַשֵּׁב

said, "I will go ahead and try." He left behind his horse and went to the castle. The soldiers didn't stop him at all, and he went from room to room. Finally, he came to the main hall. There he saw the king sitting with the crown on his head. There were many soldiers there as well as musicians with their instruments before them. It was all very beautiful and pleasant. Neither the king nor anyone else asked him any questions. He saw delicacies and fine foods there and he stood and ate. Then he went to lie down in a corner to see what would happen next.

He saw that the king requested for them to bring the queen. They went to fetch her, and there was a great uproar and tremendous joy as they brought forth the queen. The orchestra played and the choir sang. They set up a throne for her and she sat next to the king. She was the lost princess! As soon as the viceroy saw her, he recognized her. The queen looked around, and, seeing someone lying in a corner, she recognized him. She stood up from her throne and went over and touched him. "Do you know me?" she asked. "Yes," he replied. "I know you. You are the lost princess."

He then asked her, "How did you get here?" "It happened when my father, the king, threw those words from his mouth ('May the no-good one take you.')," she answered. "This is the place of no-good." The viceroy told her that her father was in so much pain and had searched for her for many years. "How can I get you out of here?" he asked. She said, "It is impossible to get me out of here unless you choose for yourself a place and remain there for a full year.

עַצְמוֹ: אֵלֵךְ וַאֲנַסֶּה. וְהִשְׁאִיר הַסּוּס וְהָלַךְ לְהַמִּבְצָר, וְהָיוּ
מַנִּיחִים אוֹתוֹ, וְלֹא עִכְּבוּהוּ כְּלָל, וְהָיָה הוֹלֵךְ מֵחֶדֶר לְחֶדֶר
בְּלִי עִכּוּב. וּבָא לְאַרְמוֹן אֶחָד וְרָאָה שֶׁיּוֹשֵׁב שָׁם הַמֶּלֶךְ בַּעֲטָרָה,
וְכַמָּה חֲיָלוֹת שָׁם וְכַמָּה מְשׁוֹרְרִים בְּכֵלִים לְפָנָיו, וְהָיָה שָׁם
נָאֶה וְיָפֶה מְאֹד. וְהַמֶּלֶךְ וְשׁוּם אֶחָד מֵהֶם לֹא שְׁאָלוּהוּ כְּלָל.
וְרָאָה שָׁם מַעֲדַנִּים וּמַאֲכָלִים טוֹבִים, וְעָמַד וְאָכַל, וְהָלַךְ
וְשָׁכַב בְּזָוִית לִרְאוֹת מַה נַּעֲשֶׂה שָׁם.

וְרָאָה שֶׁהַמֶּלֶךְ צִוָּה לְהָבִיא לְהַמַּלְכָּה, וְהָלְכוּ לְהָבִיא
אוֹתָהּ וְהָיָה שָׁם רַעַשׁ גָּדוֹל וְשִׂמְחָה גְּדוֹלָה, וְהַמְשׁוֹרְרִים
הָיוּ מְזַמְּרִים וּמְשׁוֹרְרִים מְאֹד בַּאֲשֶׁר שֶׁהֵבִיאוּ אֶת הַמַּלְכָּה
וְהֶעֱמִידוּ לָהּ כִּסֵּא וְהוֹשִׁיבוּהָ אֶצְלוֹ, וְהִיא הָיְתָה הַבַּת מֶלֶךְ
הַנַּ"ל, וְהוּא [הַיְנוּ הַשֵּׁנִי לַמַּלְכוּת] רָאָה וְהִכִּירָהּ. אַחַר כָּךְ
הֵצִיצָה הַמַּלְכָּה וְרָאֲתָה אֶחָד שֶׁשּׁוֹכֵב בַּזָּוִית, וְהִכִּירָה אוֹתוֹ.
וְעָמְדָה מִכִּסְאָהּ וְהָלְכָה לְשָׁם, וְנָגְעָה בּוֹ וְשָׁאֲלָה אוֹתוֹ:
הַאַתָּה מַכִּיר אוֹתִי? וְהֵשִׁיב לָהּ: הֵן, אֲנִי מַכִּיר אוֹתָךְ, אַתְּ
הִיא הַבַּת מֶלֶךְ שֶׁנֶּאֶבְדָה.

וְשָׁאַל אוֹתָהּ: הָאֵיךְ בָּאת לְכָאן? וְהֵשִׁיבָה: בַּאֲשֶׁר שֶׁאָבִי
הַמֶּלֶךְ נִזְרַק מִפִּיו דִּבּוּר הַנַּ"ל וְכָאן, הַמָּקוֹם הַזֶּה, הוּא לֹא
טוֹב. וְסִפֵּר לָהּ, שֶׁאָבִיהָ מִצְטַעֵר מְאֹד, וְשֶׁהוּא מְבַקְשָׁהּ כַּמָּה
שָׁנִים. וְשָׁאַל אוֹתָהּ: אֵיךְ אֲנִי יָכוֹל לְהוֹצִיא אוֹתָךְ? וְאָמְרָה
לוֹ שֶׁאִי אֶפְשָׁר לְךָ לְהוֹצִיא אוֹתִי כִּי אִם כְּשֶׁתִּהְיֶה בּוֹחֵר לְךָ
מָקוֹם, וְתִהְיֶה יוֹשֵׁב שָׁם שָׁנָה אַחַת.

"All that year you must long to free me. Whenever you are unoccupied, you must only yearn, seek, and look forward to freeing me. And you must also fast. Then, on the last day of the year, you must fast and go without sleep for the entire twenty-four-hour period."

The viceroy went and did what the princess had told him. On the final day, at the year's close, he fasted and did not sleep. He rose and began heading toward the palace. He saw a tree with very beautiful apples. It was very desirable to his eyes, and he ate an apple. Immediately after eating the apple, he fell into a deep sleep, and he slept for a very long time.

The servant tried to shake him, but he would not wake. After some time, the viceroy awoke from his slumber and asked his servant, "Where in the world am I?" The servant told him what had happened. "You slept for a very long time — for many years. I survived by eating the fruit." The viceroy was very upset at himself. He went to the palace and found the princess.

He found her and she lamented to him greatly, saying, "If you had come on that day, you would have freed me from here. But because of one day, you lost everything. However, it is very difficult not to eat, especially on the last day when the Evil Urge is very strong." (The princess is telling him that she will make the conditions easier for him by allowing him to eat on the last day, for it is very difficult, etc.)

וְכָל הַשָּׁנָה תִּתְגַּעְגַּע אַחֲרֵי לְהוֹצִיא אוֹתִי, וּבְכָל זְמַן שֶׁיִּהְיֶה לְךָ פְּנַאי תִּהְיֶה רַק מִתְגַּעְגֵּעַ וּמְבַקֵּשׁ וּמְצַפֶּה לְהוֹצִיא אוֹתִי, וְתִהְיֶה מִתְעַנֶּה. וּבַיּוֹם הָאַחֲרוֹן מֵהַשָּׁנָה תִּהְיֶה מִתְעַנֶּה, וְלֹא תִּישַׁן כָּל הַמֵּעֵת־לְעֵת.

וְהָלַךְ וְעָשָׂה כֵן. וּבְסוֹף הַשָּׁנָה בַּיּוֹם הָאַחֲרוֹן הָיָה מִתְעַנֶּה, וְלֹא הָיָה יָשֵׁן. וְעָמַד וְהָלַךְ לְשָׁם, וְהָיָה רוֹאֶה אִילָן, וְעָלָיו גְּדֵלִים תַּפּוּחִים נָאִים מְאֹד, וְהָיָה מִתְאַוֶּה לְעֵינָיו מְאֹד, וְעָמַד וְאָכַל מִשָּׁם. וְתֵכֶף שֶׁאָכַל הַתַּפּוּחַ, נָפַל וַחֲטָפוֹ שֵׁנָה. וְהָיָה יָשֵׁן זְמַן מְרֻבֶּה מְאֹד.

וְהָיָה הַמְשָׁרֵת מְנַעֵר אוֹתוֹ, וְלֹא הָיָה נֵעוֹר כְּלָל. אַחַר כָּךְ הֵקִיץ מִשְּׁנָתוֹ, וְשָׁאַל לְהַמְשָׁרֵת: הֵיכָן אֲנִי בָּעוֹלָם? וְסִפֵּר לוֹ הַמַּעֲשֶׂה [הַיְנוּ הַמְשָׁרֵת סִפֵּר לְהַשֵּׁנִי לַמֶּלֶךְ הַמַּעֲשֶׂה וְאָמַר לוֹ] שֶׁאַתָּה יָשֵׁן זְמַן מְרֻבֶּה מְאֹד זֶה כַּמָּה שָׁנִים, וַאֲנִי הָיִיתִי מִתְפַּרְנֵס מֵהַפֵּרוֹת. וְהָיָה מְצַעֵר עַצְמוֹ מְאֹד. וְהָלַךְ לְשָׁם וּמָצָא אוֹתָהּ.

וּמָצָא אוֹתָהּ, וְהָיְתָה מִצְטַעֶרֶת לְפָנָיו מְאֹד, כִּי אִלּוּ בָּאתָ בְּאוֹתוֹ הַיּוֹם, הָיִיתָ מוֹצִיא אוֹתִי מִכָּאן וּבִשְׁבִיל יוֹם אֶחָד אִבַּדְתָּ. אָמְנָם שֶׁלֹּא לֶאֱכֹל הוּא דָּבָר קָשֶׁה מְאֹד, בִּפְרָט בַּיּוֹם הָאַחֲרוֹן, אָז מִתְגַּבֵּר הַיֵּצֶר הָרָע מְאֹד [הַיְנוּ שֶׁהַבַּת מֶלֶךְ אָמְרָה לוֹ, שֶׁעַתָּה תָּקֵל עָלָיו הָאַזְהָרָה וְלֹא יִהְיֶה מֻזְהָר שֶׁלֹּא לֶאֱכֹל, כִּי הוּא דָּבָר קָשֶׁה לַעֲמֹד בּוֹ וְכוּ'].

"Therefore, return and choose for yourself a place, and sit there for a year, just as before. On the last day you will be allowed to eat, but you must not sleep and you mustn't drink wine so that you don't fall asleep, for the most important thing is that you remain awake." He went and he did so. On the final day, he began approaching the palace. He saw a flowing river. The river was red and it smelled like wine. He asked his servant, "Have you ever seen such a thing — a river of water that appears red and smells like wine!" And he went and tasted from the river. He immediately fell asleep and slept for many years, a period of seventy years.

Many troops passed, with a procession and equipment that accompanied them. The servant hid himself because of the soldiers. After the troops passed, a chariot and covered wagon approached. In it, sat the princess. The procession stopped nearby. The princess descended and sat next to the viceroy. She recognized him. She shook him very much, but he did not wake.

She began to bemoan, "How many immense difficulties and toils he has undergone for so many years in order to free me, and on the day he could have freed me he lost everything…" She began to cry greatly over all of this, [saying], "For there is great pity upon him and upon me, for I have been held captive here for so long and I am unable to leave…" She then took the scarf from her head and wrote on it with her tears. She placed it next to him. She went and sat in her chariot, and they traveled on.

בְּכֵן תָּשׁוּב לִבְחֹר לְךָ מָקוֹם, וְתֵשֵׁב גַּם כֵּן שָׁנָה כַנַּ"ל, וּבַיּוֹם הָאַחֲרוֹן תִּהְיֶה רַשַּׁאי לֶאֱכֹל, רַק שֶׁלֹּא תִישַׁן, וְלֹא תִשְׁתֶּה יַיִן כְּדֵי שֶׁלֹּא תִישַׁן, כִּי הָעִקָּר הוּא הַשֵּׁנָה. וְהָלַךְ וְעָשָׂה כֵן. בַּיּוֹם הָאַחֲרוֹן הָיָה הוֹלֵךְ לְשָׁם, וְרָאָה מַעְיָן הוֹלֵךְ, וְהַמַּרְאֶה אָדֹם וְהָרֵיחַ שֶׁל יַיִן. וְשָׁאַל אֶת הַמְשָׁרֵת: הֲרָאִיתָ שֶׁזֶּה מַעְיָן, וְרָאוּי שֶׁיִּהְיֶה בּוֹ מַיִם. וְהַמַּרְאֶה אֲדֻמִּית וְהָרֵיחַ שֶׁל יַיִן! וְהָלַךְ וְטָעַם מֵהַמַּעְיָן, וְנָפַל וְיָשַׁן מִיָּד כַּמָּה שָׁנִים, עַד שִׁבְעִים שָׁנָה.

וְהָיוּ הוֹלְכִין חֲיָלוֹת רַבּוֹת עִם הַשַּׁיָּךְ לָהֶם, מַה שֶּׁנּוֹסֵעַ אַחֲרֵיהֶם, וְהַמְשָׁרֵת הִטְמִין עַצְמוֹ מֵחֲמַת הַחֲיָלוֹת. אַחַר כָּךְ הָלְכָה מֶרְכָּבָה וַעֲגָלוֹת־צַב, וְשָׁם יָשְׁבָה הַבַּת מֶלֶךְ, וְעָמְדָה שָׁם אֶצְלוֹ, וְיָרְדָה וְיָשְׁבָה אֶצְלוֹ וְהִכִּירָה אוֹתוֹ, וְהָיְתָה מְנַעֶרֶת אוֹתוֹ מְאֹד, וְלֹא נִנְעַר.

וְהִתְחִילָה לְקַבֵּל עָלָיו, אֲשֶׁר כַּמָּה וְכַמָּה יְגִיעוֹת וְטִרְחוֹת גְּדוֹלוֹת מְאֹד שֶׁהָיוּ לוֹ זֶה כַּמָּה וְכַמָּה שָׁנִים כְּדֵי לְהוֹצִיא אוֹתִי, וּבִשְׁבִיל אוֹתוֹ הַיּוֹם שֶׁהָיָה יָכוֹל לְהוֹצִיאֵנִי וְאִבְּדוֹ. וְהָיְתָה בּוֹכָה מְאֹד עַל זֶה, כִּי יֵשׁ רַחְמָנוּת גָּדוֹל עָלָיו וְעָלַי, שֶׁכָּל כָּךְ זְמַן שֶׁאֲנִי כָאן, וְאֵינִי יְכוֹלָה לָצֵאת. אַחַר כָּךְ לָקְחָה מִטְפַּחַת מֵעַל רֹאשָׁהּ וְכָתְבָה עָלָיו בַּדְּמָעוֹת שֶׁלָּהּ, וְהִנִּיחָה אֶצְלוֹ. וְעָמְדָה וְיָשְׁבָה בְּמֶרְכַּבְתָּהּ, וְנָסְעָה מִשָּׁם.

After this, the viceroy awoke and asked his servant, "Where in the world am I?" The servant told him (the viceroy) the entire story about the many soldiers that had passed, the chariot, the princess, and her great crying and grief. Suddenly he looked and noticed the headscarf next to him. "Where is this from?" he asked. The servant answered that the princess had written on it with her tears. The viceroy took the scarf and held it up to the sun. He began to see letters. [He read that] at this time, she is no longer in the previous palace. "Rather, you will need to search for a mountain of gold and a palace of pearls, and there you will find me."

He left his servant behind and went to search for her, alone. His search for her lasted many years. Eventually, he came to the realization that this mountain of gold and palace of pearls certainly does not exist in the settled parts of the world, for he was an expert in all the maps of the world. [He said,] "I will go to the deserts," and he went to search for her in the deserts for many years. After this, he saw a tremendously large person, who didn't seem to be human at all because of his enormous size. He carried a huge tree — no tree in the settled world was as large as this tree. The giant asked him: "Who are you?" He responded, "I am a human." The giant was astounded, and he said, "It has been so long since I have been in this desert, and I have never seen a human here!"

The viceroy told him the whole story, and about how he was searching for a mountain of gold and a palace of pearls. The giant responded, "Certainly, this place doesn't exist."

אַחַר כָּךְ הֵקִיץ וְשָׁאַל אֶת הַמְשָׁרֵת: הֵיכָן אֲנִי בָּעוֹלָם? וְסִפֵּר לוֹ כָּל הַמַּעֲשֶׂה, וְשֶׁחֲיָלוֹת רַבּוֹת הָלְכוּ שָׁם, וְשֶׁהָיְתָה כָּאן מֶרְכָּבָה הַנַּ"ל, וְשֶׁהָיְתָה בּוֹכָה עָלָיו, וְהָיְתָה צוֹעֶקֶת שֶׁיֵּשׁ רַחֲמָנוּת עָלָיו וְעָלֶיהָ כַּנַּ"ל. בְּתוֹךְ כָּךְ הֵצִיץ וְרָאָה, שֶׁהַמִּטְפַּחַת מֻנַּחַת אֶצְלוֹ, וְשָׁאַל: מֵאַיִן זֶה? וְהֵשִׁיב לוֹ, שֶׁהִיא כָּתְבָה עָלָיו בְּהַדְּמָעוֹת. וּלְקָחָהּ, וְהֵרִים אוֹתָהּ כְּנֶגֶד הַשֶּׁמֶשׁ וְהִתְחִיל לִרְאוֹת הָאוֹתִיּוֹת. וְקָרָא מַה שֶּׁכָּתוּב שָׁם כָּל קְבִלָתָהּ וְצַעֲקָתָהּ כַּנַּ"ל, וְשֶׁכָּעֵת אֵינֶנָּה שָׁם בַּמִּבְצָר הַנַּ"ל, כִּי אִם שֶׁיְּבַקֵּשׁ הַר שֶׁל זָהָב וּמִבְצָר שֶׁל מַרְגָּלִיּוֹת, שָׁם תִּמְצָאֵנִי.

וְהִשְׁאִיר אֶת הַמְשָׁרֵת וְהִנִּיחוֹ, וְהָלַךְ לְבַדּוֹ לְבַקְשָׁהּ. וְהָלַךְ כַּמָּה שָׁנִים לְבַקְשָׁהּ, וְיִשֵּׁב עַצְמוֹ שֶׁבְּוַדַּאי בְּיִשּׁוּב לֹא נִמְצָא הַר שֶׁל זָהָב וּמִבְצָר שֶׁל מַרְגָּלִיּוֹת, כִּי הוּא בָּקִי בְּמַפַּת הָעוֹלָם, וְעַל כֵּן אֵלֵךְ אֶל הַמִּדְבָּרִיּוֹת. וְהָלַךְ לְבַקְשָׁהּ בַּמִּדְבָּרִיּוֹת כַּמָּה וְכַמָּה שָׁנִים. אַחַר כָּךְ רָאָה אָדָם גָּדוֹל מְאֹד שֶׁאֵינוֹ [בְּגֶדֶר] אֱנוֹשִׁי כְּלָל שֶׁיִּהְיֶה אָדָם גָּדוֹל כָּל כָּךְ, וְנָשָׂא אִילָן גָּדוֹל, שֶׁבַּיִּשּׁוּב אֵינוֹ נִמְצָא אִילָן גָּדוֹל כָּזֶה. וְאוֹתוֹ הָאִישׁ שָׁאַל אוֹתוֹ: מִי אַתָּה? וְאָמַר לוֹ: אֲנִי אָדָם. וְתָמַהּ, וְאָמַר שֶׁזֶּה כָּל כָּךְ זְמַן שֶׁאֲנִי בְּהַמִּדְבָּר וְלֹא רָאִיתִי מֵעוֹלָם בְּכָאן אָדָם.

וְסִפֵּר לוֹ כָּל הַמַּעֲשֶׂה הַנַּ"ל, וְשֶׁהוּא מְבַקֵּשׁ הַר שֶׁל זָהָב וּמִבְצָר שֶׁל מַרְגָּלִיּוֹת. אָמַר לוֹ: בְּוַדַּאי אֵינוֹ בַּנִּמְצָא כְּלָל,

He repressed him, telling him that his mind had been led astray by folly, for it was clear that no such place existed. The viceroy began to cry very much, for he was certain that the place existed. The giant repressed him again, saying, "It is certainly folly!" And the viceroy said, "It certainly exists."

He said to him (the giant to the viceroy), "In my opinion, it is folly. But because you are adamant about it — I am appointed over all of the wild animals. I will do you a favor and call these animals, for they run all over the world. Perhaps one of them will know about the mountain and palace of which you speak." He called to all of them from the smallest to the largest, all kinds of wild animals, and he asked them. All of them answered that they hadn't seen such a place. "You see?" said the giant, "you have been told foolishness. If you will listen to me, turn back! For you will certainly not find it, for it is certainly not in the world." The viceroy adamantly insisted, saying that it must certainly exist. He said to him (the giant to the viceroy), "Further in the desert you will find my brother. He is in charge of all the birds. Perhaps they will know something, since they fly up high in the air; maybe they saw the mountain of gold and the palace of pearls. Go to him and tell him that I sent you."

The viceroy searched for him for many years, until he again encountered a giant like the previous one. He, too, carried a great tree. The giant asked him all that the first one had. The viceroy told him his whole story and how the giant's brother had sent him here. This giant began pushing him away as well, telling him that it certainly didn't exist,

וְדָחָה אוֹתוֹ וְאָמַר לוֹ שֶׁהֶשִּׂיאוּ אֶת דַּעְתּוֹ בִּדְבַר שְׁטוּת, כִּי בְּוַדַּאי אֵינוֹ נִמְצָא כְּלָל. וְהִתְחִיל לִבְכּוֹת מְאֹד [הַיְנוּ הַשֵּׁנִי לַמַּלְכוּת בָּכָה מְאֹד, וְאָמַר] כִּי בְּוַדַּאי בְּהֶכְרֵחַ הוּא נִמְצָא בְּאֵיזֶה מָקוֹם. וְהוּא דָּחָה אוֹתוֹ, [הַיְנוּ הָאָדָם הַמִּשְׁנֶה שֶׁפָּגַע דָּחָה אוֹתוֹ בִּדְבָרָיו וְאָמַר] כִּי בְּוַדַּאי דְּבַר שְׁטוּת אָמְרוּ לְפָנָיו. וְהוּא אָמַר [הַיְנוּ הַשֵּׁנִי לַמַּלְכוּת], שֶׁבְּוַדַּאי יֵשׁ.

אָמַר לוֹ [הָאָדָם הַמִּשְׁנֶה לְהַשֵּׁנִי לַמַּלְכוּת]: לְדַעְתִּי הִיא שְׁטוּת. אַךְ מֵחֲמַת שֶׁאַתָּה מִתְעַקֵּשׁ, הִנֵּה אֲנִי מְמֻנֶּה עַל כָּל הַחַיּוֹת, אֶעֱשֶׂה לְמַעַנְךָ וְאֶקְרָא לְכָל הַחַיּוֹת, כִּי הֵם רָצִים אֶת כָּל הָעוֹלָם, אוּלַי תֵּדַע אַחַת מֵהֶם מֵהַר וּמִבְצָר, כַּנַּ"ל. וְקָרָא אֶת כֻּלָּם מִקָּטָן וְעַד גָּדוֹל, כָּל מִינֵי הַחַיּוֹת, וְשָׁאַל אוֹתָם, וְכֻלָּם הֵשִׁיבוּ שֶׁלֹּא רָאוּ. וְאָמַר לוֹ: רְאֵה שֶׁשְּׁטוּת סִפְּרוּ לְפָנֶיךָ! אִם תִּשְׁמַע, שׁוּב לַאֲחוֹרֶיךָ, כִּי בְּוַדַּאי לֹא תִמְצָא, כִּי אֵינֶנּוּ בָּעוֹלָם. וְהוּא הִפְצִיר מְאֹד, וְאָמַר שֶׁבְּהֶכְרֵחַ הוּא בְּנִמְצָא בְּוַדַּאי. אָמַר לוֹ [הָאָדָם הַמִּשְׁנֶה לְהַשֵּׁנִי לַמַּלְכוּת]: הִנֵּה בַּמִּדְבָּר נִמְצָא שָׁם אָחִי, וְהוּא מְמֻנֶּה עַל כָּל הָעוֹפוֹת, וְאוּלַי יוֹדְעִים הֵם, מֵחֲמַת שֶׁהֵם פּוֹרְחִים בָּאֲוִיר בְּגָבוֹהַּ, אוּלַי רָאוּ הַר וּמִבְצָר הַנַּ"ל. וְתֵלֵךְ אֵלָיו וְתֹאמַר לוֹ, שֶׁאֲנִי שְׁלַחְתִּי אוֹתְךָ אֵלָיו. וְהָלַךְ כַּמָּה וְכַמָּה שָׁנִים לְבַקְשׁוֹ, וּמָצָא שׁוּב אָדָם גָּדוֹל מְאֹד כַּנַּ"ל, וְנָשָׂא גַּם כֵּן אִילָן גָּדוֹל כַּנַּ"ל. וְשָׁאַל אוֹתוֹ גַּם כֵּן כַּנַּ"ל, וְהֵשִׁיב לוֹ כָּל הַמַּעֲשֶׂה וְשֶׁאָחִיו שְׁלָחוֹ אֵלָיו. וְהוּא דָּחָה אוֹתוֹ גַּם כֵּן, כִּי בְּוַדַּאי אֵינוֹ בַּנִּמְצָא,

but the viceroy remained adamant. He said to him (the giant to the viceroy), "I am appointed over all of the birds. I will call them, perhaps they know." He called all the birds, and asked them all, from the smallest to the biggest. They answered that they did not know of this mountain or palace. "Now you can see for yourself that it doesn't exist in the world. If you will listen to me, turn around and go back, for it doesn't exist!" But the viceroy adamantly insisted, saying that it certainly did exist.

The giant said to the viceroy, "Further in the desert, you will find my brother. He is appointed over all of the winds which travel throughout the world. Maybe they know something." The viceroy walked for many, many years until he found another giant, carrying a tree like the others. The giant asked him who he was, and the viceroy told him the whole story. Like the others, this giant tried to discourage him, but the viceroy stood his ground. The third giant said to the viceroy that he would call all of the winds of the world on his behalf and ask them. He called them, and they came. He asked them all, and they said they had never seen such a mountain or palace. The giant said: "Now you surely see that you have been led along by folly." And the viceroy began to cry very greatly, saying, "I know with certainty that it exists."

In the middle of this conversation, they saw that another wind had come. The giant grew very angry, saying, "Why did you come so late? I decreed that all of the winds should come, why did you not come together with them?"

וְהוּא הִפְצִיר אוֹתוֹ גַּם כֵּן, וְאָמַר לוֹ [הָאָדָם הַזֶּה לְהַשֵּׁנִי
לַמַּלְכוּת]. הִנֵּה אֲנִי מְמֻנֶּה עַל כָּל הָעוֹפוֹת, אֶקְרָא אוֹתָם,
אוּלַי יוֹדְעִים הֵם. וְקָרָא כָּל הָעוֹפוֹת, וְשָׁאַל אֶת כֻּלָּם מִקָּטָן
וְעַד גָּדוֹל, וְהֵשִׁיבוּ, שֶׁאֵינָם יוֹדְעִים מֵהֶר וּמִבְצָר הַנַּ״ל. אָמַר
לוֹ: הֲלֹא אַתָּה רוֹאֶה שֶׁבְּוַדַּאי אֵינֶנּוּ בָּעוֹלָם. אִם תִּשְׁמַע לִי,
שׁוּב לַאֲחוֹרֶיךָ, כִּי בְּוַדַּאי אֵינֶנּוּ! וְהוּא [הַיְנוּ הַשֵּׁנִי לַמַּלְכוּת]
הִפְצִיר אוֹתוֹ וְאָמַר שֶׁבְּוַדַּאי יֶשְׁנוֹ בָּעוֹלָם.

אָמַר לוֹ [הָאָדָם הַב׳ הַזֶּה לְהַשֵּׁנִי לַמַּלְכוּת] לְהַלָּן בַּמִּדְבָּר
נִמְצָא שָׁם אָחִי שֶׁמְּמֻנֶּה עַל כָּל הָרוּחוֹת, וְהֵם רָצִים כָּל
הָעוֹלָם, אוּלַי יוֹדְעִים הֵם. וְהָלַךְ כַּמָּה וְכַמָּה שָׁנִים לְבַקֵּשׁ,
וּמָצָא אָדָם גָּדוֹל גַּם כֵּן כַּנַּ״ל, וְנָשָׂא גַּם כֵּן אִילָן גָּדוֹל כַּנַּ״ל.
וְשָׁאַל אוֹתוֹ גַּם כֵּן כַּנַּ״ל, וְהֵשִׁיב לוֹ כָּל הַמַּעֲשֶׂה כַּנַּ״ל. וְדָחָה
אוֹתוֹ גַּם כֵּן, וְהוּא הִפְצִיר אוֹתוֹ גַּם כֵּן, וְאָמַר לוֹ [הָאָדָם
הַשְּׁלִישִׁי הַזֶּה לְהַשֵּׁנִי לַמַּלְכוּת] שֶׁלְּמַעֲנוֹ יִקְרָא שֶׁיָּבוֹאוּ
כָּל הָרוּחוֹת, וְיִשְׁאַל אוֹתָם. וְקָרָא אוֹתָם, וּבָאוּ כָּל הָרוּחוֹת,
וְשָׁאַל אֶת כֻּלָּם, וְלֹא יָדְעוּ שׁוּם אֶחָד מֵהֶם מֵהֶר וּמִבְצָר
הַנַּ״ל. וְאָמַר לוֹ [הָאָדָם הַשְּׁלִישִׁי לְהַשֵּׁנִי לַמַּלְכוּת]: הֲלֹא
אַתָּה רוֹאֶה שֶׁשְּׁטוּת סִפְּרוּ לְפָנֶיךָ! וְהִתְחִיל לִבְכּוֹת מְאֹד,
וְאָמַר: אֲנִי יוֹדֵעַ שֶׁיֶּשְׁנוֹ בְּוַדַּאי.

בְּתוֹךְ כָּךְ רָאָה שֶׁבָּא עוֹד רוּחַ אֶחָד, וְכָעַס עָלָיו הַמְמֻנֶּה
הַנַּ״ל: מַדּוּעַ נִתְאַחַרְתָּ לָבוֹא? הֲלֹא גָּזַרְתִּי שֶׁיָּבוֹאוּ כָּל
הָרוּחוֹת, וְלָמָּה לֹא בָּאתָ עִמָּהֶם? הֵשִׁיב לוֹ שֶׁנִּתְעַכַּבְתִּי

The wind answered, "I was held up because I needed to carry a princess to a mountain of gold and a palace of pearls." And he was very joyous.

The giant asked the wind, "What is precious there?" [Meaning, which items are valuable there and held in esteem?] The wind responded, "Everything there is tremendously valuable and expensive." The one appointed over the winds said to the viceroy: "Because you have been searching for her for such a great amount of time and you've had so many struggles, it is possible that you will now have a further obstacle because of money. Therefore, I will give you a vessel. Whenever you reach inside, you will take money from there." The giant commanded the wind to bring the viceroy to this place. The storm wind came and carried him there, bringing him to the gate. There were troops there who did not let him enter the city. He reached his hand into the vessel and took out money. He bribed them and entered the city. It was a beautiful city. He went to a wealthy man and paid him for room and board, for he would need to stay a while. He would need to devote much thought and contemplation to free her.

[Reb Nosson writes:] The manner in which he freed her was not told. But in the end, he freed her.

מֵחֲמַת שֶׁהָיִיתִי צָרִיךְ לָשֵׂאת בַּת מַלְכָּה אֶל הַר שֶׁל זָהָב וּמִבְצָר שֶׁל מַרְגָּלִיּוֹת. וְשָׂמַח מְאֹד.

וְשָׁאַל הַמְמֻנֶּה אֶת הָרוּחַ: מַה יָּקָר שָׁם? [הַיְנוּ אֵיזֶה דְּבָרִים הֵם שָׁם בְּיֹקֶר וּבַחֲשִׁיבוּת.] וְאָמַר לוֹ, שֶׁכָּל הַדְּבָרִים הֵם שָׁם בְּיֹקֶר גָּדוֹל. וְאָמַר הַמְמֻנֶּה עַל הָרוּחוֹת לְהַשֵּׁנִי לַמַּלְכוּת: בַּאֲשֶׁר שֶׁזֶּה זְמַן גָּדוֹל כָּל כָּךְ שֶׁאַתָּה מְבַקְשָׁהּ, וְכַמָּה יְגִיעוֹת שֶׁהָיוּ לְךָ, וְאוּלַי יִהְיֶה לְךָ עַתָּה מְנִיעָה מֵחֲמַת מָמוֹן. עַל כֵּן אֲנִי נוֹתֵן לְךָ כְּלִי, כְּשֶׁתּוֹשִׁיט יָדְךָ לְתוֹכָהּ, תְּקַבֵּל מִשָּׁם מָעוֹת. וְגָזַר עַל הָרוּחַ הַנַּ"ל, שֶׁיּוֹלִיךְ אוֹתוֹ לְשָׁם. וּבָא הָרוּחַ סְעָרָה וְנָשָׂא אוֹתוֹ לְשָׁם, וְהֵבִיא אוֹתוֹ אֶל שַׁעַר. וְהָיוּ עוֹמְדִים שָׁם חַיָּלוֹת, שֶׁלֹּא הִנִּיחוּ לִכְנֹס אֶל הָעִיר, וְהוֹשִׁיט יָדוֹ אֶל הַכְּלִי, וְלָקַח מָעוֹת, וְשִׁחֵד אוֹתָם, וְנִכְנַס לְתוֹךְ הָעִיר, וְהָיְתָה עִיר נָאָה. וְהָלַךְ אֶל גְּבִיר וְשָׂכַר לוֹ מְזוֹנוֹת, כִּי צָרִיךְ לִשְׁהוֹת שָׁם, כִּי צָרִיךְ לָשׂוּם שֵׂכֶל וְחָכְמָה לְהוֹצִיאָהּ.

וְאֵיךְ שֶׁהוֹצִיאָהּ, לֹא סִפֵּר. וּבַסּוֹף הוֹצִיאָהּ.

PART I

DUSK

לְהַגִּיד
בַּבֹּקֶר חַסְדֶּךָ
וֶאֱמוּנָתְךָ בַּלֵּילוֹת

To proclaim
Your kindness in the morning
and Your faithfulness at night.

TEHILLIM 92:2

CHAPTER 1

Searching for
the Fire of Youth

עָנָה וְאָמַר: בַּדֶּרֶךְ סִפַּרְתִּי מַעֲשֶׂה, שֶׁכָּל מִי שֶׁהָיָה שׁוֹמְעָהּ
הָיָה לוֹ הִרְהוּר תְּשׁוּבָה. וְזוֹ הִיא:

The Rebbe spoke up and said, "While on a journey,
I told a story. Whoever heard it had a thought of repentance. This is the story."

HE STORY OF THE Lost Princess opens with a few words
of introduction: "The Rebbe spoke up and said, 'While on
a journey, I told a story. Whoever heard it had a thought
of repentance.'" On a simple level, this statement relates to the circumstances through which the tale first came to be told and the
effect it had on those who heard it. Like his great-grandfather, the
holy Baal Shem Tov, Rebbe Nachman of Breslov was known for
extensive travels throughout the Ukraine — mysterious journeys
whose urgent purpose only the tzaddik understood. On one level,
then, it is probable that Rebbe Nachman was referring to an actual

trip he had taken during which he told this story for the first time, and the reaction of those who had been present at that event.[1]

However, there is surely a deeper meaning as well. If Chazal teach that even the simple words of the tzaddikim contain tremendous depth,[2] this is certainly true of words spoken regarding stories which, as we have learned, encompass the deepest secrets of our universe.

✳ The Story of Our Lives

BETRAYED BY ITS unambiguous title, the plot of our story should not be too difficult to guess: it is about a princess who gets lost and the epic search to find her. But while the story itself is emotional, poignant, and dramatic, it leaps off the page when we realize that this story is, in fact, our own. In the words of Reb Nosson of Nemirov:

> This story occurs with every person and in every era. Each individual person experiences practically this entire tale.[3]

Paying heed to the metaphor of every twist and turn in the plot, the reader perceives a sense of intimate familiarity. One finds that the events and emotions so vividly portrayed are those he has experienced firsthand in the story of his own life; feelings he thought might never find expression, emotions assumed to defy analyzation. In the framework of this wonderful story, these feelings are free to emerge with incredible clarity, granting one the ability to examine them closely for the first time — gaining, in

---

1. Indeed, this particular story was told to the chassidim on 11 Av, 1806, following the Rebbe's mysterious journey to Medvedevka. (*Yemei Moharanat* Vol. 1, 11)
2. *Avodah Zarah* 19b.
3. Second introduction to *Sippurei Maasios*.

the process, profound insight into the great struggle and triumph of the human condition.

In our attempt to experience the tale in this manner, it is important that we first explore the identity of the princess in our lives and attain a general understanding of the manner in and degree to which she has become lost.

✳ From Wonder to Apathy

THE LIFE CIRCUMSTANCES of each Jew are replete with details unique to his or her personal circumstances — each person is an *olam malei*, an entire universe; "Just as their faces differ, so are their personalities dissimilar."[4] However, while the distance between one Jew and the next may be very great indeed, there are certain intergalactic paths that cross the great divides, universal experiences to which we can all relate.

Chief among these collectively shared adventures is the developmental journey from childhood to adulthood. Regardless of background, family circumstance, appearance, personality, abilities, habits, experiences, traumas, tendencies, or aspirations, we have all experienced that very same journey. No matter our current age, stage, or physical location, our identity as adults has been shaped by the contours of this turbulent transformation.

The journey from childhood to adulthood is remarkable in many respects. In a healthy environment, this transformation is the glorious voyage from selfishness to selflessness, irresponsibility to maturity, and small mindedness to a broader perspective.[5] More so than any other element, it is the autonomy of adult

---

4. *Berachos* 58a.
5. See *Likutei Amarim, Tanya*, Chapter 6.

independence that allows for the difficult personal decisions that result in spiritual greatness.

Yet, for all the advantage this transition implies, it oftentimes involves a profound loss. As wonderful as it is to live as an adult in a grown-up world, the journey from childhood to adulthood is often the journey from wonder to apathy, from simplicity to sophistication, from innocence to wariness, from self-confidence to self-doubt, and — most devastatingly — from spiritual sensitivity to the numbing of the soul.

Our story begins with a seemingly trivial detail: *"The Rebbe spoke up and said, 'While on a journey, I told a story.'"* But the Breslover *mashpi'im* teach that far more than merely revealing the circumstances in which the story first came to be told, these words hint to the timeless setting in which this story continually takes place — the great journey of life. Along the journey we have taken on the wondrous path of the human experience, something happens to us: *The princess of youth gets lost.* Somewhere along this journey the natural excitement for serving Hashem fades away. Anxieties, inhibitions, and phobias cast their net over our inner world, robbing us of our self-confidence. Our soaring dreams and unlimited ambitions are quashed by the apparent limitations of "the real world," triggering a deluge of cynicism, disappointment, and despair that rushes to fill the vacuum. The more accustomed we become to the norms of this bizarre reality, the more distant we grow from the norms of the spiritual world from which our pure souls descended, making it increasingly difficult to connect with matters pertaining to that realm of absolute truth and transcendent beauty. The passion, love, and excitement we experienced upon donning tefillin or kindling Shabbos candles for the first time are but a distant memory — replaced, somewhere along the way, with a feeling of onerous obligation, chore, and burden.

"The Rebbe spoke up and said, 'While on a journey, I told a story.'" Rebbe Nachman is teaching that the story of the Lost

Princess is bound up with "a journey" — *our* journey, the journey with which we are so intimately familiar. The princess represents our life-essence, the vitality so central to the holistic health of the human being, the excitement of being alive that all children seem to naturally exude. Somewhere along our journey, the princess of youth gets lost. We lose our confidence, our wonder, our faith.[6] We lose touch with the faith Hashem has in us, the pride He takes in our every movement. As the years pass by and the princess is taken further and further away, we arrive upon the desolate shores of complacency, settling into a complete and utter sense of despair — an inner dissonance masked by a fake smile, feigned interest, and the sophistication of the grown-up pursuits in which we bury ourselves, hoping to numb the throbbing pain of our meaninglessness. Instead of enjoying real relationships, deep connections, and a world seen through the wide eyes of faith as bursting with beauty and joy, we pursue wealth, power, lust, and honor. A nagging voice inside our heads may protest from time to time, reminding us that there must be a better way to live, but we tune it out, convincing ourselves that this is the way of the world — it is impossible for an adult to approach life with childlike simplicity and excitement. We simply learn to get along without it. *Baderech, "While on a journey,"* the fire of youth is extinguished, the ashes cooled, and then, as the years flash by, finally frozen in blocks of malevolent ice.

Referring to Amalek, the symbol of the wicked spiritual force

---

6. See *Midrash Tanchumah, Bereishis* 7 and *Bei'urei HaGra* to *Bava Kama* 92b. See also *Mevo L'Chassidus Ul'Darkah shel Chabad*, p. 132, where R' Hillel Zeitlin writes that the Maggid of Mezritch learned three things from children: 1. Joy is their natural state, 2. They are always busy, 3. They cry when they need something. This teaching points to a number of the positive traits associated with youth that become obscured along the journey to adulthood: joy, optimistic alacrity, and emotional sensitivity.

that reaches across generations to accost each and every Jew,[7] the verse states *"Asher karcha baderech."*[8] Translated literally, this verse means "They (the nation of Amalek) happened upon you along the way," referring to the war waged on the fledgling Jewish nation soon after their exodus from Egypt. However, Rashi reveals that while the word *"karcha"* means "happened upon," it can also mean "to cool." Based on this alternative understanding, the tzaddikim teach that with these words, the Torah is revealing to us the essence of Amalek's spiritual strategy: *Asher karcha baderech,* "That they *cooled you off* along the way." Along the journey of life, the Amalek within seeks to rob us of the spiritual fire that had once warmed and illuminated our lives. *"Asher karcha **baderech**."* *"**Baderech** siparti maaseh."* They are one and the same.[9]

It is safe to assume that many of us have experienced the loss of the princess in some area of our lives. Whether in the areas of *avodas Hashem,* marriage, parenthood, friendships, passions, or ambitions, we have experienced some level of numbing, of dimming; the cooling that takes place with the passage of time — the Amaleki chill at work. Although we live with greater prosperity

---

7. See *Kedushas Levi, Parshas Zachor.*

8. *Devarim* 25:17.

9. In *Likutei Halachos* (*Birchas HaPeiros* 5:3), Reb Nosson teaches that Amalek's primary objective was to attack the *Shevet* Dan. Along the travels through the desert, *Shevet* Dan always walked behind all other *shevatim* and served as a lost and found for the entire Jewish nation. Amalek seeks to eradicate the "lost objects" of the Jewish soul, the youthful elements of inspired living that become obscured along the journey to adulthood. It is to counter the aspect of Amalek which causes a Jew to forget about the Lost Princess of his life that the Torah commands us *"zachor"* and *"lo tishkach"* — to remember Amalek's wicked goal and the Lost Princess of youth that awaits discovery and redemption. "The main thing is that one remembers, for as long as one still remembers that things were lost and makes every effort to discover them and not to lose himself, there is yet hope. For Hashem is constantly thinking thoughts so that no soul will be lost, and in the end one will certainly find."

and comfort than any other generation in the history of the world, the ethereal spirit of contentment and true joy seems to have slipped through our fingers, lost to the subtle maladies of apathy and despair. The fact that, despite boundless opportunity waiting right outside their door, millions of people all around the world find it impossible to drag themselves out of bed in the morning is an experience unique to our broken generation.

It is along the difficult journey of our physical and emotional development that Rebbe Nachman told the first of his remarkable stories, a tale that grants us the guidance necessary to search for, discover, and recover the princess of youth. Through the medium of his holy words, Hashem has granted the Jewish nation the tools necessary to battle the frostiness of Amalek, discover lasting inspiration, and get in touch with the euphoric and heavenly spirit of the "engagement period" which, while every-present, becomes mightily concealed under the routine nature of marriage; the everydayness of *avodas Hashem*. With this story in hand, we hold the key to reestablishing contact with an *avodas Hashem* that is bursting with holy fire, a treasure that can enable us to regain feeling in all areas of our lives and — most importantly — daven, study Torah, and perform mitzvos with passion and excitement just as we did in the days of our youth.[10]

⊛ Return to Who You Are

IN THE INTRODUCTION to his tale, Rebbe Nachman states that whoever heard the story had a thought of *teshuvah*. Classically, the concept of *teshuvah*, which literally means "to return," refers

---

10. A Chassidic interpretation of Yehudah's plea, *Ki eich e'eleh el avi v'hanaar einenu iti*, "For how can I ascend to my father when the lad is no longer with me?", reads it as the prayer of each and every Jew: "For how can I ascend to my Father in heaven when the inner child of passion and wonder is no longer with me?"

to the process of returning to a life of religious commitment and realignment with Hashem and His Torah. On a deeper level, however, *teshuvah* means to return to *oneself*, to rediscover the true essence of who one is and uncover the holiness at one's core — the holy passion and wonder of our childhood which, as Rav Kook writes, represents the highest possible quality of living, an ideal we spend the majority of our adult years attempting to regain.[11] Perhaps it is this definition of *teshuvah* — which reflects the inner dimension of the classical understanding — to which Rebbe Nachman refers. Treating the discovery of our essential self and the manner in which we may regain connection with the youthful spirit of excitement, passion, joy, vitality, humility, vulnerability, sincerity, and simplicity that has gotten lost along the way, *The Lost Princess* inspired a thought of *teshuvah* in all those who heard it: "*Return, my soul*, to your place of comfort."[12] "The Torah of Hashem is complete, enabling the soul *to return to its place*."[13]

How are we to define the essential self? When a Jew returns to the root of his soul, what does he encounter?

One of the mighty foundations of the Chassidic perspective is the firm conviction that the innermost foundation of existence is rooted in goodness and holiness. Belief in the essential goodness and acute holiness present at the truest core of the Jewish identity, the tzaddikim stressed that instead of seen as working from the outside in, defined in the common Mussar axiom, "External actions *impact* the inner emotions," *avodas Hashem* must be seen as working *from the inside out*: "External actions *reveal* the inner emotions." In the circles of the Chassidic masters, the teaching of "*Mitoch shelo lishmah ba lishmah*" did not simply mean that by engaging in Torah for ulterior motives, one would eventually

---

11. *Middos HaRAYaH*, p. 230.
12. *Tehillim* 116:7.
13. *Tehillim* 19:8.

come to study it for the proper reasons. Rather, they read this teaching differently: *"Mitoch shelo lishmah,"* within the ulterior motive itself, *"ba lishmah,"* one is able to unearth the veiled presence of holy intention.[14] The Baal HaTanya saw the verse "For the soul of man is God's candle"[15] as referring to the constant inner yearning of the Jewish soul to jump out of the bodily bond into ego-obliterating union with the Master of the world, much like a flickering flame constantly jumps and dances in a desperate attempt to escape the earthly bond of the wick.[16] Beyond the layers of concealment and foreign impulses, the soul of a Jew is always flickering, constantly yearning for a life of closeness with its Creator. In the words of the tzaddik:

> *"Knesses Yisrael"* is the source of every Jewish soul and is called by the name *Libi,* "My heart." This collective soul is the inner point of each Jewish heart whose nature is to rise, like a flame, to attach itself to Hashem. This is the essence of the soul, founded in the realms of holiness, a literal portion of God on High. Its only desire and yearning is to nullify itself and to become included in Hashem's Light, to allow that light to manifest within the mental powers and emotional traits which in turn express themselves in thought, speech, and action, the "garments" of the soul...[17]

In the words of Rebbe Nachman of Breslov:

> For one who knows the holiness of the Jewish people, and the place from which they are taken, and understands their spiritual nature and sublimity — he knows, that the Jewish people are absolutely distant from sin, and that sin has no

---

14. See *Chovas HaTalmidim* 12:7.
15. *Mishlei* 20:27.
16. *Likutei Amarim, Tanya,* Chapter 19.
17. *Torah Ohr, Tetzaveh,* "Zachor."

connection with them whatsoever, in light of the tremendous holiness at their root and the awesomeness of their sublimity and spirituality.[18]

In a comment on the verse *Karov Atah Hashem*, "Hashem, You are near,"[19] the Ibn Ezra records three words which penetrate to the depths: *Karov mikol karov*, "Nearer than all near." Closeness with Hashem sits at the centermost point of the Jewish soul — *nearer than all near.* Engagement with His love is our premise, purpose, and ultimate eventuality. With it, we need nothing more. Without it, nothing else will do.[20]

Because of our essential holiness, our most familiar and natural state is the closeness with Hashem achieved through conscious alignment with His will. The Torah is a glorious tool which, when engaged with in a healthy manner, guides the Jew toward living in a way that is more natural and familiar to the soul than anything else, constantly drawing light and energy from the letter in the Torah that is her deepest source.[21] Sadly, however, when we lose touch with our true identity, we come to see the Torah as a foreign system of restrictions unjustly imposed upon us that demands grotesquely unnatural intellectual, physical, and emotional contortion, a frightful distortion of the truth. In this place of existential obscurity, we become caught in the magnetic field of the *yetzer hara* and wander away from our essence to frolic in the fields of what the tzaddikim refer to as *"machshavos zaros," strange thoughts* of impurity, anxiety, arrogance, anger, and jealousy. These thoughts are called "strange" because, inhibiting our ability to cleave to Hashem, they are

---

18. *Likutei Moharan Tinyana* 7. See also *Tzidkas HaTzaddik* 52, *Derech Pikudecha*, Introduction, 5:8, and *Maharal, Netzach Yisrael*, Chapter 14.

19. *Tehillim* 119:151.

20. See *Oros, Zeironim* 8.

21. *Zohar Chadash*, p. 74.

foreign to the nature of our being, the holiness of our eternal dignity. Their entire essence is "strangeness"; they cause a Jew to perceive Yiddishkeit as something "strange" and "foreign" to one's true identity. Rooted in the Primordial Snake which, while originally a completely external force, became included within Adam's being after the original sin,[22] the *yetzer hara* and his army of *machshavos zaros* attempt to assume our true identity. This mighty inner force, which is entirely foreign to our true essence, often succeeds in convincing us that its own physically oriented goals and desires are the defining factor of our character, not our yearning for holiness.

The tzaddikim teach that returning from a life of existential abnormality to the most familiar element of our existence — that part of us which sits in eternal communion with Hashem Who is "nearer than all near" — represents the very essence of *teshuvah*.[23] Indeed, *teshuvah* means not "to turn," but rather "to *return*." *Teshuvah* is not about attaining something new that we didn't already have before. It is simply about returning to the most natural state of the Jew, a life lived in alignment with the strivings of our innermost identity.

---

22. See *Nefesh HaChaim* 1:6.

23. The tzaddikim teach that all Jewish souls are hewn from under the *Kisei HaKavod*. This idea parallels another, that the *Kisei HaKavod* is linked to the spiritual world of *Binah-Imah* which is seen as the universal womb from which all souls emerge. This inner dimension of the *teshuvah* process is hinted to in the statement of Chazal, "*Teshuvah* is great, for it reaches the *Kisei HaKavod*" (*Yoma* 86a). In this statement, Chazal are teaching that *teshuvah* represents the Jew's returning to the *Kisei HaKavod* — the very essence of his soul. (This idea is also related to Rebbe Nachman's teaching in *Likutei Moharan Tinyana* 73 that the Forty-nine Gates of *Teshuvah* accessible to each and every Jew correspond to the forty-nine letters in the names of the *shevatim*. In pointing out this connection, the tzaddik is communicating that the *teshuvah* process is one of return to our essential and ideal state as rooted in the *shevatim*, the root of our souls.) See *Shaarei Orah*, Eighth Gate.

In the words of Rav Kook:

> When we forget the nature of our individual *neshamah*, when we divert our attention from focusing on the quality of the individual's inner life, everything becomes confused and rife with doubt. The primary *teshuvah*, which immediately illuminates all darkness, is when a person returns to himself; to the essence of his *neshamah*. Immediately, he then returns to Hashem, the Soul of souls, and proceeds onward, higher and higher in holiness and purity.[24]

In another place:

> One must learn about the greatness of his soul and its sublimity in its very essence. Even though he may become dirtied with all manners of physical dross, "even when a myrtle is found among thorns, it is still a myrtle, and we must refer to it as a myrtle"[25] — the soul forever remains shining by virtue of its essence. In truth, the mere awareness of this itself purifies, for this knowledge is one of the mighty branches of *teshuvah mei'ahavah*.[26]

In a third:

> From the side of the soul, one already has the requisite capacity to rejoice in Hashem and to take pleasure in the delight of His love and the light of expanded consciousness. It is just that the weakness or lowliness of the body prevents that light from becoming revealed. It emerges that the

---

24. *Oros HaTeshuvah* 16:10.

25. *Sanhedrin* 44a. The larger context of this phrase: "When Hashem explained to Yehoshua the reason for the Jewish people's defeat at the city of Ai, He said: 'Yisrael has sinned' (*Yehoshua* 7:11). Rav Abba bar Zavda says: 'From here it may be inferred that even when the Jewish people have sinned, they are still called "Yisrael."' Rav Abba says: 'This is in accordance with the adage that people say: Even when a myrtle is found among thorns, its name is myrtle and people call it myrtle.'"

26. *Mussar Avicha* 1:8.

essence is always already prepared. It is only the secondary element which stands in the way. Therefore, a person must be aware that the essence is primary. One should be confident that the light of Hashem already shines in his soul, although it may be hidden...[27]

Filled with a singular sense of clarity and honesty on Yom Kippur due to the gravity of the moment and our separation from the physical distractions of life, we declare, "All desire to fear Your Name."[28] In that shining moment of truth, it becomes clear to us that despite the mundanity of our diverse ambitions and goals, the burning desire for closeness with Hashem is our deepest concern. Exhausted from the strangeness of our experience, we desire nothing more than to return to our essential selves, to Hashem Who is "nearer than all near." In that moment of silent reflection, we are beckoned by the expression of Hashem's ultimate concern,[29] a universal wail that reaches our individual soul like sunlight embraces a lonely flower in a field of weeds, "Woe is to creation for the embarrassment of the Torah."[30]

When Adam and Chava hid from His presence, Hashem called out: *"Ayekah?* Where are you?" It is a call that goes out again and again. It is a still small echo of a still small voice, not uttered in words, not conveyed in categories of the mind, but ineffable and mysterious, as ineffable and mysterious as the glory that fills the whole world. It is wrapped in silence; concealed and subdued, yet it is as if all things were the frozen echo of the question: "Where are you?"[31]

27. *Pinkesei HaRayah* 11:15.
28. Yom Kippur liturgy.
29. See *Berachos* 4b, *Rashi*: "If a Jew who is accustomed to praying in the *beis knesses* does not show up, Hashem asks about him: "What is *Ploni*'s situation? Why hasn't he come?"
30. See *Degel Machaneh Ephraim, Shelach,* "*Dabeir.*"
31. *Between God and Man*, p. 69.

The word "*teshuvah*," return, can also mean "an answer." Deep within the innermost recesses of our heart and soul, we are filled with an overpowering desire to embody the spirit of *teshuvah* by answering Hashem's call to action and beginning our return to the blessings of youth. *And we can!* Reaching out to us through the nuance of this iconic tale, Rebbe Nachman of Breslov is holding our hand, whispering: "Never despair! The Lost Princess of youth is waiting for you! It is possible to free her if you only take up the search! Please allow me show you the way!"

The Breslover *mashpi'im* concur: Rebbe Nachman's statement that anyone who heard the tale of the Lost Princess had a thought of repentance is far more than a simple anecdote. It is a firm guarantee. This tale contains the wisdom, guidance, and encouragement necessary to enable us to miraculously gather our strength and begin the journey to our essential self. With faith in the tzaddik's words, Hashem's help, and a healthy dose of holy confidence, we will succeed in coming face to face with the wide-eyed youth at the core of our being and again share in the great gifts he holds. Let's begin!

LESSONS FOR LIFE

⊛ In our formative years, our transformation from children into adults is oftentimes accompanied by a loss of the innocence, excitement, wonder, passion, and joy that is so natural to youth.

⊛ The essence of *teshuvah* is the return to our essential self and the closeness with Hashem which sits at the core of our being. The ability to rediscover vibrancy in all areas of life is ever-present. It is never too late! There is no despair in the world at all!

CHAPTER 2

Our Tale Begins

מַעֲשֶׂה בְּמֶלֶךְ אֶחָד, שֶׁהָיוּ לוֹ שִׁשָׁה בָּנִים וּבַת אֶחָת. וְאוֹתָה
הַבַּת הָיְתָה חֲשׁוּבָה בְּעֵינָיו מְאֹד, וְהָיָה מְחַבְּבָהּ בְּיוֹתֵר,
וְהָיָה מְשַׁעֲשֵׁעַ עִמָּהּ מְאֹד.

There was once a king who had six sons and one
daughter. The daughter was very precious in his
eyes and he loved her very much. He took very great
delight in her.

R EBBE NACHMAN BEGINS THE first of his tales by
introducing a king and his seven children — six sons and
one daughter. Traditionally, whenever we encounter a
king in a Jewish parable, it is a reference to the King of kings, the
Master of the world. In our interpretation of *The Lost Princess*, we
will follow this assumption as well.

Although, as stated in the preface, this book is devoted to exploring the psychospiritual insight of this story, not its mystical
depth, in certain places we will need to touch upon some basic
concepts of Kabbalah so that we might attain the deepest spiritual

insight. While some of these concepts may seem challenging at first, we shall attempt to present them in a logical, down-to-earth, and practical way.[1]

✳ Stained-Glass Windows of Divine Expression

THE *MEKUBALIM* TEACH that in order to make Himself known to His creation, Hashem emanated the Ten *Sefiros*, ten spiritual channels by way of which the world was created and which continually reveal different facets of His absolute unity. Each of these *Sefiros* embodies a different aspect of the way Hashem expresses Himself in governing the world and directing the path of history. The Ramak explains this foundational concept using the analogy of stained-glass windowpanes. Just as ten different colored stained-glass windowpanes reveal various hues included in the all-encompassing sunlight which would have been otherwise undiscernible to the naked eye, the Ten *Sefiros* render different qualities of the all-encompassing Divine Light of Hashem accessible to the human mind.[2] It is important to stress that, as this parable implies, the *Sefiros* do nothing to detract from the absolute oneness of Hashem, *chas v'shalom*. They are merely spiritual tools created to render the quality of Hashem's perfect unity comprehensible to our limited intellect.

The Ten *Sefiros* are: *Kesser*-Crown, *Chochmah*-Intellect, *Binah*-Wisdom, *Chessed*-Loving-kindness, *Gevurah*-Strength, *Tiferes*-Harmony, *Netzach*-Eternity, *Hod*-Splendor, *Yesod*-Foundation, and *Malchus*-Kingship.

---

1. For a fuller exposition on these foundational concepts, see Appendix E.
2. *Sifsei Chein*, p. 93.

The Torah teaches that we are created *b'tzelem Elokim*,[3] in the form of the way Hashem (Who is, Himself, infinitely beyond form) relates to the world. The tzaddikim teach us the inner meaning of this concept: reflecting the Ten *Sefiros* through which Hashem reveals Himself in the world, the "DNA" of the soul consists of ten powers that serve as the blueprint for both the human's inner makeup as well as his external appearance.[4]

On the level of emotions, our inborn capacity for *Chessed* enables us to act with unrestrained kindness and love toward our fellow man. *Gevurah* allows us to exercise restraint, strictness, and anger — when necessary. Our inborn capacity for *Tiferes* is the seat of confidence and pride. *Netzach* is the garment through which our soul's drive toward survival and the experience of eternity is expressed and *Hod* allows for submissive gratitude and praise of Hashem and others. *Yesod* expresses our desire for social interaction and having a positive impact on the world and *Malchus* is our capacity to receive and reciprocate.

This system finds physical expression as well. The human skull is a manifestation of *Kesser*. The mind with its two hemispheres is the vessel for the mental *Sefiros*: *Chochmah*, holistic thought, and *Binah*, the ability to delve into particularities of an idea and draw parallels and distinctions. The heart consists of six emotional *Sefiros*: *Chessed* and *Gevurah* which manifest in the right and left arms, respectively; *Tiferes* which manifests in the torso; *Netzach* and *Hod* which manifest in the right and left legs, respectively; *Yesod* (Foundation) which manifests in the *bris*; and *Malchus* which manifests in the mouth and its capacity for speech, as well as in the mate.

Considering the Ten *Sefiros* in this way gives us a better understanding of how they manifest in the human experience. The

---

3. *Bereishis* 1:27.

4. This is one of the many interpretations of *"Tzelem Elokim"* found among the Rishonim. See *Rabbeinu Bachya* to *Bereishis* 1:27. See Fig. A.

Ten *Sefiros*, which enable the unity of Hashem to express itself in the realm of multiplicity, find expression in the various powers of the mind and heart which reveal the multifarious functions included as one in the unity of the soul. Created to allow the mental and emotional capacities of the heart and mind to come to expression, the body mirrors the inner Ten *Sefiros* included in the soul of man.

	Psychological Manifestation	Physical Manifestation
Kesser	Desire	Skull
Chochmah	Intellect	Right Brain (Holistic)
Binah	Wisdom/ Intuition	Left Brain (Particularities)
Chessed	Unrestrained Kindness	Right Arm
Gevurah	Restraint	Left Arm
Tiferes	Confidence/ Truth	Torso
Netzach	Dominance/ Endurance	Right Leg
Hod	Submission/ Praise	Left Leg
Yesod	Connectivity/ Impact	*Bris*
Malchus	Receiving/ Reciprocity	Mouth/Mate

Fig. A: The Ten Sefiros and Their Basic Psychological and Physical Manifestation

❊ Six Sons —
The *Quantity* of Daily Accomplishment

THE BRESLOVER *MASHPI'IM* teach that when Rebbe Nachman speaks of a king and his six sons, this is a reference to six of the seven lower *Sefiros* through which Hashem reveals Himself to the world, *Chessed* through *Yesod*. As we have learned, these six traits serve as "stained-glass windows" to allow Hashem's all-encompassing infinite light to express itself in a way that allows it to be better understood. In the same manner, these six inborn *Sefiros* allow our soul to express her ethereal essence in a perceivable way.

"*The king had six sons*": Hashem implanted the functional capacities of the lower six *Sefiros* within the soul of each and every Jew.

In the Kabbalistic literature, masculinity is associated with extroversion and overt influence.[5] The right row of the Sefirotic array, the *Middos* of *Chochmah*, *Chessed*, and *Netzach*, (right brain, right arm, right leg) are "Male *Sefiros*." *Chochmah* is revealed as the initial burst of intellect in a creative process, *Chessed* as the unrestrained desire to give, and *Netzach* as an overwhelming and dominant element in interpersonal relationships.

Similarly, taken together as a single unit in contradistinction with the final *Sefirah* of *Malchus*, the first six of the lower seven *Sefiros* are seen as a masculine force. In their emotional expression, the *Sefiros* from *Chessed* to *Yesod* are the seat of action and accomplishment. What begins as a drive toward unrestrained

---

5. This concept appears in the Talmud as well, see *Kiddushin* 2b: "It is the way of a man to go out to war," and *Kesubos* 65b: "It is the way of a man to conquer." Perhaps it is possible to suggest that it is because Dinah bas Yaakov was originally conceived as a male in Leah's womb and only later switched to a female (see *Berachos* 60a) that she was a "*yatzanis*," outfitted with an extroverted nature. (See *Rashi* to *Bereishes* 34:1.)

giving in *Chessed* culminates in *Yesod*, the channel which actualizes this extroverted ambition. In their physical expression the six *Sefiros* are external, manifesting in hands and feet, etc.[6] The *Sefer Yetzirah* teaches that these six *Sefiros* are related to the six directions of the world (North, South, East, West, Up, Down) which point and extend *outward*.[7]

Because the seven lower *Sefiros* serve as the general blueprint for our physical reality[8] they are reflected in patterns of seven scattered throughout nature. There are, for example, seven primary colors of the rainbow, seven musical notes in the chromatic scale, seven core wisdoms, seven metals of antiquity, seven classical planets, seven continents, and seven seas. But perhaps the most familiar expression of what may be referred to as the "seven-ness of nature" is the weekly cycle of seven days. As with the illustrations mentioned above, each of the units in this set of seven corresponds to one of the seven lower *Sefiros*. Sunday is associated with *Chessed*, Monday with *Gevurah*, Tuesday with *Tiferes*, and so on.[9]

---

6. As opposed to the *Mochin*-mental capacities, which are concealed within the skull.

7. *InnerSpace*, p. 75.

8. The first three *Sefiros*, the *Mochin*, represent the hidden energizing force of creation, beyond time and space, which infuses nature with spiritual vitality. This is why, as the Maharal so often writes (see, for example, *Tiferes Yisrael* Chapters 1 and 2), the number eight denotes transcendence and miraculous power. In the miracle of Chanukah, for example, the laws of nature were altered for **eight** nights (*"B'nei **Binah**, y'mei **shemonah**"* — *Maoz Tzur*). This idea is also connected to the *Bris Milah*, which is performed on the **eighth** day from birth and represents man's ability to transcend his physical desires (see *Yalkut Shemoni* 33), as well as the **eight** strings of tzitzis that enable him to do so. (See *Menachos* 44a.)

9. See *Sifsei Chein, Hakdamah* 6. The author demonstrates the relationship between the seven lower *Sefiros* and the days of the week by finding their energies reflected in the particular elements introduced during each of the original seven days of creation. For example: The creation of the first day, light, reflects

In light of our characterization of the first six of the lower seven *Middos* as a masculine unit marked by extroversion and quantitative accomplishment, it now becomes clear why the Torah labels the first six days of the week as *"yemei hamaaseh,"*[10] days of action. *Sheishes yamim ta'avod v'asisah kol milachtecha,* "For six days you shall work and do all of your labor"[11]; these are days of external accomplishment, physical improvement, and financial gain.

This introduction allows us to understand the nature of the king's six sons in our story.[12]

The six sons, many in number and extroverted in orientation, represent quantitative physical accomplishment. External, impressive, grandiose, and glamorous, the six sons of a person's

---

the positive, giving nature of *Chessed*. On the second day, the firmament was created, hardening upon Hashem's decree, an aspect of *Gevurah*, rigidity and restraint (*yiras Shamayim*). The third day saw the creation of a tremendous diversity of plants blanketing the earth in a wave of color, an aspect of *Tiferes*, which denotes beauty and harmony. On the fourth day, the sun and the moon were created, allowing for the cyclical continuity of nature, an aspect of *Netzach*, endurance (see *Bereishis* 8:22), and so on regarding the creations of the other days.

10. *Yechezkel* 46:1.

11. *Shemos* 20:8.

12. It is important to stress that this characterization and the negative connotation we shall explore refers solely to the six *Sefiros* when viewed on their own, theoretically devoid of a connection to the life-giving energy of *Malchus*. It is only in this arrangement (which, in the context of the *Sefiros* through which Hashem reveals Himself to the world, is inapplicable) that the six sons may be seen in this manner. When focused toward *Malchus*, the six *Sefiros* are absolutely pulsating with energy: *Chessed* is bursting with desire to give, *Yesod* is an active channel which pours forth life-force, etc. It is only in the theoretical absence of a connection to *Malchus*, an ultimate goal and premise, that the six sons may be seen as shallow, lifeless, and outward. The description that follows is true only in the scenario that plays out, to varying degrees, in our human experience.

life represent his collective achievement and calculable success. Financially, these six sons manifest in a thick portfolio, expensive cars in the driveways of a few beautiful homes, and money to indulge in the heart's desires. Happiness, however, they do not guarantee. Spiritually, the six sons find expression in a great many motions of religious fervor and vast accomplishment in Torah scholarship and halachah observance. Of a true relationship with the Master of the world, however, there is no assurance.

Because we live in a physical realm wherein the hiddenness of God and the obscurity of the soul give rise to shallowness and the foolish celebration of transience, the six sons are highly respected. Of the three dimensions that make up the physical realm — *time*, *space*, and the *ego* — space is by far the most tangible. We can see it, measure it, and utilize it for our purposes. The various items it holds can be touched, smelled, heard, felt, and tasted. From the perspective of the body's physical eyes, the realm of space, with its delightful palpability, represents the most concrete reality. It is only natural, then, that we would be so keen to glorify accomplishments related to the realm of space, quantity, and tangibility. And indeed, in both secular and religious circles, this triumvirate is where we place the bulk of our focus.[13] In the realm of religion, we are quick to evaluate one's spiritual status by outward appearance, level of scholarship, and degree of quantifiable conformance to the exacting stringencies of the law. Sensitivity, simplicity, humility, faith, prayer, and holy desire, while appreciated, are

---

13. "The underlying assumption of modern man's outlook is that objective reality is physical: all non-material phenomena can be reduced to material phenomena and explained in physical terms. Thus, only those types of human experiences that acquaint us with the quantitative aspects of material phenomena refer to the real world. None of the other types of our experience, such as prayer or the awareness of the presence of God, has any objective counterpart. They are illusory in the sense that they do not acquaint us with the nature of the objective world" (*Between God and Man*, p. 71).

marginalized and perhaps even degraded. In the irreligious sector of society, the picture is far more extreme. The value of a person is generally dependent upon his material accomplishments — the model car, career, size of house, attractiveness of family, and other such shallow measures.[14] In the words of R' Erez Moshe Doron:

> Our physical world is competitive and achievement oriented. When we meet someone after not having seen him in a while, we ask, "What's doing?" What we really mean is, "What have you accomplished, materially? Did you buy something? Get a promotion? Get another degree? Make more money? Do you have a new car? A house? A wife? Children? Did you travel? See the world?"
>
> If he isn't wealthier, still not married, doesn't have children, doesn't have a profession or job, we think "So what's he worth?" If he answers, "I've just spent a year touring Europe," that sounds impressive to us. But if he says, "I just spent a year undergoing an inner process that taught me a great deal about myself and helped me to make major changes in my personality," we respond with a raised eyebrow or disinterest. "That's all very well and good," we think, "but what did he *do*?"[15]

If we can't immediately measure a person's success and accomplishment, he is sullied in our eyes. Obsessed with the realm of space and the physical things that fill it, we lose sense for the ethereal realm of time and the preciousness of accomplishments which may not register on our rulers, scales, and calculators. This is the natural attitude of global society which glorifies the six sons of extroversion and calculable gain.

While the accomplishments of the six sons in both the religious and material realms are certainly necessary if one is to

---

14. See *Sunlight of Redemption*, pp. 83–84.
15. *Wings*, pp. 25–26.

fulfill his mission in life, Rebbe Nachman teaches that it is not the sons who occupy the dearest place by the King of kings. Rather, *"The daughter was very precious in his eyes and he loved her very much. He spent much time delighting in her."* It is the princess Hashem truly treasures.

❀ One Daughter: The *Quality* of Daily Living

THIS ONLY DAUGHTER of the king, the princess, is the protagonist of our tale. If the sons represent the first six of the lower seven *Sefiros* and the masculine energy of the six days of the week, the princess represents the seventh *Sefirah, Malchus,* and the feminine energy of *Shabbos Kodesh.* In stark contrast to the shallow activities of the six *Middos, Malchus* is a deeply soulful, emotional, feeling, introspective, and purposeful spirit.[16] While the six sons find expression in the six directions extending outward toward infinity, the princess is the core, the center, the middle point where the directions meet and from which they extend.[17]

As the ultimate *tachlis,* goal, of the six *Sefiros* that precede her, *Malchus* is the life-giving motor to their machine; the animating

---

16. This relationship is hinted to in *Shir HaShirim* (5:16): *"Shokav amudei sheish, meyusadim al adnei-paz."* Literally translated, this verse means "His legs are like pillars of marble, founded upon sockets of fine gold," but the Kabbalists (see *Shaarei Orah,* Third Gate) revealed a deeper, mystical interpretation: *"Shokav amudei **sheish"*** — the **six** sons, the first six of the seven lower *Sefiros,* are *"meyusadim al **adnei-paz"*** — reliant upon the *Middah* of *Malchus* which is bound with the Name *"**Adona-i"*** in addition to being the bottommost *Sefirah,* like a *socket* (see *Meor Einayim, Bereishis,* *"Bereishis bara"*) and whose vibrancy, vitality, and joy is symbolized by the preciousness of **gold.** (The connection between *Malchus* and *gold* in this verse will become exceedingly significant in the later chapters of this book.)

17. See *InnerSpace,* p. 75.

answer to the lifeless question of their existence.[18] Her presence clarifies and energizes their existence, lending meaning to their otherwise mindless pursuit. If the six sons represent *doing*, the princess represents *being*. She is the soul, the core, the essence. In the absence of her unifying energy, chaos reigns.

Although *Malchus* appears to be the lowest in rank and thus the least important of the *Sefiros*, when viewed as the final step in a creative process, we understand *Malchus* as being the focal point of creation, the ultimate culmination of all the other *Sefirah*-revelations of Hashem's unity. Similarly, while the seventh day seems to be the last and thus the "lowest" day of the week, we know that the holiness of Shabbos is beyond comprehension and that it is the "Day of the Soul,"[19] the greatest opportunity to connect with Hashem in the most genuine manner.

On Shabbos there is rest from quantitative pursuits. As we lay down our modern-day tools, we escape the concrete nature of physical space into the ethereal spirit of time whose imperceivable presence drapes the world in a mantle of holiness. This was expressed most beautifully by a great Jewish thinker who wrote:

> How should we weigh the difference between Shabbos and the other days of the week? When a day like Wednesday arrives, the hours are blank, and unless we lend significance to them, they remain without character. The hours of the seventh day are significant in themselves; their significance and beauty do not depend on any work, profit, or progress we may achieve. They have the beauty of grandeur…
>
> In the tempestuous ocean of time and toil there are islands of stillness where man may enter a harbor and regain his dignity. The island is the seventh day, Shabbos, a day of

---

18. This is hinted to in Chazal's statement "Whoever does not have a wife is not called a man." (*Yevamos* 63a)

19. *Zohar*, Vol. 3, 95a.

> detachment from things, instruments and practical affairs as well as of attachment to the spirit...
>
> We usually think that the earth is our mother, that time is money, and profit our mate. The seventh day is a reminder that God is our father, that time is life, and the spirit our mate.[20]

Our sole focus on this hallowed day is *qualitative fortification*, the strengthening and deepening of our relationships with Hashem, the people with whom we share our lives, and ourselves. Shabbos is not the *last* or the *lowest* day of the week, but rather the *deepest* day of the week; the source from which the six days of the week derive their energy: *Ki hi mekor haberachah* "For she is the *source* of blessing."[21] It may be said that without Shabbos and the core tenets of our faith embodied in this glorious twenty-five hour period, the six days of the week that precede and follow are meaningless.[22] This explains why we refer to Shabbos as

---

20. *The Sabbath*, pp. 20, 29, 76.

21. *Lecha Dodi*. See *Mei HaShiloach*, Vol. 1, *Emor*, *"Shor"* and *Tiferes Shlomo*, *Mikeitz*, *"O"y, b'derech hanal, vayizkor."* See also *Torah Temimah* on *Bereishis* 1:28, #65, where the author quotes *Tosafos* as saying that even though a woman is not obligated in the joy of Yom Tov because it is a time-bound obligation, she is included through her husband, because he cannot fulfill his obligation to be joyous without her. The feminine aspect energizes and brings joy to the masculine spectrum. (It is important to point out that the Rambam [*Mishneh Torah, Hilchos Chagigah* 1:31] argues and asserts that women are indeed obligated in this mitzvah. Indeed, this is the way the *Shaagas Aryeh* [*Siman* 66] rules *l'halachah*. I thank R' Bezalel Naor for calling this to my attention.) See also *Shabbos* 152a: *"Simchas leiv — ishah."*

22. A friend, Yitzchak Klatzko, rightly pointed out that the semantic difference between the words *"Be'er,"* a spring that serves as a source of water, and *"Bor,"* a pit that can hold water, is that in the place where the word *"Bor"* contains the letter **vav**, the word *"Be'er"* contains the letter **aleph**. The numerical value of *vav* is six, a reference to the six days of the week. The numerical value of *aleph* is one, a reference to Shabbos Kodesh. This hints to the idea that Shabbos is

"*Shabbos Malkesa*," the "Shabbos Queen," for Shabbos is the day when Hashem's sovereignty is revealed in the world through the feminine *Sefirah* of *Malchus.*[23]

The distinct energy of *Malchus*, the king's only daughter, manifests in various forms throughout the spectrum of our lives.

In marriage, the presence of the princess is an unwavering echo of the excitement and passion felt in the early days of the relationship, the engagement period. It is an animating spark of desire which, while unquantifiable, elevates marriage from a static, working relationship to a deep, loving, and passionate bond of soul to soul; the innermost point of connection that pervades the practical mundanities of married life, filling them at once with life, love, gratitude, and joy. As Chazal teach, *Ish v'ishah, zachu, Shechinah sheruyah beineihem* — "If a man

---

the "*Be'er*," the source of flowing water, from which the "*Bor*," the six days of the week, derive all meaning and vitality.

23. In their holy works, the tzaddikim highlight other elements of *avodas Hashem* which are bound with the energy of *Malchus* as well, such as **emunah, tefillah, kavanah,** and **yiras Shamayim.** In contrast with Torah study and halachic commitment that manifest externally and may thus be measured quantifiably, these qualitative elements in *avodas Hashem* are concealed within the soul, far removed from prying eyes. Because, as we have discussed, our society values the six sons far more than the princess of *Malchus*, these elements are generally overlooked — and even depreciated — while Torah scholarship and halachah observance are rewarded in our schools and celebrated in our communities above all else. In truth, however, it is the more inward, hidden expressions of *emunah, tefillah, kavanah, and yiras Shamayim* which, in tandem with conformance to halachah and mitzvah observance, most powerfully reveal Hashem's kingship over our lives. (See *Berachos* 6b: "*Tefillah* is a matter that stands at the apex of the world, yet people belittle it"; *Sichos HaRan* 33: "The world considers **emunah** to be a small thing. However, by me, *emunah* is a very great thing indeed"; *Avos* 3:9: "One whose wisdom exceeds his **yiras Shamayim,** his wisdom is not enduring"; and *Berachos* 17a: "Whether one does a lot or a little, the main thing is that his heart is focused [**mechavein**] toward Heaven.").

and his wife merit, the Shechinah dwells between them."[24]

In *avodas Hashem*, the presence of the princess ensures that the facet of the six sons in Torah study, prayer, and mitzvah observance bursts with intensity, emotional commitment, and desire — *hadar*, grandeur, filled with the spirit of *hod*, beauty.[25] This facet of the princess enables a Jew to build a personal relationship with Hashem so abiding that his commitment to Torah and mitzvos is absolute, granting him a level of *yiras Shamayim* that shines just as strongly in private as it does in public. As a Chassidic master whose sole objective was to enable his followers to maximize their spiritual potential,[26] it is this particular expression of the princess in a Jew's life that most concerns Rebbe Nachman. Indeed, throughout this book, we will be primarily focusing on this foundational facet of the princess' manifestation in our lives.[27]

Rebbe Nachman begins his first tale by underscoring what is perhaps the most fundamental concept of the Baal Shem Tov's revolutionary doctrine: Hashem desires for a Jew's *avodah* to be filled with passion, vitality, joy, and spirit. In his inimitable style, the tzaddik relays this assertion almost in passing, without any indication of the mighty implication of his words: *"The daughter was very precious in his eyes and he loved her very much. He spent much time rejoicing with her."* In this statement, Rebbe Nachman is teaching that while a life spent adhering to halachah and performing mitzvos mindlessly, by rote, may perhaps represent a life

---

24. *Sotah* 17a. The Shechinah, Hashem's in-dwelling presence that saturates our physical world, is related with the *Sefirah* of *Malchus*. (See *Sifsei Chein*, p. 132 and *Shaarei Orah*, First Gate.)

25. See *Mei HaShiloach*, Vol. 1, *Vayakhel*, "Re'u," and *Sefer Yehoshua*, "Az."

26. See *Chayei Moharan* 370 and *Sichos HaRan* 124.

27. Because spiritual growth sits at the core of the Jew's being, success in recovering the Lost Princess of one's *avodas Hashem* has ripple effects across the entire spectrum of one's personality, animating one's marriage and ambitions, and rejuvenating one's passion for living in general.

well lived, it does not fulfill Hashem's deepest desire. Chazal echo this sentiment when they teach us *Rachmana liba ba'i,* "Hashem desires the heart."[28] It is the soulful, inward, and contemplative presence of the princess that imbues observance of the mitzvos and halachah with a spirit of life, desire, and passion.[29]

Six Sons	**Princess**
Masculine	Feminine
Six days of the week, *"Yemei hamaaseh"*	Seventh day of the week, *Shabbos Kodesh*
Space/Things	Time/Spirit
Six directions	Center Point
Financial Success	Meaning, Fulfillment, Joy
Dry intellectual prowess, socially conditioned observance	*Emunah, Tefillah, Yiras Shamayim, Kavanah*
Quantity	Quality
Shallow	Deep
Doing	Being

Fig. B: Partial List of Contrasting Elements of the Six Sons and the Princess

---

28. *Sanhedrin* 106b. See also *Zohar, Yisro,* 93a.
29. See Fig. B.

✳ In the Absence of the Princess

AS WE HAVE discussed in the previous chapter, the primary focus of our tale is the loss of the princess in our lives and the desperate search to rediscover her animating energy. Having delved a bit deeper into the daughter's identity and the magnificent spirit she represents, we are in the position to better understand what life looks like in her unfortunate absence.

By now it should be clear that the loss of the princess is not synonymous with spiritual, emotional, or physical shutdown and the inability to function in a given area of life. It is far more subtle. Because the six sons exist even in her absence, the loss of the princess in our lives will not necessarily affect our ability to function, accomplish, and even thrive. For example, a marriage in which the princess has been lost will not automatically end in divorce. Everything may continue to appear just fine; both husband and wife might affirm that they feel no enmity toward the other and that there has never been any abuse, physical or otherwise. The six sons of their marriage enable them to present themselves to the world as if they are as happy together now as they were on their wedding day. But deep down in the recesses of their hearts they know that something is terribly wrong. Although they may be unable to point to an exact time and place when things changed, or even cite a concrete example of their hidden grievance, there is a general feeling that the mighty flame flickering between eyes locked and hearts beating to the tune of the greatest passion, adoration, and respect has been blown out, leaving them in the chilly darkness of a shared loneliness. Somewhere along the way, the common everydayness of their relationship has crushed the closeness and love they had once felt for one another. He still says, "I love you" and celebrates birthdays and anniversaries, but it has been years since he knew what it felt like to yearn for her even as she stood right next to him. She may appreciate the advantages in sharing her life with someone else, but no longer feels as if it would be simply impossible to live life any other way. Although their marriage may be fully functional, *they have stopped being engaged.*

Similarly, with six healthy and productive sons keeping the ship afloat, the loss of the princess in one's *avodas Hashem* doesn't automatically translate into an abandonment of a Torah lifestyle. It simply means that the normalcy and everydayness of one's halachah observance and *avodas Hashem* has caused the excitement, wonder, passion, and yearning of encountering the Master of the world to disappear. Instead of activating the soul and elevating the entirety of one's life to consciousness of and closeness with our Father in heaven, his Torah study and mitzvah observance are relegated to rote, societal obligations. Instead of maintaining a feeling that one is forever "engaged" with the Master of the world (*"V'eirastich li l'olam"*[30]), he simply trudges along the well-trodden roads of religious life, failing to recognize the glory, wonder, and nobility in Yiddishkeit. As a result, his *avodas Hashem* gives him no joy.

In the words of Rebbe Nachman:

> For there are people who are sleeping away their days. Even though it appears as if they are busy with Torah and *tefillah,* even so, Hashem does not have pleasure from them, for all of their *avodah* remains below and is not able to rise above.[31]

❄ A Pointed Illustration

REB SHLOMO CARLEBACH would often contrast the candle lighting of two Jews on the first night of Chanukah to illustrate the difference between an *avodas Hashem* filled with the presence of the princess and its uninspired counterpart.

---

30. *Hoshea* 2:19.
31. *Likutei Moharan* 60:6.

The first Jew comes home from *kollel* or the workplace a few minutes before it is time to light. He hastily puts together his menorah, making sure his lighting will fulfill all of the *halachos* regarding the placement of the menorah, the menorah itself, the wicks etc. — all in the choicest manner, *mehadrin min ha-mehadrin*. As his wife is gathering the children together, the phone rings, his great-aunt Hilda calling from overseas. It has been so long since they have spoken! Excitedly, he begins catching up with his great-aunt, holding phone to ear with his shoulder as he finishes setting up his menorah. Soon, he is ready to light. With the menorah beautifully arranged and his children surrounding him, he asks his aunt to stay on the line for a moment. Phone in one hand, candle in the other, he proceeds to recite the *berachos*, light, and sing a hasty *"Haneiros Hallalu"* and *"Maoz Tzur."* When he has finished, he is back on the phone, walking into a different room so he can hear his great-aunt's voice over his children's excitement. "So, how is Uncle Shmuel?"

The second Jew has been preparing for this exalted Yom Tov for a month, learning everything he can get his hands on regarding the inner soul of Chanukah and the awesome nature of the spiritual energy revealed during these eight glorious days — particularly during the lighting of the Menorah. By the time the clock is changed and Chanukah peeks over the horizon, this Jew is bursting with the most unbearable excitement for the Yom Tov. His heart could melt from the heat of his desire. What an honor, what a privilege to be able to kindle these holy lights and reveal Hashem's presence in the depths! As the week before Chanukah approaches, he can no longer contain his yearning. Although the *chag* is still a few days away, he lovingly sets up his menorah, taking care to ensure that his lighting will fulfill all of the *halachos* which he understands to be overflowing with spiritual meaning and personal relevance. Finally, it is Erev Chanukah. This Jew makes a special effort to go the *mikvah* to prepare for this glorious *avodah*. The deep thirst for a relationship with Hashem engulfs his soul in flames of excitement. A half-hour before the lighting begins, he sits and says all of the *tefillos* penned by the tzaddikim in preparation for the lighting. Each *"L'sheim Yichud"* activates another facet of his soul, and they rise above to bask in the light of his holy desire. Finally, at long last, the time has arrived. Heart overflowing, he stands with his children before the menorah — the same menorah lit by the generations before him in the most unimaginable circumstances. The gravity of the moment overwhelms him, moving him to tears. Candle in one hand, his youngest child's hand in the other, he recites the blessing slowly, with the deepest intention and feeling born of the intensity of his anticipation. He savors each word as if it were a cold glass of water in an endless desert. After lighting, he spends an hour by the holy candles, singing sweet songs, reciting various *tefillos*, and simply looking at the candles — allowing their illumination to enter his soul and shine Hashem's light into his essence.

On the level of the six sons, *quantity*, and halachah observance alone, both Jews accomplished the same exact thing. Both lightings fulfilled the identical halachic requirements — the *avodah* of the first Jew impacts all of creation just the same.[32] But

---

32. See *Nefesh HaChaim* 1:22, and *Perakim*, Chapter 2. See, however, *Likutei Amarim, Tanya*, Chapter 39 where the Baal HaTanya presents somewhat of a less favorable view on inattentive *avodah*. Yet even from the perspective of the *Nefesh HaChaim's* stress on the importance of pure action in *avodas Hashem* despite being devoid of feeling, it is abundantly clear that Rav Chaim of Volozhin never intended to propose that a Jew should settle, *l'chatchilah*, for mindless service alone. As he makes it quite clear, his primary intention in stressing this unequivocal truth was simply to fortify one's deep respect for even a mindless act of *kedushah* performed without holy intention and desire so that we never *chas v'shalom* A) come to disparage any mitzvah as worthless, regardless of how uninspired it may be, or B) come to break halachah if we perceive our breach as being beneficial for our *kavanah*. (See *Nefesh HaChaim, Perakim*, Chapters 3 and 4.) Throughout *sefer Nefesh HaChaim* (see 1:6, 21, 22; 2:8, 11, 14; *Perakim*, Chapters 5, 6; and 4:3, 6, 7) the author discusses the tremendous qualitative difference between mindless service and a service bursting with passion, desire,

it is plainly clear that these two scenarios are not identical. On the level of *quality*, the difference between them is unimaginable. While the first Jew will most certainly receive his portion in Gan Eden, it is the Gan Eden in *this world* he is missing.[33] Instead of piercing his soul and satisfying him in the deepest way, filling his life and the lives of his family members with the glorious spirit of Chanukah, the absence of the princess in his mitzvah robs his service of the joy that is rightfully his.

In the words of Rav Shlomo Wolbe:

> The majority of our mitzvah observance is simply to fulfill the law. What would our lives — both communal, personal, and spiritual — be like without these laws? However, even so: "Yerushalayim was not destroyed until they fulfilled Torah law but did not act beyond the letter of the law."[34] The letter of the law represents the boundaries within which we live our lives. However, life itself is to be found *within* these very boundaries, "*lifnim meshuras hadin.*" It is impossible to found one's life upon the boundaries alone. It is only *beyond the surface* of the boundaries that one finds kindness and love. It is our obligation to give them space and to bring them from potentiality to actuality.[35]

---

and holy intention, stressing that we should certainly always strive for the latter — while respecting, and never negating the value of, the former.

33. See *Noam Elimelech, Bereishis*, "*Bereishis Bara,*" *Vayeishev*, "*O"y Vayeishev Yaakov*"; *Meor Einayim, Vayeitzei*, "*Vayeitzei Yaakov*"; and *Nefesh HaChaim*, Chapter 11. See also *Hachsharas HaAvreichim*, pp. 16–17: "Let it be clearly stated that not only one who experiences complete rapture (*hislahavus*) in his *avodah*, but also one who is merely impacted on an emotional level (*hisragshus*); this feeling is the early stages of his soul's emergence upon which dwells lofty, elevated light. The pleasurable feelings and holy emotions experienced by this person in his prayer, mitzvos, and Torah study, and the eruption of sparks of pleasure and holy fire, *are from his portion of Gan Eden* which he will experience in full, for eternity, after the completion of his days and years."

34. *Bava Metzia* 30b.

35. *Alei Shur*, Vol. 2, p. 202.

✳ Paradise in This World

VIRTUALLY ALL OF the Chassidic masters stress that it is not enough for a Jew to simply follow the ways of the Torah for the sake of earning reward in the World to come. Rather, Hashem intends for our *avodah* to be bursting with passion, excitement, vitality, and meaning to the point that we experience a taste of paradise in this world. With this, they interpreted the words of the Mishnah, *"Sechar mitzvah mitzvah"* not as, "The reward for a mitzvah is the opportunity to perform another mitzvah," but rather as, "The reward of a mitzvah is *the mitzvah itself."*[36]

In the words of Rebbe Nachum of Chernobyl:

> The primary reward for a mitzvah is the mitzvah itself; the Divine binding and the spiritual pleasure involved in the action which is an aspect of "Greeting the face of the Shechinah." Without this, it is called "an empty mitzvah", for it is missing the life-force and the soul, leaving only the "body" of the act. It is only truly called a "mitzvah" by means of the desire and the cleaving (*"tzavsa"*) of the inner spark of Godliness with its Source...[37]

This idea is one of the main themes discussed in a previous work, *Sunlight of Redemption.*[38] There, we learn that a primary teaching the Baal Shem Tov and his students sought to convey was the idea that it is possible for a Jew to tap into the glorious spirit of *Olam HaBa* even while living life in *Olam HaZeh*. The early Chassidic masters trained their followers to sense the rays

---

36. See *Kesser Shem Tov* #96; *Likutei Moharan* 5:2; *Likutei Amarim, Tanya,* Chapter 39; *Kedushas Levi, Eikev, "V'hayah eikev tishma'un"*; and *Degel Machaneh Ephraim, Korach, "Ani Chelkecha."*

37. *Meor Einayim, Vayeira, "B'shaas d'Shabbos."* See also *Vayeishev, "V'yisrael ahav"* and *Behaalosecha, "Vayedaber Hashem."*

38. Feldheim, 2018. See pp. 161–165.

of presence filtering through the curtain of concealment and encounter the truth behind the falsehood, the infinite behind the limited, and the eternal light of Hashem illuminating the transience of our reality.[39] They taught that the collective exile of the Jewish nation is mirrored by a personal servitude of confusion, lowliness, and despair experienced by each and every individual and that, while the collective redemption may be beyond the influence of any one individual, it is well within a Jew's capacity to free himself from the bonds of his personal exile. By endeavoring to attain existential lucidity and religious clarity through engagement with the teachings of our tzaddikim, the Jewish person is able to transform his or her consciousness into one of *emunah* and *bitachon*, living life with ultimate peace of mind, gratitude, vibrancy, and boundless joy despite the multifarious troubles of this-worldliness. Although one's feet may yet walk in exile, his heart and mind are imbued with the transcendent spirit of the *neshamah*, lifted on wings of love and awe to a world beyond. Instead of seeing a natural world of absurdity where lusts, jealousy, and base desires reign supreme, a *Malchus D'Sitra Achra*, it is possible for a Jew to see past the illusory silence of our physical realm and attain a deep and abiding awareness of the purposeful, meaningful, and glorious spiritual element underlying

---

39. In *Sunlight of Redemption*, we learn that the ability to discern the spirituality of *Olam HaBa* within *Olam HaZeh* was granted to the Jewish nation in Yitzchak Avinu's *berachah* to Yaakov. (See p. 164, note 44) While Eisav received the pure physicality of nature, Yaakov Avinu received the spiritual energy which infuses all of nature. In Chapter 21, "The (Endless) End!", we will explore the manner in which the attitude of simple faith and *bitachon* enables a Jew to experience boundless contentment despite his limitations. There, we will learn that *bitachon* is linked to Yaakov Avinu as well. Indeed, this trait of *bitachon* is one expression of the Jew's ability to experience the infinite pleasure of *Olam HaBa* within the broken vessels of *Olam HaZeh*. This is in contrast to Eisav, who, unable to rise above the angst of this world, experiences constant lack and endless frustration.

our perspective of reality that renders this world a *Malchus D'Kedushah,* a unified kingdom in which each and every facet of existence joins all others in the quest to bring about the ultimate honor of Hashem.[40] Faced with the same facts as everyone else, his interpretation of those facts, so vastly different from that of the nations of the world, alters his experience, entirely. The laws, concepts, customs, precepts, and ideals of our holy Torah form a portal through which the Jew can travel to a world of transcendent lucidity and draw down streams of other-worldly clarity to illuminate the topsy-turvy world of darkness, transforming reality with the brilliance of his spiritual perception. Thoughts, words, and actions of holiness that are granted permission to reach into the Jew's core to consciously engage his *neshamah* with sincerity, joy, confidence, and humility, draw the spirit of *Olam HaBa* into his soul and fill his world with the scent of paradise.

The story is told about a rabbi who visited paradise in a dream. Entering the hall where the Tannaim were enjoying their eternal reward, he saw that they were all sitting around a plain wooden table, studying Torah. Disappointed, the rabbi asked an angel, "Is this all? This is what paradise looks like?" He received the following reply: "The Tannaim aren't in paradise. Paradise is in the Tannaim."

The tzaddikim desired to demonstrate how the other-worldly joy of paradise present in each mitzvah and every word of Torah and prayer could spill over into one's mundane activities, filling them all with meaning and contentment. The goal, they taught, is never for one to remove himself from this world and cleave

---

40. This outlook of *Malchus D'Kedushah* fills our world with the spirit of the princess, the aspect of Shabbos, which is *"Mei'ein Olam HaBa"* (*Berachos* 57b, *Zohar*, Introduction, 1b). In addition, as discussed in an earlier note, *teshuvah*, the process of discovering and recovering the Lost Princess, is related to *Binah* which is the realm of *Olam HaBa* itself. (For more on the deep and intimate relationship between the *Sefiros* of *Binah* and *Malchus*, see *Shaarei Orah*, Eighth Gate.)

solely to the spiritual glory of the next, but rather to allow the spirit of *Olam HaBa* to illuminate his daily experience, *"Olamcha tir'eh b'chayecha."*[41] When set in the context of a personal bond with our Father in heaven, one's mundane responsibilities are elevated to the realm of the sacred. They, too, are considered *avodas Hashem.*[42] They, too, become filled with a sense of joy and ultimate fulfillment. This is an important point: Rather than being castigated and abandoned, the six sons of our lives are to be imbued with the energizing spirit of the princess, serving as a vessel for her awesome light. Indeed, when it comes to *avodas Hashem*, it is the structure of practical halachah and mitzvah observance that provides a framework, the *only* framework, in which the spirit of the princess can truly flourish.

Rebbe Nachman begins his book of tales by teaching that of all his children, the king loves his daughter the most. Hashem seeks the heart and soul of His holy nation, awaiting the unification of the daughter and the six sons in their service; exacting halachah observance activated and energized by the life-giving spirit of yearning, longing, sincerity, and passionate excitement.

Unfortunately, as we walk along the difficult journey of life, we often find ourselves bereft of the princess. Our impressive accomplishments seem to be matched only by the ever-growing emptiness within. We desperately thirst for meaning and the lost joy of our youth, but do not know where to search. In this story, Rebbe Nachman reveals to the final generations before the coming of Mashiach just when and where it is that the princess of our *avodas Hashem* has gotten lost and how we might locate and free her, allowing for her exuberance to animate our lives once more with the passion, wonder, and excitement of youth; the holiness of Shabbos Kodesh.

---

41. *Berachos* 17a.
42. See *Noam Elimelech, Toldos, "O"y V'Avraham"* and *Likutei Moharan* 280.

LESSONS FOR LIFE

❋ All of life is made up of two contrasting components; a quantifiable measure of external, shallow accomplishment and a qualitative and inward spirit of depth, purpose, meaning, and vibrancy.

❋ While it is possible to maintain an *avodas Hashem* that consists of pure action alone, Rebbe Nachman teaches us that Hashem delights in the desire of the heart more than anything else. He relishes the spirit of faith, passion, excitement, and youthful wonder that so animates the halachic experience.

CHAPTER 3

A Grave Error

פַּעַם אַחַת הָיָה מִתְוַעֵד עִמָּהּ בְּיַחַד בְּאֵיזֶה יוֹם, וְנַעֲשָׂה
בְּרֹגֶז עָלֶיהָ, וְנִזְרְקָה מִפִּיו דִּבּוּר: שֶׁהַלֹּא טוֹב יִקַּח אוֹתָךְ.
בַּלַּיְלָה הָלְכָה לְחַדְרָהּ, וּבַבֹּקֶר לֹא יָדְעוּ הֵיכָן הִיא.

On one occasion, when the king was together with
her on a certain day, he grew angry with her and
threw the following words from his mouth: "May
the no-good one take you." That night she went to
her room, and in the morning, no one knew where
she went.

I N THE PREVIOUS CHAPTER, we learned that the king
loved his only daughter very much and immensely enjoyed
the time they would spend together. Yet immediately after
revealing their close bond, Rebbe Nachman tells of a horrific
event in which their relationship appears to have been shattered.
On a certain day, something the princess does or doesn't do
seems to anger the king terribly, compelling him to utter terrible
words that ultimately lead to his beloved daughter's disappear-
ance. Although Rebbe Nachman does not overtly reveal what it

was that so greatly upset the king, the Breslover *mashpi'im* teach that the original Yiddish wording of this sentence hints to the nature of her misdeed.

"Epes Ah Tug": Just Another Day

IN HEBREW, THIS line of the story tells us that the king was together with his beloved daughter *"b'eizeh yom,"* which we rendered as "on a certain day." While lost in translation, *"epes a tug,"* the original Yiddish words used by Rebbe Nachman when he first told this story, hint at what it was that so angered the king.

The phraseology of *"epes ah tug"* carries a connotation of triviality, as if the day in question holds no significance at all and is barely worth mentioning. *"Epes ah tug"* is the answer one gives when asked what day an event took place if that information is entirely inconsequential. It is akin to responding: It isn't important what day it was; *"Epes ah tug."*

The Breslover *mashpi'im* teach that when Rebbe Nachman uses this particular phrase to describe the day of this shocking and heartbreaking event, he is hinting what it was that the princess did wrong: she stopped appreciating the preciousness of her daily meetings with her father. While the king treasured every moment spent with his beloved daughter and derived the greatest joy and pleasure from their meetings, the princess began to grow accustomed to these visits. Although she loved her father deeply, with time her excitement slowly grew stale. She began considering a day with her father to be *"epes ah tug,"* just another day — devoid of wonder, awe, and yearning. Her passion began to fade, she began to approach her relationship with the king flippantly, as if it were a given, natural occurrence. Perceiving this change in his daughter was what caused the king such intense pain and drove him to his drastic response.

It is human nature to grow accustomed to even the most

wondrous of things. Life flourishes upon an ocean of astounding miracles, and yet, with the passage of time, we begin to accept them as part and parcel of our status quo, taking them for granted. Sunrise and sunset, a baby's giggle, the whisper of a bird's wings, the marvels of modern technology, a loving word, a full moon, a thunderstorm, not to mention seeing, breathing, hearing, etc. — these are mind-blowing occurrences, sublime hints to the transcendent. But as we grow accustomed to the realities of our world, they cease to evoke wonder in our hearts. The messages they carry fall on deaf ears.

Shifting to the realm of *avodas Hashem*, the daily life of an observant Jew is packed with the most incredible gifts. The mitzvos we merit to perform on a daily basis provide us with a direct line to the King of kings, the Author of existence. Each time we wrap tefillin around our arm or kindle the Shabbos candles, we are fulfilling the purpose of creation, imbuing all of physicality with greater meaning, relevance, and holiness.[1] Above all, the mitzvos embody the awesome love Hashem has for every single Jew and the extent to which every act of holiness, no matter how slight, is precious in His eyes. In the words of Chazal: "Hashem wanted to grant merit to the Jewish nation, therefore He gave them an abundance of Torah and mitzvos."[2] The King of kings delights in us and the pleasure He receives from our relationship is unimaginable. How fortunate we are to be the recipient of such love, the subject of the most powerful, unconditional adoration! What an awesome privilege it is that Hashem takes pride in every Jew to the point that, in the words of Rebbe Nachman:

---

1. See *Likutei Moharan* 52. Elsewhere (*Likutei Moharan* 21:11), Rebbe Nachman writes that the simplest Jew's experience of the mitzvos will be the paradise of the non-Jews in the world to come.
2. *Makkos* 23b.

Every Jew is cause for a unique pride, and Hashem takes pride in him individually. Even the lowliest among the Jews, indeed even Jewish sinners — all the while that they are still called "Jews" — offer a unique pride, for Hashem takes pride in each one individually.... There are times when some lowly Jew twirls one of his *peyos*, and Hashem has tremendous pride from this.[3]

Is there anything greater in the world than to have the undivided attention of the Creator of existence, a deep, personal bond that He cherishes above all else? *Ashreinu, mah tov chelkeinu!* From this perspective, the performance of a single mitzvah or the opportunity to communicate with the Creator of heaven and earth just one time should be reason enough to dance for two thousand years. In the tear-soaked words of Reb Nosson's prayer:

The great amount of joy and delight that I should rightfully feel over my portion is immeasurable and beyond calculation — this that You have granted me the merit, in Your great Mercy, to be counted among the Jewish nation, the nation chosen from all of the nations and elevated beyond all languages — for You express Your fondness for us using all terms of endearment, and You love Your nation, Yisrael, with a great love and an utterly eternal bond. And, because of Your love and mercy toward Your nation, Yisrael, You granted us a large measure of Torah and mitzvos, such that we ought to feel endless joy, celebration, and elation over each and every mitzvah which revives the soul and gladdens the heart...[4]

But alas, disconnected from the very essence of the religious consciousness, the perpetual sense of wonder that the mitzvos

---

3. *Likutei Moharan* 17:1.
4. *Likutei Tefillos*, Vol. 1, 89.

are intended to preserve, we grow unfeeling. In the weeks and months following a boy's bar mitzvah, his excitement toward putting on tefillin wanes. It is no longer clear to him that Hashem needs him to wear tefillin in the grand scheme of His Master plan and that every morning he wraps these holy straps on his arm he is bringing unimaginable joy to the King of kings. Although Hashem creates each day anew, completely fresh and bursting with opportunities to grow close to Him, we approach the new day just like the last; *"od eizeh yom,"* just another day, just another twenty-four-hour period of stumbling through the motions of Torah observance, oblivious to the joy and wonder hidden beneath the surface of each and every act of holiness. Just another day of sitting in front of the Gemara, frequently glancing at the clock to see how much time is left before *seder* concludes. Just another day of swiftly skimming through the agenda at three exclusive meetings with the Infinite One, Shacharis, Minchah, and Maariv, oblivious to the enormity of this gift and opportunity to commune with the King of kings.[5]

When the princess of youth in our *avodas Hashem* begins to

---

5. The latter example is all the more tragic, for one of the important functions of daily *tefillah* is to reinforce the Torah consciousness of the wonder and amazement with which a Jew is supposed to approach space, time, nature, history, and all other aspects of life. In the words of a great Jewish thinker:

"Three times a day, we pray, 'We thank You... for Your miracles which are with us daily, for Your constant marvels...' In the evening liturgy we recite the words of Iyov, 'Who does great things beyond comprehension, marvelous things without number.' Every morning we recite, 'He created light and makes the dark.' Twice a day, we say, 'He is One.' What is the meaning of such repetition? A scientific theory, once it is announced and accepted, does not have to be repeated twice a day. The insights of wonder must be constantly kept alive. Since there is a need for daily wonder, there is a need for daily worship." (*Between God and Man*, p. 43)

When we begin to approach the very tool that enables us to preserve our sense of wonder in a way of rote and apathy, it is particularly devastating.

cool, the King is pained beyond words. How can we be so obtuse so as to ignore the great kindnesses that He has bestowed upon us? Can't we feel the love in His constant gaze? Can't we sense just how precious we are to Him and how desperately He desires for us to reciprocate by showing interest and gratitude for the gifts we have been given? With time, the King grows more and more saddened by our spiritual blindness. Eventually, He resolves to bring us to our senses with a powerful wake-up call.

The King's Strategy

AT FIRST GLANCE, the opening lines in this story are extremely difficult to swallow. The reader is left confused, incredulous, and confounded. One minute we are told about the king's wonderful relationship with his loving daughter whom he cherishes beyond all else, and in the very next he seems to transform into a horrible man with mood swings who is capable of uttering terrifying words about a gentle, innocent princess! The stark change in tone leaves us confused as to what has happened. It's as if the joyful, cheery soundtrack with which our story opened has suddenly changed, with no warning, to a dark, ominous score well-suited for a horror film. What did the princess do to receive such awful treatment? How could the king's love be so easily shattered?

These questions become even stronger when we look toward the *nimshal*. As we have learned, the king in the story represents our Father in heaven, the King of kings. Does Rebbe Nachman mean to suggest that in response to an apathetic approach to the privilege of a relationship with Him, Hashem grows angry to the point that He cuts us off entirely, allowing the "no-good one" to take us away? How can this possibly be?

The Breslover *mashpi'im* explain that while the king's response to his beloved daughter's apathy appears horrible and unfair to the extreme, it is only on the surface. In truth, this response is an expression of his never-ending love, a ploy to rekindle the passion of his most precious relationship. Delving beneath the surface allows us to explore the king's true intention.

Earlier, we touched upon the distinction between the elements of engagement and marriage, two stages of the spousal relationship which are often vessels for the contrasting elements of passionate yearning on the one hand and the everydayness of having settled into a new reality on the other.

Much of the excitement and intensity of an engaged couple's relationship is founded upon the all-consuming yearning they had very recently felt for the sense of completion and spiritual stability that only reuniting with the other half of one's soul can bring. Acutely aware of just how blessed they are to have had their primary prayer fulfilled, they are completely overwhelmed with gratitude and cherish the subject of their newfound contentment.

However, as the passage of months and years takes the newly married couple further and further away from the experience of singlehood and the lack that had so entirely consumed them, they no longer relate to each other in the same way they had during the whirlwind period of their engagement. The more detached they become from their single days, when the pain over the absence of companionship was constantly at the forefront of their minds, the more they take their new status quo for granted, and the less passionate they are about their relationship.

Thankfully, this model isn't at all an ironclad rule. While admittedly rare, there are many couples who are indeed able to preserve a spirit of "engagement" in their relationship that enlivens the day-to-day facets of their marriage with passion, excitement, and intense love. The key to acquiring this kind of marital bond is *gratitude*. Gratitude is a vessel that preserves — in the present moment — the very same levels of excitement, passion, and desire we felt toward something in the past. When a couple is grateful for one another and constantly express their thanks and appreciation to Hashem for having given them the ultimate gift of companionship and completion, they remain bound to their past experience of lack and the yearning it fosters even while experiencing its very fulfillment. As a result, the spirit of newness, excitement, and desire never leaves them.[6]

Of course, the gift of gratitude and its special qualities extend far beyond the realm of marriage to all areas of life. No matter what it is that we are truly grateful for, we are sure to experience that thing, experience, pleasure, or circumstance in a significantly more desirable manner. Far more than merely representing a positive trait, gratitude is a wondrous key that unlocks deeper levels of quality, depth, and desire in all areas of life, immeasurably enhancing our relationships with others and the wondrous goodness that surround us "at all times, in the evening, morning, and afternoon."[7]

---

6. Rebbe Nachman stressed the importance of preserving the feeling of "engagement" in *avodas Hashem*. See *Chayei Moharan* 518 where Reb Nosson recounts: "I heard that Rebbe Nachman once said the main thing is to hold onto the feelings one has when he starts serving Hashem. When a person makes a start he is filled with tremendous enthusiasm. One should make every effort to retain this initial enthusiasm for as long as possible."

7. *Shemoneh Esrei* prayer. A great Jewish thinker posited that it is for the preservation of this sense of gratitude that we make so many *berachos* on experiencing life:

"No routine of the social, physical, or physiological order must dull our sense of surprise at the fact that there is a social, a physical, or a physiological order. We are trained in maintaining our sense of wonder by uttering a blessing before the enjoyment of food. Each time we are about to drink a glass of water, we remind ourselves of the eternal mystery of creation, "Blessed are You... by Whose word all things come into being." A trivial act and a reference to the supreme miracle. Wishing to eat bread or fruit, to enjoy a pleasant fragrance or a cup of wine; on tasting fruit in season for the first time; on seeing a rainbow, or the ocean; on noticing trees when they blossom; on meeting a sage in Torah or in secular learning; on hearing good or bad tidings — we are taught to invoke

Aside from the amazing strategy of *quality preservation via gratitude*, there is another, considerably less desirable, way of reawakening the spirit of "engagement" in a given area of life.

A well-known maxim states, "We don't know a good thing until it is gone," and how very true it is! When we lose something special, we truly begin to appreciate the extent of its goodness. When one finds it impossible to feel grateful for something any longer and loses touch with his lack and desire by taking it for granted, the only way he will be able to regain the passionate appreciation he once had is by having that thing taken away, thus allowing him to again experience its absence.[8]

The tzaddikim saw the destruction of the Beis HaMikdash as a drastic demonstration of this model. Reb Nosson writes:

> All salvation, all closeness between Klal Yisrael and our Father in heaven, all livelihood, and all bounty — everything is drawn from that place, the place of the Beis HaMikdash about which the verse states, "And he saw the place from

---

His great name and our awareness of Him. Even on performing a physiological function we say "Blessed are You... Who heals all flesh and does wonders." This is one of the goals of the Jewish way of living: to experience commonplace deeds as spiritual adventures, to feel the hidden love and wisdom in all things." (*Between God and Man*, p. 43)

8. Our Sages teach that the laws of *niddah*, monthly physical separation between husband and wife, is a response to the general loss of appreciation for the marital union with the passage of time (see *Niddah* 31b). In another place, Chazal compare the exile of Klal Yisrael from their land to the temporary separation of *niddah* (*Taanis* 20a). The Meor Einayim likens the Sefirah period to the *niddah* period as well. The tzaddik writes: "As a general rule, constant pleasure is not pleasurable. Therefore, 'the Chayos were running and returning.' But they do not depart entirely — they leave a residual impact. In their departure, they create a vessel so that pleasure may be experienced. Were they not to depart, there would be no vessel and thus no pleasure... Therefore Hashem commanded, 'You shall count seven weeks' which parallel the seven clean days of *niddah* so that we should be able to receive the ultimate pleasure of *Kabbalas HaTorah*." (*Meor Einayim, Emor, U'sefartem lachem*.)

afar." And even when one stood in the Beis HaMikdash at the time of its standing, it was necessary to realize how far one was from the holiness of this awesome place. Indeed, the primary reason for the destruction stemmed from this — that they caused a blemish in thinking that "all good was in their hands" [it was coming to them, no longer seen as a gift], and thus they rebelled against Hashem, as the verse states, "When I fed them they were satisfied, they were satisfied and they grew proud, therefore they have forgotten Me."[9] This is in accordance with Rashi's comment on the verse, "Turn your eyes away from me"[10] — as a result of the love He showed them in the first Temple, they rebelled against Him. *For at the time of closeness, one must be aware of the distance.* It is only then that one can truly come close without erring, for one needs to remember his distance and rejoice in Hashem's kindness that He draws him near with such awesome closeness.[11]

Reb Shlomo Carlebach explains:

We went into exile because we stopped dreaming dreams about the Beis HaMikdash while we had the Beis HaMikdash. There was no other way of making us dream again. Do you know what's so special about today? Why doesn't God give us back Yerushalayim in its entirety, right now? Obviously, *we haven't dreamt enough about it yet.* We have it, we are slowly coming home, but are still given the privilege to dream about it.[12]

---

9. *Hoshea* 13:6.

10. *Shir HaShirim* 6:5.

11. *Likutei Halachos, Shiluach HaKein* 5:17

12. Recording, May 1987, Yerushalayim. A friend, Yitzchak Meir Malek, suggested that perhaps this idea — that the reason we have not yet merited the rebuilding of the Beis HaMikdash is because we haven't yet dreamed about it to the necessary extent — can provide a deeper understanding of the verse:

The destruction of the Beis HaMikdash was not a *cause,* but an *effect.* The true cause was that we lost touch with the preciousness of the Beis HaMikdash. It became such a concrete part of our reality that we took it for granted and began acting in ways that reflected our obliviousness to the presence of Hashem that rested among us. In response, Hashem took it away from us — not as a punishment, but rather to enable us to regain the all-important yearning, excitement, and passion which is so dear to Him; *"The daughter was very precious in his eyes and he loved her very much. He spent much time rejoicing with her."*

The Breslover *mashpi'im* teach that the king's outburst in our story may be understood in the same vein. When the king utters the dreadful words, "May the no-good one take you," he intends merely to remind the princess of the great preciousness of their relationship by allowing her to temporarily feel its absence. The anger he displays is only a front, a desperate attempt to shake the princess from her apathy. At no point does the king truly desire for the "no-good one" to take her away. His concealment is simply a method of bringing his beloved daughter closer to him than ever before.

Throughout the journey of life there are times we feel as if Hashem has distanced us from His closeness. Drowning in shame, guilt, and existential loneliness, we sense His absence from our lives and feel as if it is impossible to break past the obstacles that prevent us from reaching Him. When the words *"Shuvu banim shovavim, chutz mi'..."*[13] — with our name as the exception to

---

B'shuv Hashem es shivas tzion hayinu k'cholmim, "When Hashem returned the captives of Zion, it was as if we were dreamers" (*Tehillim* 126:1). When the time comes for the entirety of the Jewish nation to finally return home, we will be "like *dreamers,"* for this will serve as proof that we have successfully yearned and dreamed to the greatest possible extent.

13. See *Chagigah* 15b, where the Gemara relates that a voice emerged from heaven, declaring, "Return my wayward children — except for Acher." The

this invitation — echo in the recesses of our soul, we feel that all hope is lost. Our perception of Hashem's wrath overwhelms us. Persuaded that Hashem no longer desires our closeness, we convince ourselves that it is impossible for us to return, that the "no-good one" has taken us and Hashem is no longer interested in building a relationship.[14]

However, Rebbe Nachman teaches that, "All apparent acts of distancing are only for the purpose of bringing us close."[15] The deepest secret of life is the understanding that all darkness is for the purpose of ensuing light; constriction is only to bring about expansion, night is a preparation for the dawn, mistakes are for the purpose of growth, and concealment is for the sake of ultimate revelation.[16] Just as a child must overcome the frightening challenge of a parent's distance if he is to learn how to walk, true growth is achieved only when a deeper insight into Hashem's apparent detachment enables us to cross the great divide and

---

Maharsha explains that this was merely a test, an obstacle arranged for the purpose of allowing the wayward sage to express his true yearning for holiness.

14. Regarding the episode referenced in the previous footnote, Rabbi David Bashevkin writes: "Acher is convinced that he is hopeless. A cursory reading would suggest that he has good reason to believe so. No less than a voice from heaven proclaims him irredeemable. Each child in the study hall quotes a verse pointing to his bleak fate. Everyone has hope except for him. But what if Acher only hears what he wants to hear? Neither heavenly voices nor exegetical divination provide definitive judgment... Acher doesn't become hopeless because he heard a heavenly voice; his hopelessness is the filter through which he hears all heavenly messages... Heaven does not reject Acher; Elisha ben Avuyah rejects Acher. He could not reconcile his Torah with the direction of his life. He therefore begins to interpret all Torah and divinity as pointing him in the direction away from God." (*Sin•a•gogue*, p. 93)

15. *Likutei Moharan Tinyana*, 48.

16. See *Midrash Shocher Tov* 22: "Our sages taught: From amidst anger comes goodwill. From amidst darkness, light. From amidst anger, mercy. From amidst constriction, an expanse. **From amidst distancing, closeness.** From amidst descent, ascent." See also *Zohar*, Vol. 2, 184b.

discover His love once more.[17] While, by all appearances, it may seem as if Hashem has forsaken us, the tzaddikim teach that He is ever waiting behind the curtain, hoping that we will be compelled to seek Him once more and rekindle the love of our youth. Therefore, when the King says, "May the no-good one take you," it is simply a test, a desperate attempt to help us realize what living a life devoid of spirituality feels like so that it may trigger our return to His loving arms. "We must first peer into the darkness, feel strangled and entombed in the hopelessness of living without God, before we are ready to feel the presence of His living light."[18] "All barriers are only for the sake of increasing desire."[19]

In the words of R' Hillel Zeitlin:

> There are times when the world is completely unified with its Creator. Joy and rejoicing are then found on the face of all worlds and upper realms. Godly beauty then shines clearly, illuminating everything and within everything... This is the unity between *"Kudsha B'rich Hu"* and *"Shechintei,"* the bond between God and the world, God and man, heaven and earth. There are also times when the world rests in the darkness, distant from its Creator, locked within itself, separate. The Shechinah is exiled and distanced from *Kudsha B'rich Hu.*
>
> The pain of the Shechinah is great at this time. Beauty longs after its Godly Source. She yearns to be elevated and freed. However, She has long been entrenched within the world. The darkness of the world blackens all, She is trapped in its cords. Now, She is bound in the captivity of the world without any ability to return to Herself, to free Herself from Her pain.
>
> However, in accordance with Her great pain, so is the depth of Her yearning for the Godly beauty. Her yearning

---

17. See *Degel Machaneh Ephraim, Behaalosecha,* "*Al pi*" and *Kedushas Levi, Shemos,* "*V'zeh lecha.*"

18. *Between Man and God,* p. 70.

19. *Likutei Moharan* 66.

continuously grows, until, slowly but surely, the cords that bind her begin to weaken, and in their place wings begin to sprout. The pain of separation becomes diluted with yearning, and this yearning takes on the hue of longing for closeness with the Divine. The Shechinah slowly begins to become redeemed, and unity is achieved anew; first for a few fleeting moments at a time, and then more and more commonly as the day of reunification grows closer and closer.[20]

"To *Her* Room" — Not Back to His

UNFORTUNATELY, WE OFTENTIMES misinterpret the true intention of Hashem's anger. Paralyzed by the darkness enveloping our spiritual clarity, we fail to realize that the shadow has been cast by Hashem's outstretched hand.[21] Instead of using the miserable angst of failure as a catalyst for spiritual renewal, we get caught up in the illusory force of Hashem's apparent rejection and sink into despair. Never having been taught about Hashem's unconditional love and His unwavering desire for our return to the Torah's ways or sufficiently convinced by our current spiritual numbness to deny this abiding truth,[22] we lack the ability to navigate the stormy waters of renewal and begin to drown.

Sadly, when we are unable to access a level of conviction necessary to utilize this "rock bottom" in our lives to spark a spiritual renaissance, we run away. Devastated by the severity of her father's comment, the princess takes it at face value and escapes "to her room" — to *her* room, instead of back to his. This is a grave error indeed.

---

20. *Mevo L'Chassidus Ul'Darkah shel Chabad*, p. 25.
21. See *Yeshayahu* 49:2 and *Sanhedrin* 38b.
22. See *B'Ibei HaNachal* to *Likutei Moharan* 17:2.

Throughout his writings, Rebbe Nachman teaches about the necessity for a Jew to employ *"Azus D'Kedusha,"* holy stubbornness, in his or her *avodas Hashem.* In *Sichos HaRan*, the Rebbe writes:

> It is very good for one to pour out his heart before Hashem with genuine supplication as a child who has sinned before his father, for Hashem has called us His children, as the verse states, "You are children to Hashem your God." ... And even if it appears to a person that as a result of his sinful actions he is no longer considered a child to Hashem, Hashem has already called us His children without exception (as the Gemara teaches, in the name of Hashem), "Regardless of their spiritual state, they are My children."[23] (Therefore, one must say:) "If You are driving me away from the aspect in which I am your child, do what is good in Your eyes. It is still my obligation to act as Your son."[24]

Rebbe Nachman wanted his followers' commitment to Yiddishkeit to be so incredibly resolute that nothing — *not even Hashem's rejection* — could drive them away. Intimate knowledge of, and staunch faith in, the countless Torah sources that reflect Hashem's awesome love for His holy nation,[25] His eternal desire for their return to *avodas Hashem*,[26] and the ever-present prospect of *teshuvah mei'ahavah* that can transform even the greatest sins into merits[27] would enable them to understand Hashem's distance as being a challenge — instead of the resolute rejection the Satan would like them to perceive.[28]

---

23. *Kiddushin* 36a.
24. *Sichos HaRan* 7.
25. See, for example, *Shemos Rabbah* 1:3.
26. See, for example, *Yechezkel* 18:23.
27. See, for example, *Yoma* 86b.
28. See *Sichos HaRan* 22.

Sadly, like the princess in our story, we so often lack this conviction. As children exploring the strange new realities of adolescence, we make mistakes and feel, for the first time, a shattering of our innocence and the accompanying pain of Hashem's sudden distance. Somewhere along the way a classmate whispers something on the bus, we look somewhere we shouldn't, and a flare of rebellion lights in our heart, launching a mighty assault on our sense of identity as "Mommy's sweet little boy," or "Daddy's precious little girl." Immediately, despair begins to creep in. We feel alone in our shame, convinced that nothing could ever be built on the rubble of our destruction. Like Adam HaRishon after the first sin, it seems clear to us that the world can no longer continue to function, that nature must break her silence. We are certain that the devastating darkness we feel descending upon the world is a direct result of our iniquity. But then, to our great dismay, we realize that the cause of this darkness is merely sunset — a sunset like any other. In the morning, dawn rises once more and the streets teem with life, business as usual.[29] "That's all?" we think, frightful astonishment echoing urgently in calm tremors of innocence. "No lightning bolt, no devastation? Am I so insignificant that the enormity of the sin that has so demolished my inner world has no effect on the world beyond my heart and mind? Is Hashem so distant from me that punishment is itself pointless?"

In this significant moment, basking in the oppressive heat of an indifferent morning sun whose nauseating illumination appears to downplay the human sentiment that our actions truly matter, something dies inside. *"In the morning, no one knew where she*

---

29. See *Avodah Zarah* 8a: "On the day of Adam's creation, the sun began to set. He said, 'Woe is to me, for it is because I have ruined the world it is growing dark around me. Certainly, it is returning to nothingness and emptiness, and this is the death that was decreed upon me!' He sat and cried the whole night, and Chava cried opposite him. When the sun rose in the morning, he said, 'This is the way of the world.'"

went." We are alone in an unfeeling world, distant from all meaning, cast away to the dungeons of an inconsequential existence. The seeds of apathy have been planted, and there is no one that can shake us out of this nightmare. Once this occurs, it is only a matter of time before the sparkle in our eye dims, our wonder disappears, and the princess of youth begins to slowly slip away.

Ironically, and most devastatingly, it is this very error that makes the princess susceptible to actual abduction by "the no-good one." Her conviction that the king desires for her to be taken away is what causes her to become truly concealed from her father. Unaware that Hashem is only hiding Himself from us on the surface, desperately hoping that we will be inspired to seek Him from behind the veil, we despair of regaining the innocence, passion, and excitement of former good days. Instead of picking ourselves off the floor and returning to Hashem with *"Azus D'Kedusha,"* holy stubbornness built on unwavering confidence in His unconditional love and eternal desire for our service, we fall prey to His apparent anger and slink off to our own room of despair, hopelessness, and self-loathing. In the process of entering the darkness of this bitter place, we leave the door wide open for the *yetzer hara* to waltz on in and take hold of the reins.

At this point, it is all over. The "no-good one" has grabbed us. We become stuck in a consciousness of "no-good," experiencing life with a gloomy pessimism that causes us to see even the most exciting aspects of life as being drab and tedious. The light that so illuminated our world as a sweet little child has dimmed. Devoid of all meaning, we perceive our circumstances, experiences, and relationships with our spouse and children as being "no-good," lending us no joy or peace of mind.[30] In such a situation, even

---

30. In the previous chapter, we have described *Malchus* as representing the concept of purpose and meaning that is bound with this *Middah*'s serving as the ultimate goal, the final step in the process of creative manifestation — the vessel that receives that which was stirred solely for the purpose of filling it.

when Hashem pulls back the curtain to check on our progress and reveals Himself to us in whatever which way, we experience this opportunity itself as being similarly unattractive and pointless.

But Rebbe Nachman teaches us there is a way out of this terrible darkness. Deep down, every Jewish soul yearns for the Lost Princess of youth, and she yearns for home in the same measure. She is waiting, ever waiting for redemption. And each and every one of us has the ability to free the princess from her bonds and bring her back home.

In our own experience of personal expression, our desires, thoughts, wisdom, kindness, severity, pride, endurance, submission, and drive to connect must find a *"Malchus"* in order to properly manifest. Generally, one's *Malchus* is defined by one's sphere of influence; spouse and children, co-workers and students, family members and friends (see *Likutei Moharan* 56:1). It is the potential receptivity of his surroundings that enables the Jew to fully manifest the silent potency that roils within. His particular surroundings and the unique circumstances of his life allow him to properly express that which would otherwise remain forever hidden within.

When a person is satisfied with his position in life and attains the recognition that his circumstances represent the perfect *Malchus*-receptacle which enables him to express the powers of his inner world, his life is saturated with a sense of serenity, stability, and a deep joy that reaches the core of his being. Here, however, Rebbe Nachman speaks of a scenario in which one's *Malchus* is taken by the "no-good one." This means that the Jew feels as if the *Malchus* allotted to him in his experience is not adequate for that which he wishes to disclose. Instead of one's spouse, home, and other "vessels" broadening one's mind by granting him the ability to express himself in full (see *Berachos* 57b), one feels as if they constrict him in failing to provide context for the content of his particular character. When one falls into this mistaken view, a view unhinged from simplicity and the faith in *hashgachah pratis*, he sees everything in his life as being *"lo-tov."* All of the elements of his personal *Malchus* are sub-par; his wife, his children, his co-workers etc. are the cause for a deep and abiding anxiety and the urge to escape to a different place with other vessels he is certain will better match the powers of his soul. This illustration provides a deeper insight into understanding what it means when *Malchus* is taken by the "no-good one." This important idea is discussed by the *Degel Machaneh Ephraim, Re'eh, "V'chol gevuleich."*

LESSONS FOR LIFE

✳ When one of the parties in even the closest of relationships ceases to appreciate the gift of their bond and begins taking the other's love for granted, it is incredibly painful and destructive.

✳ Gratitude preserves the excitement, passion, and desire we once felt toward something even after attaining it. When we stop being grateful for the gifts in our lives, we have lost touch with the deep feelings we have toward those gifts and they cease to inspire wonder and joy in our hearts.

✳ All apparent Heavenly distancing is only for the purpose of bringing us closer. While it may seem as if Hashem is driving us away, in truth He wants us to use this challenge as an opportunity to express how much He means to us by returning to His service.

✳ When we make the mistake of thinking that Hashem's apparent rejection is for real and run away from His fury, this devastating error leaves us susceptible to the evil forces.

CHAPTER 4

The Viceroy's
Three Requests

וְהָיָה אָבִיהָ מִצְטַעֵר מְאֹד, וְהָלַךְ לְבַקְשָׁהּ אָנֶה וָאָנָה. עָמַד
הַשֵּׁנִי לַמַּלְכוּת, מֵחֲמַת שֶׁרָאָה שֶׁהַמֶּלֶךְ מִצְטַעֵר מְאֹד,
וּבִקֵּשׁ שֶׁיִּתְּנוּ לוֹ מְשָׁרֵת וְסוּס וּמָעוֹת עַל הוֹצָאוֹת,
וְהָלַךְ לְבַקְשָׁהּ. וְהָיָה מְבַקְשָׁהּ מְאֹד, זְמַן מְרֻבֶּה מְאֹד
עַד שֶׁמְּצָאָהּ. [עַתָּה מְסַפֵּר אֵיךְ בִּקְשָׁה עַד שֶׁמְּצָאָהּ.]

Her father was very pained, and he went here and
there looking for her. The viceroy stood up, for he
saw the king's pain. He requested a servant, a horse,
and money for expenses, and he went to search for
her. He searched for a very long time until he found
her. (Now we will tell of how he searched until he
found her.)

I N THE PREVIOUS CHAPTER, we learned that the king
had hoped his show of anger and the terrible statement he
had uttered would frighten his daughter into sober awareness
of how badly her appreciation for their relationship had waned,
bringing them closer together than ever before. Certainly, he

never truly desired the abduction of his precious daughter. It was only a show, an ingenious plan to bring her back. Sadly, this plan had gone miserably awry. Instead of returning to his room with holy stubbornness and an outpouring of renewed desire, his precious princess ran away to her room where she was seized by the forces of "no-good."[1] Devastated by his tremendous loss, the king set out to search for her.

❋ The King Does Not Find the Princess

THROUGHOUT THE JOURNEY of life, there are times that we find ourselves, like the princess, convinced by Hashem's outward show of impatience and anger. The voice that echoes within validates all but the consciousness in which it resonates, proclaiming that Hashem no longer desires our service and that we have fallen too far to again rise to a new beginning. It seems so true, so very real! The arguments it makes are so logical and in step with rational consequence! In a short time, we are swayed by its words. We submit to the position that we deserve this feeling of disconnection, that we have brought it upon ourselves, and that this death sentence of the soul is the direct result of our spiritual crimes. Drowning in an ocean of choking despair and hopelessness, we give up fighting and sink to the depths. Our childhood dreams of spiritual fulfillment are shattered; leaving in their place a charred and tortured monument to what might

---

1. Those familiar with my previous work, *Sunlight of Redemption*, will remember the two features of the moon's constriction which A) conceals the presence of Hashem, and B) allows His presence to be discovered in the world. The reaction of the princess to her father's distance aligns with the outlook of Eisav — the *Moon of the Other Side* (see p. 134). This outlook similarly misinterprets the *tzimtzum*-constriction, failing to recognize the positive end toward which the negative event serves as a means.

have been, a broken vision of what closeness with Hashem might have felt like.

Once a Jew has been deceived into making this tremendous mistake, it is exceedingly difficult to become inspired from an external source. Having "heard" Hashem Himself declare that there is no longer hope, nothing else seems to be able to bring one to the revelation that, in fact, there always is hope, and that even when the gates of *teshuvah* are closed, they are never locked — all one needs to do is turn the doorknob.[2]

In this story, the king isn't the one to find the lost princess. Rebbe Nachman is teaching us that heaven-sent inspiration is often not enough to undo the terrible damage of our mistaken belief. If we are to rediscover our passion and excitement for a relationship with Hashem, someone else must be sought to carry on the search, someone with an entirely different perspective. This character is represented by the royal viceroy.

✳ An Inner Point of Holiness

THE MAJORITY OF our story is devoted not to the princess mentioned in its title, but to the viceroy, his mighty efforts on behalf of the king, and the progressions and failures he experiences along the way. Consequently, his role is perhaps even more important than that of the princess herself. It is therefore necessary to explore the viceroy's inner essence and the element he represents in the story of our own lives.

Throughout their writings, the tzaddikim stress that every Jew, regardless of his or her spiritual standing, has a point deep inside that is always perfectly pure. No matter how removed one

---

2. See *Mishneh Torah, Hilchos Teshuvah* 6:3; *Peleh Yoetz,* "*Hisorerus*"; and *Tzidkas HaTzaddik* 45, *Kesser Shem Tov* #82. See also *Oros HaTeshuvah* 14:3.

may become from holiness or how badly one has sinned, that pilot light continues flickering, ever defiant.[3] Much like the sole jug of oil found among the rubble of the Beis HaMikdash during the times of the Chashmonaim, this inner point remains ever untouched by any level of impurity. When a Jew encounters this essential core of his identity, it enables him to rededicate his inner temple and reignite the flame of his passion toward serving Hashem.

The *sefarim hakedoshim* refer to this element in different ways. Some tzaddikim called it the *"Pinte'le Yid"* (Point of Jewishness). Others referred to it as the *"Cheilek Eloka mimaal"* (Portion of God Above). Rebbe Nachman of Breslov famously called it the *"Nekudah Tovah,"* (Drop of Goodness). In his magnum opus, *Likutei Moharan*, Rebbe Nachman writes: "And even when we encounter one who is completely wicked, we must search and seek within him to find some tiny drop of goodness in which he isn't wicked."[4] This untainted portion of holiness is hinted to in the inner "Yaakov" within which Hashem sees no iniquity.[5] It is this element that enables the prophet to refer to every member of our holy nation as "tzaddikim."[6]

The Breslover *mashpi'im* teach that the viceroy in our tale refers to this special element in the Jewish soul, the "tzaddik" within.[7]

---

3. See *Nefesh HaChaim* 1:18.

4. *Likutei Moharan* 282.

5. *Bamidbar* 23:21. See *Machshavos Charutz* 7.

6. *Yeshayahu* 60:21: "And your entire nation is righteous." The second half of the verse states, "they will inherit the land (*'eretz'*) forever." In the deeper *sefarim*, "Eretz" is a reference to the *Sefirah* of *Malchus*. Thus, this verse can be understood as hinting to the viceroy's eventual success in locating and freeing the lost princess.

7. The Hebrew term for the viceroy, *"Sheni L'Malchus,"* literally "Second to Kingship," connotes the *Sefirah* of *Yesod*, which is positioned directly above *Malchus*. This *middah* is bound with the concept of the tzaddik, as the verse states, *V'tzaddik yesod olam*, "The tzaddik is the foundation (*Yesod*) of the

world." Additionally, the Gemara (*Shabbos* 156a) states, "One who is born on Friday will be a seeker" — the day associated with the sixth *middah*, *Yesod*, contains the energy of the ever-seeking point of holiness within. Indeed, Yosef, the biblical figure who serves as the chariot for the *middah* of *Yesod*, is referred to as "Yosef **HaTzaddik**." This is the deeper meaning of the verse, "He (Pharaoh) had him (Yosef) ride in the chariot of the second-in-command" (*Bereishis* 41:43); the viceroy is the "*Sheini l'melech*," *middas Yesod*, the tzaddik within. (Mordechai **HaTzaddik** became the "*mishneh lamelech*," second-in-command, as well [see *Esther* 10:3].)

The connection between the *Sefirah* of *Yesod*/viceroy and Bris allows us deep insight into a fascinating teaching from Chazal. Chazal state (*Menachos* 43b) that when David HaMelech went into a bathhouse and saw that he stood without tefillin, tzitzis, or mezuzah, he said, "Woe is to me that I stand naked, without mitzvos!" But then he remembered his *bris milah*, and he was appeased. This Gemara is teaching us that even when a person is sunk in the depths of spiritual rot, devoid of all mitzvos, the aspect of *Bris/Yesod*/Viceroy never leaves him — the inner flame of holiness remains ever flickering within.

It is important to note, however, that in addition to connoting ultimate goodness and contact with the ever-present validating factor within oneself as well as within the world, *Yesod* embodies a certain danger. Because it is the culmination of the six sons, when disconnected from *Malchus*, a relationship with a valid goal, *Yesod* comes to represent the absolute pinnacle of meaninglessness and wastefulness. On the most basic level, *p'gam habris* represents the physical expression of essential potentiality with no hope for substantive development embodied in a mate. In verbal expressivity, *p'gam bris halashon* represents excessive and inane speech that conveys no essential point or relevance. In portraying the proper *Yesod/Malchus* relationship, Chazal teach, "One who toils on Erev Shabbos will have what to eat on *Shabbos*" (*Avodah Zarah* 3a). However, *Yesod* on its own, disconnected from the life-giving receptivity of *Malchus*, may be likened to toiling to prepare food on Friday in the total absence of a seventh day — surely a pointless and vain endeavor.

The tzaddikim teach (see, for example, *Rabbeinu Bachya, Bereishis* 2:3), that just as the week is divided into seven days — mirroring the seven lower *Sefiros*, as we have learned — all of history is divided into seven millennia, a period of seven thousand years. Presently, we are living within the sixth millennia — corresponding to Erev Shabbos, the *Sefirah* of *Yesod*. It is in our time, then, that the worldview of the six sons, a perspective of post-modernistic meaninglessness, shallowness, and secularism has become so powerfully pervasive. This explains why the quintessential expression of the six sons, the selfish wastefulness of *p'gam habris*, is the undisputed battle of our generation.

When a Jew sinks into despair and loses the princess of wonder and passion in his or her *avodas Hashem,* the *Nekudah Tovah* within acutely senses the King's devastation over His great loss and resolves to do everything in its power to find the princess and free her from the influence of the evil forces that have taken her away. It may take days, weeks, or even years for the call of the inner tzaddik to reach us from below the rubble, but eventually we are stirred by a nagging feeling of unfulfillment, existential unrest, and guilt — the *Nekudah Tovah* at work.[8] With no warning, a torpedo of wastefulness and lack bursts through the deceptively

---

This struggle, which has been a part of the human experience from the beginning of time, has been magnified in our times to a frightening extreme by an overwhelming onslaught of promiscuity and a cultural atmosphere of immorality that ultimately champions the total cheapening of what should rightfully be revered as the most meaningful of all human actions — the act of procreation bursting with a spirit of devotion, care, and the deepest love. Whereas previous generations took speech (*bris halashon*) very seriously, intensely deliberated upon it and treated it with utmost seriousness, the rise of social media has transformed the way we use our words, cheapening our speech and robbing our verbal expression of the meaning it once held. The concept of truth and the weightiness of facts has gone in much the same way. In our generation, a time when *Yesod* is so often detached from the purposeful, deep, and sensitive nature of *Malchus,* we are experiencing the deadening of wonder, depth, and the increasing sense that life has no meaning.

However, for all the impurity of our times, there is a unique opportunity here as well. Because ours is the generation of *Yesod,* if we succeed in living a life of engagement with *Malchus,* saturated with ultimate purpose and meaning, we can merit to live lives of unparalleled depth and quality. The sixth millennium, mirroring Friday, has the potential to become included in the great *Shabbos* to come, to be infused with an other-worldly experience of transcendent spirit.

In a world filled with viceroys wandering aimlessly on a journey with no objective, it is of utmost importance that we take stock of the unique opportunity of our time to connect the *Yesod* of our lives to the purposeful spirit of *Malchus,* gathering our strength to discover and become united with the princess of youthful passion in life and in our *avodas Hashem.*

8. See *Likutei Moharan* 274 and *Sichos HaRan* 10.

calm surface of our consciousness, exploding the illusion of stability and shaking us from our dark reverie. Suddenly, the realization that a life lived apart from the Torah is no life at all compels us to think deeply about how frozen and stagnant we have become since our fire was extinguished so many weeks, months, or even years ago by the cool winds of despair. As the echo of the *bas kol, Shuvu banim shovavim*, "Return, my wayward children" rings in our ears once more, this time naming no exception in its urgency, it begins to attract our attention.[9] The inner viceroy runs in circles, frantically gathering all holy forces working on our behalf and energetically waving the banner of hope in an effort to remind us that we can still turn things around and regain what we've lost. As we groggily wake to the truth and sincerity of his words, the viceroy begins packing his bags for the long journey ahead. Our validation is all that is required. If we trust in its existence and allow it to guide the way, this tiny drop of untouched goodness will search for and eventually discover the Lost Princess of passion and wonder in *avodas Hashem*. From its ever-glowing embers, a great fire of holiness will rise once more.

⁑ Provisions for the Journey

BEFORE SETTING OUT to search for the passion and excitement toward the service of Hashem lost to "the no-good one," spiritual devastation founded upon the mistaken belief that one's efforts are no longer desirable, the viceroy makes three requests from the king.

The viceroy's first request is to be granted a *mishareis*, a **servant**. The Breslover *mashpi'im* teach that this servant represents the powers of intellect. Because the viceroy's search for the lost

---

9. See *Toldos Yaakov Yosef, Vayikra,* "*Vayikra el Moshe.*"

princess essentially symbolizes a *teshuvah* process, it will require a mature and openminded intellectual capacity if it is to meet with success. As we shall see, in addition to aiding the Jewish person in his search for truth, an intellectually sound relationship with the tenets of our faith will preserve one's appreciation for the framework of *avodas Hashem* even when he is emotionally exhausted.

The second request is for a **horse**. This refers to a strong and healthy body. The Rambam writes that "for the body to be healthy and sound is of the paths of G-d."[10] It is impossible for one to embark on a campaign of Torah and *tefillah* if his body lacks the level of functionality necessary for this adventure. Indeed, the Maggid of Mezeritch is quoted as having said, "A small hole in the body makes a large hole in the soul."[11] Although it is a commonly neglected *avodah*, Rav Kook stressed that maintaining physical health is a major element of *avodas Hashem*. In his masterpiece on *teshuvah*, the tzaddik writes that a weak body is oftentimes the cause for the lessening of holy desire and that, in the *teshuvah* process, we must seek to strengthen the force of the body in order to fortify the courage of the soul and grant wings to its aspirations.[12]

In another place, Rav Kook teaches:

> The demand for physicality is enormous. We need healthy bodies. But we have been so focused on our souls that we have forgotten the holiness of the body. We have neglected our health and strength and have forgotten that we possess holy bodies no less than we possess holy souls.[13]

In the coming chapters, we will read about the tremendous difficulties the viceroy will face in his search for the lost princess;

---

10. *Mishneh Torah, Hilchos Dei'os* 4:1.

11. See *I Will Write It in Their Hearts*, Vol. 7, Letter 899.

12. *Oros HaTeshuvah*, Chapters 1 and 14:20.

13. *Oros HaTechiyah* 33.

mighty obstacles that will push the viceroy to the limits of his endurance. Physical strength and the vibrancy and vigor that accompany it are thus crucial for the success of his mission.

There is another level here as well. Rav Kook writes that when a Jew embarks on a *teshuvah* journey without first working on matters related to the body such as his mannerisms, behaviors, and habits, he may achieve spiritual insight and elevation only to return to a broken body that cannot adequately serve as a vessel for his newfound illumination. This can cause tremendous anguish and spark a destructive inner battle in which, no matter who wins, the Jew's emotional health always emerges the loser. Therefore, it is of utmost importance to work on body-related spiritual development first — relationships, habits, behavioral traits etc. — before proceeding to greater levels of spiritual elevation.[14]

The third and final element the viceroy requests from the king is the most straightforward. The Breslover *mashpi'im* teach that "**money** for expenses" means just that. The search for the Lost Princess in our lives has a far greater chance of success if our waking hours are not consumed with worry over how we are going to pay the rent or our child's tuition. Financial difficulties and the anxiety they cause can be absolutely debilitating to the early stages of spiritual growth. When a Jew gathers his strength and resolves to search for the princess of youth, he requires *yishuv hadaas*, requisite peace of mind and the ability to devote himself fully to the task at hand. While it is certainly true that money can't buy happiness, and that — as we shall learn — *emunah* and *bitachon* can enable us to serve Hashem with joy regardless of our circumstance, financial stability goes a long way in granting the peace of mind necessary for one to achieve these levels. It is important to stress that we are not talking here about attaining

---

14. *Oros HaTeshuvah* 14:2.

fabulous wealth or amassing riches. Rebbe Nachman teaches that the viceroy requests only the money *"for expenses"* — the basic funds to cover the costs of a reasonable lifestyle, all for the sake of *avodas Hashem*. As Rebbe Levi Yitzchak of Berditchov teaches: "When one requests kindness from Hashem, he should not focus upon the personal gratification he will receive from this thing. Rather, his primary focus should be that this thing will enable him to serve Hashem with peace of mind."[15]

Explaining why Zevulun received his *berachah* from Yaakov before Yissaschar despite being the younger of the two, the *Kli Yakar* writes:

> Although it is true that acquiring Torah takes precedence over the acquisition of mundane wares, for "her wares are better than all others," Zevulun's *berachah* preceded Yissaschar's because "if there is no flour, there is not Torah." If one does not have what to eat and drink, how will his limbs be strong and healthy for the sake of toiling in Torah? Therefore Zevulun, who brings bread from afar, preceded Yissaschar so the latter could sit in the tents of Torah.[16]

In a similar vein, Reb Nosson records:

> The Rebbe said that he wanted very much that we should have a sure source of income. To have *bitachon* is certainly very good, but it is also very good when one has a steady income as a base. Then, instead of working on developing trust he can work on a different area of devotion. A person without a steady income is always anxious about his financial situation and he has to work constantly to strengthen his trust. Instead of this he could be working on a different area of devotion.[17]

---

15. *Kedushas Levi, Shemos, "Vayomer Hashem."*
16. *Kli Yakar* to *Bereishis* 49:15.
17. *Chayei Moharan* 501.

The requests the viceroy makes before setting out on his journey represent the three most fundamental elements for which a Jew must beseech the Master of the world before setting out to search for his lost princess. In *Likutei Moharan*, Rebbe Nachman teaches that the verse "And Yaakov arrived, complete, to the city of Shechem"[18] refers to the necessary elements that must be attained before global society can properly seek the truth.[19] Commenting on the word "complete," Chazal write, "Complete in his *physical health*, complete in his *financial state*, and complete in his *Torah knowledge*."[20] These three aspects in which Yaakov achieved completion correspond to the servant, horse, and money requested by the viceroy. Mental, physical, and financial well-being are the three pillars that put a person in position to succeed in matters of spirituality.[21]

Because they are so imperative to spiritual growth, one can rest assured that these three elements are not easily attained. The *yetzer hara* works overtime to damage these pillars, doing all in his power to spread illness, promote financial failure, and corrupt our intellectual integrity. However, if one approaches Hashem with simplicity and sincerity and expresses in prayer that his desire for these physical blessings is solely for the assistance of his spiritual pursuit, his prayers will be graced by a special measure of Divine attention.[22]

---

18. *Bereishis* 33:18.

19. *Likutei Moharan* 27.

20. *Shabbos* 33b.

21. The *gemara* in *Berachos* (57b) teaches that three things broaden the mind of a person: a beautiful house, a beautiful wife, beautiful furnishings. Perhaps it is possible to suggest that these correspond to the three requests of the viceroy: a beautiful house — financial security; property is often a reference to a person's wealth. Beautiful furnishings (*"keilim"*) — intellectual clarity; Torah is referred to as *"Kli chemdah"* (*Avos* 3:14). A beautiful wife — physical health; *"Ishto k'gufo"* (*Berachos* 24a).

22. See *Likutei Halachos, Hilchos Rosh Chodesh* 5:4. A closer look at the text

✹ Failure in the Context of Triumph

BEFORE BEGINNING TO detail the viceroy's epic journey and the many obstacles and disappointments he meets along the way, Rebbe Nachman strengthens us by disclosing that in the end, the viceroy's mission emerges a success. While it doesn't seem like the best idea for a storyteller to give away the ending of his tale before it even begins, Rebbe Nachman does so here for the purpose of granting his reader the retrospective viewpoint that will allow us to view the viceroy's devastating failures in the broad context of his ultimate triumph.

Our sages teach that when David HaMelech composed *"Ashrei"* according to the *aleph-beis*, he skipped over the letter *"Nun"* so as not to include the negative topic of *"Nefillah,"* falling and failing. Yet, while not overtly, David in fact mentions falling and failure in the verse that begins with the letter *"Samech,"* *Someich Hashem l'chol hanoflim*, "God supports all those who fall."[23] This teaches us that while it is too difficult and perhaps counterproductive to discuss failure and descent on its own, it becomes possible and proper to mention it in the context of a positive eventuality. Once Hashem's unconditional support, *"Someich Hashem"* has been evoked, it is now possible to mention

---

reveals that the viceroy doesn't wait for his requests to be filled before setting out on his journey. "וּבְקֵּשׁ, שֶׁיִּתְּנוּ לוֹ מְשָׁרֵת וְסוּס וּמָעוֹת עַל הוֹצָאוֹת, וְהָלַךְ" "לְבַקְּשָׁה — He makes his requests and departs. Although, in the chapters ahead, we will learn that his requests were indeed granted, it is possible to suggest that the lack of overt attention paid to this detail teaches us a lesson: although one must ask Hashem for physical, intellectual, and financial well-being, he mustn't wait until his prayers are answered before embarking on his spiritual odyssey. Rather, he should begin his search in tandem with constant prayer. If he does so, he will find that, with time, his requests will be granted. See also footnote 9 in the following chapter regarding *hishtadlus*.

23. *Berachos* 4b.

the painful facts of spiritual failure *"l'chol **hanoflim**."* Having laid a foundation of triumph and ultimate success, it is now possible for Rebbe Nachman to lead us by the hand through the viceroy's journey with all its heartbreak and trouble.[24]

Throughout the tale, we are going to encounter the words, "a very long time," over and over again. The epic search for the essence of Yiddishkeit is neither short nor easy. It takes a long time, spanning many years and even decades.[25] Because it is such an awesome privilege to return to a life of communion with the Master of the world, the purpose of our entire existence,[26] tremendous patience and fortitude are required. It is in order to provide us with the strength to endure the woeful tale of the viceroy's struggle that Rebbe Nachman encourages us with the liberating knowledge of a happy ending. If we accompany our inner viceroy on his search for the princess of passion, purpose, meaning, excitement, vitality, and vibrant faith, we are sure to find her in the end.

---

24. This is an important lesson for life. As social beings, situations invariably arise that require us to provide guidance and attempt to assist someone in fixing the wrongs in his life. This is especially true of parents and teachers whose responsibility it is to make sure that the children in their charge are developing in a proper, healthy way. However, before talking about any wrongdoing, misdeed, or sin, it is important that we first create the supportive *"Samech"* of *"Someich Hashem,"* prefacing our rebuke with words of comfort and encouragement in praising the child for all the things he is doing right, providing context that lessens the severity of the misdeed, and communicating to him just how much Hashem loves him. The only way to focus on *"noflim,"* the unpleasant deeds that need fixing, is to first lay a general foundation of *"someich"* — love, comfort, and support.

25. See *Likutei Moharan Tinyana* 48.

26. See *Likutei Moharan Tinyana* 73.

LESSONS FOR LIFE

❋ Oftentimes, because it is our perception of heavenly wrath that drives us away from *avodas Hashem*, heaven-sent inspiration will not suffice to convince us of our error. Instead, we need to feel an awakening from within.

❋ Every Jewish person contains an inner point of perfect purity, a place which remains ever untouched by past misdeeds regardless of their severity. It is this *Nekudah Tovah* within which gives us no rest and relentlessly compels us to pursue a relationship with Hashem.

❋ Three elements create an emotional foundation conducive to spiritual searching: *intellectual*, *physical*, and *financial* wellbeing. Even though we have not yet been granted these three blessings, it is proper to set out on our spiritual journey in tandem with sincere prayer.

❋ It is only possible to discuss the pain of failure when it is enveloped by a spirit of hope and ultimate triumph. When we must rebuke a child or a friend, it is imperative that we lay a foundation of comfort and support before focusing on the misdeed.

CHAPTER 5

The Side Path to Spiritual Success

וְהָיָה הוֹלֵךְ אָנֶה וָאָנָה זְמַן רַב, וּבַמִּדְבָּרִיּוֹת וּבַשָּׂדוֹת
וּבַיְּעָרִים וְהָיָה מְבַקְשָׁהּ זְמַן רַב מְאֹד, וְהָיָה הוֹלֵךְ בַּמִּדְבָּר,
וְרָאָה שְׁבִיל אֶחָד מִן הַצַּד, וְהָיָה מְיַשֵּׁב עַצְמוֹ: בַּאֲשֶׁר
שֶׁאֲנִי הוֹלֵךְ כָּל כָּךְ זְמַן רַב בַּמִּדְבָּר וְאֵינִי יָכוֹל לְמָצְאָהּ אֵלֵךְ
בַּשְּׁבִיל הַזֶּה, אוּלַי אָבוֹא לִמְקוֹם יִשׁוּב. וְהָיָה הוֹלֵךְ זְמַן רַב.

The viceroy traveled here and there for a long time
through deserts, fields, and forests. He searched
for her for a very long time. Finally, while traveling
through the desert, he saw a path to the side, and
thought it over. "Since I have traveled for so long in
the desert and I cannot find her, let me follow this
path. Perhaps it will bring me to an inhabited area."
And he walked for a very long time.

❋ Deserts, Fields, and Forests

AT THE OUTSET of the viceroy's journey, he travels through three
distinct landscapes: deserts, fields, and forests. What is the
spiritual significance of these three terrains, and what do they

represent in our search for the Lost Princess of youth? The Breslover *mashpi'im* teach that deserts, fields, and forests hint to three major stages in the process of spiritual recovery. Let us explore them one by one.

A **desert** is a place of desolation and very little growth. Its cracked ground and dusty air conjure the brokenhearted cries of David HaMelech, "My soul is like parched land for You"[1] and "My soul thirsts for G-d."[2] At this initial stage of growth, the heart is closed, the mind numb, and the barren earthiness seems to stretch on forever. Here we feel directionless and lost amidst winds of doubt which whip up blinding clouds[3] of anguish and a renewed sense of hopelessness. Our Torah study and *tefillah* have no taste, the atmosphere of our *avodas Hashem* is arid and dry. This is the desert, the deathly silence within which the viceroy's journey begins.

The *avodah* of the desert is to serve Hashem even without feeling and even when devoid of inspiration — to keep showing up for minyan, continuing to study Torah in whatever way we can, and holding tight to our observance of halachah no matter how difficult it seems.[4] *Naaseh v'nishma*, "We will do and we will hear" — the declaration of our ancestors who received the Torah in the Sinai *desert* — has multiple meanings, and one hints to this *avodah*. Even before "hearing," experiencing the sweetness of spiritual illumination, we are satisfied with "doing," engaging in *avodas Hashem* simply because we know that it is what Hashem desires, what our soul craves, and what we need to do in order to

---

1. *Tehillim* 143:6.

2. Ibid. 63:1.

3. See *Likutei Moharan* 2.

4. See *Likutei Moharan* 155. See also *Torah Ohr, Tetzaveh, "Zachor,"* where the Baal HaTanya explains why, after leaving Mitzrayim, Klal Yisrael needed to travel through the desert before entering Eretz Yisrael.

put our lives in order.[5] Because life is marked by many ups and downs, the winters and summers of the human condition, the ability to push forward in a time of constricted consciousness is a necessary condition to attaining true spiritual fulfillment.

In *Kesser Shem Tov*, we read:

> Hashem held the mountain over the Jews to teach that even when one feels no desire for Torah and *avodas Hashem*, he is not free to sit idly. Rather, he must act — even against his will — as if he was being forced. And this is a good path for the Jewish person in a time of "*katnus*," never to interrupt his *avodah* simply because he feels little desire, but rather to nevertheless perform acts of holiness.[6]

In teaching that the viceroy begins his search in a desert, Rebbe Nachman intends to invoke the principle revealed by our Sages that *kol haschalos kashos*, "all beginnings are difficult."[7] One does not attain spiritual illumination in one day. However, knowledge that we must experience this doubt and confusion as we set out on our search gives us the strength to carry on, to keep on moving. Eventually, we enter the next stage of development — the field.

The **field** hints to the second stage of spiritual recovery. A field is a place of growth and production, of healthy crops and lush vegetation. However, the field is a place of tremendous toil. While at this stage the searching soul begins to witness some degree of progress, it is only by way of strenuous work and persistent effort. "Those who plant with tears reap with joy"[8] sang David

---

5. See *Mei HaShiloach*, Vol. 2, *Vayikra*.

6. *Kesser Shem Tov* #47.

7. *Rashi* to *Shemos* 19:5. See also *Mei HaShiloach*, Vol. 1, *Ki Savo*, "*Es Hashem he'emarta.*"

8. *Tehillim* 126:5.

HaMelech; any fruit we may cultivate in the field is a product of our tireless labor. Ultimately, while tasting the sweet fruits in the field of growth is certainly a positive and rewarding experience, the princess is still nowhere to be found, and the viceroy must move on.

The next phase in the viceroy's search is the **forest**. This landscape is teeming with all levels of life, a place of abundant growth and development. Kabbalistically, the forest represents the powers of intellect and the unique capacity of the human mind to contemplate lofty ideas of transcendent spirituality. After spending a long time in the fields of toil and labor, the Jew is elevated to a realm of resplendent clarity where he finds it easy to ponder the spiritual nature of the world and his Divine mission within it. Still, Rebbe Nachman teaches that this is not yet the ultimate level. While the forest's mighty trees represent existential lucidity and spiritual accomplishment, they simultaneously represent the ability for one to hide, a previous impossibility in the desolation of the desert and the limited growth of the field. It is possible for a Jew to spend all his life plumbing the depths of spiritual philosophy and halachic intricacies in a manner of arrogance and sophistication, remaining disconnected from his princess — the vitality, passion, and joy that simple faith and a true relationship with Hashem engenders. In addition, the forest presents another danger: having tasted true enjoyment in Torah and *avodah*, one may feel that it is no longer necessary to seek the princess of youthful passion. Acutely aware of these points and the abundant peril presented by the forest, the viceroy continues his search.[9]

---

9. In addition to this *avodah*-oriented interpretation, perhaps it is possible to suggest that the desert, field, and forest allude to the viceroy's *hishtadlus* toward attaining the horse, money, and servant he requested in the previous chapter. The desert refers to the viceroy's *Teshuvas HaGuf*, rectification of his physical health by way of proper eating and exercise. The field refers to efforts to attain financial security, as the field is always a symbol for a person's wealth.

✳ The Tail of the Lion

HAVING EXPLORED THE symbolism of the three landscapes experienced by the viceroy, it may seem strange that it is a path found in the *desert* which allows the story to proceed. Hadn't the viceroy already mastered the desert of physical desolation and attained the forest of spiritual success? Didn't he already grasp a profound clarity into the spirituality that pulses within corporeality? How did our hero fall back to the parched plains of the desert, and why is it here, of all places, that he discovers a path that will bring him closer to his goal?

Rebbe Nachman teaches that the growth process is a multi-tiered system. There are a great many segments along the path toward finding the Lost Princess of our lives — *each* of which contains aspects of "desert," "field," and "forest" unique to that particular stage. Thus, after spending much time in the forest of the first segment, we proceed onward — to the *desert* of the second segment; from the head of the fox to the tail of the lion. Battling our way up to the forest of the second segment, we proceed yet again, entering the desert of the third segment, and the pattern continues.[10]

Understandably, while the desert of a greater level is more elevated than the forest of the level preceding it, it is still a desert — complete with all manners of desolation a desert embodies. Because of this, one necessarily experiences a lull in his *avodah* upon crossing the threshold into a new stage in his development. Old desires awaken, ancient doubts arise, and the vulnerabilities inherent in the human condition are once more exposed. All of

---

Finally, the forest hints to the viceroy's attempts to reach intellectual clarity, as the *Mekubalim* teach that a forest is related to the *Mochin*, the mental processes.

10. See *Liktuei Amarim, Tanya, "Chinuch Katan."*

this is because in order for a glorious new building to be erected, the old foundation must be torn down.[11] However, if misunderstood, these feelings can give the impression that one has fallen back to square one. This, in turn, may cause him to fail these tests and fall further into the darkness. Rebbe Nachman refers to this error in his magnum opus, *Likutei Moharan*. There he teaches:

> And the chassidim often err in this matter, for it suddenly appears as if they have fallen from *avodas Hashem*. But in truth this is not a descent at all! It is only that they need to proceed from level to level.[12]

When a Jew who has begun to taste the sweetness of *emunah* and conscious *limud haTorah* suddenly finds himself back in the desert of *avodas Hashem* — numb to spirituality and overcome by baser inclinations, it may appear that all his effort has gone to waste and that he has fallen right back where he started. But this couldn't be further from the truth! On the contrary! A Jew's re-entry to the level of the desert is oftentimes the greatest sign that he has progressed to the next major segment of growth. To reinforce this point, Rebbe Nachman tells us that it is in the *desert* of a higher level, not the *forest* of a lower level, that the viceroy begins to make real progress in his search for the lost princess.

This leads us to another, related idea. One of the mighty implications of the Baal Shem Tov's doctrine of perceiving the Godly holiness within everything is the redeemable nature of life: every part of the human experience can be used as a tool to discover and cleave to Hashem's presence.

---

11. See *Maharal, Netzach Yisrael*, Chapter 35.

12. *Likutei Moharan* 25:5. See also *Sichos HaRan* 79 and *Meor Einayim, Lech Lecha*, "*V'es Hanefesh*."

In the words of R' Hillel Zeitlin:

> This is the nature of every circumstance and every desire, everything a person thinks and wills: Whether one will be merciful or cruel, angry or compassionate, speak curses or soft words, hate or love, conduct oneself with pride or lowliness, sit in solitude or together with people, live a life of austerity or with family, withhold from the world or enjoy everything the eye sees — everything can be good, and everything can be bad. Everything is good when the gain is refined, elevated, filled with the presence of the living God, and performed in relation to the Godly life. Everything is bad when the gain descends, sinks, when one forgets the God Who gives birth to him and recognizes only his individual desire and personal gain.[13]

One area that received special focus from the Baal Shem and his students was *"Haala'os HaMiddos,"* the process of elevating one's traits and emotions. The tzaddikim taught that every emotional state represents a potential doorway into closeness with Hashem if we are wise enough to seize it and walk through its gates to a loftier perception.

Chief among the emotions that may be elevated is that of sadness and brokenness. The Ishbitzer writes that when a Jew is sad, this is a tremendous *eis ratzon* for prayer.[14] The Baal HaTanya teaches that the best time for heartbroken contemplation over one's distance from Hashem and the search for more effective strategies going forward is a time when one is in a bad mood caused by mundane reasons. Channeling this energy to *avodas Hashem*, one is able to elevate this mood and refine it so that it becomes transformed into something that is deeply meaningful

---

13. *Mevo L'Chassidus Ul'Darkah shel Chabad*, p. 65.
14. *Mei HaShiloach*, Vol. 2, *Mikeitz, "HaElokim matza."*

and productive.[15] To facilitate this exercise, the Piaseczner Rebbe
Hy"d lists specific chapters in *Tehillim* to be recited when a wave
of sadness washes over a person so this negative mood, which is
truly an awesome opportunity for true spiritual growth, can be
seized and fulfilled before it passes.[16]

The desert of *avodas Hashem* provides us with the opportunity to expand the emotion of brokenness through contemplation
and prayer in a way that can create a more productive level of
commitment.[17]

Rebbe Ephraim of Sudylkov writes:

> It is known in the name of the Baal Shem Tov that "the *cha-
> yos* were running and returning" — it is impossible to con-
> stantly remain on one level. Rather, one is always rising and
> descending. But the descent is for the sake of ascent — *when
> one focuses his heart to know and to feel that he is in a state
> of "smallness,"* and he calls out to Hashem...[18]

In the words of Reb Tzadok HaKohen:

> A time of descent, when a person has no desire for Torah and
> *avodah*, is a preparation for a great ascent, [by way of] the
> cry that one emits *when he contemplates his lowliness and
> descent.* Like the verse states "They traveled from *Refidim*

---

15. *Likutei Amarim, Tanya,* Chapter 32. See also *Degel Machaneh Ephraim,
Mishpatim, "M'lei'ascha."*

16. *Hachsharas HaAvreichim,* Chapter 9. The chapters recorded are: 3,6,10,
13,16,17,22,25,31,38,42, and specifically 51, among others.

17. It is important to note that after this period of brokenness, one must open
himself up to the subsequent level by inspiring great joy in his heart. This is
accomplished by remembering that he has merited to begin drawing close to
Hashem and the tzaddikim. Joy over the successes of the past — after the brokenness of his contemplation — enable him to break past the shell guarding the
next rung in the ladder and continue his ascent. (See *Likutei Moharan* 25:5.)

18. *Degel Machaneh Ephraim, Vayeitzei, "Vayeitzei Yaakov."* See also *Kesser
Shem Tov* #10.

and came to *Midbar Sinai.*"[19] Chazal famously comment: "Their hands weakened (*rafu yedeihem*) from Torah study."[20] This weakening was a preparation for the giving of the Torah which was the ultimate "strengthening of hands" in the study of Torah.[21]

Seizing the great opportunity granted by his re-entry into the desert of lowliness, the viceroy engages in deep contemplation. Thus far along the highway of *avodas Hashem* in Torah, *avodah*, and *gemillus chassadim*, he has not yet been successful in discovering the lost princess. Perhaps it is time for him to take a different way?

"Finally, while traveling through the desert, he saw a path to the side, and thought it over. 'Since I have traveled for so long in the desert and I cannot find her, let me follow this path. Perhaps it will bring me to an inhabited area.'"

The viceroy's discovery of a path to the side in the desert of spiritual brokenness represents the first breakthrough in his journey. As we shall read in chapters ahead, it leads him directly to the place where the princess is being held. It is therefore important for us to examine the nature of this path, exploring its symbolism as well as the significance of its being "to the side."

✳ The Fullest Expression of Unity

A WELL-KNOWN TEACHING from the holy *Zohar* states that every Jewish soul is sourced in one of the Torah's 600,000 letters — each different from the next, each with a unique path to spiritual

---

19. *Shemos* 19:2.
20. *Sanhedrin* 106a.
21. *Tzidkas HaTzaddik* 151.

success.[22] Deceptively simple, the implications of this teaching are extremely deep.

One of the theological foundations of Yiddishkeit is the idea of essential collectivism. This means that all members of our holy nation make up one organism; individual cells in a singular structure, drops in a vast ocean, sparks of a single torch. Each Jewish soul represents a shard of stained glass, unique in its hue. Taken as a whole, the Jewish nation serves as a glorious stained-glass window through which Hashem's light shines to illuminate the world. Lacking even a single shard, a single hue, that window would stand incomplete. Indeed, *Knesses Yisrael*, the collective soul of the Jewish nation, is bound with the concept of *"Malchus — Peh,"*[23] the mouth, for we are Hashem's "mouthpiece" in the world. We share messages from a spiritual realm beyond through our attempt to embody the Torah's ideal in holy thoughts, words, and actions of holiness. Our holy nation serves as a constant reminder of an omnipotent Creator and humanity's responsibilities to Him: "You are My witnesses, says Hashem."[24]

It is possible to suggest that this is one aspect of what the *Zohar* intends to communicate in drawing a connection between the root souls of the Jewish nation and the letters of the Torah. A gathering of Jews for a holy purpose represents a collection of letters into sentences and words, an expression of the Shechinah's Presence.[25] Much like the stained-glass analogy above, missing

---

22. *Zohar Chadash*, p. 74; *Megaleh Amukos, Va'eschanan* #186. Many answers have been suggested as to how to reconcile this teaching with the fact that there are only 304,805 letters in the Torah and many more than 600,000 Jews. See, for example, *Pnei Yehoshua* to *Kiddushin* 30a and *Pri Tzaddik*, beginning of *Parshas Shemos*.

23. *Pasach Eliyahu*, introduction to *Zohar*.

24. *Yeshayahu* 43:10.

25. Perhaps this explains why our Sages placed such a stress on praying with a congregation and the concept of *"b'rov am hadras Melech"* (see *Berachos* 53a

letters will detract from the coherence of the message; the participation of every Jew is a required element for the ultimate success of our shared mission.

However, there is a deeper level as well. In addition to communicating the idea of essential collectivism, this analogy expresses an almost paradoxical condition necessary for the expression of our collective soul and her mission: maintenance of and respect for uniqueness and individuality. There is another factor that detracts from the coherence of a sentence in much the same way as missing letters, and that is a lack of requisite space between the letters. If all the Torah's letters were to be blended into a giant mass of ink, it would be impossible to discern its messages. It would be impossible to read or study, and humanity would be deprived of this enormous treasure chest of objective morality and absolute truth. Paradoxically, because it will destroy any hope for coherence, a sense of extreme, individuality-negating unity will in fact obscure the messages these letters have joined together in the hope to convey. Indeed, if it is to be kosher, the letters of a Sefer Torah need to be completely surrounded by parchment.[26] If any two letters are touching one another to the point that their forms are indistinguishable, the entire Sefer Torah is invalid.[27]

The fact of our essential unity does nothing to negate the value of our uniqueness. On the contrary, each member of *Knesses Yisrael* is charged with utilizing his or her unique talents and propensities for the purpose of our shared mission of revealing Hashem's light

---

and *Beitzah* 39a). Indeed: **"B'rov am,"** the more Jews that gather and cause their letters to combine, **"hadras,"** this accentuates the communication of **"Melech,"** "*Malchus-Peh,*" our expression of Hashem's sovereignty over the world.

26. *Shulchan Aruch, Orach Chaim* 32:32.

27. See *B'Pardes HaChassidus*, p. 126. See also a similar idea from the *Tiferes Shlomo, Shavuos*, p. 141a.

in the world.[28] It is only when the letters of the Torah scroll that is the Jewish nation are properly separated in their unique expression that our unified and singular message will be coherent to the world. In sum, instead of detracting from it, Jewish individuality expressed in both the mundane areas of life as well as in *avodas Hashem* allows for the fullest expression of our essential oneness.[29]

✳ Making Yiddishkeit Our Own

IN THE FIRST passage of Kri'as Shema, we read that each member of our holy nation is commanded to serve Hashem *b'chol levavcha, b'chol nafshecha, uv'chol meodecha*, "with all of one's heart, all of one's soul, and with all of one's might." Chazal expound on this verse, teaching that serving Hashem "*b'chol levavcha*" means with the inclination for both good and evil, "*b'chol nafshecha*" refers to *mesiras nefesh*, and "*b'chol meodecha*" means to serve Hashem with all of our assets.[30] The tzaddikim revealed that while "*b'chol meodecha*" can be translated as "with all your might" or "with all your assets," there is a deeper level as well.

Although it is difficult to translate, the Hebrew word *meod*

---

28. See *sefer Hakitzu V'Ranenu*, Chapter 1.

29. Parenthetically, when a Jew utilizes his or her uniqueness for the purpose of the singular mission of our general, collective soul, the single and ultimately limited letter of their individuality becomes seen as a "*rashei teivos*," revealing hidden abilities and powers that are far greater than the limit apparent on the surface. Using this idea, perhaps it is possible to draw a relationship between the Chassidic fascination with "*rashei teivos*" and the stress on individuality in the Chassidic teachings. Perhaps the focus upon the depth hidden beyond the surface of a simple letter enabled the tzaddikim to believe in the incredible power packed into the soul of each individual Jew. (For a deeper exploration of "*Notrikon*" and its relationship with personal ability, see *Ein Ayah, Shabbos* 12:33.)

30. *Berachos* 54a.

connotes "more" or "very," as in the phrase *tov meod, "very* good." This means that literally translated, the words *b'chol meodecha,* "with all of *your meod,"* means "with all of your *very"* — with that which is *especially you,* that one thing that is more related to your essence than that of anyone else.[31] Read in this manner, this verse encourages each member of the Jewish nation to find his or her *"meod"* — that one special area in which we can particularly excel, and use it to serve Hashem.[32]

In addition to the general, universal mission of the Jewish nation as a whole, each individual Jew was sent down to this world to accomplish something specific and unique, to perfect one particular aspect of his relationship with Hashem, others, and himself. The Malbim explains that the verse describing the Torah, "Its ways are pleasant ways and all of its paths are peaceful," refers to

---

31. For a sampling of the many sources that abound to this effect, see *Shabbos* 118b, "What was your father particularly scrupulous in?", and *Shabbos* 156a, "One who was born under the mazel of *Madim* (which grants him a murderous nature) should become a ritual slaughterer or a *mohel."* See also the Gra's comments to *Mishlei* 16:4, "For each person has his own, individual path..."; *Sichos Mussar* 33; *Klach Pischei Chochmah* #8; *Mei HaShiloach,* Vol. 1, *Tetzaveh, "V'eileh habegadim," Ki Sisa, "Vayomer Ani"; Chochmah u'Mussar* 2:62; and *Mei HaShiloach,* Vol. 2, *"Lo taasun iti,"* where the Ishbitzer points out the *Avos's* unique paths in *avodas Hashem.* Yitzchak Avinu represented the *middah* of *Gevurah,* while his father, Avraham, represented the *middah* of *Chessed* — this demonstrates, says the Ishbitzer, that every Jew must find his own way of serving God that is unique from the paths of his father or teacher. See also *Mishnas HaMaggid M'Zlotchov,* p. 220.

32. The Ishbitzer teaches that this is why, in the second paragraph of Shema which switches from the singular *b'chol levavcha,* "with all your heart," to the plural *b'chol levavchem,* "with all your hearts," only *livavchem* and *nafshichem* are mentioned — there is no mention of *b'chol meodeichem.* Because *b'chol meodecha* refers to each individual's special mission that is unique to him, it is inherently singular, something which the Torah can only command each individual in particular — and not the entire Jewish nation as a whole. (See *Mei HaShiloach, Va'eschanan, "V'ahavta."*)

these two modes. The *"ways"* of Torah refer to the broad, general guidelines of Jewish living, while the *"paths"* of Torah refer to the individual mission of each Jewish soul, the *avodah* specific to his or her *tikkun* alone.[33] While the entirety of the Jewish nation will merit redemption, its members "will be gathered up *one by one.*"[34] Rav Kook writes:

> The difference between slavery and freedom is not only a matter of external status, where one person is imprisoned to a master while another person is not imprisoned. For it is possible to find an intelligent slave whose spirit is full of freedom and it is also possible to find a free person who has the spirit of a slave. True freedom is when a person or nation is driven by an exalted spirit to stay true to the inner essence and Divine image within.[35]

In the words of Reb Shlomo Carlebach:

> The book of Psalms is not just a book of prayer; it's the book where King David is teaching the world how to serve God. There's a passage in the psalms that says, *"Ner l'ragli*

---

33. *Malbim* to *Mishlei* 3:17.

34. *Yeshayahu* 27:12. This "path to the side" ultimately brings the viceroy to the princess, *Malchus*, which, being the lowest *Sefirah*, is referred to as *"aretz*," earth/land. Perhaps this is hinted to in the following verse: *Echad hayah Avraham, vayirash es ha'aretz,* "Avraham was unique, and he inherited the land" (*Yechezkel* 33:24). When a person discovers his unique path in *avodas Hashem,* this enables him to "inherit the earth," *Malchus* — to free the Lost Princess of his life (see *Shaarei Orah,* Eighth Gate). Subsequently, I found a remarkable teaching from Reb Tzadok (*Pri Tzaddik, Ki Savo, "B'sof Haftorah"*) that echoes this sentiment. In this discourse, Reb Tzadok teaches that the five appearances of various forms of the phrase, "will inherit the land" in *Tehillim* Chapter 37, refer to five paths with regard to rectifying the sin of immorality (fulfillment of the viceroy — *Bris/Yesod*) and redeem the Shechinah (*Malchus*/the princess). These methods are: 1) Torah study, 2) Constant prayer, 3) Humility, 4) One who never sinned, 5) Yearning for Hashem's assistance and rectification.

35. *Oros HaRAYaH* 2, p. 245.

divarecha" — Your words are a candle for my feet, *"Ve'ohr l'nesivasi"* — and a light for my path.[36]

The Ishbitzer says that this is what King David is saying: There are two things in life that I have to do. First, I have to be like everybody else; I have to follow every word of the Torah, the 613 laws. But then there is something which only I can do. God has chosen me to do something very special.

In a nutshell, the Ishbitzer says: *There is a light which lights up the path, but every person needs a candle for each step of the way.*[37]

⚛ Individualized Torah Study

IN THIS VEIN, Chazal teach us that while Torah study is the essential life-force of a Jew's spirituality, *"Ein adam lomeid elah bimakom shelibo chafeitz,"*[38] a person can only truly connect to Torah that his heart is drawn toward. What works for one may not work for another; what worked for a rebbi might not work for his student, because although all of Torah is equally accessible to every Jew, each soul is particularly connected to a specific portion of Torah.[39] As one grows in spiritual maturity and becomes more attuned to the yearnings of his soul he must search for the specific area of Torah that feeds a personal flame of connection. Whether it be new vistas of Aggadah, Chassidus, Mussar, Machshavah, or areas of halachah that are not as widely studied, becoming the best "me" requires that I stop attempting to impersonate the *avodah* of others and finally follow the impulses of my very own

---

36. *Tehillim* 119:105.

37. *The Soul of Chanuka*, p. 41.

38. *Avodah Zarah* 19a. See *Shevet Mussar*, Chapter 41, where this idea is expounded upon at length. See also *Oros HaTorah* 9:6, 12, and 10:14.

39. See *Mei HaShiloach*, Vol. 2, *Tehillim*, *"Oheiv Hashem Shaarei Tzion"*; *Likutei Amarim*, *Tanya*, Chapter 4.

soul.[40] If I continue to force myself to engage in Torah study that is not fitting for my *shoresh neshamah*, I risk growing frustrated and losing desire for Torah entirely *R"l*. In the words of Rav Kook:

> There are those who went in a bad way because, in their path of study and attainment of completion, they rebelled against their personal, unique nature. One person may be primed for the study of Aggadah, and matters of halachah are not in accordance with his nature that he should busy himself with them consistently, and because he doesn't recognize or value his special aptitude, he delves into the study of halachah — as is the accepted way — and he feels within his soul an aversion to these matters, because his immersion in them is not in accordance with the nature of his personal propensity. If, however, he would discover his purpose and fulfill it by constantly involving himself with this portion of Torah which fits his soul's nature, he would immediately understand that the aversion he felt when he was studying halachah did not come about because of an inherent lack in these holy and necessary studies, but rather because his soul was seeking involvement in a different area of Torah. Then, he would remain faithful to the holiness of Torah in an elevated manner, performing "acts of valor" in the area of Torah which is pertinent to him, and helping those whose hands are mighty in halachah by granting them a taste of the sweetness of Aggadah. However, since he does not realize the source for this feeling of aversion to his study, and continues to negate his nature, when some way of freedom opens before him, he immediately escapes and becomes a foe and a stranger to Torah and *emunah*...[41]

---

40. The tzaddikim spoke very harshly regarding those who attempt to imitate the *avodah* of others instead of discovering their own "style" in *avodas Hashem*. See, for example, *Noam Elimelech, Kedoshim, "Al tifnu el ha-elillim."*
41. *Oros HaTorah* 9:6.

In another place, the tzaddik writes:

> *V'ani b'soch hagolah,* "And I am in the depths of exile."[42] This
> refers to the inner, essential "I," whether individual or col-
> lective... And the world continues, descending into the de-
> struction of every "I," both individual and collective. Expert
> teachers come and focus on the superficial. They too distract
> their student's awareness from the "I." They add straw to the
> fire, give vinegar to the thirsty, and fill minds and hearts with
> everything that is impersonal to them. Little by little, the
> "I" becomes forgotten. And when there is no "I," there is no
> "He,"[43] and how much more so is there no "You."[44,45]

Over the past few decades, a phenomenon has emerged which
some have recently gone so far as to brand a "crisis." This phenomenon involves yeshivah students who studied Torah with great diligence for many years who lose touch with their Yiddishkeit when it
comes time to leave the *beis midrash* and head out into the world
of marriage, parenthood, and *parnassah*. A similar iteration of
this "crisis" applies to current yeshivah students who, during *bein
hazemanim* or on a day when the *maggid shiur* is absent, feel no
urge to open a *sefer* or consciously engage with Yiddishkeit in any
manner. Although many explanations have been given for this, Rav
Kook goes straight to the root of the problem, without any stops
along the way. Here, the tzaddik teaches that this problem derives
from a student's lack of engagement with his personal portion in
limud haTorah and *avodas Hashem*. When one never gets in touch
with the singular area of Torah study that touches the very core of
his soul, he feels no intrinsic draw toward the studies in yeshivah,

---

42. *Yechezkel* 1:1.
43. A way of referring to Hashem indirectly.
44. A way of addressing Hashem directly.
45. *Oros HaKodesh* 3, pp. 140–141 (*The Spiritual Revolution of Rav Kook*
pp. 12–13.) See also *Ibn Ezra* to *Shemos* 31:16.

110	PART I: DUSK

even if he is the biggest *lamdan*. Therefore, the moment the framework of a yeshivah schedule falls away and this student no longer feels compelled — by an external power — to learn, he abandons it completely *R"l*, and it is only a matter of time before *tefillah* and *yiras Shamayim* follow suit. The sudden collapse of this student's commitment to Yiddishkeit is caused not by a traumatic experience or a theological crisis but by a purely external and practical modification in his life. Everything that relates to the essential nature of his relationship with Judaism is exactly the same as it was yesterday. The fact that an external change like the arrival of *bein hazemanim* or pursuing a *parnassah* can have such a devastating effect on one's relationship with *avodas Hashem* demonstrates that even his apparent devotion of the past was incredibly weak, never coming close to touching the innermost point of his life. In the words of Rav Yitzchak Hutner: "It is entirely possible for one to learn with diligence in yeshivah, and yet, based on that, one still cannot evince the person's relationship with Torah."[46]

On the other side of the coin, those who manage to make Yiddishkeit their own even while still within the framework of the yeshivah's general guidelines, working on *tefillah* and *emunah*, and seeking their own portion in Torah study in their free time, experience little change during *bein hazemanim* or when it comes time to leave the yeshivah and support their families in accordance with the will of Hashem. Such spiritual seekers experience no crisis at all. Everything continues as it always had, because their relationship to Yiddishkeit is part and parcel of their very being, dependent upon no external factor, and is recognized as encompassing and retaining relevance to every area of life.

A chassid once complained to the holy Rizhiner, "During the hours I study Torah in the *beis midrash*, I experience light and clarity. But the moment I stop studying, it's all gone! What should I do?"

---

46. *Pachad Yitzchak: Igros U'Kesavim* 112.

The tzaddik replied with the following analogy: "When a man walks through a dark forest at night and is joined by a comrade with a lantern in hand, his path is illuminated — until they reach a crossroads. Then he must continue on his own, groping in the dark to find the way. However, when a man carries a lantern of his own, he never needs to fear the darkness."

❂ Unique Spiritual Expression

IN ADDITION TO seeking a unique portion in Torah study, it is similarly imperative for a Jew to search for the mitzvos and *hanhagos* with which he feels most connected and build on them, taking special care to fully involve himself with those avenues of illumination. A particular Yom Tov, a specific *tefillah*, a special gathering of Jews for a *tisch* or *farbrengen*; the opportunities are truly endless.[47] In the words of the *Mesillas Yesharim*:

> And whatever one thinks might be a means to attaining this closeness (with Hashem) he should pursue it, grab hold of it, and never let go.[48]

In another place:

> It is not that the idea of piety changes, for it is certainly accessible to all — being nothing other than doing things in which Hashem takes pride. However, because the subjects change, it is impossible that the means toward attaining this goal should not also change, each person in accordance with his nature.[49]

---

47. It goes without saying that all innovation in this area must remain within the boundaries of halachah. Acting contrary to the will of Hashem as expressed in halachah in the name of spiritual growth is certainly counterproductive.

48. *Mesillas Yesharim*, Chapter 1.

49. Ibid., Chapter 26.

When we make Yiddishkeit our own by discovering those elements of our sacred tradition that are most attuned to the nature of our particular soul, we will watch as our *avodas Hashem* is transformed from a cold chore to a vibrant, passionate relationship bursting with utmost wonder and excitement.

> Indeed, when one walks down this secure path, one's own unique trail, in a way of righteousness that is unique to oneself, he is filled with the strength of life and the joy of spirituality. The light of God will shine upon such a person, and strength and light will come from his special letter in the Torah.[50]

On a mission to free the Lost Princess of youth, the viceroy must discover a *path to the side*, a personal involvement with Torah and mitzvos.[51]

---

50. *Shemoneh Kevatzim* 4:6 (*The Spiritual Revolution of Rav Kook*, p. 18).

51. Many of the tzaddikim see the concept of holy individualism in *avodas Hashem* communicated through various aspects of the *chag* of Chanukah. The following are a few of the many symbols. A] The Gemara teaches that fulfilling the mitzvah of *hadlakas ner Chanukah* in a way that is *mehadrin* requires, "*ner l'chol echad v'echad*" (*Shabbos* 21b). The allusion here is that each and every Jew has their own light to share to the world. B] As opposed to "*Meorei Eish*," an illumination deriving from fire which consumes the fuel, the illumination of Chanukah is "*Meorei Ohr*," deriving from a fire that does not consume; the oil lasted for eight days. (This is one of the answers to the *Beis Yosef*'s famous question of why we celebrate eight days if the first night wasn't a miracle — although one night's worth of oil was indeed available, none of the oil was consumed.) These two kinds of illumination, "*Meorei Aish*" and "*Meorei Ohr*" symbolize two kinds of educators, both of whom intend to illuminate the lives of the students in their charge. However, the "*Meorei Aish* teacher" accomplishes this by "consuming" the student, forcing him to change fundamental aspects of his identity and thus robbing his individuality. The "*Meorei Ohr* teacher*," on the other hand, imparts illumination in such a way that nothing is consumed — the student is able to maintain his or her personal path toward a relationship with Hashem. (See *The Soul of Chanukah*, pp. 35–36.) C] Lighting the menorah on Chanukah is bound with the Kohen Gadol's lighting the menorah in the

✻ Personal Prayer — *Hisbodedus*

ANOTHER, CONCURRENT, INTERPRETATION sees the "path to the side" as referring to *hisbodedus* — daily personal prayer composed of original words spoken in one's own language — an *avodah* upon which Rebbe Nachman famously placed tremendous focus. As the viceroy walks through the *midbar*, searching for the princess of youthful passion, innocence, and simplicity, he becomes a *midabeir*[52] — he discovers the awesome path of *hisbodedus*.

In the early days of Reb Nosson's relationship with Rebbe Nachman, the Rebbe put an arm around his prized student's shoulder, saying, "And further, it is very good to open up your heart before Hashem as you would to a truly close friend."[53] These words express the very foundation of *hisbodedus* — the idea that although Hashem is our Father and our King, he is also our very closest and dearest Friend[54] Who is intimately involved in all details of our lives and may be addressed as such. Just as close human relationships are formed through expressive communication, a personal relationship with the Master of the world is fortified

---

Beis HaMikdash. (See *Ramban* to *Bamidbar* 8:2.) About this lighting, Chazal teach that the Kohen Gadol would hold his candle to the wick *ad she't'hei shalheves oleh **mei'eileha***, "until the wick would begin to burn *on its own*" (*Shabbos* 21a). This is another allusion to the necessity for each and every Jew to ensure that his *avodas Hashem* is in a way of *"mei'eileha"* — deriving from the source of the unique spark of the Shechinah, the collective soul of the Jewish nation, that he alone can, and must, reveal. D] The Kozhnitzer Maggid (*Avodas Yisrael*, Chanukah) sees the word "Chanukah" as deriving from the verse **Chanoch l'naar al pi darko**, "Educate the child according to his way" — each child must be guided along the path of *avodas Hashem* to which his unique soul is attuned.

52. See *Kedushas Levi, Korach, "Vayikach Korach."*

53. *Hishtapchus HaNefesh*, Introduction.

54. See *Rashi* to *Bamidbar* 23:19, *Rashi* to *Mishlei* 27:10, *Rashi* to *Tehillim* 122:8, *Midrash Tehillim* 8:3, and *Midrash Tanchuma* 5:1.

with direct conversation.[55] While the three standardized prayers, instituted to maintain the "quantity" of *tefillah* in ensuring that Jews would be able to pray despite the inability to originate, can easily result in a loss of "quality," lacking individual spontaneity and prone to distraction and mindless recitation, personal prayer in one's own words demands true faith, personal investment, and emotional inspiration.

In the words of Rebbe Nachman:

> *Hisbodedus* is a most wonderful practice — it is greater than anything else. That is, to set aside at least an hour or more[56] to seclude oneself in a room or in the fields and to express oneself directly to his Creator... This prayer and conversation should be in the language that one is accustomed to speaking. In Hebrew, it is difficult to express oneself properly — the heart is not drawn after the words because we are not so accustomed to speaking this language. However, when we speak in the vernacular, which we are accustomed to speaking, it is easier for one to come to a broken heart, for the heart is more naturally drawn to the language we are used to speaking.[57]

Rebbe Nachman teaches that just as well-known roads are often stalked by thieves who wait in hiding for the unassuming passerby, the general road of standardized prayer is stalked by

---

55. See *Alei Shur*, Vol. 2, Chapter 4: "In order for human beings to build a society, Hashem gave us a tool — the power of speech. It follows that not only is our relationship with other humans built using the power of speech, but so is our relationship with the *Creator* as well."

56. In a personal conversation, Rav Yaakov Meir Shechter *shlita*, one of the leading lights of the Breslover community in Yerushalayim, told me that although this amount of time is certainly preferable, even five or ten minutes of personal prayer qualifies as *hisbodedus* as well — each person in accordance with what he or she is able.

57. *Likutei Moharan Tinyana* 25.

all kinds of damaging angels which seek to prevent our *tefillos* from rising to the proper place. Therefore, in the same way one who wishes to avoid the danger of being ambushed and robbed must take a side path which is not known to the masses, it is similarly beneficial to take the alternate route of *hisbodedus*, setting time for personal and unscripted prayer in addition to the three standard *tefillos*, in order to slip past the negative forces unnoticed.[58]

In addition to this teaching and Rebbe Nachman's use of the term *"derech yechidi,"*[59] a singular *path*, and *"tzayid b'fiv,"*[60] a *side* prayer, to describe *hisbodedus* elsewhere,[61] there is another element that makes it clear that the "path to the side" in our story is a reference to this special practice and the vital role it plays along the journey toward recovering the princess of youth in *avodas Hashem.*

Throughout the vast Breslov corpus, we find that *hisbodedus* is synonymous with *yishuv hadaas*, a settled mind — mental clarity and existential lucidity. Referring to the hour-long daily *hisbodedus* session he advocated, Rebbe Nachman writes, "One requires a very great merit to settle oneself (*'l'yasheiv atzmo'*) for one hour each day."[62] This, then, is the essence of *hisbodedus* — to attain true clarity into the meaning of our lives and untangle the absurdities of our daily experiences by delving deep within our psyche to encounter the point where faith kisses truth at the center of our being. As the Rebbe writes, the merit needed to experience this amazing inner peace is very great indeed. A sizeable number of people on this planet will live their entire lives without even

---

58. *Likutei Moharan Tinyana* 97.
59. *Avos* 3:5.
60. *Bereishis* 25:28.
61. See *Likutei Moharan* 9 and 52.
62. *Sichos HaRan* 47. See also 228.

once setting aside time to settle themselves and seek the inner meaning of their existence. In a different teaching, the tzaddik explains that this is the primary reason so many people are distant from Hashem:

> This that the world is distant from Hashem and do not draw themselves closer to Him is only because they do not have *yishuv hadaas* and do not settle themselves. Therefore, it is vital for one to attempt to settle himself well; what is the meaning of all his drives toward the pleasures of this world... in this way, he will certainly return to Hashem.[63]

In our tale, Rebbe Nachman writes that when the viceroy sees the path to the side, he is *"miyasheiv atzmo,"* he contemplates his next move and strives to attain clarity. In using this particular expression at this juncture, Rebbe Nachman is further hinting to us that this "side path" that will take him to the lost princess is the path of *hisbodedus*. Setting aside time each day to talk to Hashem in our own words and pour out our heart to Him as we would to our very best friend is the primary path that leads to the Lost Princess.

While there are a great many benefits to this wonderful practice about which Rebbe Nachman (and many other tzaddikim) spoke so highly, the greatest value of *hisbodedus* is that is represents the easiest way to build a deeply personal relationship with the Master of the world. It is this element of *personal commitment* and *spiritual relevance* stressed in both interpretations of the "path to the side" which plays such a vital role in locating and freeing the Lost Princess of youth. *"A voice calls out, 'Clear a path for Hashem in the desert!'"*[64]

---

63. *Likutei Moharan Tinyana* 10.
64. *Yeshayahu* 40:3.

LESSONS FOR LIFE

✳ *Avodas Hashem* contains various stages, including spiritual desolation, toil, and a success that presents a challenge of its own; the ability to hide from oneself and others behind the veneer of accomplishment.

✳ As we proceed from one level of spiritual development to another, we must leave the highest stage of level one and enter the lowest stage of level two. Although this lull may be seen as a *yeridah*, a spiritual descent, it is, in fact, the surest sign of progress.

✳ It is imperative for each Jewish person to search for his or her unique pathway in *avodas Hashem*. One way to accomplish this is by finding the areas of Torah that speak to our particular soul and allocate time to exploring them. Another is to discover the mitzvah, minhag, or *hanhagah* with which we feel most connected and focus our attention on that particular area of *avodas Hashem*.

✳ The primary manner in which one can merit to build an intimate relationship with the Master of the world is by engaging in *hisbodedus*, personal prayer in one's own words. Setting aside time each day to speak candidly with the Creator of all solidifies our *emunah* and enables us bring Hashem into every detail of our lives.

CHAPTER 6

The Pleasant Façade of Evil

אַחַר כָּךְ רָאָה מִבְצָר, וְכַמָּה חֲיָלוֹת הָיוּ עוֹמְדִים שָׁם סְבִיבוֹ,
וְהַמִּבְצָר הָיָה נָאֶה וּמְתֻקָּן וּמְסֻדָּר מְאֹד עִם הַחֲיָלוֹת. וְהָיָה
מִתְיָרֵא מִפְּנֵי הַחֲיָלוֹת, פֶּן לֹא יַנִּיחוּהוּ לִכְנֹס. וְהָיָה מְיַשֵּׁב
עַצְמוֹ: אֵלֵךְ וַאֲנַסֶּה. וְהִשְׁאִיר הַסּוּס וְהָלַךְ לְהַמִּבְצָר, וְהָיוּ
מַנִּיחִים אוֹתוֹ, וְלֹא עִכְּבוּהוּ כְּלָל, וְהָיָה הוֹלֵךְ מֵחֶדֶר לְחֶדֶר
בְּלִי עִכּוּב. וּבָא לְאַרְמוֹן אֶחָד וְרָאָה שֶׁיָּשַׁב שָׁם הַמֶּלֶךְ
בַּעֲטָרָה, וְכַמָּה חֲיָלוֹת שָׁם וְכַמָּה מְשׁוֹרְרִים בְּכֵלִים לְפָנָיו,
וְהָיָה שָׁם נָאֶה וְיָפֶה מְאֹד. וְהַמֶּלֶךְ וְשׁוּם אֶחָד מֵהֶם לֹא
שְׁאָלוּהוּ כְּלָל. וְרָאָה שָׁם מַעֲדַנִּים וּמַאֲכָלִים טוֹבִים, וְעָמַד
וְאָכַל, וְהָלַךְ וְשָׁכַב בְּזָוִית לִרְאוֹת מַה נַּעֲשֶׂה שָׁם.

After some time, he saw a castle. Many soldiers
stood around it. The castle was very beautiful and
neat, and the troops were very orderly. The viceroy
was afraid that the soldiers would not let him enter.
But he thought it over and said, "I will go ahead and
try." He left behind his horse and went to the castle.
The soldiers didn't stop him at all, and he went
from room to room. Finally, he came to the main
hall. He saw the king, with his crown, sitting there.

> Many soldiers were there as well as musicians with
> their instruments before them. It was all very beau-
> tiful and pleasant. Neither the king nor anyone else
> asked him any questions. He saw delicacies and fine
> foods there and he stood and ate. Then he went to
> lie down in a corner to see what would happen next.

❋ Well-Mannered Amalek

AFTER TRAVELING THE "path to the side" of *hisbodedus* and the
other elements of a personal relationship with Hashem, the viceroy arrives at a large and beautiful castle. As we shall see, this
castle represents the realm of "no-good," a place of pure physicality, utterly devoid of faith in a spiritual realm. Many sessions of
deep introspection enable the searching Jew to confront a deep
darkness, a darkness within which he suspects the princess has
disappeared.

An *oveid Hashem* views physicality as a vessel for Divine vitality that is brought into existence each moment by sparks of
spiritual energy for the purpose of enabling us to attain closeness
with Hashem. The secular viewpoint, however, sees this world not
as a means, but as an end unto itself. With no guiding principle
in life other than one's egotistical desire for hedonistic pleasure,
power, and personal gain, it is all too easy for the beast at the core
of the human identity to burst forth and wreak havoc on one's
own life, the lives of others, and society at large. The castle before
which our hero now stands is the headquarters of this perspective. It is a dark and dismal place and represents a perilous risk
for the weary soul.

Although one would expect such an evil place to appear physically as it does spiritually, Rebbe Nachman is teaching us that

this is not always the case. Instead of describing an old, haunted compound covered in vines and infested with bats flitting menacingly in the eerie yellow moonlight, the tzaddik tells of a castle that is "very beautiful, neat, and orderly." His message is clear: counterintuitive as it may seem, evil does not always appear the way we would naturally assume.

Indeed, many of those who have been tricked by the silent physical smokescreen into believing in the paramount importance of this fleeting world oftentimes appear to live lives that are "beautiful, neat, and orderly." David HaMelech observed, "Behold, such are the wicked; *they are always at ease* and they increase their riches."[1] Exceedingly moral and polite, their lives are tidy and orderly. No one would ever suspect what motive stirs beneath the surface; the disdain lurking behind the smile, the hate prowling behind words of love, and the anger roiling beneath the veneer of a kindly spirit.

In the words of the Vilna Gaon:

> The majority of heretics and those who sin in the realm of "between man and God" appear to be good-natured. This is one of the strategies of the *yetzer hara*, to spread a snare before those who may be led astray and drawn after them.[2]

This is something we are seeing more today than ever in the proliferation of otherwise normal, polite citizens perpetrating mass murder in school shootings and other terror attacks. Such a transformation doesn't occur in one day. This phenomenon indicates that the anger, meaninglessness, anxiety, depression, and confusion which suddenly burst through the surface in a single senseless act of madness had been hidden away for many long years under the guise of external pleasantness.

---

1. *Tehillim* 73:12.
2. *Even Sheleimah* 4:13.

Another, less extreme, example may be found in the so-called "social justice warrior" groups on college campuses around the country and other socially and politically far-left organizations around the world. While the values these groups promulgate — such as unity, freedom for the oppressed, respect for minorities, tolerance, kindness etc. — are all beautiful ideals, the bigoted, belligerent, antireligious, rude, and otherwise bizarre behavior of many of their affiliates paints a very different picture; another reminder that talk is cheap and appearances aren't everything.

Perhaps the most extreme example of this terrifying truth is Nazi Germany. As is well known, the Nazis prided themselves on being the most cultured nation in the world, excelling in the arts, sciences, and humanities. They were neat and orderly to the extreme, their etiquette unmatched. Yet this obsession with ethics and politeness did nothing to prevent them from perpetrating the greatest atrocity known to mankind. On the contrary, this appearance of decency was so rooted in falsehood that it accompanied the very acts of evil themselves. Survivors of the Holocaust relate that before shooting a barrage of bullets, the Nazis would address the battered Jews lying before the mass grave they had dug for themselves: *"Shtei ouf, bitte"* — "Stand up, *please."*

The tzaddikim teach that this is the mark of Amalek. Unlike Eisav and Yishmael who make no attempt to conceal their wicked intentions, Amalek appears cultured, moral, ethical, and neat — the very opposite of how one would assume evil to appear. And this is precisely why the *kelipah* (malevolent force) of Amalek is the most dangerous of all. Amalek's deceptive nature gives it the ability to lure a Jew into his faithless, soulless trap of existential confusion (Amalek [עמלק] shares the same numerical value as the word ספק, doubt) and loss of faith.[3]

---

3. See *Likutei Moharan Tinyana* 19 where Rebbe Nachman connects the concept of Amalek with philosophical speculation. Many in the revered academic

> In the realm of evil there is also "good" and "evil"; *desire* is
> the "good in the evil," and *anger* is the "evil in the evil." The
> good in the evil, desire, is worse than the evil in the evil, be-
> cause it is by way of the "good" of the *Sitra Achra* that man is
> seduced… desire requires an extra distancing, because it has
> a smooth tongue — it presents itself to a person as a beloved
> friend, to give him all the goodness of this world…[4]

This is the beautiful and orderly palace of evil that Rebbe
Nachman describes. A rollicking volley of murderous gunfire
framed by the poisonous sweetness of classic German etiquette.
Shtei ouf, bitte — Stand up, *please.*

In contradistinction to Amalek's shallow façade of politeness
and order, the true spiritual seeker may appear uncouth and rag-
ged. Eschewing the false grace, the *sheker hachein*, of the world,
he may appear gruff and uncultured in comparison. But under the
surface, the glory of his staunch commitment to a truly ethical,
moral, and kindly lifestyle far surpasses any level the nations of
the world claim to have attained.[5]

Can you imagine how the viceroy appears after his long travels
through deserts, fields, and forests? Surely, he is unwashed, dusty,
and disheveled. Perhaps the neat and orderly soldiers guarding
the palace of evil even mock his ghastly appearance. Yet those

---

circles of German philosophical society willingly threw themselves into the
Nazi effort, their civilized appearances only a mask for the faithless, murderous beasts within.

4. *Even Sheleimah* 2:3.

5. The discerning reader will realize that this dichotomy is another expression
of the six sons and the princess. In line with their outwardly impressive accomplishments, the six sons appear cultured and well-mannered in comparison to
the princess whose glory is inward (as the verse states, *Kol kevudah bas melech
penimah*, "the glory of the princess is hidden" [*Tehillim* 45:13]). When disconnected from the faith embodied by their sister, the six sons exemplify external
glory masking internal desolation.

who have the eyes to peer beyond the surface understand just how beautiful the viceroy truly is — not despite, but *because* of his appearance and the special journey it implies. People like the viceroy aren't fooled when they see the beautiful castle and the orderly troops. Looking beyond the impressive facade, they can perceive the confusion, sadness, and spiritual devastation that lurks underneath.

Sefer *Ish Chassidecha* is a remarkable biography of Rav Levi Yitzchak Bender, one of the leading *gedolei Breslov* of the previous generation who established Breslover Chassidus in Eretz Yisrael. In this fascinating and important work by R' Betzalel Freedman, a story is brought about the visit of a high-ranking government official to the Polish city of Grodzhinsk. The official's tour around the city included two special stops, one at the main shul and the other, *l'havdil*, at the Catholic church. At the reception in the shul, the rav was honored to say a few words. This rav, who was a tremendous *talmid chacham* and *tzaddik*, was very poor and not versed in proper practices of etiquette. In addition, his Polish was far from fluent. Much to the horror of his congregants, toward the end of the rav's barely comprehensible speech, he suddenly wiped his nose with the corner of his coat! The organizers of the event lowered their heads in shame, fearful that the rav's coarse mannerisms would give the official an unfavorable impression.

When the event was over, the official took leave of the committee and proceeded to his next stop, the Catholic church. There, he was treated to a glorious sight of wealth and splendor. The bishop's speech, filled with flattery and honor, was delivered with grace and clarity.

Upon completion of his tour, the bishop presented his impression of the city's religious institutions. "I was very impressed by the culture and elegance of the Catholic place of worship. There I saw beauty and splendor. But in the Jewish place of worship, I saw truth."

Rav Levi Yitzchak would recount this story often, always accentuating the last line: "There I saw beauty, but there I saw truth."

✸ Don't Be Afraid!

AS HE GROWS nearer to the castle where he suspects the princess is being held, doubts begin to arise in the viceroy's mind as to whether he will be successful. Although he has already come so far and overcome so much, it is here that the *yetzer hara* begins his attack in earnest. "There is no point in attempting to explore this castle," he says. "The soldiers won't even let you in! Better not to waste your time trying. It is entirely futile!"

How many of us have experienced this voice on previous journeys to the Lost Princess of our lives? How many times in the past have we turned around just when we might have reached our goal because a little voice in our head has convinced us that we are destined to fail?

Luckily, the viceroy isn't shaken by this inner attack. He remembers Rebbe Nachman's iconic proclamation that "The whole world is a very narrow bridge, and the main thing is not fear at all."[6] "If I make an attempt," he thinks to himself, "there is a *chance* that I will fail. However, if I surrender before even attempting, I am submitting to *certain failure*! Let me go and try!"

Here, too, Rebbe Nachman uses the words *"V'hayah meyasheiv atzmo,"* a reference to *hisbodedus*. Talking through our difficulties in the loving presence of the Master of the world enables us to attain true *yishuv hadaas*. We leave the session filled with *emunah*; settled, without anxiety, free of cumbersome calculations and overthinking, and open to any eventuality. The simplicity of the viceroy's approach to this apparent obstacle, "I will go and try!", is a direct result of his efforts to settle himself by means of *hisbodedus*. Utilizing this "side path" to again realign himself with his mission, he soon realizes that he has nothing to lose. Fearlessly, he marches

---

6. *Likutei Moharan Tinyana* 48.

ahead. "Though I walk in the valley of the shadow of death, I fear no evil, for You are with me."[7]

Curiously, Rebbe Nachman relates that "the soldiers didn't stop him at all" — the viceroy meets with zero resistance. Here, the tzaddik is teaching us an important lesson: while the obstacles arranged along the path to spiritual success may appear to be impassable, it is all one giant optical illusion.

In *Likutei Moharan*, we read:

> There was once a king who placed a great treasure in a certain place and enclosed the treasure within many illusory walls using various optical illusions. When people came to these walls, it seemed to them that the walls were real and thus difficult to breach. Some immediately turned back. Others broke through the first wall and reached the second one, only to find that they could not breach it. A few broke through further walls but could not breach the rest. Finally, the prince arrived. He said, "I know that all the walls are only an illusion, and that, in reality, there isn't any wall at all!" He proceeded confidently until he had passed through them all.
>
> One who is wise will understand the parable as referring to all the obstacles, lures, and enticements which represent conceptual walls surrounding the treasure house of *yiras Shamayim*. In reality, they are nothing. The main thing is a mighty and courageous heart, for then, one has no obstacles — especially the physical kind, such as on account of money, those his wife, children, father-in-law, or parents set in his way, or anything similar. They are all completely nullified when one's heart is mighty and courageous for God.[8]

Obstacles along the path to closeness with Hashem may seem menacing and impossible to overcome. But the tzaddik teaches

---

7. *Tehillim* 23:4.
8. *Likutei Moharan Tinyana* 46.

that if we are committed to victory at all costs, we can proceed confidently with the knowledge that the barriers will fall away on their own. Courage founded in the *emunah* fostered during *hisbodedus* is the key that unlocks these optical illusions, revealing that there was never any danger to begin with. When we meet with a challenge on our journey, it is so important to forge ahead and give it our best shot instead of automatically assuming failure and heading back home. Rebbe Nachman taught: "It is forbidden to overthink!" Go with simplicity, faith, and courage, and you will succeed beyond your wildest imagination.

✺ Leaving the Body Behind

IN CHAPTER FOUR, we learned that the viceroy's horse represents the physical body. Rebbe Nachman teaches that before the viceroy approaches the castle, he leaves his horse behind. Here, there are two layers of meaning.

Firstly, the viceroy's leaving his horse behind symbolizes the inner tzaddik's rejection of physical desire and his total focus on spirituality. In his Torah and *tefillah*, the recovering Jew can reach a state which the Piaseczner Rebbe refers to as "*Hislahavus*," a state of such closeness with the Master of the world that he is divested of his physicality and all of his earthly desires are completely nullified.[9] In the words of Rav Chaim of Volozhin:

> The love in one's soul toward Hashem can proliferate and burn to the point that he truly desires, in speaking a given word from the daily prayers, for his soul to leave his body entirely, rising to commune with Hashem.[10]

---

9. See *Hachsharas HaAvreichim*, Chapter 2.
10. *Nefesh HaChaim* 2:14.

Similarly, Rebbe Nachman writes:

> The essence and completion of *hisbodedus*, direct conversation between man and his Creator, is when he expresses himself before Hashem to the point that his soul is very close to leaving him... his soul is unhinged from the body, bound only by a thin thread, due to the awesome pain, yearning, and pining for Hashem.[11]

The *Meor V'Shemesh* offers this glorious portrayal:

> When a person is alive, he is forced to eat and drink etc. However, the path of truth demands that one center the entire focus of his life — in all of his endeavors and pursuits — around Hashem alone in order to perceive His pleasantness and for his soul to thirst for a taste of the sweetness, closeness, and pleasantness of Hashem's Godliness, constantly longing; "when will I come to see the illuminated face of the Living God?"[12] The soul of a person who has set this as his goal tastes — at the time of *tefillah* when he removes his thoughts from this-worldliness — a bit of this sweetness, the pleasantness of this elevated light. His soul desires with all of its might to bind itself to those lofty lights. At the time of this intense desire, he is disgusted with his life; if it would be possible to shed the body from upon his soul and bind himself to the other-worldly illumination he would gladly do so. His heart is pained over his soul's connection with the body which prevents him from rising to bind himself to these lights. In this moment, his body is purified as well as a result of the great yearning that burns within him like a mighty torch; the desire to align himself with the spiritual realm. Even though after the *tefillah* his yearning is no longer as strong as it had been, it is still beneficial, for his body is no

---

11. *Likutei Moharan Tinyana* 98.
12. Paraphrase of *Tehillim* 24:3.

longer as attracted to physicality, leaving him free to serve Hashem in all of his ways. If he is consistent with his yearning, strengthening his longing for *deveikus* with Hashem each and every day, his body will become purified until the physical matter becomes transformed into spiritual form.[13]

When a Jew is in close proximity with the princess of youthful passion, he is able to attain *hislahavus*, a deep yearning for Hashem before which all physical desires disintegrate. Coming into contact with his essential core, he discovers that the physical desires with which he was so preoccupied just a short time ago no longer interest him at all. Having risen above the body and its false seductions, escaping from the realm of *machshavos zaros*, foreign thoughts, and encountering his true desire for holy connection, the viceroy leaves his horse behind.

A second understanding refers to the *avodah* of attaining physical health so that one may serve Hashem in the best possible manner. Having laid a proper foundation for a healthy lifestyle throughout his journey across the deserts, fields, and forests of spiritual development, the viceroy sets this goal aside and proceeds with higher aspirations in mind. At this point, he devotes all of his energy to the spiritual battles that await him.

✷ Fleeting Honor, Eternal Disgrace

EARLIER, WE DISCUSSED two major approaches toward the great question mark of existence. One view sees our world as being the greatest revelation of Godliness and can pick up on the perpetual Divine speech that echoes within the silence of nature.[14] The

---

13. *Meor V'Shemesh, Pinchas*, "Oh yevuar vayidabeir Hashem."
14. See Tanya, *Shaar HaYichud V'HaEmunah*, Chapter 1. Perhaps it is possible to suggest that this perspective is hinted in Yechezkel's vision of the

other sees nature as being devoid of any transcendent spiritual quality — an end unto itself, a bizarre realm of meaningless-ness trapped in an endless cycle of futility. For the purpose of free choice, the latter option must necessarily remain viable; the impossibility for the human mind to grasp that which is beyond its categories necessitates that no proof will ever be adequate for the committed non-believer. Provided by God with the license to deny His own existence, many take advantage of this reality and live their lives without ever coming to recognize the pres-ence of the transcendent peering through the cracks of existence, *"meitzitz min hacharakim."*[15]

When a person lives life in this manner, denying Hashem's sovereignty over every aspect of the physical realm, he comes to crown himself king over his life, crediting his accomplishments solely to his own efforts. Blind to the intrinsic weaknesses built into the human condition, man without God becomes convinced that he is all-powerful and in total control — much like a child who is oblivious to the extent of his reliance on his parents. His very being bespeaks the verse, "My power and the strength of my hand have produced this wealth for me."[16] This worldview, which fails to recognize all of existence as being unified under the ab-solute rule of Hashem, is represented in our tale by the kingdom of evil, "the no-good one," which Rebbe Nachman refers to as

---

"*Chashmal*" amidst the fire (*Yechezkel* 1:4). The word *Chashmal* may be seen as a conjugation of the words *Chash* (silence) and *mal* (speech). (See Chagigah 13b) Therefore, "*Chashmal*" may be seen as implying "the speaking silence"; a lofty level of faith-based perception which sees nature's silence as being ever permeated with the Ten Utterances with which Hashem created, and contin-ually re-creates, the world.

15. *Shir HaShirim* 2:9. For an in-depth study of these contrasting approaches, see my book *Sunlight of Redemption: An Illuminated Path Toward Inner Free-dom*, on the first lesson in *Likutei Moharan* (Feldheim, 2018).

16. *Devarim* 8:27.

Malchus d'Sitra Achra.[17] A person who harbors this arrogant approach and sees himself as being in control of his life takes the form of the "king" whom the viceroy encounters in the castle. In the words of R' Hillel Zeitlin:

> The desire for sovereignty, the desire to reveal the "I," the experience of being — is, according to classical thinkers, the inheritance of every living thing. However, in the worldview of the Chassidim, this path leads us to a "shattering of the vessels." The very self-perception of being and individualism that, to Nietzsche and the modern philosophers, represented the *beauty* of nature and of each individual creation was, to the Chassidim, the great sin of the world and its downfall, descent, and shattering. The idea of *"Malchus,"* sovereignty, belongs only to the truly existent Being, *the Creator.* When the *creation,* too, strives to rule, its being is shattered into tiny particles, each of which proclaim, "I shall rule."[18]

In another place:

> *Malchus*-Kingship is not always unified with her Beloved. There is an aspect in which the external revelation of the spiritual worlds is perceived as an independent existence, a separate being detached from any Godly Source... This is the exile of the Shechinah which has taken place over the course of creation, exile after exile: through the sin of the *Eitz HaDaas,* through the sins of each person, and the sins

---

17. See *Likutei Moharan* 1.

18. *Mevo L'Chassidus Ul'Darkah shel Chabad,* pp.19–20. The castigation of individualism from the perspective of Chassidus presented here by R' Zeitlin refers only to an individualism that functions as an end unto itself, ignoring the true *Malchus* of Hashem. The individualism discussed in the previous chapter represents the polar opposite of this approach: the Jew's desire to utilize his individual talents, circumstances, and propensities for the purpose of the collective mission of the entire Jewish nation, to further reveal Hashem's *Malchus* in the world.

of Am Yisrael as a whole. She is in exile at all times — in every detail, in every action big or small, *in every distancing of nature, the external revelation of the spiritual worlds, from its hidden Source.*[19]

"There were many soldiers there as well as musicians with their instruments before them." A person who lives life in this castle of evil, wearing the crown of self-aggrandizement and convinced that he alone rules over his life, finds it necessary to invest much effort into surrounding himself with "soldiers" and "musicians"; all manners of illusion to make it seem as if he is, in fact, a legitimate king. He proudly displays his diplomas on the wall and speaks in grand terms about past accomplishments. His speech is full of pride, he loves nothing more than to share his delusions of grandeur with those around him. Indeed, the realm of evil seems to be "very beautiful and pleasant," perfectly manicured and under control. He enjoys beautiful music, a gourmet meal, and fine wines. All the pleasures of this world are rightfully his for the taking — after all, he has earned them with his hard work.

But the moment comes when the true source of this person's life-force is revealed and the skyscrapers he has constructed immediately fall away, nullified like a ray of light in the face of the sun.

In the words of Rebbe Nachman:

> One who desires honor is a fool. This may be explained with the following parable. A king once sent a viceroy to a faraway place (to serve as the minister). This viceroy took all the grandeur for himself to the point that the commoners, not knowing he was merely a servant of the true king, began to think that he was the king. When they needed something,

---

19. *Mevo L'Chassidus Ul'Darkah shel Chabad*, p.85.

they would fall before his feet and refer to him with all the terms of honor which are appropriate for a king. One day, the king visited this place. He commanded the viceroy to appear before him and asked him why certain citizens weren't performing adequate labor. The viceroy called for a policeman to question him about the details of the city. When the policeman arrived, he didn't recognize the king — only the viceroy. He fell at the viceroy's feet, granting him tremendous honor, and answered his questions. The viceroy was mortified, for there was no greater embarrassment than for him to be treated like a king in the presence of the true king.[20]

The day will come when, face to face with the King of kings, those who have assumed false positions of royalty will be shamed by the very objects of honor they so relished. They won't be able to get rid of the crown of their arrogance fast enough, they will franticly rush to hide their pathetic throne. In a flash, the mirage of their beautiful, orderly, and neat lives will be torn away to reveal the true ugliness of every despicable trait imaginable that lurks underneath.

Until this wondrous time, however, yet unchallenged by the true sovereignty of Hashem — which will remain hidden until Mashiach's arrival and the fulfillment of such prophecies as, "The world will be filled with knowledge of Hashem like water covers the sea,"[21] and "Your Teacher shall no longer be concealed"[22] — the king sits in his beautiful castle, surrounded by soldiers and musicians. Much like the etiquette and politeness of Amalek mentioned earlier, everything looks beautiful, orderly, and impressive. But one who has a sense for the truth understands that something

---

20. *Likutei Moharan* 194. See also 66:3.
21. *Chabbakuk* 2:14.
22. *Yeshayahu* 30:20.

is very, very wrong. Describing the illusory beauty of hedonistic luxury, Rebbe Nachman compares this-worldly pleasure to sun beams filtering through the window. Although they appear to be solid columns composed of concrete matter, when one tries to grasp them, he feels nothing at all.[23] While the headquarters of *Malchus d'Sitra Achra* appears to be filled with all sorts of wonderful delights, it is all a grand illusion. Full of life, this place is entirely devoid of soul.

It is in this palace of *Malchus D'Sitra Achra* that *Malchus D'Kedusha*, the faith-filled spirit of the lost princess, is trapped. Ironically, as we shall see, her very energy, when seized and corrupted, animates this realm of arrogance and allows for the place of no-good to flourish. Convinced of his autonomy and self-made success, the old and foolish leader of this kingdom[24] fails to realize that his life is an illusion made possible by the very holiness he so vehemently denies.

Total Accessibility

THE BRESLOVER *MASHPI'IM* point out a peculiar element which further supports the notion that this palace is a place of great impurity and disconnection from the Master of the world. In these lines, Rebbe Nachman twice points out that the viceroy seems free to explore the palace at will — the soldiers do not stop him at the palace gates, and he is able to go from room to room without anyone asking him any questions. This seems quite strange, as we would expect such a beautiful palace housing an important king and filled with high-ranking officials attending a

---

23. *Sichos HaRan* 6.
24. See *Koheles* 4:13.

ball to be strongly guarded! And yet there seems to be no guest list or any measure of supervision as to who attends this royal event; *"Neither the king nor anyone else asked him any questions."* What is going on here?

The Vilna Gaon writes:

> In order to attain holiness, one must exert a tremendous amount of toil and effort. But when it comes to the *Sitra Achra*, the opposite is true.[25]

This is the nature of impurity. Unholiness is always at hand and eternally accessible. When Rebbe Nachman writes that the viceroy is able to waltz right into this glamorous palace without anyone asking him a single question, he is further intimating the dark nature of this place. While it takes many years of toil and struggle to rise above the ego in communion with Hashem through faith, holiness, humility, and purity, the *yetzer hara* is as close as a thought in our mind and the phone in our pocket. Nobody asked the viceroy any questions — there is no special qualification for engaging with the *yetzer hara*. This element of Rebbe Nachman's description is another indicator that while it appears to be quite beautiful, friendly, and delightful, the air of frivolity masks a palpably sinister energy.

✳ Eating: A Lofty Form of *Avodas Hashem*

REBBE NACHMAN TEACHES that the viceroy "stood and ate" from the delicacies and fine foods in the palace. The Breslover *mash-pi'im* teach that his perfect awareness of the sparks of holiness filling the spiritual desolation around him enabled the viceroy to eat from the food without being affected. Seizing on the term

---

25. *Even Sheleimah* 4:21.

"stood and ate," they teach that in mentioning this seemingly insignificant detail — that the viceroy stood up before partaking of the food — Rebbe Nachman means to teach us something about this act.

We Jews have a special relationship with food. A well-known quip notes that all Jewish holidays have a similar storyline: "They tried to kill us, we survived, let's eat!"; food is an integral part of our tradition. However, all jokes aside, Judaism is the only religion in which eating is so often consecrated as a holy act. Sacrifices in the Beis HaMikdash, Shabbos and Yom Tov meals, matzah and marror at the Pesach Seder, and Kiddush over a cup of wine are only a few examples of physical acts of consumption that represent the loftiest form of spiritual engagement and *avodas Hashem*.

The Chassidic masters took this one step further and taught that *all* acts of eating[26] — even the most mundane — can become holy with the proper intentions.[27] If a Jewish person sits down to his lunch on a Tuesday afternoon and eats with the intention of giving his or her body strength for the purpose of serving Hashem through Torah, prayer, and acts of kindness, the food becomes part and parcel of this *avodah*[28] — all the more so if he remains cognizant that the food he eats contains a Divine spark, and that it is this spark of spirituality that gives him strength and is thus elevated.[29]

---

26. Of kosher, permissible food.

27. Rebbe Nachman goes so far as to say that *avodah* involved in the eating and drinking of a lofty soul is more illuminated than even the Torah and *tefillah* of a lesser soul. (*Likutei Moharan* 25:3)

28. *Likutei Amarim, Tanya*, Chapter 7. See also *Mishnah Berurah* 170:22.

29. Although full treatment of this concept is beyond the scope of this work, the *mekubalim* reveal that in the process of creation, the spiritual vessels (*Sefiros*) created to reveal Hashem's unified light in a realm of multiplicity were overwhelmed by the light with which they were filled and shattered. This stage/

In the words of Rebbe Nachum of Chernobyl:

> If at the time of his eating, a Jew is sure to look toward the interiority of the act, seeing to it that all of his actions are for the sake of Heaven in fulfillment of the verse "In all of your ways, know Him"[30] — attaining the mystery of knowledge which is to know that there is nothing separate from His service and that, on the contrary, through his eating in this manner he is growing closer to Hashem — this eating is considered as if it were a Korban-sacrifice to Hashem, the bringing close ("*mekareiv*") of holy elements from below to their Source above. This strengthens the connection of his inner portion of Godliness, and Hashem has great joy from this.[31]

---

event is referred to as "*Sheviras HaKeilim.*" This process is alluded to in the Torah's description of the "*Misas HaMelachim,*" the eight kings of Edom who ruled and died in succession (see *Bereishis* 36:31–39). The tzaddikim explain that the Torah uses the imagery of deceased **kings** to describe the shattering of the vessels as this shattering occurred because each vessel forgot its Source and desired to **rule** ("*ana emloch*") over the others. (*Shaarei Gan Eden* 2:2:2, *Avodas Yisrael, Bo,* "*Hachodesh.*") Although, when this shattering occurred, much of the spiritual light that could not be contained returned to its source, 288 sparks of holiness descended with the material of the vessels so that they could ultimately achieve rectification. These 288 sparks are the source for all latent holiness in physicality that may be elevated when utilized for a positive, spirituality-oriented purpose. (See *B'Pardes HaChassidus,* p. 28 and *Mevo L'Chassidus Ul'Darkah shel Chabad,* p. 50.)

These basic introductions allow us to understand why it is specifically after describing the arrogant nature of this faithless kingdom, "*Malchus d'Sitra Achra,*" that Rebbe Nachman makes a veiled reference to the sparks of holiness in food that may be elevated when that food is eaten in a way of holiness. The source for this process is the nature of the very place in which the viceroy stands, the arrogant and faithless realm of *Malchus D'Sitra Achra* — the perception of our physical world as concealing Hashem's presence. (See *Innerspace,* p. 81.)

30. *Mishlei* 3:6.

31. *Meor Einayim, Emor,* "*Eileh moadei Hashem.*"

The Kozhnitzer Maggid teaches:

> All kinds of food are elevated when they are eaten by a devoted Jew. When a Jew eats and serves Hashem with the strength derived from this meal, the foods rise from the levels of inanimate, plant life, or animal to the level of human.[32]

Paraphrasing another teaching from the *Meor Einayim*,[33] R' Hillel Zeitlin explains:

> Every single thing in this world contains a holy spark which emanates from the Word of Hashem to animate this thing. When a person eats food that is sweet to the palate, the holy spark remains within the person and becomes unified with his life-force, adding vitality and vibrancy. When a person believes with perfect faith that within this food exists spiritual sustenance, Hashem's Godliness, and focuses his heart on this perspective, binding himself to the Source of all, he brings this holy spark — which was previously trapped in the brokenness of exile — to Hashem. Hashem has great pleasure from this, for this is the foundation of our *avodah*, to lift all holy sparks which fell into the realms of impurity after the shattering, to a place of holiness.[34]

The positive implication of the viceroy's *standing* to eat contains another facet as well. One of the ultimate objectives of a Torah lifestyle is to illuminate the physical elements of life with the spiritual light of the soul. The Baal HaTanya famously stresses that Hashem created the world because He desired a *"dirah*

---

32. *Avodas Yisrael, Acharei Mos.*
33. *Parshas Mattos, "Vayedabeir Moshe."*
34. *Mevo l'Chassidus Ul'Darkah shel Chabad*, p. 57.

b'tachtonim," a dwelling place in the lower realms.[35] This is the foundation for the practical mitzvos involving physical materials and objects; they provide us an opportunity to sanctify the physical world in Divine service.

In the same vein, the human soul, which is a portion of God on High,[36] desires to permeate the depth of the body's physical drives in an attempt to sanctify and elevate all areas of the human experience.[37] The physical act that most unifies body and soul, physical mass and spiritual life-force, is eating. Eating food infuses a person with strength and vibrancy by strengthening the relationship between body and soul.[38] Therefore, in a very deep way, the act of physical consumption encapsulates the very purpose of creation — to draw the light of spirituality into the darkness of physical dross.[39]

Rebbe Nachman relates that the viceroy didn't merely partake in the food of this miserable place. The viceroy *stood to eat*; his eating was an act of ascension and elevation, carried by the loftiest intention. More specifically, the viceroy's holy, God-conscious eating served to remind him that a Jew's primary battle in this world is to illuminate the darkness of existence with the light of spirituality. Surrounded on all sides by the deepest impurity and arrogant frivolity, this was a message the viceroy needed to believe in now more than ever.

Now, all he could do was to wait for something to happen. And it wasn't long before something did.

---

35. *Likutei Amarim, Tanya,* Chapter 37.
36. *Likutei Amarim, Tanya,* Chapter 2.
37. *Likutei Moharan* 22:5.
38. See *Nefesh HaChaim* 2:6.
39. See *Likutei Halachos* Vol. 2, *Netillas Yadayim L'Seudah* 6:1, and *Likutei Moharan* 62.

LESSONS FOR LIFE

❋ The worst kind of evil is that which appears, on the surface, to be moral, ethical, polite, and socially correct. Don't be fooled! Everything is not always as it appears!

❋ While it may be possible for one who denies the active presence of Hashem in existence to attain glory and honor that accompany accomplishments he proudly claims to be his very own, the shame he will feel when the mask is removed and the true King is revealed will be commensurately overwhelming.

❋ Although it takes many long years of effort and toil to attain elevated levels of holiness and purity, the *yetzer hara* is readily accessible to everyone, at all times.

❋ Even a mundane meal can be considered a holy act if one eats with the proper intention. In a deep way, eating symbolizes the very essence of life, as it fills the desolate body with the great light of the soul.

CHAPTER 7

Discovery

וְרָאָה שֶׁהַמֶּלֶךְ צִוָּה לְהָבִיא הַמַּלְכָּה, וְהָלְכוּ לְהָבִיא אוֹתָהּ
וְהָיָה שָׁם רַעַשׁ גָּדוֹל וְשִׂמְחָה גְּדוֹלָה, וְהַמְשׁוֹרְרִים הָיוּ
מְזַמְּרִים וּמְשׁוֹרְרִים מְאֹד בַּאֲשֶׁר שֶׁהֵבִיאוּ אֶת הַמַּלְכָּה
וְהֶעֱמִידוּ לָהּ כִּסֵּא וְהוֹשִׁיבוּהָ אֶצְלוֹ, וְהִיא הָיְתָה הַבַּת
מֶלֶךְ הַנַּ"ל, וְהוּא [הָיְינוּ הַשֵּׁנִי לַמַּלְכוּת] רָאָהּ וְהִכִּירָהּ.
אַחַר כָּךְ הֵצִיצָה הַמַּלְכָּה וְרָאֲתָה אֶחָד שֶׁשׁוֹכֵב בַּזָּוִית,
וְהִכִּירָה אוֹתוֹ. וְעָמְדָה מִכִּסְאָהּ וְהָלְכָה לְשָׁם, וְנָגְעָה בּוֹ
וְשָׁאֲלָה אוֹתוֹ: הַאַתָּה מַכִּיר אוֹתִי? וְהֵשִׁיב לָהּ: הֵן, אֲנִי
מַכִּיר אוֹתָךְ, אַתְּ הִיא הַבַּת מֶלֶךְ שֶׁנֶּאֶבְדָה.

He saw that the king requested of them to bring the queen. They went to fetch her, and there was a great uproar and tremendous joy as they brought forth the queen. The orchestra played and the choir sang. They set up a throne for her and she sat next to the king. She was the lost princess! As soon as the viceroy saw her, he recognized her. The queen looked around, and, seeing someone lying in a corner, she recognized him. She stood up from her throne and went over and touched him. "Do you know me?" she asked. "Yes," he replied. "I know you. You are the lost princess."

✳ Not Extinguished, But Usurped

IN THE OPENING chapters, we explored the identity of the princess. We explained that the lost princess represents the flames of innocence, passion, and excitement that grow dim during the journey from childhood to maturity. At length, we attempted to paint a portrait of the way this loss manifests across the broad spectrum of the human experience, leaving a particularly gaping hole in our service of God and the natural Jewish drive toward matters of faith and holiness. However, although we have treated the loss of this fundamental element of our existence, we have not yet touched upon what happens to the lost princess in the place to which she is taken.

The natural assumption is that the lost princess is being held in a dark dungeon, the underbelly of an ominous and forbidding palace, where she spends her days weeping over her predicament and waiting longingly for a savior. Surely, the reader opines, the princess is broken, living a life of pain and suffering. But Rebbe Nachman teaches that this isn't the case at all.

In this segment of the story, the viceroy discovers that the lost princess is indeed being held in this palace, but another piece of information follows: The princess has become the *queen* of this miserable place! She now sits on a throne next to the faithless king and enjoys all imaginable luxury!

With this counterintuitive twist, the Rebbe is teaching us a profound lesson. When one loses the princess of youthful passion and excitement for a vibrant relationship with the Master of the world, she is not taken away in chains to be locked away in an abandoned compartment of our heart. Instead, upon her capture by the realm of "the no-good one," the princess becomes the *queen* of the evil kingdom, the source of life and vitality to the opposing powers in the great struggle over our identity.

Throughout the development of an adolescent, there is an almost direct correlation between the loss of passion toward matters of the spiritual and transcendent and the intensification of physical desires and a drive toward this-worldly success. The difficulty a teen encounters in waking up early for davening is usually matched by the alacrity and excitement he exhibits when waking up early to go on vacation or for the purpose of some other enjoyable activity. Torah study and *tefillah* lose their draw as the child begins discovering the marvels of modern technology and the meaningless entertainment that seem so much more exciting. Over the years, the focus of the child's life shifts. Those things that used to excite him now embarrass him. As his parents watch the wonder and natural excitement for life, family, and spirituality fade from his eyes, his friends witness its miraculous revival when he is involved with his newfound, increasingly self-centered, teenaged interests. Absent from her proper place, the princess of youth re-emerges in a very different guise.

When the fire of youth is concealed from its place, it is not extinguished. It is rather *usurped*, its treasures seized and channeled for expression in material-oriented pursuits. Although a mitzvah or Yom Tov which, only a few short years ago, would evoke a sense of wonder, pleasure, and comfort in the child now conjure cynicism, apathy, and perhaps even disdain in the mind of the teenager, it doesn't mean that he has lost the capacity to feel wonder, pleasure, or comfort. Rather, it is his perception of worthy catalysts for those feelings that has changed. As the years progress and the young adolescent becomes further acquainted with what appears to be a purely physical reality, the notion of a spiritual realm gradually loses its draw, overshadowed by ever more tangible pursuits.

Perhaps this is what Rebbe Nachman means to communicate in relating that the lost princess has become the queen of this miserable place: oftentimes, the Lost Princess is hidden right under our very nose. After the developmental process of self-discovery that takes place in the deserts, fields, and forests of *avodas Hashem*, we come to the realization that the true objective lies not in *finding* the Lost Princess but rather in *recognizing* her from behind the disguise and bringing her home.

In the words of two *kohanim gedolim*:

> The powerful, boundary-shattering desire which caused sin itself becomes a vibrant force which can accomplish great and lofty things in the ways of goodness and blessing.[1]

> Each person must know that in the specific area where his *yetzer hara* is particularly strong, he has the ability to be particularly clean and refined. And in the areas where he has sinned abundantly, he must know that he is a ready vessel for cleanliness and purity of heart.[2]

✸ Alive with the Sound of Music

AS WE HAVE learned, this evil kingdom of *Malchus d'Sitra Achra* has transformed the lost princess into a source of energy and vitality for the pursuit of this-worldly, physical gratification. It is no wonder, then, that her entrance triggers a joyous uproar and a proliferation of energy in the hall.

In addition to describing the excitement in the room, Rebbe Nachman relates that the orchestra struck up a lively tune, filling the room with music. The Breslover *mashpi'im* teach that the concept of music shares a deep connection with the current

---

1. *Oros HaTeshuvah* 12:1. See also *Tzidkas HaTzaddik* 76.
2. *Tzidkas HaTzaddik* 49. See *Mei HaShiloach* Vol. 1, *Korach,* "*U'maduah,*" for a possible source for this teaching in the words of Reb Tzadok's Rebbe, Rebbe Mordechai Yosef Leiner of Ishbitz. See also ibid., Vol. 2, *Toldos,* "*Vayichar Af,*" and Vol. 1, *Metzora,* "*Zos,*" where the Ishbitzer sees this idea hinted to in the rectification for the *Metzora's* improper speech. The *Metzora* is not charged with abstention from speech, but rather, his rectification involves further speech — channeled in a positive manner. For another example, see *V'nichtav B'sefer,* Vol. 1, third discourse. See also *Sparks from Berditchov,* pp. 350–352.

position of the lost princess and the queen she has been forced to become.

In many ways, the body-soul dichotomy finds a parallel in an orchestra and a choir. Much like the soul provides vitality for the body, serving as a premise to its postulation, a cause to its effect, and an answer to its question, music serves as the life-force for those whose spirits are moved to sing. The music is the canvas, the singer the paint. The chords created by the various instruments serve as the backdrop for the melody intoned by the vocalist; necessary for the experience but decidedly secondary. Thus, in the relationship between an orchestra and a choir, the former may be compared to a body, and the latter, the soul. Just like the entire existence of the body is predicated upon that of the soul which provides life and vitality both in a literal sense and as a theological premise, the orchestra is predicated upon the choir and their singing a melody that will provide context and coherency to the musical soundscape.

This parable enables us to understand why it is that the lost princess' entrance as the royal queen is accompanied by an orchestra and a choir.

We have seen that the special and inherently holy nature of the lost princess has been usurped by this faithless kingdom and now serves as the life-force and vitality for its wicked pursuits. Seized from the chambers of her father's spirituality, her precious gifts have been channeled to the realm of the "no-good one." In this sense, she has become the "soul" of this kingdom.[3] It is only by virtue of her presence that any of this is possible at all; it is the possibility of one's coming to recognize the world as being a *Malchus D'Kedusha* that necessitates the ability to view it as a

---

3. See *Sanhedrin* 97b, where Chazal count *Malchus* being transformed into *Minus*, heresy, as one of the signs of the final generation before the coming of Mashiach.

Malchus D'Sitra Achra as well. Therefore, on a very deep level, the relationship between the orchestra and the choir — which begin to play upon the queen's entrance — serve as an expression of the relationship between herself and the kingdom of evil. Just as the choir acts as the "soul," the life-force and vitality upon which the orchestra is predicated, the holy passion and excitement of the Lost Princess has become the "soul" of the evil realm, the excitement we come to feel toward the pursuit of physical gratification, material success, and increasingly self-centered aims.[4]

In addition to this approach, another, related, lesson may be learned from this segment as well. The tzaddikim teach that evil exists solely for the purpose of holiness. Closeness with Hashem and true levels of elevation are the raison d'être of distance from Him and spiritual rot. The sole purpose of evil is to level the playing field and create the necessity for us to *choose* the path of life from among a plethora of other paths whose tantalizing appearance conceals their deadly nature. Evil is there, as Rav Yaakov Meir Shechter *shlita* so emphatically stressed in a personal meeting, solely to be ignored, nothing else. In this vein, the tzaddikim teach that the *kelipos*, negative spiritual forces, draw all of their vitality from sparks of holiness that they surround and latch onto for their very sustenance, like the worst kind of parasite.[5] In associating the relationship of the queen and wicked assembly with that of the orchestra and the choir, Rebbe Nachman is hinting to this important truth: just as the orchestra is only there to create a musical setting for the choir, so is the wicked kingdom only for the sake of perfecting the existence of the queen. Just as, in serving as the premise for the music, the choir gives it life and the vitality born of a purposeful existence, so does the queen, in

---

4. For a deep Kabbalistic insight into the relationship between the *Sefirah* of *Malchus* and the concept of music, see *Likutei Moharan* 3.

5. See *Likutei Moharan* 17.

creating the necessity for a backdrop of evil, bring this miserable place to life.[6]

❋ Three Essential Recognitions

AFTER A LONG journey of self-improvement and deep introspection, the viceroy has finally discovered the lost princess. Although her powers have been usurped by the enemy, she appears to be otherwise unharmed. The burning question now is — how to bring her home?

Before examining this issue, Rebbe Nachman accentuates the flash of recognition that lights between the viceroy and the lost princess when she enters the room.[7] The recognition goes both ways; the princess recognizes the viceroy, and he expresses his recognition of her identity. As we shall see, each carries an important lesson. In addition, the Breslover *mashpi'im* teach that a third recognition is at play here as well; the queen's noticing the viceroy leads to her recognizing *herself*, her true identity as the lost princess.

While the viceroy looks vastly different as a result of his arduous journey, when the princess notices his figure lying in a corner, she recognizes him instantly. The viceroy's nobility, dignity, and inner grace shine brilliantly in contrast with the cheap imitation surrounding her. There is no question about it — this is her father's trusted official, a central figure in her childhood and development.[8]

---

6. See *Avodas Yisrael, Mikeitz, "Vayitzbor"*; and *Mevo L'Chassidus Ul'Darkah shel Chabad*, pp. 52–53.

7. See *Avodas Yisrael, Mikeitz, "V'henei hiksheh hatzaddik"* for a very deep idea that can explain the reason the viceroy's recognition of the princess precedes her taking notice of him.

8. As an aside, the Breslover *mashpi'im* size upon the fact that only the princess notices the viceroy, no one else. They explain that all of the other people

Simultaneous to her recognition of the viceroy comes the *self-recognition* of the princess. While the classical definition of the term "the lost princess" refers to her being concealed from the eyes of those who are searching for her, there is a deeper meaning as well. Although she is perfectly aware of her whereabouts, having been cast away by her father, she too sees herself as "the *lost* princess." Her entire experience may be summed up in the term "the lost princess"; the feeling that her status of "princess" has been lost, that she no longer has any connection to her father, the

---

attending this ball of base physical pleasure are far too occupied with themselves to survey their surroundings. The ability to see beyond oneself and notice one's surroundings is uniquely related to the energy of *Malchus*, a spiritual energy which is affected by the others in a major way.

In *Kochvei Ohr* (*Anshei Moharan* 5), a story is brought regarding one of Rebbe Nachman's students, Chaikel, a successful businessman. One day, Rebbe Nachman looked out of his window and saw Chaikel running through the marketplace in a big hurry. The Rebbe called through the window and asked him to come upstairs. "Tell me Chaikel," said the Rebbe. "Have you looked up at the sky today?" "No Rebbe," answered the bewildered student, "I haven't had the time." Rebbe Nachman motioned toward the window and they looked down upon the marketplace. "Believe me," said the tzaddik. "In fifty years from now, everything you see here will be gone. There will be another fair, with different horses, different wagons, and different people. You won't be here then, and neither will I. So why don't you have the time to look up at the sky?"

With these powerful words, Rebbe Nachman was gently reminding his student that instead of spending so much time engaging the six sons of financial accomplishment, he should reconnect with the inward spirit of *Malchus* and look beyond his personal pursuits to take in his surroundings.

In a powerful appeal, Rav Wolbe writes: "A person who is constantly entrenched in his own pursuits doesn't even see the other. Such a person must make an effort to leave his personal space and forsake his pursuits from time to time. We must not give the impression that this is unimportant, for how can a *ben Torah* remain an egoist? May Hashem save us from this! Even one who isn't an egoist in the true sense of the word, but someone who is constantly preoccupied with building his inner world, contemplating deep thoughts of Torah and *yir'ah* — it will be similarly difficult for such a person to be aware of things happening around him." (*Alei Shur*, Vol. 2, p. 204)

king. Now she is the queen of an evil place, a million miles away from the sweet holiness she once tasted in her father's embrace. In her mind, she is the *lost princess*, certain that this aspect of her identity has been wrested out of her hands, never to return. However, when the queen beholds the shining presence of the inner tzaddik, the place where every Jew maintains an unbreakable bond with the Master of the world, she is immediately realigned with the beauty she carries within herself and her undying propensity toward matters of holiness. All at once, her identity as the king's lost princess comes rushing back to her. Although, as we shall see, the princess still requires external validation on the part of the viceroy to confirm her position, she has already experienced an inner revolution, a paradigm shift. While perhaps still lost to the others, she is no longer lost to herself.

The third and most crucial recognition that takes place is viceroy's identification of the lost princess. The inner tzaddik's ability to look beyond the false identity of the queen to discern the holiness of the innocent princess is absolutely vital for the success of his mission. It is this wisdom that paves the way to his ultimate triumph.

As we have discussed at length, the appearance of a "queen" who grants energy and vitality to this evil constituency is created by the forced corruption of an inherently holy force. Instead of indicating moral rot and essential impurity, passion for sin and physical indulgence often represent mischanneled desire for true spiritual satiation. The teen's passionate interest in trivial pursuits of fleeting pleasure oftentimes signifies a deeply hidden hunger for spirituality — "It is not a hunger for bread and it is not a thirst of water, but to hear the word of God."[9] In the words of Rav Chaim Cohen, the "Chalban":

---

9. *Amos* 8:11.

It was about this that Rav Nechunia ben Hakanah wrote his prayer upon leaving the *beis midrash* and seeing the whole world running around the externalities of life, and, at times, impurity and corruption. He came and said, *Anu ratzim v'heim ratzim*, "We are running, and they are running"; the inner kernel of these pursuits is one, the power of movement is rooted in a single source. The great difference is only in the *direction* of the running; between moving in a way that will bring one to personal fulfillment or moving in a way that will bring one to an empty pit which pains the spark of Godliness within and increases the feeling of distance.[10]

The great running toward physical desires and lowly behaviors is rooted in intense holiness — the soul's desire to run toward the Master of the world. Rav Nechunia ben Hakanah realized that his running to the *beis midrash* and the world's pursuit of this-worldly pleasure were both sourced in the very same feeling of being compelled to run, the passionate longing for connection to Hashem. Underneath the layers of the dust and impurity that has usurped this holy longing, the princess remains, waiting for redemption.[11] The Kozhnitzer Maggid writes:

---

10. *Tallelei Chaim: Ana B'Koach*, p. 82.

11. The tzaddikim teach that this is the deeper meaning of our response to the wicked son's question on Seder night: *"hak'heh es shinav,"* we are charged to "knock out his teeth." While the word *"shinav"* literally means "his teeth," it can also be seen as referring to the letter *"shin"* which sits at the center of the word *"rasha,"* surrounded on both sides with letters that spell *"ra,"* evil. This letter *"shin"* stands for *"shoresh,"* the holy roots of the wicked son's soul. Its three branches represent Avraham, Yitzchak, and Yaakov, the *rasha's* ancestors who bequeathed to him a spiritual inheritance of *ahavas Hashem* (Avraham), *yiras Shamayim* (Yitzchak), and Jewish pride over the great beauty and truth of our tradition (Yaakov). The opening letters of the verse in *Tehillim* (3:8), *Shinei resha'im shibarta,* "You have broken the teeth of the wicked," spell the word *shoresh,* root, core. In response to the wicked son's heretical challenge on Seder night, we are *"mak'heh es shinav,"* we knock out his roots, reminding him of

There is no Jew who doesn't feel yearning, love, and inspiration toward Hashem at one time or another. The Godly
portion within the Jewish soul feels the sweetness and truth
of Hashem. However, because of one's sins and the residual
experience of lowly pleasures that remains in the heart, his
holy thoughts of closeness with and love toward Hashem are
terminated because the impure love he tasted in the past has
been awakened.[12]

The story is told that one year on the eve of Yom Kippur, Reb
Levi Yitzchok of Berditchov rose to the heavenly realms. When
his soul returned to his body, he reported what he had experienced to the chassidim. "In heaven, I saw many white angels
that were produced by our holy actions and proper decisions.
Some of these angels were healthy and others were sick. I saw
also black angels, created by our negative actions and decisions,
but these angels were *all* sick. Many of them had heart failure
or were completely brain-dead. They were all sluggish or crip-
pled." The Berditchover stopped for a moment, deep in thought,
and then continued. "The explanation of this vision is that a Jew
can perform a mitzvah with his entire heart and mind, with
the whole of his being. But a Jew can never do an *aveirah* with
his whole heart. Deep inside, beyond the negative garments of
misguided action, his heart and mind are somewhere else, where
they really want to be, with the *yetzer tov*. The forces created
by our errors are never whole. These mistakes are merely an
expression of a misguided desire for spiritual connection, an

---

the holy inheritance that permeates his holy essence and that the wickedness
("*Ra*") with which he behaves is simply an external expression which obscures,
but never destroys, this essential purity and holiness. (Indeed, when the numerical value of "*shinav*" [366] is subtracted from the word "*rasha*" [570], we
are left with the word "*tzaddik*" [204]. The key to spiritual transformation is
the realization of our true essence.)

12. *Avodas Yisrael, Bamidbar, "Vayedaber."*

awesomely holy desire that continues to shine at the core of the Jewish heart."[13]

While it may have been easy for these tzaddikim to see this deep and glorious truth, it is exceedingly difficult for us to attain this perspective which seems so far removed from our experience. Understandably, a parent or educator is far more likely to bemoan or reprimand a negative action than to seek the positive energy concealed within because the pain of the moment makes it near impossible to see the bigger picture. The same applies to our own "self-education." Instead of seeing our negative drives as a corruption of an inherently holy energy, we grow disgusted with ourselves and feel that we will never be able to change. Having never been taught about the true nature of our impure desires, the capture of our holy princess and the channeling of her energies to the palace of impurity casts us into a terrible state of confusion and despair.

Shaken by the appearance of the viceroy in this desolate place, the princess is able to remember her true essence and the glory of her past life. But she is yet unsure. She needs some external validation — the viceroy's confirmation of the feelings burning in her heart. She needs him to water the seed of her holy conviction with his confidence in her ability to cast off this guise and reassume her proper place as the daughter of the King of kings. Shyly, filled with uncertainty, the princess of passion approaches the viceroy of perfect holiness, the essence of each and every Jew, and touches him. The question she asks is bursting with a great mixture of feelings. Sadness over what has happened to her joins hands with the desperate hope that she may return home to her father once again. Finally, she musters up the courage to ask her all-important question. "Do you recognize me?" she asks him. *"Are you able to see me for who I really am?* Do you believe in your ability to redeem me from this place, to extract me from this

---

13. *The Depth of Our Connection,* p. 160.

misery and reinstate me as the pure, refined, and holy princess that am supposed to be?"

When this encounter occurs in our inner world along the journey of spiritual return, many make the terrible mistake of ignoring the queen. Faced with ugly passion that appears hopelessly evil, many of us find it impossible to recognize the princess behind the guise, turning our backs instead to her silent plea. Others recognize the queen's holy essence but have long ago given up on the notion that her energies can possibly be channeled correctly and used once more for holiness. Unable to come to this belief in our ability to change, we give up.

In our tale, Rebbe Nachman teaches that the princess is able to get the viceroy's attention by touching him. Countless other lost princes and princesses are often not so lucky. Drowning in the waters of self-doubt and shame, our students, children, and friends desperately yearn for a life jacket, a word of encouragement, of support, for us to let them know that they are yet precious in our eyes and in Hashem's eyes and that everything can be turned around. But they find it impossible to get our attention. In their own way, they jump up and down, waving their hands and shouting at the top of their lungs. The princess within their soul is tapping us on the shoulder, but we feel nothing at all, because we insist on looking at them in a shallow manner. If we would be able to recognize the diamonds hidden below the garbage heap, the holy yearning peeking out from behind the mask of lowliness and spiritual rot, we would immediately pick up on the silent cry, the unasked question of "Am I still holy? Am I still worth it?" When we are not able to hear this question screaming from every movement of the souls in our care, when we cannot respond correctly with strength and confidence, this can *chas v'shalom* cause them to be lost forever. It is truly a question of life and death.[14]

---

14. See Rav Kook, "A lack of faith in the essential goodness (*in oneself and*

If the viceroy cannot honestly tell the princess that despite the role she has unfortunately come to play in this terrible place, her beauty is still recognizable, his mission ends right here, as this will shatter her confidence and break her heart into a million pieces. However, by recognizing her holiness from under the ugly mask she wears, he is able to transform her external guise and reveal her true beauty, as Rebbe Nachman famously teaches:

> Know, that one must judge everybody favorably. Even if one is completely wicked, it is necessary to search and find within him some small bit of goodness wherein he is not wicked. By finding the *Nekudah Tovah* and judging him favorably, through this we literally elevate him to the side of merit, and we are able to help him return in *teshuvah*.[15]

In the words of the Ishbitzer:

> Each and every Jewish soul contains within it a *Nekudah Tovah* which Hashem granted it in particular. However, in this world, this point is clothed within a garment that appears to be the very reverse of its nature.[16]

Everything depends on how the viceroy answers the princess's question. Existence itself hangs in the balance. Fortunately, he recognizes the inner intention behind her words and responds encouragingly, *"Yes! I know you! You are the lost princess!"* With these words, the viceroy affirms the princess's essential identity

---

others, friends, children and students etc.) brings to the weakening of the heart. This weakening prevents a person from accessing the spiritual nature of elevated structures. One worries that one is perhaps not fit for elevated yearnings which the soul so desperately expresses. Because of this, one proceeds and falls, dwindling. This is the entire foundation of a person's downfall which brings to various spiritual ailments, hate, and *much spilling of blood*: a lack of faith in the essential light of goodness that shines within the soul."

15. *Likutei Moharan* 282.

16. *Mei HaShiloach*, Vol.1, *Korach*, *"U'maduah."*

and grants her the ability to teach him how he may extricate her from this terrible place.[17]

LESSONS FOR LIFE

❊ When energy and excitement toward matters of holiness gets lost, it reemerges under the disguise of the passion for physical pleasure and worldly pursuits. Although it may seem as if we lose our excitement for holiness due to a separate passion toward sin and negative traits, it is, in fact, the very same passion in disguise.

❊ It is crucial that we recognize the holy potential of our passion from behind the guise of impurity. It is only when we affirm the essential goodness of these energies and see their redeemability that we can then channel them toward positive use once more. The same applies for others. Recognizing the holy energy hidden within decidedly unholy pursuits can enable our children, students, friends, and the Jewish nation as a whole to rediscover their essential selves and begin the journey toward spiritual redemption.

---

17. The viceroy's recognition stands in contradistinction with the fool about whom the verse states, *"U'chesil lo yavin es zos"* (*Tehillim* 92:6), The fool does not understand this. In the deeper texts, the word *"Zos"* is a hint to the *Sefirah* of *Malchus* (the first time we find this word in the Torah it is in reference to Chava, the feminine energy of *Malchus* — *Bereishis* 2:23). Thus, the fool does not understand *"zos,"* he is unable to discern the holy energy of the princess from behind the mask of her impurity.

PART II

NIGHT

נַפְשִׁי לַה'
מִשֹּׁמְרִים לַבֹּקֶר
שֹׁמְרִים לַבֹּקֶר

My soul is to Hashem —
more than those who yearn for the morning,
I yearn for the redemption.

TEHILLIM 130:6

CHAPTER 8

Stirrings
of Redemption

וְשָׁאַל אוֹתָהּ: הָאֵיךְ בָּאת לְכָאן? וְהֵשִׁיבָה: בַּאֲשֶׁר שֶׁאֲבִי
הַמֶּלֶךְ נָזְרַק מִפִּיו דִּבּוּר הַנַּ"ל וְכָאן, הַמָּקוֹם הַזֶּה, הוּא לֹא
טוֹב. וְסִפֵּר לָהּ, שֶׁאָבִיהָ מִצְטַעֵר מְאֹד, וְשֶׁהוּא מְבַקְשָׁהּ
כַּמָּה שָׁנִים. וְשָׁאַל אוֹתָהּ: אֵיךְ אֲנִי יָכוֹל לְהוֹצִיא אוֹתָךְ?
וְאָמְרָה לוֹ שֶׁאִי אֶפְשָׁר לְךָ לְהוֹצִיא אוֹתִי כִּי אִם כְּשֶׁתִּהְיֶה
בּוֹחֵר לְךָ מָקוֹם, וְתִהְיֶה יוֹשֵׁב שָׁם שָׁנָה אַחַת.

He then asked her, "How did you get here?" "It
happened when my father, the king, threw those
words from his mouth ('May the no-good one
take you')," she answered. "This is the place of
no-good." The viceroy told her that her father
was in so much pain and had searched for her for
many years. "How can I get you out of here?" he
asked. She said, "It is impossible to get me out of
here unless you choose for yourself a place and
remain there for a full year."

❋ Setting the Record Straight

IN THE PREVIOUS chapter, we learned that the unmistakable holiness of the princess jolted the viceroy's recognition of her presence behind the false identity of the queen. It is this awareness of her exalted nature that now prompts a question saturated with bewilderment and incomprehension: *"How did you get here?"* The opening letters of the Hebrew words *Heich bas l'kan,* "How did you get here," spell הבל, vanity. Overcome by the shallowness of this faithless kingdom, the viceroy expresses his pained surprise to the princess. How could such a holy power have ended up in a place of such devastating vanity and spiritual bankruptcy?

The response of the princess takes us through the agony and inner turmoil she has experienced. She recalls the anger her father had displayed, the terrible words he uttered, and the dark cloud of hopelessness that had settled upon her world. She remembers how she had run away to her room, tears streaming down her face, giving up on ever having a relationship with her father again. She recounts the feeling of *yi'ush,* despair, that made her vulnerable to the advances of the realm of evil; the feeling that, bereft of her connection with her father, she no longer had anything to lose. This feeling allowed her holy energies to be seized and redirected for a foreign pursuit. She relates how, like an unanchored ship lost at sea, her perceived lack of unconditional connection to the dock of holiness caused her to be swept away and controlled by the furious waves of evil, "and the wicked are driven like the troubled sea, unable to rest."[1]

If the princess had formerly believed, albeit mistakenly, that her father had stopped caring for her on that fateful day, there was hardly a doubt in her mind that now, after what had become of her in the evil place, she was completely hopeless. Certainly,

---

1. *Yeshayahu* 57:20.

she assumed, the king had only grown angrier with her as the years passed. Surely, she was seen as an embarrassment to the family, her name rarely mentioned and even then, only in hushed tones. What her future in this place looked like she knew not, but of one thing she was unequivocally certain: there was no use in dreaming about going home. There was nothing there for her anymore.

Picking up on the emotions latent in her words and the sentiments they suggest, the viceroy sets the record straight and informs the princess that she is sorely mistaken. As we have discussed, the inner point of untainted holiness within the Jewish soul is the headquarters for an unconditional relationship with the King, an abiding truth with which the princess has lost touch. It is the place within the Jew which the King always cherishes, regardless of how far one has fallen into the pits of depravity and distance from Hashem. Even when all hope seems lost and darkness settles on the face of the deep emptiness one has sadly embraced, the inner tzaddik remains ever shining, an abiding testament to the inherently pure essence of the Jew, ever awakening the unconditional love that Hashem has for His beloved children.

It is only the viceroy, the inner tzaddik, who can shake the Princess of youth out of her devastating despair and convince her that the sun of her renewed closeness with the King is sure to rise once more.[2] Striking at her mistaken assumption regarding the king's feelings toward her, the viceroy tells the princess that, in addition to her father's positive intention behind his angry outburst, his love had, in fact, only grown with the distance between them. *"He had searched for her for many years"*, over time the king has forgiven the princess for her apathetic attitude, loving her now even more than he had ever loved her before.[3]

---

2. See *Mei HaShiloach*, Vol. 1, *Ki Sisa*, *"Vayomer panai."*

3. See *Tomer Devorah* 1:5.

Slowly but surely, the viceroy's words penetrate the thick walls of sadness with brilliant rays of hope. The dark clouds of despair begin to fade as the princess embraces a bright image so starkly different from the one she has lived with for so many years. Each word is a bombshell. She can hardly believe her ears!

"My absence has caused my father pain?"

"He has been looking for me for many years?"

"You have been sent here to free me?"

As she grapples with the implications of what the viceroy is telling her, she begins to formulate a plan for her escape. She is ready to return home!

✳ Finding Our Place

HAVING SUCCESSFULLY CONVINCED the lost princess of her father's unconditional love and his overwhelming desire to bring her home, the viceroy asks what must be done to remove her from this place. Because she has lived here for a very long time, the princess is intimately familiar with the inner workings of the palace. The viceroy trusts that she will come up with an effective plan for her rescue.

The lost princess is not a standard captive, so she cannot be freed by ordinary measures. A military raid on the beautiful and orderly palace of evil will not do the trick. Instead, the plan must consist of spiritual guidelines to be carried out by the Jewish person with the aid of the confidence emanating from the inner tzaddik. Only when these goals are reached will it be possible to extricate the princess of youth from her captivity and redirect her energies toward the pursuit of holiness.

The initial guidelines dictated by the princess relate to the two primary realms within which human life exists: the realm of *space* and the realm of *time*.

1. **Space:** *"Choose for yourself a place"*: One of the foundational prerequisites for building an intimate relationship with the Master of the world is stability. A person who lacks a secure identity has no place in the world. With no personal address, no element of certainty in one's life, it is very difficult for one to muster up the conviction necessary to forge an abiding bond with Hashem. Instead of clarity into his mission in life and the realization of how wonderful it is to be a Jew, muddled thoughts of anxiety, self-doubt, and bitterness cloud his vision. Lacking a strong sense of identity, such a person sees no purpose in trying yet again after so many disappointments, no use in expending effort in endeavors he is certain will fail. Unable to access an ever-present core belief for the purpose of gathering his strength and beginning anew, all he can do is mope, blame others, and mourn his hopeless situation in life. In this spiritually, emotionally, and intellectually toxic mind-space, it will be impossible to rekindle the spark of youthful excitement toward a life of *avodas Hashem.*

In the words of R' Moshe Rosenstein, Mashgiach of the storied Lomza yeshivah:

> Every person needs a home, a dwelling wherein they may rest. A place where they may find relief for their body and soul whenever they may need it, so that even when they find themselves wandering outside they will know that they have a space to which they may return. In that space they will find all that they need, prepared and arranged for the rectification of their body and soul. Woe to the person who wanders incessantly with no permanent space to which they may return, dragged throughout the marketplaces and roads without comfort, with no place to hide from the stormy winds and pouring rain.
>
> Every person — wherever they find themselves — knows where their dwelling of comfort is, so that they may return there to find relief and comfort. So too, each person as a thinking soul must know where their place of comfort is. A

comforting space that is always with them even when they
are forced to leave it, wandering away for the sake of this-
worldly needs. They must know — even then — that they
have a place of rest to which they may return. Woe to the
person who has no answer when asked where their place of
comfort is so that they may find relief. For this person is in-
cessantly wandering with no place of comfort wherein they
may find relief from the onslaught of the stormy winds we
find ourselves in. Wandering from place to place without any
permanent space within which they may hide and find relief.[4]

The first condition for the redemption of the princess is the
need for one to establish his or her *place in the world*. Only from
this place of stability, identity, and existential comfort will it be possible to undertake the measures necessary to free the Lost Princess.

What are some of the elements that constitute this "place" of
spiritual and emotional stability?

Rebbe Nachman teaches that before a person commits to
change, it is as if he is not in the world at all. Having only been
created for the purpose of striving to live life in perpetual embrace with the Master of the world, a person who does not as-
pire to this ideal is considered to be inexistent, an outlier to the
system of reality. It is only when one returns to the pursuit of
meaning, saying "I am ready to become," that he or she has a
place in a world that was created to assist us in growing close to
our Father in heaven.[5] Therefore, on the most basic level, finding
a place in the world means definitively resolving to grow and to
change our ways.

The Breslover *mashpi'im* reveal a deeper level. One of the ap-
pellations we use to refer to Hashem is *HaMakom*, "the Place of

---

4. *Ahavas Meisharim* 79. Translation by R' Joey Rosenfeld (https://residual-speech.wordpress.com).

5. See *Likutei Moharan* 6.

existence." Rebbe Nachman explains that this term refers to the ability of every Jew to find a place by Hashem. He writes that Hashem is called *"HaMakom"* because "every single person has a place by Him."[6] Thus, on a deeper level, the princess is telling the viceroy that if he is to attain the emotional stability necessary to free her, he must allow a single truth to penetrate to the core of his consciousness: no matter what may occur in his life, he always has a place by Hashem, the *Mekomo shel Olam.* Survival of the difficult trials the viceroy is sure to encounter on the long road ahead requires the staunch knowledge that Hashem loves him unconditionally, that He trusts in his ability to right all of the wrongs in his life and that, having been at his side every step of the journey, Hashem knows all that he has experienced and uses this knowledge to judge him in the most favorable manner.

Once we have discovered the Lost Princess of our lives and expressed our recognition of her untainted holiness, we must find our place in the world; an island of stability, focus, confidence, and commitment. The way to do this is by binding ourselves to the *"Mekomo shel Olam,"* our Father in heaven. It is in this aspect of Hashem's relationship with creation that we may find both the strength and confidence to begin once more and the perseverance to overcome any challenge that may arise.

Digging even deeper, we discover a third level. The specific words used by the princess to express this first task, *"Choose for yourself a place,"* hint to the primary element of how a Jew may go about establishing a sense of identity and stability in his or her life. While the simple translation of the Hebrew words *"Bocheir lecha makom"* reads, "Choose for yourself a place," they may also be read, *"The ability to choose shall be your place."* Here, the princess is teaching the viceroy that the foundational element of individual stability is the ever-present capacity to make choices in

---

6. *Likutei Moharan Tinyana* 1:14.

one's life. "*Bocheir*": the knowledge that, at every moment of life, you have the ability to choose properly, irrespective of how many times you have abused this privilege in the past, "*lecha makom*": shall provide you with the ability to create a new foundation upon which to build the life of your dreams.

In the words of Rav Kook:

> One of the foundations of teshuvah in the mind of a person, is the recognition of culpability for his actions *which is an extension of one's faith in his ability to choose freely.* This is the content of the *vidui* (confession) composition which is so bound with the mitzvah of teshuvah — a person admits there is nothing and nobody else to blame for his sins and their effects but himself alone.[7]

When one comes to a place in life where he feels that he no longer has the ability to choose freely and make his own decisions, he loses control and forfeits his "place" in the world. Such a person cannot enjoy a sense of stability and identity because he is beholden to the forces that overpower him. Instead of choosing a path for himself and standing strong to his principles, he is whatever those powers dictate to him that he is.

But, in truth, this is merely an illusion. As one of the basic definitions of our humanity, freedom of choice remains ever-present and undeniable. No matter how strongly one may feel that a negative cycle of behavior or destructive habit influences his decisions or that he has an uncontrollable propensity toward certain actions, his freedom of choice (as difficult as it may be to activate) remains forever intact. So abiding is this ability to choose freely that even those helpless victims throughout history who were indeed robbed of the ability to act as they pleased, found their humanity preserved in their ability to choose how

---

7. *Oros HaTeshuvah* 17:2.

to react emotionally to the injustice cast upon them. Come what may, the human spirit is free, and it is in this glorious freedom that man may find his "place" in the world, his identity, the *terra firma* upon which to build something of true meaning. In the words of Reb Nosson of Nemirov:

> I heard that somebody once asked him (Rebbe Nachman), "How is [one to understand] free choice?" The Rebbe answered him with simplicity: "Choice is in the hand of man. If he wants, he acts. If he does not want, he does not act." I recorded this, for it is very necessary. For there are many people who are extremely confused in this matter since they are accustomed to acting in certain ways from a very young age and it therefore appears to them as if they have lost the ability to choose and that they can no longer change their ways. But in truth, this is not so, for every person certainly always has free choice, regarding every aspect of life, and "If he wants, he acts." Understand these words very well.[8]

Dr. Viktor Frankl was a world-famous psychiatrist who survived the Holocaust and used his experiences to fortify the fundamental tenets of Logotherapy, his liberating theory that man's primary drive is neither pleasure nor power but rather his desire for meaning. In his magnum opus, Frankl writes:

> To be sure, a human being is a finite thing, and his freedom is restricted. It is not a freedom from conditions, but it *is* freedom to take a stand toward the conditions. As I once put it: "As a professor in two fields, neurology and psychiatry, I am fully aware of the extent to which man is subject to biological, psychological, and sociological conditions, But in

---

8. *Likutei Moharan Tinyana* 111. A precedent for this idea may be found in the works of the Rambam, *Mishneh Torah, Hilchos Teshuvah* 5:2; *Shemoneh Perakim* 8; and *Moreh Nevuchim* 3:51. See also *Alei Shur*, Vol. 2, Chapter 11; and *Likutei Halachos, Netillas Yadayim* 6:43.

addition to being a professor in two fields I am a survivor of four camps — concentration camps, that is — and as such I also bear witness to the unexpected extent to which man is capable of defying and braving even the worst conditions conceivable."[9]

"Bocheir lecha makom" says the princess. Take refuge in your ever-present ability to exercise the willpower necessary to alter the course of your existence. Utilize this inner strength to take a stand against the winds of the world which ceaselessly seek to uproot your sense of identity and establish your place. Stand up and stake your claim: "This is who I am, and this is what I stand for. My realization of the abiding ability to choose life along my journey and my belief in *HaMakom*, Hashem's love for me and His confidence in my ultimate success, combine to form a powerful mission statement that guides my daily life. I *can* make the right choices. I *can* begin again, as if for the very first time. I *can* rectify the many years spent surviving a meaningless existence and redeem the Lost Princess of youthful wonder. I *can* truly begin to live my life to the fullest!"

2. **Time:** *"And remain there for a full year"*: After establishing this place of identity, the viceroy is to remain there for a specific amount of time, a full year. Once one has used the deep-rooted confidence of the inner tzaddik to attain tranquility, health, confidence, and stability, he must now maintain his position for this specific unit of time. Only after maintaining this level of health for twelve months — each with its own energy, the roller coaster ride of the four seasons and all of the various holidays,[10] can a person proceed with the certainty that he has truly discovered an island of safety in an unstable world. In the next chapter, we will explore the final conditions necessary to free the Lost Princess.

---

9. *Man's Search for Meaning*, p. 132.
10. See *Shabbos* 151b: "For twelve months, his soul rises and falls."

LESSONS FOR LIFE

❋ In order for the spiritual healing process to begin, we must believe, wholeheartedly, that Hashem yearns for our return and is pained over our distance from Him.

❋ A basic prerequisite for freeing the Lost Princess is the discovery of one's "place" in the world, a strong sense of identity and stability founded upon a resolve to change and grow.

❋ There are two elements that enable one to begin finding his place in the world — the awareness of Hashem's unconditional love, and belief in one's ability to succeed and the ever-present ability to make the right choices in life.

❋ It takes a full year for lasting spiritual transformation to take place.

CHAPTER 9

Holy Desire

וְכָל הַשָּׁנָה תִּתְגַּעְגַּע אַחֲרַי לְהוֹצִיא אוֹתִי, וּבְכָל זְמַן
שֶׁיִּהְיֶה לְךָ פְּנַאי תִּהְיֶה רַק מִתְגַּעְגֵּעַ וּמְבַקֵּשׁ וּמְצַפֶּה
לְהוֹצִיא אוֹתִי, וְתִהְיֶה מִתְעַנֶּה. וּבַיּוֹם הָאַחֲרוֹן מֵהַשָּׁנָה
תִּהְיֶה מִתְעַנֶּה, וְלֹא תִישַׁן כָּל הַמֵּעֵת־לְעֵת.

"All that year you must long to free me. Whenever
you are unoccupied, you must only yearn, seek, and
look forward to freeing me. And you must also fast.
Then, on the last day of the year, you must fast and
go without sleep for the entire twenty-four-hour
period."

H ERE, THE PRINCESS DETAILS the most substantial
requirement for her redemption: After securing a place
for himself, the viceroy must spend the entire year
yearning and longing for the release of the princess. The Breslover
mashpi'im reveal the tremendous depth hidden beyond the surface of this strange condition.

✳ The Spirit of Gan Eden

TRADITIONALLY, YEARNING FOR success in *avodas Hashem* is seen as a means to an end, valuable only as an emotion which may or may not lead to holy acts of *emunah*, Torah study, mitzvah observance, and kindness. Those who hold this view dismiss yearning that doesn't directly lead to action as wasteful and useless, a stance which seems logical enough. What value is there in desire if it does not merit actualization?

However, Rebbe Nachman of Breslov reveals a deeper perspective. In a number of places, the tzaddik writes that aside from the value associated with its purely pragmatic function, holy desire and yearning is a precious *avodah* in and of itself.[1] Hashem derives tremendous pleasure from the Jew who struggles to lift his head above the surface of the filth in which he is drowning and, in a shining moment of clarity, lets out a deep sigh and verbalizes how strongly he desires to rid himself of these actions and return to a life of Torah and mitzvos. In the eyes of our Father in heaven, it was worth creating the whole world just for this one sigh to rise to the heavens. We haven't the slightest inkling of what kind of impact this small expression of holy desire has in all of the spiritual worlds.

Reb Nosson takes this idea one step further. In *Likutei Halachos*, Reb Nosson explains that, in a certain way, the creation of the world was only for the purpose of creating a barrier that would put distance between the Jewish soul and the Master of the world so as to create a situation in which yearning for His closeness would be possible.[2] This is an incredibly powerful idea. Holy desire is not simply "tolerated" by Hashem — it represents the

---

1. See, for example, *Sichos HaRan* 12, 259, *Likutei Moharan* 31 and 109, *Siach Sarfei Kodesh* 91.
2. *Likutei Halachos, Hilchos Areiv* 3:4.

very purpose of creation! In the same vein, the *Zohar HaKadosh* teaches that no good desire is ever dismissed by Hashem, even those that do not seem to materialize in concrete action.[3] Regardless of whether it merits actualization in actions of holiness, the very feeling of yearning and desire to change one's life and grow closer to Hashem is extremely valuable and precious in His eyes.

In the soaring description of Rav Kook:

> It is impossible to imagine or measure the great pleasure that a person must feel within himself — along with great satisfaction, from within the gentle ache which pains him at the time when the pure and holy spirit of *teshuvah* rests upon him; at the time when he proceeds and soars in thoughts that are burning with the fire of utter regret regarding all of his sins, misdeeds, and iniquities; at the time when his soul lovingly embraces the glory of holiness and completion — her Beloved, her Creator, her Maker, the Maker of all, Blessed be He; at the time when he desires with all of his heart and with all of his soul with the deepest depths of awesome yearning to go in a simple and straight way, to become a tzaddik and to perform righteousness, to be straight and to walk in the proper path. Even though it is undecided how he will remove his feet from the filth of his sins; even though it is yet completely unclear how he will manage to rectify the past; even though the practical pathways are not yet cleared before him and are cluttered with large stones, *the desire to be good — this is the spirit of Gan Eden* which is blown into the soul and fills it with an endless joy, until even the fiery Gehinnom of his deep pain is transformed into a stream of pleasantness.[4]

---

3. *Zohar, Terumah* 150b.
4. *Oros HaTeshuvah* 17:3.

In the words of Reb Nosson:

> One time, Rebbe Nachman spoke with me in grand terms regarding the greatness of yearning, pining, and longing for holy activities — even if one does not merit to actually perform them. Even so, the yearning and longing are, themselves, very great. He brought a proof to this from a halachah in *Shulchan Aruch*[5] which states that if one finds himself in an unclean place where he isn't able to recite Keri'as Shema, he should think the words in his heart. The halachic authorities[6] explain that when one thinks in his heart that he needs to recite Keri'as Shema now but cannot, and feels pained by this, he receives reward.
>
> This demonstrates that the yearning and longing one feels toward a mitzvah — even if he is unable to actually perform the mitzvah — are extremely precious and one receives reward for them.[7]

❋ The Most Elevated Capacity

THE TZADDIKIM TEACH that while the *yetzer hara* has the license to steal away the holiness and purity from a person's life, there is one element he is never allowed to touch: the Jew's desire for holiness.[8] While, on a simple level, the saying, *Ein davar ha-omeid bifnei haratzon*, "Nothing stands in the way of desire,"[9] is

---

5. *Orach Chaim* 62:4.

6. *Magen Avraham* 62:2.

7. *Sichos HaRan* 260. See also *Sichos HaRan* 27.

8. *Likutei Halachos, Hilchos Areiv* 3:5 and *Netillas Yadayim L'Seudah* 6:34. See also *Nefesh HaChaim* 1:18. This idea is hinted to in *Likutei Moharan Tinyana* 12.

9. Popular saying quoted in the name of the Chida. It is possible that it is based on *Zohar*, Vol. 2, 162b. See *Sefer Maamarim* 5703, p.12, where the

the Hebrew equivalent of "When there's a will there's a way," Reb Nosson teaches that there is a deeper meaning: *nothing can ever prevent a Jew from desiring holiness.* "Even when there is in fact no way, there is always potential for will."[10] Even in the darkest, filthiest pit of spiritual rot and distance from Hashem, the Jew has the ability to desire closeness with Him once more. Trapped by the bonds of addiction, possessed by a wicked force intent on destroying every last vestige of his connection to spirituality, the Jewish person yet maintains his capacity to yearn for the holiness he is so distant from.

In the deeper *sefarim*, we find that a person's faculty of desire is considered to be the loftiest part of his being. As we have learned in the second chapter, human beings express feelings using the six emotional *Sefiros* that manifest in the heart, and think using the three intellectual *Sefiros* that are revealed in the mind. But the headquarters for *ratzon*, holy desire, is sourced in the uppermost *Sefirah* of *Kesser*,[11] the very peak of our personality which transcends the haphazard structures of negative actions, words, and thoughts to portray a shining blueprint for spiritual, emotional, intellectual, and physical health. Regardless of how miserably wrong things may have gone in the life of a Jew, the *Kesser-Ratzon* of his soul is indestructible and contains the core ingredients necessary to realign himself with his mission.

So abiding is a Jew's capacity to yearn for holiness, that even when one level may be absent, a deeper level always remains. Therefore, while a Jew may be in such a poor state that he can't honestly express a desire for closeness with Hashem, he can always

---

Lubavitcher Rebbe writes that while it is quoted in many places, he is unsure of its exact source.

10. *Likutei Halachos, Hilchos Areiv* 3:5.

11. See *Tehillim* 5:13: *Katzinah* **ratzon** *ta'atrenu*, "You **crown** him (*Kesser*) with **desire** (*Ratzon*) like a shield."

penetrate deeper within his core and express a *desire to desire*. If that desire is also lacking, he can *desire to desire to desire*, and so on, ad infinitum. No matter how far away a Jew may wander from the gates of righteousness, *Ein davar ha-omeid bifnei haratzon* — nothing can prevent him from yearning to return home.

The princess tells the viceroy: *"Whenever you are unoccupied,"* whenever you manage to lift your head above the ocean of vanity that seeks to drown your vitality and snuff out your relationship with the Master of the world, *"you must only yearn, seek, and look forward to freeing me,"* you can always access your innermost desire, the blueprint of who you truly are, what you truly want, and how you can again pick up the broken pieces of your life to form the image that dances, elusively, before your tear-filled eyes. Even when all other lanes seem closed, yearning for holiness (or even yearning to yearn, and so on) remains an ever-accessible method of serving Hashem in each situation and can succeed in refreshing our deepest goals and strengthening our conviction toward reaching them.[12]

Reb Nosson writes:

> The main thing is: There is no despair in the world at all! Even if a person is the way he is [lowly and blemished], all the while that he still remembers Hashem and has a desire to return to Him — even though he has pined for Hashem for so long and has still not merited to return, and on the contrary, he has only intensified his blemishes and added

---

12. Perhaps it possible to suggest that the awesome strength afforded to a Jew by contacting the place of *Kesser-Ratzon*, the essential beauty of the Jewish personality, is reflected in the juxtaposition of two blessings in *Birchos Ha-Shachar*: *Oter Yisrael b'sifarah*, "Who crowns the Jewish nation with splendor," and *Hanosein laya'eif koach*, "Who grants strength to the weary." The more we tap into the "crowning jewel" of our holy desire, the source of our splendor, the more we will find the strength to carry on searching for the Princess of spiritual vitality.

sin onto iniquity *chas v'shalom* — even so, he should encourage himself to yearn and long for Hashem constantly,
at all times. Through doing this, he will undoubtedly merit
to eventually break free from his folly and will certainly
do *teshuvah*. This path is good and proper advice for every
person in the world, no matter how big or small; whether
a big tzaddik, a truly good Jew who must rise from level to
level, Jews who are spiritually very small, or even those who
are placed in the depths of [a metaphorical] purgatory, filthy
from their wicked actions — even so, through the aspect of
desire, all of them can merit to rise from the lowest possible
extent to the pinnacle of all heights. It is impossible to explain the tremendous benefit of holy yearning and longing —
in accordance with what we have brought from the words of
our holy Rebbe of blessed memory and in accordance with
what we heard from his own mouth — because in writing,
it is impossible to describe even a little bit, even one thou-
sandth. He revealed many lofty lessons about this in the past
which have already been printed. But even more than this
are the lessons we heard from his holy mouth and perceived
from his holy movements and awesome hints when he spoke
about this, time and time again. And it is impossible for one
who wants to heed this advice to corrupt or negate it in any
manner. For, although it is possible for the *yetzer hara* to
overpower a person and prevent him from fulfilling all other
advice, it is impossible to negate positive will, because — regardless of the state one is in — even so [he can always say],
"I want to return to Hashem with a powerful desire." For
who is the fool or the deranged one who does not desire the
true and everlasting good? Certainly, it may be difficult for
one to overcome what one must overcome. But surely, every
Jew who believes in Hashem has an extremely strong desire
to return to Him. Unfortunately though, one does not know
the value of desire or appreciate the fact that desire is — on
its own — a very valuable thing. As a result, when he sees
how many times he has longed to come close to Hashem and

yet still not merited to succeed, or even blemished further, he gives up on himself and forgets to continue yearning, until the point that his holy desire becomes concealed. In truth, this blemish is worse than all others, because no matter what, one mustn't slack or forsake his holy desire. Rather, on the contrary — one should accustom himself to continuously yearn and long with increasing intensity. This desire is itself very good, and through it, one will merit complete *teshuvah* and all levels of holiness.[13]

In another place:

For the primary encouragement derives from desire, that regardless of what a person goes through, no matter what, *no matter what*, he must nonetheless strengthen himself with extremely powerful desire toward Hashem, and nonetheless long and yearn to return to Hashem from whatever place he might be. For in the end, what will remain of him? Particularly after the true tzaddikim have revealed to us that positive desire is itself exceedingly precious and valuable...[14]

However, despite (or perhaps specifically because of!) the ease and accessibility of expressing our *gaaguim*, our powerful desire to grow close to Hashem, we rarely engage in doing so. Somehow, this all-important aspect of *avodas Hashem* suffers continual neglect, both personally and communally. The primary reason for this abstention is our lack of faith in the inherent value of yearning for holiness. Deep within our hearts, an inner voice mocks this *avodah* as a waste of time and energy. "Yearning for holiness is worthless," it says. "Something as simple as merely expressing desire is far too easy to have a true effect on your spiritual position."[15]

---

13. *Likutei Halachos, Hilchos Areiv* 3:5.
14. *Likutei Halachos, Hilchos Netillas Yadayim L'Seudah* 6:51.
15. See *Chayei Moharan* 492: "There are times when a person shirks from

Friends, let us make no mistake about it — this is the voice of the *yetzer hara*. His great awareness of just how precious a Jew's holy desire is to the Master of the world compels him to do everything in his power to ensure it is never expressed.

But the princess knows the truth. She knows that not only isn't holy desire a waste of time and energy, it represents the very purpose of creation, the quintessence of being. *"All that year, you must long to free me"* — recovering the princess in our lives will require us to engage in this unique and all-important *avodah* of holy desire.

✳ Emulative Extraction

WE HAVE LEARNED that holy yearning is a key element to a healthy *avodas Hashem*. But the question begs: Why it is so imperative for the success of the viceroy's mission? What is the significance of this particular *avodah* to freeing the lost princess? Revisiting the core identity of the princess and the unique spirit she represents sheds brilliant light on this seemingly obscure connection.

In Chapter Two, we learned that the princess in our story represents an animating spirit of purpose and meaning that brings our otherwise inert endeavors to life. Counterintuitively, although she is the primary, essential point of being, the princess is — in contradistinction to the six sons of outward accomplishment — an unquantifiable entity, a nearly imperceivable force that imbues those accomplishments with ultimate quality. As a result, she is

---

carrying out a certain holy task because of its difficulty and the obstacles in his way. He simply does not exert himself enough to break them. At other times, it is the other way around. He holds back from the task because it is too easy — he looks at it as something so simple that he cannot believe that the very life of his soul could depend on something so insignificant."

commonly ignored and neglected in exchange for those pursuits that seem to be more tangibly worthwhile.

If there is one human capacity that most closely embodies this nature of the princess, it is the capacity of holy desire. Compared to the quantifiable value of the six sons, desire seems entirely useless. The voice of the *yetzer hara* convinces us to leave cultivating our desire for holiness aside, that our time is far better spent on the more distinguished areas of *avodas Hashem* such as amassing Torah knowledge — which can be measured and thus respected. We are inclined to maximize on life's opportunities at the expense of the wonder, awe, and amazement that is founded upon a deep desire for life itself, the essence of living. In so doing, we run the risk of reaching the end of our days only to find that we have never truly lived at all. While it may be difficult to assess with our human measurements, desire represents the core ingredient of life, the spirit that lends meaning and vitality to all of our endeavors.[16] Seen in this manner, we can understand that *holy desire is one of the primary elements of the lost princess.*

We have learned that because freeing the lost princess from the faithless kingdom is an essentially spiritual task, the strategy used must share this nature. The spiritual premise of the present strategy is that unlike a classic rescue operation which might include a raid and the immediate release of the captive, the princess must be freed in a very different manner — *extraction via emulation.* Because the princess is only useful to the faithless kingdom inasmuch as her powers are vulnerable to misuse and usurpation, when the viceroy utilizes the powers unique to her spirit for the ultimate pursuit of good once more, the princess is naturally extracted from her captivity, bit by bit, until she can finally achieve total freedom.[17] Following the princess's conditions

---

16. See *Likutei Moharan* 31, and *Pri Tzaddik, Va'eschanan* #13.

17. This interpretive model is founded upon *Likutei Halachos, Rosh Chodesh*

are not a *cause* that leads to the ultimate *effect* of freeing the princess. Rather, using the directives of the princess to cultivate her spirit of meaning, wonder, and passion in his own experience, the viceroy is *actively engaged in freeing her.* Like fine sand quietly slipping from one half of an hourglass to the other, the passion of the lost princess is transferred through the walls of the orderly palace of evil and back to the realm of holiness.

Having explored the relationship between holy desire and the spirit of the lost princess, we can now understand why the viceroy's passionate yearning to free her is so critical for her actual redemption. As a core element of the princess's identity, holy yearning serves as the very foundation for the delicate process of her complete return to the pursuit of holiness. The stronger the viceroy's yearning for the princess grows over the year he spends in the place he has chosen, the more of her holy fire he extricates from the realm of evil and returns to its intended purpose. When the year reaches its end, her essence will have been completely transferred, leaving only the purely technical task of bringing her back to her father's embrace.

✳ Separation from Physicality

THE PRINCESS'S FOURTH condition is that the viceroy must fast throughout the year. Although, as we have learned, eating can be an incredibly elevated act, in its simplest form, eating is among the most physical activities a human being can engage in. There is hardly anything so egotistical as taking physical items and consuming them so that they become a part of our own physicality. The act of eating essentially reinforces our physical identity by increasing our corporeal mass, further strengthening the material

---

5, where Reb Nosson discusses the process of transforming *Malchus* into her own *Partzuf* by turning Torah into *tefillah.*

bonds that trap the soul in this world. As a result, excessive fixation on food and eating can shift one's focus away from spirituality to the point that one loses touch with his soul's mission in the world, as the verse states, "Lest you eat and be satiated... and your heart grows haughty and you forget Hashem your God."[18]

In our holy tradition, eating is not seen as something inherently impure — in fact, the Torah's guidelines for eating turn it into an act of sanctity. However, there is a recognized spiritual benefit in abstaining from this physical act at the appropriate times. Fasting on Yom Kippur, for example, enables us to better focus on the spiritual significance of the day. Weakening the body by temporarily denying it sustenance allows us to tap into the true desires of the soul.

Another element to the viceroy's task of emulative extraction is intermittent fasting. Refraining from excessive involvement with matters of physicality will strengthen his desire for spiritual matters and closeness with Hashem.

It is important to note that the princess doesn't prescribe specific days or times for fasting. This is because fasting is generally frowned upon[19] for a few reasons, one of which is the fear that, in our weakened state, we will be unable to properly serve Hashem through Torah study and prayer.[20] Rather, the princess advises the viceroy to fast (an umbrella term accommodating all forms of separation from hedonistic indulgence) at his own discretion, to make boundaries for himself and abstain from physicality in a healthy, balanced way. Chazal teach: "Before you pray for Torah to fill your stomach, pray that food and drink do not fill your stomach."[21] Separation from a consuming involvement with the

---

18. *Devarim* 8:12, 14.
19. See *Nedarim* 10a, *Taanis* 11a.
20. *Taanis* 11b.
21. *Tanna D'vei Eliyahu Rabbah*, Chapter 26. See also *Parparaos L'Chochmah*

body and its desires will enable the viceroy to focus on his yearning for the princess and his overwhelming desire to free her, at long last.

⊛ The Final Day

THE TZADDIKIM TEACH that there is nothing the *yetzer hara* despises more than when a Jew manages to complete a matter of holiness. Beginning a new project in *avodas Hashem*, such as learning a new *masechta* of Gemara only meets with faint protest on the *yetzer hara*'s part. It is only when it comes to *finishing* a project that that he invests tremendous effort in the attempt to stop us. (This is one of the reasons that a *siyum* is such a joyous occasion.)[22] Due to the *yetzer hara*'s aim to prevent a Jew from attaining his spiritual goals, the final few feet to the finish line are always met with the most fearsome obstacles. Just before his defeat, the evil inclination expends every last bit of effort in attempt to prevent the Jew from completing his goal.[23]

To protect against this fearsome attack, the princess warns the viceroy that on the final day of the year of longing, he must put in extra effort to battle the evil forces — which are sure to unleash all of their energy to prevent him from freeing her. On this final day, he must abstain from food and drink to maintain perfect focus on his goal. In addition, he must remain awake, physically and spiritually — laser-focused on the awesome task at

---

to *Likutei Moharan* 17:3.

22. Rav Yaakov Meir Shechter *shlita* quotes *kadmonim* as saying that the name of the Satan, "**Samae-l**," is a mnemonic for the phrase *Siyum masechtos ein la'asos*, "One must not complete tractates of the Talmud." (Heard from R' Judah Klein.)

23. See *Likutei Moharan Tinyana* 48.

hand. Because eating and sleeping can grant entry to the creeping seductions of the desperate *yetzer hara*, enabling him to ruin the entire plan, the viceroy must steer clear of these activities on the final day.

Sadly, as we shall see, these measures ultimately prove insufficient.

LESSONS FOR LIFE

❂ Even if it does not merit actualization in acts of holiness, yearning for elevation and a relationship with the Master of the world is inherently valuable and precious in the eyes of Hashem.

❂ As the loftiest and most essential element of his being, nothing can prevent a Jew from desiring closeness with Hashem. Even when the desire is lacking, one can *desire to desire*, ad infinitum.

❂ When one devotes himself to fulfilling the directives of the Lost Princess — finding stability, yearning for her, removing himself from physicality etc. — he is emulating her nature, and, in the process, actively extracting her from the faithless kingdom.

❂ The *yetzer hara* detests the completion of a holy endeavor. Just when a project is about to come to fruition, he launches a mighty attack in an effort to prevent it from happening.

CHAPTER 10

So Close,
Yet So Very Far

וְהָלַךְ וְעָשָׂה כֵּן. וּבְסוֹף הַשָּׁנָה בַּיּוֹם הָאַחֲרוֹן הָיָה מִתְעַנֶּה,
וְלֹא הָיָה יָשֵׁן. וְעָמַד וְהָלַךְ לְשָׁם, וְהָיָה רוֹאֶה אִילָן, וְעָלָיו
גְּדֵלִים תַּפּוּחִים נָאִים מְאֹד, וְהָיָה מִתְאַוֶּה לְעֵינָיו מְאֹד,
וְעָמַד וְאָכַל מִשָּׁם. וְתֵכֶף שֶׁאָכַל הַתַּפּוּחַ, נָפַל וַחֲטָפוֹ
שֵׁנָה. וְהָיָה יָשֵׁן זְמַן מְרֻבֶּה מְאֹד.

The viceroy went and did what the princess had told
him. On the final day, at the year's close, he fasted
and did not sleep. He rose and began heading toward the palace. He saw a tree with very beautiful
apples. It was very desirable to his eyes, and he ate
an apple. Immediately after eating the apple, he fell
into a deep sleep, and he slept for a very long time.

EBBE NACHMAN RELATES THAT the viceroy fulfilled all of the conditions given to him by the princess.
Utilizing his freedom of choice to re-establish a sense of
identity, stability, and staunch commitment to meaningful values,
the viceroy spent the year expressing his powerful yearning to

free the lost princess and again enjoy her precious gifts of passionate living founded upon *emunah, tefillah, hisbodedus,* humility, simplicity, God-consciousness, joy, *yiras Shamayim,* and deeply meaningful relationships. All of this was done with a sense of fulfillment and confidence. Finally, he had a concrete plan of action! The vision of his homecoming often filled his mind, images of the masses celebrating the success of his mission. Victory was so near; he could practically taste it!

We might imagine that the year was filled with a spirit of intense purpose and tremendous resolve. As the weeks and months passed by, his excitement grew by leaps and bounds, ultimately reaching a fever pitch as the long year finally drew to a close. This was it! All of his efforts were about to pay off! He was about to reach his awesome objective!

✷ The Viceroy's Error

AT LONG LAST, the great day arrived. Taking care to heed the final directives of the princess, the viceroy fasted and made sure not to fall asleep. Finally, the darkness melted away and the glowing orb of the sun breached the horizon, filling the deep blue sky with a brilliant flood of illuminated colors. His heart was exploding with pride. He had practically done it! Just a few more hours left! Carried by a tremendous spirit of confidence and relief, the viceroy joyfully set out for the palace of evil to collect his prize.

Unfortunately, while blissfully riding the waves of his imminent success, the viceroy made a devastating error: he let his guard down at perhaps the most crucial juncture in the entire operation.

As we have learned,[1] the moments before a Jew reaches a new

---

1. See Chapters 6 and 9.

spiritual plateau are the most treacherous of the entire journey, for it is then that the *yetzer hara* launches his greatest assault on the soul. When the *yetzer hara* of a particular level[2] feels as he is going to be defeated once and for all, he focuses every ounce of his remaining energies toward one final attempt at preventing the Jew from experiencing true spiritual success.

In the words of Rebbe Nachman:

> There are Jews who, when they are very near the door [to the halls of holiness], are accosted by the *Sitra Achra* (the impure forces) and the *yetzer hara* in a very mighty assault, and they do not let him enter through the door. Because of this, he turns around. For this is the way of the *yetzer hara*: when he sees that a person is very, very near to the gates of holiness and is about to enter, he attacks with tremendous ferocity. Therefore, great encouragement is necessary.[3]

In addition to the intensity of the *yetzer hara*'s final attack, an additional factor present at the very end of a particular phase of *avodah* contributes greatly to our chances of failure. This factor is the hubris, pride, and self-assurance caused by the many successful steps along the journey one is about to complete. Referring to this common error, David HaMelech sings, "And when I was untroubled, I said, 'I shall never be shaken'… when You hid Your face, I was terrified."[4]

So often in our journey, progress in the areas of *emunah*, *lashon hara*, *tefillah*, *shemiras einayim*, Torah study, or *middos*, causes us to grow over-confident as a result of our initial success. Certain that we are "over this" or "past that," a voice in our head begins to proclaim, *"I shall never be shaken,"* like David HaMelech describes. We come to believe that we are no longer susceptible to

---

2. See *Likutei Moharan* 72 and *Meor Einayim, Lech Lecha*, "*Vayeilech*."
3. *Likutei Moharan Tinyana* 48.
4. *Tehillim* 30:7–8, see the *Radak's* explanation ad loc.

the urges of yesterday, that we have successfully left our negative impulses in the past where they can no longer hurt us.

However, this is a tremendous mistake. Hillel HaZakein taught us, *Al taamin b'atzmecha ad yom moscha,* "Do not trust yourself until the day of your death."[5] No matter how many walls we have built to protect ourselves from his seductions, the *yetzer hara* is constantly lurking in the shadows, silently plotting his next strategy. We must remain ever wary of our fragile human nature, celebrating our successes with caution, along with the awareness that although battles may have indeed been won, the war is still in progress and our position yet uncertain: *"When You hid Your face, I was terrified."*[6]

Although the viceroy surmounted the first major barrier presented by an earlier form of the *yetzer hara* in not allowing the fierce-looking soldiers stationed at the gate of the orderly palace of evil to discourage him from approaching, this time around, the *yetzer hara* gets the best of him. Tragically, after an entire year of unimaginable growth, doing everything exactly as the princess

---

5. *Avos* 2:5. See also *Mei HaShiloach* Vol 2, *Tetzaveh*, "*V'asisa tzitz*," where the Ishbitzer explains that, by juxtaposing the *Tzitz* and the *Michnasayim* in its account of the *Bigdei Kehunah*, the Torah intends to teach us that even the Kohein Gadol, who had attained an awesome level of holiness that enabled him to wear the *Tzitz* with Hashem's Name on his forehead, needed constant vigilance over his physical desires (hinted to by the *Michnasayim* that cover the body's lower, more physical elements.) In the tzaddik's words, "This is to teach that even a very precious soul that has purified itself to the core requires constant guarding and vigilance." See also *Mei HaShiloach*, Vol. 2, *Eikev*, "*Uv'taveirah*."

6. It is interesting to note another verse in *Tehillim* that seems to provide the contrast for this erroneous approach. Elsewhere, David HaMelech sings, *Im amarti matah ragli, chasdecha Hashem yisadeini,* "If I said, 'My foot has slipped,' Your kindness, Hashem, will support me." (*Tehillim* 94:18). While in saying **"Bal emot l'olam,"** one's overconfidence renders him vulnerable to a surprise attack, if he recognizes his abiding susceptibility to failure, saying **"Matah ragli,"** then "*chasdecha Hashem yisadeini*" — he can rest assured that he will enjoy continued protection from the *yetzer hara*'s attacks.

had told him, hubris and overconfidence on the final day prove to be his undoing. In a moment of weakness, the Spirit of Folly that immediately precedes every sin[7] fills the viceroy's mind, causing him to forget the enormity of what is at stake and how incredibly close he is to achieving his goal. The combination of the *yetzer hara*'s vicious attack and the viceroy's vulnerability lead to a catastrophic outcome.

⊛ Flourishing in the Courtyards of Life

ON HIS WAY to the palace to redeem the lost princess, the viceroy sees a tree with beautiful apples. The Breslover *mashpi'im* note the similarity between the phrase used by Rebbe Nachman to express the appeal of this tree to the viceroy, "It was very desirable to his eyes" (*misaaveh l'einav*), and a verse in *Bereishis* that describes Chava's attraction to the *Eitz HaDaas Tov v'Ra*, an episode that closely mirrors the viceroy's downfall, "*V'chi **taavah** hu l'einayim.*"[8] The same visual perception that led to introduction of sin in the infancy of creation causes the viceroy to be led astray. Chazal refer to the eyes as the agents of the body that lead man to sin: "The eyes see, the heart desires, and the body performs the transgression."[9] The Gemara teaches that Hashem says, "Let your fear of Me be opposite your eyes, and guard your mouth from sin."[10] It all begins with the eyes, an innocent glance at the realm beyond the boundary of holiness which results in spiritual calamity.[11]

---

7. See *Sotah* 3a.

8. *Bereishis* 3:6.

9. *Midrash Tanchuma, Shelach* 15. See also *Yerushalmi Berachos* 1:8.

10. *Berachos* 17a.

11. The Rambam (*Moreh Nevuchim* 1:2) famously understands the original fall,

If guarding one's perception of truth is always an important factor in protecting against sin, it is even more necessary at this point, when the viceroy must temporarily leave the place in which he has established his identity. Sitting in the *beis midrash* surrounded by an aura of holiness, constant renewal of one's commitment to *avodas Hashem* is unnecessary. However, when we leave our *makom* and wander out onto the streets of the world, guarding our eyes and their perception of truth becomes an exceedingly crucial element of our spiritual survival.

In Chapter Five, we discussed the unfortunate phenomenon of Jews who lose their connection to Hashem upon leaving yeshivah for the workplace. We explained that this occurs when one has not focused on building an abiding personal relationship with *avodas Hashem* that can remain intact regardless of external circumstance. A yeshivah student who has managed to "make Yiddishkeit his own" by discovering the elements of *avodas Hashem* that fit his personal abilities and unique *kochos hanefesh*, and has "chosen a place" of stability, commitment, and resolute identity will not be threatened when the time comes for him to

---

Adam's eating from the *Eitz Ha'Daas Tov v'Ra*, as involving Adam basing his choice not on "**Emes**" and "**Sheker**," that which is objectively true or false, but rather on "**tov**" and "**ra**," that which he subjectively perceived to be "pleasant and unpleasant, comfortable and uncomfortable, delightful and ugly" (Rav Yosef Dov Soloveitchik, *Worship of the Heart: Essays on Jewish Prayer*, p. 47). This shift in utilization of free will was considered a very grave sin indeed. Seen in this light, one may suggest that the "beautiful and orderly" palace of *Malchus D'Sitra Achra* represents the pinnacle of the post-sin utilization of free choice, making decisions based on a preference for what appears to be beautiful, comfortable, and pleasant instead of the truth. In this challenge, the viceroy is being given the opportunity to affirm the correct approach to life by making the difficult decision to choose the truth, difficult and unpleasant as this may appear: "There I saw **beauty**, there I saw **truth**." Instead, he falls prey to the perspective of the princess' captors, following his eyes and their perception of good, even at the expense of that which is truly important.

leave yeshivah and support his family. His personal bond with the Master of the world forged through Shabbos Kodesh, *tefillah*, and God-conscious Torah study that touches his very essence will enable him to incorporate every life-circumstance into his *avodas Hashem*.

There is a *pasuk* about these Jews whose relationship with Hashem reaches the very essence of their being. Regarding one whose connection to his "place" is sufficiently powerful, the verse states, *Shisulim b'veis Hashem, b'chatzros Elokeinu yafrichu*, "Planted in the house of Hashem, they will flourish in the court-yard of our God."[12] David HaMelech is teaching us that if one is firmly "planted in the house of Hashem," when it comes time for him to wander into the courtyards of life, he is still able to flourish.

The Baal Shem Tov taught: *B'machshavto shel adam, sham hu ha'adam*, "Man is where his thoughts are."[13] Immediately upon set-ting out for the palace, it became necessary for the viceroy to close his eyes to the outside world and mentally bind himself to his *ma-kom* with a mighty bond. As the verse states: "And Avraham lifted his **eyes** and he saw the place (*hamakom*) from **afar**"[14]; lifting our eyes away from the desires of the physical world allows us to re-main ever connected to our *makom*, even when we are "*rachok*," far removed from our comfort zone. Another verse hints to this idea as well: *Mah tovu ohalecha Yaakov, mishkenosecha Yisrael* — "How goodly are your tents, Yaakov, your sanctuaries, Yisrael." The "tents" in this verse hint to the journeys a Jew must sometimes make outside the four *amos* of his "*makom*" — at which time he

---

12. *Tehillim* 92:13.
13. See *Likutei Moharan* 21:11; *Tzidkas HaTzaddik* 144; *Degel Machaneh Ephraim, Bereishis*, "*Vayomer Elokim*"; and *Mei HaShiloach* Vol. 1, *Emor*, "*Emor el.*"
14. *Bereishis* 22:4.

is referred to as "Yaakov," a lower level. But *"mah tovu ohalecha, Yaakov,"* these journeys can be exceedingly positive, providing that *"mishkenosecha Yisrael"* — he always remains rooted in the sanctuary of his ideal identity, the lofty character of "Yisrael."[15] In the holy words of the Ishbitzer:

> Similarly, each person, all the while that he has not yet turned to the occupations of this world, is obligated to implant the words of Torah in his heart, so that its holiness will remain with him and enable him to overcome anything that arises against him.[16]

Reb Nosson writes:

> For this is the primary perfection of Man, for one to become so very established in Torah and *avodah* that no matter where he might find himself, in all of the various situations in the world, he will always return from there to his established place; his connection to Torah where he finds peace and stability...[17]

The viceroy's inability to guard his eyes upon leaving the confines of his holy foundation indicate that he had not yet fortified his sense of identity to the proper degree.[18]

---

15. See *Degel Machaneh Ephraim, Masai, "Od yeish l'vaeir vayichtov."*

16. *Mei HaShiloach* Vol 1, *Naso, "Vayidaber."* See also *Re'eh, "Asser,"* and Vol. 2, *Eikev, "U'maltem."* See also *Likutei Halachos, Betzi'as HaPas* 5:19.

17. *Likutei Halachos, Betzi'as HaPas* 5:46.

18. Because, as we have discussed in an earlier note, *teshuvah* is essentially a process of return to the root of our souls in *Binah/Imah/Kisei HaKavod*, not having, or losing touch with, one's *"makom"* is indicative of some flaw in that process. "When a soul is cut off from its source (*Binah*), it is cast from place to place..." (*Shaarei Orah*, Eighth Gate)

✳ The Princess's Intuition

LOOKING BACK TO the guidelines, the princess had told the viceroy that on the final day of the year, *eating* was prohibited. None of her conditions included anything about *looking* at food. Similarly, Rebbe Nachman doesn't say that the viceroy approached the tree with the intention of eating from it. He simply says that the viceroy stopped along his triumphant journey to the palace of evil to *look* at the tree, for *"it was very desirable to his eyes."* This, friends, is one of the most beloved strategies of the *yetzer hara*.

Referring to the modus operandi of this damaging inner force, Chazal teach, "Today, he tells you to do this [commit a seemingly minor sin] and tomorrow he tells you to do that, until, eventually, he gets you to worship idols."[19] Much like the cunning primordial snake in Gan Eden, the *yetzer hara* whispers into the viceroy's ear: "Look at how beautiful those apples are! Did the princess say you couldn't look at food? She only said you couldn't *eat* the food! Come on, don't be such a *machmir* (one who is overly stringent)! Just look at how beautiful these apples are!"[20]

Here we come to a very deep point. Approached with the mentality of the six sons, there is indeed nothing wrong with looking at the apples. On a purely intellectual level, there is nothing perceivably forbidden about stopping to behold this beautiful sight — after all, it's well within the boundaries of the princess's guidelines. But the viceroy is not on his way to free the six sons. It is the *princess* he intends to redeem, by way of the emulative

---

19. *Shabbos* 105b.

20. It is also possible that the *yetzer hara* utilizes the fact that the *Sefirah* of *Malchus* is referred to as a "Field of Apples" (*Zohar, Haazinu,* 257a) to attempt to convince him that eating from the apple tree would, in fact, aid him in his mission to free the lost princess.

extraction process we have described. *Her* standard in this situation is quite different from that of her brothers.

On the level of the princess of soul and depth, an action's essential permissibility is not the only factor to be taken into account when deciding whether or not to perform it, engage with it, or introduce it into one's life. The princess contributes a deeper element to the decision-making process, a certain sensitivity, an intuitive sense for the inner spirit of Torah and the true *ratzon Hashem* in a given situation. In the words of the Ishbitzer Tzaddik:

> On Shavuos, at the giving of the Torah, Hashem implanted *Binah*-intuition into the heart of every Jew, that they should be able to perceive the will of Hashem on their own. This *Binah*-intuition is referred to as the "Moon." The "Sun" hints to *Chochmah*-intellect, the 613 mitzvos which enable a person to assess each situation and understand how to act, if a given thing is forbidden or permitted. The "Moon" hints to the heart's intuition which enables man to sanctify himself even in that which is officially permitted[21]; the ability to draw an inner boundary and say, "Until here is the will of God. Past here is no longer represents the will of God."[22]

Even though a given activity may be halachically permissible according to the letter of the law, a Jew who is in touch with the holy princess of *avodas Hashem* knows intuitively to stay away. Although he may intellectually understand why a certain thing has been formally permitted by the authorities, his heart tells him that all is not right, that while this activity may fit the Torah's official requirements, it is out of touch with the *spirit* of the Torah.

Throughout the generations, our tzaddikim have warned us about the possibility of becoming what the Ramban famously

---

21. See *Yevamos* 20b.

22. *Mei HaShiloach* Vol. 1, *Emor*, *"V'heiveisem es omer."* See also *Chayei Moharan* 197.

calls a *"naval b'reshus haTorah,"* a scoundrel within the boundaries of the Torah.[23] It is possible to do everything right by the book, and yet remain completely out of touch with what it is that Hashem truly desires of His holy nation. Focused solely on Yiddishkeit's realm of the six sons of outward accomplishment to the exclusion of the princess, one runs the risk of doing everything wrong even while doing everything right; "For it is possible to be both a *lamdan* and completely wicked."[24]

This concept is addressed by Rav Itamar Schwartz, author of *Bilvavi Mishkan Evneh*:

> The soul can feel all kinds of contradictions in this world. One example is when a person indulges in permitted pleasure; this is called a "disgusting one who indulges within the permission of the Torah." When a person indulges in desires, even desires that are permissible and not forbidden by the Torah, his soul can feel disgust inside. This is a simple example of materialism that makes our soul recoil.
>
> But in our generation, there is a new kind of problem, in which people around us engage in certain actions that appear to be mitzvos, but a person can sense that if he does such an act, it will further him from holiness. There

---

23. *Ramban* to *Vayikra* 19:2.

24. *Likutei Moharan* 31:9. The Gemara in *Berachos* 35b relates that the later generations would bring the grain into the silo through the window, roofs, and other alternate entrances so that the grain would be exempt from *maaser*. In the version of this Gemara brought in *Ein Yaakov* (*Berachos* 102), a few additional words appear: "*Lefikach, lo nisbarchu peiroseihen*." Although, according to the letter of the law, it was halachically permitted for them to do this and their grain was indeed exempt from *maaser*, the *Ein Yaakov* teaches that because of their intentional circumvention of this mitzvah, their grain did not enjoy bountiful blessing. On the level of the six sons, these Jews were in the clear, but the princess demanded more. Indeed, the word "*Berachah*" is related to the *Sefirah* of *Malchus*. (*Shaarei Orah*, First Gate.) Because the action of these Jews lacked the intuitive spirit of the princess, their fruits were devoid of *berachah*.

are things which other people do which appear to be fine, but just because others are doing it doesn't mean it's fine for *you* to do. When a person only has intellectual prowess and doesn't develop his soul's sensitivity, he will not be sensitive to things which harm his soul. Besides for learning Torah in-depth, we also need to develop our soul's sensitivity to feel what is holy and what isn't, what is true and pure, and what isn't. Our soul can become sensitive to what truth is; even if we are not prophets, we are "sons of prophets," which implies that our soul can still have an inner sense for what is and isn't the truth.[25]

Here, Rebbe Nachman is teaching us that although looking at the beautiful apples was not officially forbidden, at this point the viceroy should have been connected enough with the Lost Princess of *avodas Hashem* to be able to discern the intuitive truth that, while formally permitted, stopping to look at these beautiful apples at this critical juncture ran contrary to the spirit of his holy mission. With his guard down and assaulted by a mighty *yetzer hara*, the viceroy ignores the impulses of the princess so near to freedom, beginning a process that leads to his downfall and the frustration of his effort to complete his mission.

While every Jewish person contains *Binas haLeiv*, the intuitive sense for the true will of Hashem, most have not sufficiently strengthened this spiritual muscle. The way to fine tune this sense is by studying the behavior, decisions, and mannerisms of true *ovdei Hashem*. When we read stories about the tzaddikim and learn about the ways they lead their affairs, we gain something perhaps even more important than we do when we hear Torah from their mouths: the refinement of our inner intuition, the *Binas haLeiv* that rests in the heart of each and every Jew. Perhaps

---

25. *Elul Talks*, p. 42.

this is the intention of Rav Elazar when he taught, "One who has studied Torah and Mishnayos but has not served *talmidei chachamim* is considered to be an ignoramus."[26] Despite the scholarship of such an individual, his lack of expertise regarding his teacher's conduct *outside* the *beis midrash* points to a tremendous deficiency in his *avodas Hashem*. He is surely missing what Rav Soloveitchik famously referred to as "the Jewish tremor" — the special sensitivity that allows one to intuit the *ratzon Hashem* in situations that fall outside of the strict boundaries of halachah. The following story expresses this point in a beautiful way.

In the days when the great Chassidic master, Rebbe Simchah Bunim of Peshischa, traded in lumber, a number of merchants in Danzig asked him why he went to visit tzaddikim if he was so well versed in the *sefarim hakedoshim*. What could they tell him that he could not learn from the *sefarim* just as well? He answered them, but the response did not satisfy their curiosity.

That evening, they invited the soon-to-be rebbe to go with them to a play, but he refused.

When they returned from the theater, they told him they had seen many wonderful things.

"I know all about those wonderful things," he replied. "I have read the program."

"But from that," they retorted, "you cannot possibly know what we have seen with our own eyes!"

Rebbe Simchah Bunim smiled. "That's just how it is," he said, "with the *sefarim* and the tzaddikim."

While each and every Jew carries a guitar of his own, we must tune our strings against those of the tzaddikim who, in turn, have tuned theirs against Hashem's perfect pitch.

---

26. *Sotah* 22a. See also *Berachos* 7a, "*Gedolah shimushah shel Torah yoser m'limudah.*"

✹ Spiritual Slumber

DRAWN AFTER HIS eyes and the *yetzer hara's* seduction, the viceroy eats from the tree, breaching the princess's directive to fast on the final day. Immediately, he falls into a deep slumber.

In the deeper texts, sleep is synonymous with a lower level of consciousness, a spiritual descent into the terror, confusion, and emotional numbness that accompanies distance from Hashem.[27] When the viceroy fails to fulfill the lost princess's conditions, he loses the insight and elevation gained over the course of the year, toppling from the tower of spiritual brilliance into a deep pit of profound darkness. The Spirit of Folly that has entered his heart — blurring his sense of priority to the point that he was willing to sacrifice a full year of painstaking effort for the fleeting taste of the fruit on his palate — has extended itself throughout his being. He has forgotten who he is, where he is, and what he has come here to get.

Sometimes, a moment is all it takes to lose everything.

✹ An Unlikely Beginning

IF THE STORY ended here, how do you think we would feel? In all probability, we would feel sad, frustrated, and confused. Perhaps we would even feel irate. But we wouldn't think it unfair. Although he put up a mighty fight and made great strides toward his goal, the viceroy has, in the end, failed. His convictions were strong, founded on his great love for the king and his desire to free the lost princess, but they seem not to have been enough. He has fought so hard to attain so much, but has foolishly chosen to

---

27. See *Likutei Moharan* 60:6.

forfeit it all. In a moment of mindless passion, he has blown the single opportunity he had to reach his goal.

However, in truth, it is this kind of absolute, definitive, and ultimately shallow thinking that Rebbe Nachman intends to counter with this marvelous tale in the first place. Thoughts like these emanate from a consciousness of the six sons and scream of disconnection from the princess of youth. Indeed, regarding the spiritual journey of life, Shlomo HaMelech teaches "The tzaddik falls seven times and again rises."[28] It is when the failing reaches the aspect of "seven," the deeply intuitive insight of *Malchus*, that all failures can be used as a springboard for growth. With the eyes of the princess we are able to see that the seven fallings in fact aided us in attaining a greater degree of clarity, *Mezukak shivasayim*, "refined *seven*fold."[29] An old shoemaker once told Reb Yisrael Salanter, "As long as the candle is still burning, it is possible to make repairs."[30] Although the viceroy has fallen into a deep sleep — his spiritual strivings frozen over and his priorities in disarray — he is still alive. The flame of his soul yet flickers. Rotting away deep inside the earth of faith, the seeds of hope are consolidating their conviction to the innermost core, preparing to push upward toward the heavens once again. *Ani yesheinah, v'libi eir*, "I am asleep, but my heart is awake."[31]

For the world, this is where our story would end.

For Rebbe Nachman of Breslov, the master of hope, this is where our story truly begins.

---

28. *Mishlei* 24:16.
29. *Tehillim* 7:6.
30. *Avodas HaMiddos*, p. 34.
31. *Shir HaShirim* 5:2.

LESSONS FOR LIFE

❊ After one has experienced a measure of success in *avodas Hashem*, he may begin to grow proud, self-assured, and overly confident. Letting his guard down, he becomes vulnerable to the *yetzer hara*'s attacks once more.

❊ When it is time for a Jew to wander onto the streets of the world, it is important for him to remain bound with his core identity and guard his eyes from exploring his surroundings lest he be drawn astray.

❊ Even while a certain thing may be halachically permissible, Hashem has granted His holy nation the ability to access an inner intuition that dictates the proper standard. This intuition lends an additional level of sensitivity to a decision-making process, ensuring that one will stay aligned with the true spirit of our holy Torah.

CHAPTER 11

"Where in the World Am I?"

וְהָיָה הַמְשָׁרֵת מְנַעֵר אוֹתוֹ, וְלֹא הָיָה נֵעוֹר כְּלָל. אַחַר כָּךְ
הֵקִיץ מִשְּׁנָתוֹ, וְשָׁאַל לְהַמְשָׁרֵת: הֵיכָן אֲנִי בָּעוֹלָם? וְסִפֵּר
לוֹ הַמַּעֲשֶׂה [הַיְנוּ הַמְשָׁרֵת סִפֵּר לְהַשֵּׁנִי לַמֶּלֶךְ הַמַּעֲשֶׂה
וְאָמַר לוֹ] שֶׁאַתָּה יָשֵׁן זְמַן מְרֻבֶּה מְאֹד זֶה כַּמָּה שָׁנִים,
וַאֲנִי הָיִיתִי מִתְפַּרְנֵס מֵהַפֵּרוֹת. וְהָיָה מִצְטַעֵר עַצְמוֹ מְאֹד.
וְהָלַךְ לְשָׁם וּמָצָא אוֹתָהּ.

The servant tried to shake him, but he would not wake. After some time, the viceroy awoke from his slumber and asked his servant, "Where in the world am I?" The servant told him what had happened. "You slept a very long time — for many years. I survived by eating the fruit." The viceroy was very upset at himself. He went to the palace and found the princess.

❀ "And Draw It Down to Your Heart"

IN A PREVIOUS chapter,[1] we learned that the viceroy's servant represents the powers of human intellect. When the inner tzaddik falls into spiritual slumber along the journey toward discovering the fire of youth in *avodas Hashem,* the intellect attempts to rouse him to his mission once more.

Implicit in this detail is an important message: the servant cannot continue the journey to free the lost princess alone. Here, Rebbe Nachman is teaching us that a dry, intellectual understanding of the importance of Judaism and the value of a life spent serving Hashem cannot itself put a person in touch with the Lost Princess. Although the Torah enjoins us to engage with Torah and Hashem on an intellectual level, the *avodah* of *V'yadata hayom,* "You shall know, today,"[2] is, alone, not enough. In order to truly get in touch with *avodas Hashem* in the ultimate manner, the verse continues, revealing a second, vital, condition: *v'hasheivosa el livavecha,* "and you shall draw it down to your heart." The ultimate goal of holy knowledge is to inspire the emotions of love and awe for the Master of the world. "It is not study that is primary, but the deed."[3]

The viceroy, the inner *tzaddik yesod olam,* is the channel bridging the fearful expanse between mind and heart. Only that abiding point of holiness and piety which has a sense for the ineffable presence of God and in comparison, the vanity of all other pursuits, is able to utilize the intellectual information of the mind to set the heart aflame with the fire of youthful passion, excitement, and vitality.

Still, although the servant cannot do it alone, he tries his best

---

1. Chapter 4, "The Viceroy's Three Requests."
2. *Devarim* 4:39.
3. *Avos* 1:17.

to wake the viceroy from his slumber by reminding him of the task at hand. Unfortunately, he is unsuccessful. But when the viceroy awakens on his own, the intellect is able to remind him of what had happened.

The intellect tells the inner tzaddik that while he slept, he continued to eat the fruits, a reference to the Torah and mitzvos.[4] Even though his service was devoid of feeling and holy intention, it was enough to keep the fire burning while the viceroy slept.

✳ A Cry from the Depths

THE MOMENT THE inner tzaddik wakes up from his deep sleep he asks one simple but incredibly powerful question. *Heichan ani b'olam?*, "Where in the world am I?" The ability of the viceroy to wake up and *stay* awake instead of turning over and going back to sleep is a major element of his success. Unlike Pharaoh, about whom the verse states, "Pharaoh awoke and went back to sleep and dreamed a second time,"[5] the viceroy stubbornly fights to remain awake and rectify his error.

It is perfectly clear to any student of Rebbe Nachman's works that when the viceroy asks, "Where in the world am I?", he is not simply wondering where he is currently located in a geographical sense. Instead, the viceroy is responding to his lowly spiritual

---

4. See *Peah* 1:1: "The following are the things for which a man enjoys the *fruits* in this world while the principal remains for him in the world to come..." Interestingly enough, the servant survives by eating the fruits of the very same tree that caused the viceroy to fall asleep. This seems to parallel Adam and Chava's covering themselves with leaves from the *Eitz HaDaas* after they had sinned by eating its fruit. (See *Rashi* to *Bereishis* 3:7.) Chazal learn from here that the very thing that causes ruin can itself bring rectification. (*Sanhedrin* 70b)

5. *Bereishis* 41:5.

standing. This question bursts forth from the deepest essence of the viceroy's soul, piercing the heavens with its bitter anguish: "Where in the world am I? Look what has happened to me! I have fallen so far from my Maker, so alienated from my deepest essence and removed from my mission in this world!" This rhetorical expression of spiritual bewilderment is an important element in *avodas Hashem*, utilized by the Breslover chassidim until this very day.

A familiar scene: A skinny chassid with a small blond beard walks the singular path of *hisbodedus*, engaged in a one-on-one conversation with the Master of the world in the forest behind his home. He nervously twirls his long *payos* around his finger and paces back and forth, at a loss for words. Suddenly, a long sigh escapes his lips and he lifts his eyes through the leafy cover toward the blue sky above. "Oy!" he softly cries, *"Abba she'baShamayim!* Father in heaven! *Heichan ani b'olam*?! Where in the world am I? *Heichan ani b'olam*?! I am so far from my true mission; I have strayed so far from the path of light and truth! How long will I continue to forsake you, Father in heaven? How much longer will I turn my back to the well of living waters and drink from this dirty pit of lowliness and filth?[6] Is this where a soul like mine, hewn from the *kisei hakavod*, belongs? Is this what You sent me to this world for? I am ready to return to Your loving arms, my dear Father! I am ready to stand up from this place and continue my journey toward closeness with You!"

In *Likutei Moharan* we find what appears to be a parallel teaching. There, Rebbe Nachman teaches that when a Jew feels so disconnected from Hashem that he is drifting off in a sea of darkness and physical obsession, he should muster up his strength and utter, in the final moments of his defeat, a single word: *Ayeh?*, *"Where?"* — "Where is Hashem? Where is the place of His glory?

6. See *Yirmeyahu* 2:13.

How can I have fallen so far that my soul has lost sight of her Source for which she so desperately yearns?" It matters little whether one screams this word or whispers it, regardless, it serves to express an inner anguish otherwise inexpressible, to make a crack in the hard shell covering his heart and to allow the *neshamah* to peek out at the great expanse above from which she has fallen.

Rebbe Nachman teaches that when this cry of *"Ayeh?"* leaves a Jew's mouth, it is the beginning of his salvation — it holds the power to extract him from the dark pit into which he has descended:

> A person can fall into spiritually vile places, experiencing doubts, negative thoughts, and tremendous confusion. But if while evaluating himself and his great distance from Hashem, he begins to ask *Ayeh mekom kevodo*, "Where is the place of His glory"? — for he recognizes that he has fallen so far into such places, this is the foundation of his *tikkun* and spiritual ascent.[7]

The honesty, simplicity, and humility packed into this little question lend it incredible power. It is a wonderful lifejacket to use in our own journey toward the Lost Princess of *avodas Hashem*.

❋ *"Where* am I?", Not *"Who* am I?"

IN THIS ROAR of pain, the viceroy expresses his shame, guilt, and regret over having lost touch with his true nature — "Where in the world am *I*?" He feels that he has lost touch with his "I," that he is floating out into the open sea of strange thoughts and

---

7. *Likutei Moharan Tinyana* 12.

feelings, lost and alone. As we have seen, the only way to anchor himself and regain his footing is by asking this very question.

The viceroy doesn't ask, "How did I get here?" or, "What will become of me?" The question, "Where in the world am I?" concerns itself neither with the past nor the future, but rather with the *immediate present*: "I need to regain my sense of direction." Expressing his present disbelief at how he has failed so miserably, the viceroy succeeds in reminding himself of who he truly is and of the exalted nature of the mission he has undertaken. Asking this question allows the viceroy to contrast the dark depravity of his current state (*"Where in the world"*) with the sweet holiness of his true essence (*"am I"*). Assessing the ugly damage of his misdeed by holding it up to the light of his essential self, the viceroy is able to appreciate the gravity of his error without falling into despair. The construction of his question reminds him that his act in the passion of the moment does not define his true essence. While he has made a mistake and will certainly suffer consequences, he realizes that this misstep doesn't have any bearing on the truth of his identity and the path toward the shining goal which yet lies before him. *Where* he is does not define *who* he is.[8]

In the nuance of the viceroy's words, Rebbe Nachman is teaching us a tremendous rule in *avodas Hashem*: An error *never* results in the termination of our holy mission. We may fall, yet we never shatter; our light may be dimmed, but it is never extinguished. When we wake from our spiritual slumber and behold the devastation around us, our first question should never be *"Who* have I become?" In order for us to heal, we must instead ask *"Where* in the world am I?" — lamenting our current state

---

8. It is important to note that the ability to phrase the question in this manner is a direct result of the viceroy's quality year during which he found his place of identity and got in touch with the core of his personality expressed in holy desire. It is these elements that allow him to cling tightly to the reality that his misdeed does not define him and that there is yet hope.

while never losing sight of our awesome holiness and the all-encompassing mission for which we were sent to this world.[9]

In the words of Rav Kook:

> The Jewish person is obligated to believe that a Godly soul rests within him, that his entire being is a letter in the Torah — each of which is an entire world that proceeds and expands to an infinite degree. The spiritual extension of even a single grain of sand is also without boundary or measurement; all the years of one's life would not suffice to explicate the many laws which are founded in the deepest wisdom, bound with the knowledge and strength he carries within. How much more so does a member of our holy nation need to believe with a lucid and passionate faith in his life-force...[10]

Reb Tzadok adds:

> The same way one needs to believe in Hashem, so too must he afterward believe in himself; that Hashem has an interest in him and that he is not toiling for naught.[11]

⊛ The Value of a Broken Heart

IN *SICHOS HARAN*, Rebbe Nachman draws a vital distinction between a broken heart and debilitating sadness. In the strongest terms, the tzaddik stresses that they are not the same thing at all — while a broken heart is "beloved to Hashem and extremely precious in His eyes," sadness is "from the Side of Impurity and is hated by Hashem."[12]

---

9. See *Likutei Tefillos* Vol. 2, 12.
10. *Oros HaTorah* 11:2.
11. *Tzidkas HaTzaddik* 154.
12. *Sichos HaRan* 41.

What is the defining difference between these two emotional states? How are we to differentiate between sadness and a broken heart?

The Piaseczner Rebbe *Hy"d* gives us the following definition: A wealthy person who suddenly loses his entire fortune becomes inconsolably *saddened.* A pauper who knows with absolute certainty that a treasure is buried deep under the ground in the exact place he is standing, yet meets with obstacles in digging it up, feels *brokenhearted.*[13]

What emerges from this definition is that sadness is the reaction to what one perceives as a completely hopeless situation. In the Piaseczner's parable, the formerly wealthy man despairs of ever regaining his wealth and the accompanying prestige, therefore growing angry, bitter, and resentful. Seeing all avenues to financial survival closed to him, he shuts down and falls into a deep, dark depression. Brokenheartedness, on the other hand, is founded upon hope, yearning, positive expectation, and confidence. Although the pauper may be frustrated over his inability to dig deeply enough to reveal his treasure, never does that frustration obscure his joyful confidence and deep-seated certainty that he will indeed, with time, reach his objective. In a similar vein, Rebbe Nachman teaches that while a depressed person is angry and belligerent over his spiritual failures,[14] a brokenhearted Jew

---

13. *Chovas HaTalmidim,* Chapter 2. The term used by the Piaseczner Rebbe as the parallel to depression is *daagah,* "worry," but the distinction fits *shivron lev,* "brokenheartedness," as well.

14. *Sichos HaRan* 42. See also ibid. 43, where Rebbe Nachman says that sadness causes a person to "forget his name." The tzaddikim teach that a person's name is his essence and embodies his mission in life. (See *Sotah* 12a; *Berachos* 7b and 39b; *Pesachim* 4a; *Esther Rabbah* 6:3; *Kesser Shem Tov* 104; *Likutei Moharan* 56:3; *Meor Einayim, Vayakhel, "Re'u ki kara"*; and *Bamidbar, "Vayedaber"*; *Noam Elimelech, Shemos, "Oh yevuar v'eileh shemos"*; and *Sichos HaRan* 95.) Perhaps when Rebbe Nachman teaches that sadness makes a person forget his name, his intention is that the hopelessness that accompanies sadness

still sees the benefit in lifting his eyes heavenward and begging Hashem for Divine assistance.[15]

To Rebbe Nachman, a broken heart represents the healthy strivings of an honest soul pained by the appearance of its reflection in the great ocean of Hashem's unconditional love. While the intense yearning for closeness with Hashem may elicit tears of guilt and frustration, it is, at its very essence, founded upon the certainty that the great treasure house of *yiras Shamayim* is ever in reach, that there is yet hope, and that regardless of how many times the *yetzer hara* has prevented us from fulfilling our innermost desire to serve Hashem, "there is no despair in the world at all." Like the pauper who maintains perfect belief in the treasure under his feet and requires only the fortification of his belief that he will yet reach it, we are able to lift our aching hands to the Master of the world and cry out from the deepest depths of our being.

Founded upon the stark awareness of the essential holiness that forms the core of his identity, the viceroy experiences not debilitating sadness, but rather a healthy broken Jewish heart. His cry, "Where in the world am I?" embodies his abiding connection to the true "I," the flickering flame of holy desire that never goes out. Were the viceroy to approach this situation "from the outside, in," he might despair of ever attaining the spiritual wealth he perceives as being external to him and near impossible to attain. However, because he approaches his descent from the perspective of *penimiyus*, "from the inside out," the viceroy is able to consider *teshuvah*, the passionate *re*turn to the treasure he knows for certain is buried within.

---

causes a person to lose his sense of identity and self-worth. Consequently, he forgets his mission in the world.

15. *Sichos HaRan* 231.

✳ Holy Stubbornness

"THE VICEROY WAS very upset at himself. He went to the palace and found the princess." Despite being overcome by the immensity of his error, the viceroy stands up and heads for the palace, continuing to fight toward his goal. As indicated by his question, "Where in the world am I?", the viceroy's sorrow over his current spiritual state has not washed away his faith in the mission he has undertaken and his ability to triumph despite his failure. Instead of running away, the viceroy forges on.[16] Although he spends some time thinking about the extent and implication of the damage he has done, he does not allow those thoughts to drag him under. When he feels he has mourned his loss for long enough, he removes those thoughts from his mind and presses on, eager to correct his error.

On one occasion, Rebbe Nachman said to his chassidim:

> You certainly hold me to be a perfect tzaddik. But even if I were to commit a grave sin *chas v'shalom*, even so, the sin wouldn't cast me away at all. I would remain a good Jew after the sin just as I was before. Only afterward, I would do *teshuvah*.[17]

With this shocking statement, Rebbe Nachman intended to demonstrate the theoretical reach of his holy stubbornness. The tzaddik had reached such a level of clarity that nothing in the world could ever hold him back from returning to the Master

---

16. The astute reader will notice that the viceroy's current decision is in direct contrast to the princess's reaction to her father's show of anger. Forgetting her true nature, the princess had given up on herself and run away to her room, yet the viceroy refuses to give in, and stands ready face his failure and make things right. In so doing, he is emulating another essential characteristic of the princess, thus extracting her from her captivity.

17. *Chayei Moharan* 453.

of the world. The deep recognition of his eternal holiness would allow him to hold his ground and perform *teshuvah* instead of falling into despair.

Each of us find ourselves, from time to time, in the viceroy's situation — crushed by the awesome weight of a misdeed and chasing the shadow of a lost opportunity. The question that must echo in our mind is: *What do I do now? Where do I go from here?* Rebbe Nachman uses the medium of this tale and the viceroy's response to teach us how to recover from a spiritual failing. Somehow, despite his acute awareness of the terrible damage he caused by eating the apple, the viceroy finds the inner strength, the *"Azus d'Kedusha"* — holy stubbornness Rebbe Nachman so often spoke about — to get back up and face the princess. Uncomfortable as their meeting is sure to be, he knows that it is the right thing to do. Moping around and wallowing in guilt will not help anyone. Instead, he must pick himself up, dust himself off, and forge ahead with great joy, as this is the only way he will emerge victorious from this quest. In the words of the Baal HaTanya:

> At this point there is a general principle you need to know. Let's compare this to winning a competition in the physical realm, such as a match between two wrestlers. Each one attempts to throw the other down. If one of them would be lazy and sluggish, he would be easily beaten — even if he were stronger than the other. The same applies when it comes to winning against the *yetzer hara*: One cannot beat the *yetzer hara* while in a state of laziness and sluggishness, which are symptoms of depression and a fossilized heart. The only way to emerge victorious is with the zeal that derives from joy and a wide open heart, free from any trace of worry or anxiety.[18]

---

18. *Likutei Amarim, Tanya*, Chapter 26.

This attitude is so fundamentally unique to the Breslover path to *avodas Hashem*. Humility, simplicity, courage, determination, hope, clarity, honesty, and faith — all pillars of the Breslov way — meet in this line of our amazing story. This unique spirit is something to keep in mind and to strive for, ceaselessly.

The journey continues.

LESSONS FOR LIFE

❋ A purely intellectual engagement with Torah and *avodas Hashem* fails to engender the passion, wonder, desire, and qualitative spirit represented by the princess. It can, however, maintain one's general connection with Judaism in the event of a momentary lapse of commitment and the spiritual numbness that ensues.

❋ When a Jew cries out from the core of his being, expressing deep anguish over his spiritual failures and his distance from Hashem, this is the beginning of his salvation.

❋ It is important to remember that even when one falls into the foreign world of negative desires and sinful behavior, his essence remains pure and bound to the realm of holiness. *Where* one is does not define *who* one is.

❋ After a spiritual descent, a Jew must exhibit *Azus D'Kedusha*, holy stubbornness, summoning the courage necessary to stand up from that place and seek out ways to make things right.

CHAPTER 12

Reconciliation

וּמָצָא אוֹתָהּ, וְהָיְתָה מִצְטַעֶרֶת לְפָנָיו מְאֹד, כִּי אִלּוּ בָאתָ
בְּאוֹתוֹ הַיּוֹם, הָיִיתָ מוֹצִיא אוֹתִי מִכָּאן וּבִשְׁבִיל יוֹם אֶחָד
אָבַדְתָּ. אָמְנָם שֶׁלֹּא לֶאֱכֹל הוּא דָּבָר קָשֶׁה מְאֹד, בִּפְרָט
בַּיּוֹם הָאַחֲרוֹן, אָז מִתְגַּבֵּר הַיֵּצֶר הָרַע מְאֹד [הַיְנוּ שֶׁהַבַּת
מֶלֶךְ אָמְרָה לוֹ, שֶׁעַתָּה תָּקֵל עָלָיו הָאַזְהָרָה וְלֹא יִהְיֶה
מֻזְהָר שֶׁלֹּא לֶאֱכֹל, כִּי הוּא דָּבָר קָשֶׁה לַעֲמֹד בּוֹ וְכוּ'].

He found her and she lamented to him greatly, saying, "If you had come on that day, you would have
freed me from here. But because of one day, you
lost everything. However, it is very difficult not to
eat, especially on the last day when the Evil Urge is
very strong." (The princess is telling him that she
will make the conditions easier for him by allowing
him to eat on the last day, for it is very difficult etc.)

SHAKEN, YET GROUNDED BY the holy stubbornness
founded upon his sense of stability and identity, the viceroy
returns to the palace and finds the princess. As we might
imagine, she is devastated. Rebbe Nachman relates that upon
seeing the viceroy's face, the princess begins to express her pain.

210

✴ Cry of Pain, Whisper of Hope

IT WOULD APPEAR that the princess is extremely angry at the viceroy, and rightfully so. How could he have made such a poor decision? What could possibly have compelled him to trade away an entire year of effort and the all-important goal of bringing her home to her father for a silly little apple? How could he have blown such an incredible opportunity? However, a closer look at her words reveal that, while theoretically justified, this sentiment is very far from the spirit of the princess's intention.

Looking carefully at the way Rebbe Nachman writes these sentences, we find that the princess is not yelling at the viceroy in an angry attempt to take make him feel even worse than he already does. Such a move would undoubtedly break the viceroy's heart and drag him to the depths of despair, resulting in the mission's automatic termination. Rather, with her impassioned words, the princess intends to *strengthen* the viceroy. In revealing to him how much she had yearned for him and anticipated his success throughout the year, the princess stresses how much faith she has in his ability to fulfill the conditions and free her from this place. Rebbe Nachman does not write that the princess yelled at the viceroy. Nor does he tell us that she cried with despair as if all is lost. Instead, the tzaddik tells us that the princess is *"mitzta'eres lifanav,"* she expresses her brokenheartedness, softly communicating a pain that bespeaks the hope she had *and still has* in the viceroy and her ironclad conviction that although he has failed in his first attempt, he will yet succeed in the future — as long as he is wise enough to use this failure as a learning experience.

The same holds true in our personal attempt to redeem the Lost Princess of our *avodas Hashem*. Like the viceroy in our tale, we fall prey to the *yetzer hara*'s final attack as we toe the threshold of a spiritual breakthrough. When this happens, we hear the voice of the princess echo through our being, expressing her pain over our folly and the opportunity lost at our hands. It is easy to mistake her cry as one of anger, anguish, and despair. When we do, it cripples us by bolstering the lingering notion that there is no longer any hope for us, that we will never be able to change — the venom that is injected with the bite of the snake. In this line of our tale, the tzaddik teaches that this is a tremendous mistake. The voice we hear is not one of hopelessness and despair — *on the contrary!* It is a voice of strength and hope, reminding us just how much the princess is relying on our efforts and how deeply she believes in our ability to free her from the darkness of her captivity.

❋ No Progress Is Ever Lost

HAVING STRENGTHENED THE viceroy by reminding him how desperately she is depending on him and how strongly she believes that he can, with the proper focus, free her from the place of her captivity, the princess further appeases him by validating his struggle and understanding how difficult it must have been to face such a powerful *yetzer hara*. For this reason, she hints that she will give him a new set of conditions, and that they will be easier to fulfill — it will no longer be forbidden for him to eat on the final day.

At first glance, it seems difficult to understand why the conditions for freeing the princess lighten after the viceroy's botched first attempt. Logic seems to dictate that the conditions should grow even more strict and demanding in light of his initial failure! What of Chazal's teaching that a *baal teshuvah* needs stricter fences than does the perfect tzaddik to protect against sin?[1]

However, exploring the deeper meaning behind this element of our story, we understand that Rebbe Nachman is teaching us one of the deepest and most important secrets in *avodas Hashem*.

---

1. *Menachos* 29b.

The Breslover *mashpi'im* teach that the princess does not intend to lighten the conditions because she doubts the viceroy's abilities. Rather, on a very deep level, the princess is telling the viceroy that even though he had ultimately failed, his effort and *mesiras nefesh* throughout the year in the area of eating accomplished a tremendous amount. Therefore, this time around he needn't refrain from eating on the final day, because there is no longer a necessity for him to work on this condition. The princess's decision doesn't stem from the viceroy's inability to make it through the final day without succumbing to the temptation of satisfying his hunger. Rather, there is simply *no need* for him to work on that condition again. Despite his general failure to complete the mission, his effort in this particular area of *avodas Hashem* met the individual goal of this isolated condition.

This idea is crucial for a healthy experience along the journey toward spiritual success. Unfortunately, many of us have been conditioned to believe that our relationship with Hashem through Torah and mitzvos is all or nothing. Therefore, if we *chas v'shalom* succumb to a temptation and think, speak, or act in a manner contrary to the Torah, we assume that all is lost — nothing positive we have done in the past or may currently be involved with seems to be of any consequence. Seeing *avodas Hashem* like a broad mission in which multiple micro successes in various arenas are required for the sole purpose of a single, primary objective, we are convinced that the final result is all that matters: did we succeed in our mission, or did we fail? After assessing our situation and coming to the resolute conclusion that we have failed, we relegate the various successes along the way to waste and oblivion.

Here, Rebbe Nachman tells us that this couldn't be further from the truth. In Chapter Nine, we learned about the preciousness of holy desire that doesn't merit actualization. There, we learned a teaching from the *Zohar HaKadosh*: *Leis reiusa tava d'isavad*, "No good desire is ever lost." If this is true for pure desire, how much more so does this apply for actions of holiness! Present failure does not erase past progress. Every step toward Hashem's outstretched arms remains forever etched in the scroll of eternity, irrespective of how many steps one subsequently takes in the opposite direction. No matter how strong our feeling of failure may be, as long as life is still being breathed into us by the Master of the world, our mission is yet in progress. There is no despair in the world at all! And the rules of this mission dictate that every success along the way, no matter how small, is collected and cherished and ultimately comes to our assistance in a time of need.

In the words of Rebbe Nachman:

> And know, that every movement and detachment you make, that each time you separate yourself — even if only a little bit — from your physicality and turn toward Hashem, they are all collected and bound together, and they come to your assistance in a time of need.[2]

In another place:

> Regarding the individuals who grow close to *avodas Hashem* only to subsequently grow distant again, Rebbe Nachman declared: Even so, this fleeting closeness is still precious to Hashem.[3]

Even when a Jew is ultimately unable to hold on to a particular devotion and falls, his holy thoughts, words, and actions are celebrated in heaven and Hashem takes eternal pride in them. Although it may seem as if his efforts did not produce tangible results, they are all lovingly gathered and used for his aid in future battles.

This is the message Rebbe Nachman is teaching us in this line

---

2. *Likutei Moharan Tinyana* 48. See also *Sichos HaRan* 11.
3. *Sichos HaRan* 123.

of our tale. Despite his ultimate fall, the viceory's *avodah* in his time of elevation did, in fact, accomplish great things. While he may have been unable to complete this phase of his holy mission, this does not mean that his year was entirely wasted. *Avodas Hashem is not all or nothing.*[4] Each and every positive effort toward holiness is precious to Hashem and represents progress that can never be washed away. When he was forced to stop printing one of his *sefarim* because of a paper shortage, Reb Nosson wrote:

> The difference between something that is holy and something that is not holy is as follows: When building a house, if it is not finished, all efforts have been wasted. But in a holy project, anything that is done is already an accomplishment. I am satisfied with what I have accomplished. Whatever I have printed until now is not wasted.[5]

---

4. An interesting source that further supports this assertion may be found in the Rambam's explanation of the halachah allowing a known sinner to perform *birkas kohanim*. There, the Rambam writes: "We do not tell a wicked person, 'Add on to your wickedness and desist from performing mitzvos.'" (See *Mishnah Berurah* 128:146.) This demonstrates that, despite his current spiritual failings, every act of holiness is considered by itself. Another expression of this idea may be found in the concept of *"tashlumin,"* making up a *tefillah* that was accidentally missed by davening Shemoneh Esrei twice in the following *tefillah*. The halachah states that, when performing *tashlumin*, one must intend for the first Shemoneh Esrei to fulfill the obligation of the current *tefillah* and the second to make up the previous *tefillah* he missed. Perhaps the Torah is teaching us that despite our tendency to assume that we can only move forward once we fix the past, we are still perfectly eligible for Minchah despite having missed Shacharis — each element of *avodas Hashem* is precious in and of itself, irrespective of the past or the future. (*The Depth of Our Connection*, pp. 126–127). See also *Tzidkas HaTzaddik* 58 where Reb Tzadok discusses the concept of a *"tzaddik l'oso davar,"* one who — despite massive failure in other areas of *avodas Hashem* — has perfected a specific element of his personality and may thus be considered a tzaddik with regard to that particular *avodah*. See also *Shmuel I* 12:20–22 and *Shabbos* 31b.

5. *Siach Sarfei Kodesh* #181.

Having perfected his eating the first time around, the viceroy no longer needs to focus on this area of *avodas Hashem*.

LESSONS FOR LIFE

✳ The cry of our *neshamah* that echoes through our being after a devastating fall from our devotions, expressing pain over our failure to live up to her expectations, should not be interpreted as a cry of anger, anguish, and despair. Rather, her expression of just how much she is depending on us to redeem her is intended to reveal her staunch faith in our ability to succeed.

✳ *Avodas Hashem* is not all or nothing. Present failure does not erase past progress. Every step in the direction toward closeness with the Master of the world is valuable in and of itself and its positive effect survives any subsequent downfall.

CHAPTER 13

The Trap of the Fascinating Permitted

בְּכֵן תָּשׁוּב לִבְחֹר לְךָ מָקוֹם, וְתֵשֵׁב גַּם כֵּן שָׁנָה כַּנַּ"ל, וּבַיּוֹם הָאַחֲרוֹן תִּהְיֶה רַשַּׁאי לֶאֱכֹל, רַק שֶׁלֹּא תִּישַׁן, וְלֹא תִּשְׁתֶּה יַיִן כְּדֵי שֶׁלֹּא תִּישַׁן, כִּי הָעִקָּר הוּא הַשֵּׁנָה. וְהָלַךְ וְעָשָׂה כֵּן. בַּיּוֹם הָאַחֲרוֹן הָיָה הוֹלֵךְ לְשָׁם, וְרָאָה מַעְיָן הוֹלֵךְ, וְהַמַּרְאֶה אָדֹם וְהָרֵיחַ שֶׁל יַיִן. וְשָׁאַל אֶת הַמְשָׁרֵת: הֲרָאִיתָ שֶׁזֶּה מַעְיָן, וְרָאוּי שֶׁיִּהְיֶה בּוֹ מַיִם. וְהַמַּרְאֶה אֲדֻמּוֹמִית וְהָרֵיחַ שֶׁל יַיִן! וְהָלַךְ וְטָעַם מֵהַמַּעְיָן, וְנָפַל וְיָשֵׁן מִיָּד כַּמָּה שָׁנִים, עַד שִׁבְעִים שָׁנָה.

"Therefore, return and choose for yourself a place, and sit there for a year, just as before. On the last day you will be allowed to eat, but you must not sleep, and you mustn't drink wine so that you don't fall asleep, for the most important thing is that you remain awake." He went and he did so. On the final day, he began approaching the palace. He saw a flowing river. The river was red, and it smelled like wine.

He asked his servant, "Have you ever seen such a thing — a river of water that appears red and smells like wine!" And he went and tasted from the river. He immediately fell asleep and slept for many years, a period of seventy years.

✳ Choosing a New Place

THE FIRST OF the new set of conditions is that the viceroy is to again choose a place and remain there for a year. It is interesting to note that the princess doesn't merely tell the viceroy to return to the original place he had already chosen. Instead, he must find a new location in which to do his holy work.

Here, Rebbe Nachman is teaching us that each time a Jew returns to *avodas Hashem* after a *yeridah*, a spiritual descent, it is imperative that he becomes a new person, rooted in a "different place" with an informed perspective.

One of the possible benefits of unfortunate mistakes is the ability to learn from them so that we might succeed in the future. If one remains unchanged after erring and simply returns to the same failed strategy, nothing was gained.

The verse states: *K'chu imachem devarim v'shuvu el Hashem*, "Take words with you, and return to Hashem."[1] On a simple level, the commentators explain that *devarim*, words, in this verse refer to the words of Torah, *tefillah*, and confession. But the word "*devarim*" has another meaning as well. In addition to meaning "words," *devarim* can also mean "things." Perhaps on a deeper level, the verse is teaching us that in our return to Hashem, we must "take things" with us — the lessons of what worked and what hasn't; to pick up the broken pieces of our lives and rebuild something stronger with them.

Reb Nosson of Nemirov was once walking with some students through the streets of Breslov. They passed a house that had burned down to the ground. A man, the owner of the house, was searching through the rubble, hoping to salvage some wood to rebuild his home. "Pay close attention to what that man is doing," Reb Nosson told his students. "For this is indeed the proper

---

1. *Hoshea* 14:2.

response to destruction. One must search within the rubble to find the good points that will enable him to carry on."

The good points referred to by Reb Nosson may be seen as the mighty lessons that may be discerned from beneath the smoking rubble of spiritual destruction. If we analyze our errors and use them to inspire positive change and developmental reinforcement, then every mistake we make is one we'll never make again. In the words of the Sfas Emes:

> *Teshuvah* rectifies sin. In truth, the vitality of sin is the existence of [the potentiality for] *teshuvah*, which is enhanced by the existence of sin. It is this factor which provides sin with its life-force.[2]

The potential lessons to be learned from a misstep along the path to *avodas Hashem* provide a premise for the concept of sin. When those mistakes are learned from and *teshuvah* is achieved, those sins are transformed into something else entirely.

Upon finally succeeding to invent a functioning lightbulb after one thousand failed attempts, Thomas Edison was asked by a news reporter: "How did it feel to make a thousand mistakes?" Thinking for a moment, Edison responded, "I didn't make a thousand mistakes. Inventing the lightbulb was simply *a thousand-step process*."

Before reaching his goal, it is indeed likely that Edison viewed those mistakes as serious failures. However, turning around to survey his creative journey from the elevated platform of success, his newfound perspective afforded him the realization that each and every mistake was necessary for his ultimate triumph; each taught him a particular lesson that he would not have been able to learn any other way.

---

2. *Sfas Emes, Chukas*, 5637. See also *Oros HaTeshuvah* 6:2.

In the words of Rav Kook:

> This level of *teshuvah*, which includes those previously mentioned, is already filled with an endless light. It comes to turn all sins into merits; *from all mistakes it derives lofty lessons, from all descents, awesome elevation.*[3]

This is what the princess implies in directing the viceroy to choose a new place.[4] If he returns to his old strategy and level of commitment, things are sure to stay the same. It is only if he succeeds in taking a lesson from his experience that he has any chance of succeeding this time around.[5]

Don't Fall Asleep!

IN THE FIRST set of conditions, holy yearning was to serve as the primary focus of the viceroy. While it appears that the previous conditions must also be met this time as well, the primary focus seems to center around the necessity of the viceroy's remaining awake on the final day.

---

3. *Oros HaTeshuvah*, Chapter 1.
4. See *Menachos* 29b: the *baal teshuvah* must enter the letter "*hei*" via a different entrance than that used by the tzaddikim.
5. It is important to stress that "learning from mistakes" is only possible if that is truly what they are — mistakes. Actively giving in to temptation or acting against one's better judgement for the purpose of discovering a lesson is counterproductive.

In the words of Rabbi David Bashevkin: "There is much to learn from failure. But in order to learn from failure, first every effort must be made to avoid it.... Educational failures emerge from concerted and sincere efforts to succeed that naturally fall short. Pursuing failure in order to learn will just leave a mess. Life will provide plenty of opportunities to learn from failure — but don't go looking for them. You can be sure that they will find you. And when they do, there will be lots to learn." (*Sin•a•gogue*, p. 106)

Reb Nosson writes that sleep is a physical manifestation of a lesser consciousness; a numbing of the soul and a lack of spiritual awareness.[6] When one is far from Hashem and has difficulty allowing his awareness of Hashem's imminence to serve as the deciding factor in his personal choices, he is "asleep" in a spiritual sense. Clarity into his mission in this world and the importance of his every action obscured, he wanders around the arenas of daily life like one who sleepwalks — externally functioning but internally inert.

In order to ensure that the viceroy remains at his pinnacle of spiritual alertness throughout the harrowing period of the final day, the princess forbids him from drinking wine. In a different place, Reb Nosson explains that just as drinking wine induces physical slumber, it can also bring a person to this place of spiritual sleep, causing him to lose touch with his perception of the spiritual realm.[7] It is of utmost importance that the viceroy steer clear of anything that may cause him to lose focus.

✳ The Satan's Deception

FOR A FULL year, the viceroy focused all of his energy toward fulfilling the directives of the princess. Every free moment was spent yearning for her and waiting anxiously for the year's completion when he would be able to redeem the princess at long last. Finally, the long-awaited day arrived! Filled with joy at having reached the climax of this long journey the viceroy walks purposefully toward the palace, just as he had the last time around. This time,

---

6. *Likutei Halachos, Hashakamas HaBoker* 1:2.

7. *Likutei Halachos, Netillas Yadayim Shacharis* 2:16. See also *Likutei Moharan Tinyana* 26.

however, he is far more cautious, weary of temptation and the weakness inherent to his humanity.

As he walks, he suddenly comes upon the strangest sight. A river flows, yet in the place of clear water, he sees a deep red liquid! The air around him is filled with the scent of delicious wine! Awed, the viceroy stops for a moment to behold this wonder. This is the beginning of the end.

Friends, what do you think would have happened if the path to the palace had been lined with barrels of the world's most exquisite wine? Fully aware of his susceptibility to falling, particularly on the final day, the viceroy would surely have turned his eyes from them and continued with confidence. Knowing full well that such an obvious affront would produce no results, the *yetzer hara* cast a much subtler net. Because the viceroy would never knowingly approach the forbidden, the *yetzer hara* clothes the forbidden in the *fascinating permitted.*

"What harm is there in simply approaching this wondrous river?" The voice of the Snake echoes in the viceroy's mind. "It is certainly not wine (despite the fact that it looks and smells that way). Whoever heard of a river of wine? This must be some strange kind of water. You simply *must* get a closer look at this amazing sight!" Despite the fact that chances of a liquid that looks and smells like wine being water are very slim, the slight possibility created by this illusion provides the justification necessary for the viceroy to approach for a closer look. Such is the power of the *yetzer hara.*

This strategy is a favorite with the *yetzer hara* and one that he commonly employs. So often, the *yetzer hara* clothes the forbidden in the fascinating permitted, convincing us that the innocent curiosity drawing us to a story, food, experience, or website negates any chance of the story being *lashon hara*, the food being less than kosher, the experience being improper, and the website being inappropriate. So often, seemingly innocuous curiosity serves as the doorway to the lowest places. This is the sly deception of the *yetzer hara* who, as Rebbe Nachman writes, clothes himself in that which is permitted, sometimes even convincing us that what he wills us to do is a mitzvah![8]

This strategy is even more effective since it thrives on the Jew's confidence in his ability to guard against sinning overtly. It is the Jew's certainty, founded on the lesson learned from previous failures, that — due to his increased vigilance — he will not fall, which provides the license to explore the fascinating permitted. True, he isn't exactly sure what this experience is (which is what makes it so intriguing in the first place), but one thing he knows for sure: if at any point this experience is revealed as being improper or sinful, he will immediately escape back to the safety of the straight and narrow.

Unfortunately, however, this often isn't the case. The moment he lets his guard down to investigate even the permissible garment of sin, it is already too late. While he hasn't yet been chewed up and swallowed, his head is already caught in the lion's jaws.

If the *yetzer hara* was desperate on the final day of the previous year, now, knowing that the viceroy's guard would be up against overt temptation this time around, he is even more frantic. As we have learned in Chapter Ten, the *yetzer hara* saves his best for last — this strategy is the sneakiest and most effective in the Satan's playbook.

Tragically, the viceroy falls for the *yetzer hara*'s nefarious ruse and drinks from the river. It is incorrect to suggest that the viceroy's tasting from the river represents his falling for the temptation of drinking wine. Rather, tasting from the river is itself still a part of his investigation of the fascinating permitted, this marvel

---

8. *Likutei Moharan* 1. See also *Derech Chaim* on *Avos* 1:1, *"V'chein mah she'amar v'asu."* Alternatively, it is possible that the *yetzer hara* attempts to utilize the fact that the *Sefirah* of *Malchus* is related to the concept of "grapes" (see *Zohar, Vayechi*, 238a) to convince the viceroy that even if the water were in fact to be wine, drinking from it would somehow aid him in his goal of freeing the lost princess.

of a river whose water looks and smells like wine.[9] It is in the midst of an innocent quest to satisfy his curiosity that he steps on the land mine which explodes in his face, completely destroying the entirety of his mission. The *yetzer hara* is victorious once again, and the viceroy has blown his second opportunity to free the lost princess.

A Lifetime of Despair

AFTER FALLING FOR temptation the previous time, the viceroy had slept for many years. This time, he sleeps for seven decades. The Breslover *mashpi'im* teach that while after his initial failure the viceroy had fallen into spiritual slumber, this time, giving up on his ability to free the princess, he forgets about her entirely. Traumatized by a devastating downfall caused by innocent curiosity, the tzaddik within feels that he will never again be able to free the holy fire of youth and conquer the Jew's being. If everything in the world represents an obstacle to serving God, how can he possibly move forward?

In *Tehillim*, David HaMelech sings, *Yemei shenaseinu bahem shivim shanah*, "The days of our lives are seventy years."[10] The viceroy sleeps in the darkness of his confusion for a full lifetime; many Jews in this sorry situation remain in a perpetual state of hopelessness for the remainder of their days. Indeed, the viceroy no longer makes it back to the orderly palace of evil. This time, the lost princess will need to come to him.

---

9. The Breslover *mashpi'im* teach that while the viceroy's first failure parallels the *Cheit Eitz HaDaas*, which was founded upon physical desire, the second failure parallels the *Cheit HaEigel*, which was more intellectual/spiritual in nature.

10. *Tehillim* 90:10.

LESSONS FOR LIFE

✹ When returning to *avodas Hashem* after a fall, it is important to begin anew from a post-fall perspective, built on the lessons that were learned and the perspective gained. Eventually, one will come to see all of his mistakes as having been steps along the path to success.

✹ Just as wine has the ability to induce physical slumber, if used improperly, it can bring a state of "spiritual sleep" upon the Jew, numbing his sensitivities and causing him to lose his perception of the spiritual realm.

✹ Having learned a lesson about his vulnerability after initial failure, the Jew can no longer be easily seduced by overt temptation. Instead, the *yetzer hara* lures him in with the fascinating permitted — that which appeals to our innocent curiosity and sense for novelty. Once caught in the trap, it is very difficult to pull away.

CHAPTER 14

The Strategy of Emunah

וְהָיוּ הוֹלְכִין חֲיָלוֹת רַבּוֹת עִם הַשַּׁיָּךְ לָהֶם, מַה שֶּׁנּוֹסֵעַ
אַחֲרֵיהֶם, וְהַמְשָׁרֵת הִטְמִין עַצְמוֹ מֵחֲמַת הַחֲיָלוֹת. אַחַר
כָּךְ הָלְכָה מֶרְכָּבָה וַעֲגָלוֹת־צָב, וְשָׁם יָשְׁבָה הַבַּת מֶלֶךְ,
וְעָמְדָה שָׁם אֶצְלוֹ, וְיָרְדָה וְיָשְׁבָה אֶצְלוֹ וְהִכִּירָה אוֹתוֹ,
וְהָיְתָה מְנַעֶרֶת אוֹתוֹ מְאֹד, וְלֹא נִנְעַר.

Many troops passed, with a procession and equipment that accompanied them. The servant hid himself because of the soldiers. After the troops passed,
a chariot and covered wagon approached. In it, sat
the princess. The procession stopped nearby. The
princess descended and sat next to the viceroy. She
recognized him. She shook him very much, but he
did not wake.

✳ The Intellect Hides

AFTER MANY DESPERATE years of numbness and despair, something finally happens — soldiers pass by the place where the viceroy slumbers. These troops belong to the Other Side, the army of the *yetzer hara*. Having triumphed over the viceroy and disrupted his holy mission, the *yetzer hara* travels with free rein, parading his forces with great pomp and ceremony.

The Breslover *mashpi'im* teach that this is *all* the *yetzer hara* truly has — pomp and ceremony. The desires of this world are so transient that they have no real influence over a thinking person. "Vanity of vanities," cried Shlomo HaMelech, wisest of men. "All is vain."[1] The Gemara teaches, "A person only sins if a spirit of folly has entered him."[2] And Rebbe Nachman echoes, "For, in truth, to a person who has even a slight measure of wisdom, the yetzer hara is folly and madness."[3]

Chazal teach that in the world to come, the wicked will be able to see the *yetzer hara* for what it really was — a tiny hair.[4] In this world, however, the *yetzer hara* puffs itself up (much like chametz, which, as the *Rishonim* write, symbolizes the *yetzer hara*) and makes itself look fearfully seductive. Here he travels with many troops, outfitted with frightful weapons and a powerful artillery, creating the illusion that there is no escape from his reach.

In Chapter Four, we learned that the viceroy symbolizes the tzaddik within, the point of holiness that constantly seeks to expand, rise, and conquer the Jew's being and set his or her heart aflame with the service of Hashem. When the viceroy is awake, the strength of his passion is such that nothing can get in his way.

---

1. *Koheles* 1:2.
2. *Sotah* 3a.
3. *Likutei Moharan* 72.
4. *Sukkah* 52a.

Regardless of what the *yetzer hara* might do to frighten him into submission, nothing works — his courage allows him to overcome every obstacle with ease. Therefore, the only way for the *yetzer hara* to overpower him is by using that very confidence to his benefit. Both times, it was the viceroy's overconfidence that allowed him to fall prey to the *yetzer hara*'s cunning traps. Now, with the viceroy in a deep sleep and the servant — who symbolizes the powers of intellect — on his own, the *yetzer hara* reverts to scare tactics to dispose of him as well.

Rebbe Nachman teaches that in response to terrible intimidation from the troops, the servant's response is to hide. What is the deeper meaning?

Throughout the journey of life, there are times we feel as if we are disconnected from our mission. Be it a result of physical desires, fear, financial stress, sadness, confusion, or the myriad responsibilities of daily life, we become detached from the foundations of our existence — the inner viceroy falls asleep. In this sorry scenario, the servant — our intellect — remains awake, and attempts to "rouse the viceroy" by helping us rediscover the rational truth of our holy tradition. However, when the terrifying troops of the *yetzer hara* arrive and threaten to compromise the servant's intellectual integrity, there is only one thing he can do to save himself, and that is to hide.

When Rebbe Nachman writes that the servant hid from the soldiers, he is teaching that when the *yetzer hara* assaults our ideas as the inner tzaddik slumbers, the powers of intellect must temporarily cease and give way to pure, unadulterated *emunah*, simple faith. Philosophizing and attempting to counter the *yetzer hara*'s reasoning never yields success. The *yetzer hara* is a consummate academic, rooted in the forces of Amalek, a power Rebbe Nachman equates with the cool, "rational," heresies of secular thought.[5] *Emunah*,

---

5. See *Likutei Moharan Tinyana* 19.

however, is beyond his reach. When the intellect hides itself and the Jew shifts gears from intellectual clarity to simple faith, neither the intimidation nor the philosophizing of the *yetzer hara* can make any impression on his relationship with the Master of the world.

In *Likutei Moharan*, Rebbe Nachman writes:

> And the same applies to prayer. At first, one experiences many obstacles with regard to prayer. Afterward, when he overcomes them all and arrives to pray, only to find that his heart is crooked and perverse before Hashem, this is the greatest obstacle of all. This is an aspect of, "My heart was engulfed," which Onkelos renders as "Surrounded." Meaning, his heart is surrounded and engulfed with challenges, questions, and heretical ideas regarding Hashem... the questions in one's heart are the greatest obstacle.

In this passage, Rebbe Nachman paints a portrait of a Jew who finds his heart engulfed in doubt, numb to any perception of a Creator or His presence in our cold, dark world. This crisis of faith serves as a fearful obstacle that prevents him from engaging in a Torah lifestyle. In the lines that follow, Rebbe Nachman outlines the unlikely remedy.

> In such a situation, one must scream to our Father in heaven with a powerful scream from the depths of one's heart. Hashem will then hear his voice and turn toward his cry. It is possible that this will itself cause the failure and nullification of all of his questions and obstacles.

With these words, the tzaddik is teaching us an amazing thing. When one is challenged with questions and doubts that eat at his or her faith, instead of seeking to respond to the issue directly through philosophical clarification or theological fortification, one must simply cry out from the depths of one's heart. When a Jew cries out to the very God he is having trouble believing in, this expression activates the hidden love and concealed faith latent in the very core of the Jewish soul in the most wondrous way.

Immediately, the insanity implicit in all arrogant thoughts of existential independence fades away, revealing the simple bond of utter clarity that pulses in our veins as *maaminim b'nei maaminim*. Perhaps this is what Chazal are communicating in their teaching that in the heat of a battle with the *yetzer hara*, a Jew should recite Krias Shema.[6] In that moment, the Jew must distance himself from philosophical calculations and simply express his faith in Hashem and in the paramount importance of adhering to His Will. Hiding away and allowing simple faith to flourish is the only manner in which the intellect can emerge victorious.

Under attack by the challenge to faith potentially embodied in the entirety of our existence, the Jewish response is to close our physical eyes to the external smokescreen and open our inner, spiritual eyes. This allows us to perceive the intuitive awareness of Hashem's light that shines through the prisms of our many conscious and subconscious memories of contact with His presence, all rooted in the constant kiss between creation and Creator which brings all of existence into being, each and every moment.

In the words of a great Jewish thinker:

> The essence of Jewish religious thinking does not lie in entertaining a concept of God but in the ability to articulate a memory of moments of illumination by His presence. Am Yisrael is not a people of definers but a people of witnesses: "You are My witnesses."[7] Reminders of what has been disclosed to us are hanging over our souls like stars, remote and of mind-surpassing grandeur. They shine through the dark and dangerous ages, and their reflection can be seen in the lives of those who guard the path of conscience and memory in the wilderness of careless living.[8]

---

6. *Berachos* 5a.
7. *Yeshayahu* 43:10.
8. *Between God and Man*, p. 70.

❋ A Tragic Indicator

WE HAVE LEARNED that all the forces of impurity in the world derive their strength from the side of holiness. Therefore, amidst the troops of the *yetzer hara* sits the princess, the fire of youth in captivity. Wherever they go, she must go as well. Better stated — *if they are to go*, the princess must go as well, for she is their source of energy.

While the nature of this reality is tragic, it carries an exceedingly positive implication. In these words, Rebbe Nachman is reinforcing the notion that wherever the troops of impurity and concealment are found, one can discover the Lost Princess of holiness from deep beneath the rubble — if he is only wise enough to search. Regardless of how far one has fallen and the mighty onslaught of lowly temptation he faces, he can be sure that commensurate with the *yetzer hara's* awesome energy are the powers of holiness that lie dormant in that struggle, simply waiting to be discovered and channeled again toward the pursuit of a relationship with the Master of the world.

❋ Ever Recognizable

"SHE RECOGNIZED HIM." Despite his mighty failures and the deep spiritual slumber into which he has fallen, Rebbe Nachman teaches that the viceroy never loses his recognizability. Despite his tremendous errors and the untold damage his actions have caused in the spiritual realm, he never stops being the viceroy, the person who sacrificed so much, who yearned so much, who refuses to give up in his quest for holiness.

There comes a time in the life of the Jew where he reaches spiritual "rock bottom." In that moment, he becomes entirely unhinged from the mission he set out upon, to the point that he feels he has lost his identity. Instead of saying, "Where in the world am I?" like the viceroy did in the past, he unfortunately wonders, "*Who* in the world am I?" — from his current perspective, he is unable to perceive his true essence. All he sees is desolation — the result of his mistakes which led to such drastic failures that he doubts he will ever recover.

But in truth, there is no such thing. Although he may not be able to truly experience this view in his current, lowly state, a Jew must always believe that regardless of how much dirt he has on his face, he is forever recognizable to the Shechinah, the Lost Princess of passion and youthful excitement in *avodas Hashem*. She is able to behold the viceroy's true essence, the brilliant rays of light shining forth from all he has done *right* over the course of his journey — his consuming desire to free the princess and the many difficulties he has faced fighting for this noble cause; the deserts, fields, and forests he needed to pass through before finding her; his years of yearning for the lost princess as he carefully followed her instructions, and so on. Internally, the viceroy has lost his ability to perceive the truth of his essence and realign himself with the mission he has set out to accomplish. However, from an external perspective, he looks just the same. The mistakes he has made have done nothing to obscure his true nature to an observer with an elevated perspective.[9]

> With these words, the holy Rebbe is speaking to our souls: "Don't think that after you have fallen these two times and deserted the Shechinah that they no longer recognize you above. On the contrary; the Shechinah descends to you and recognizes you — they still take tremendous pride in you above."[10]

---

9. See *Even Sheleimah* 3:2 which is rooted in the Gra's explanation to the *aggados* of *Sabei D'bei Atunah* where the tzaddik writes that the goodness of one's heart expressed in *bitachon* can yet be maintained despite terrible transgressions, mere actions that do not reflect one's essence.

10. *Orach Mishor*, p. 49.

The viceroy's failure to free the lost princess has required her to become proactive in winning her freedom. Despite the great pain and frustration she is certainly experiencing due to the mistakes of the viceroy that have led to his repeated failure, the princess is still relying on the viceroy's help to free her from captivity. She has stopped here not to yell at the viceroy and berate him for his folly, but because she still believes in him despite his many failures. She still has faith in his ability to learn from his mistakes, trusting that he can again gather his strength, summon his courage, and resume the struggle.

But the viceroy is so deeply sunk in his slumber of despair, apathy, confusion, and spiritual disorientation that even her positive expression of faith and encouragement fails to wake him. This is a step he will need to take on his own, when the night of his despair gives way and a dawn of hope breaks once more.

LESSONS FOR LIFE

❋ With the inner point of righteousness obscured by spiritual slumber, the *yetzer hara* attacks the intellect of a Jew, attempting to destroy his rational commitment to Torah and *avodas Hashem*. In this situation, one must exchange his intellectual understanding for simple faith; super-rational belief in God that is not contingent upon human reasoning.

❋ The evil forces cannot exist without drawing energy from the realms of holiness. Therefore, wherever a proliferation of spiritual darkness appears, one can rest assured that there is a large measure of holiness concealed within, waiting to be discovered and redeemed.

✳ When the motivating force of purity within a Jew
is overcome with spiritual numbness and despair, it
loses the ability to grasp its true essence — it ceases
to recognize the holiness at its core. However, the
passion of youth forever maintains the ability to penetrate beyond the surface, perceiving the true nature
of the inner tzaddik's identity.

CHAPTER 15

Teachings
Awash with Tears

וְהִתְחִילָה לִקְבֹּל עָלָיו, אֲשֶׁר כַּמָּה וְכַמָּה יְגִיעוֹת וּטְרָחוֹת
גְּדוֹלוֹת מְאֹד שֶׁהָיוּ לוֹ זֶה כַּמָּה וְכַמָּה שָׁנִים כְּדֵי לְהוֹצִיא
אוֹתִי, וּבִשְׁבִיל אוֹתוֹ הַיּוֹם שֶׁהָיָה יָכוֹל לְהוֹצִיאֵנִי וְאִבְּדוֹ.
וְהָיְתָה בּוֹכָה מְאֹד עַל זֶה, כִּי יֵשׁ רַחֲמָנוּת גָּדוֹל עָלָיו
וְעָלַי, שֶׁכָּל כָּךְ זְמַן שֶׁאֲנִי כָּאן, וְאֵינִי יְכוֹלָה לָצֵאת. אַחַר
כָּךְ לָקְחָה מִטְפַּחַת מֵעַל רֹאשָׁהּ וְכָתְבָה עָלָיו בַּדְּמָעוֹת
שֶׁלָּהּ, וְהִנִּיחָה אֶצְלוֹ. וְעָמְדָה וְיָשְׁבָה בְּמֶרְכַּבְתָּהּ, וְנָסְעָה
מִשָּׁם.

She began to bemoan, "How many immense difficulties and toils he has undergone for so many years
in order to free me, and on the day he could have
freed me he lost everything..." She began to cry
greatly over all of this [saying], "For there is great
pity upon him and upon me, for I have been held
captive here for so long and I am unable to leave..."

She then took the scarf from her head and wrote
on it with her tears. She placed it next to him. She
went and sat in her chariot, and they traveled on.

⊛ Outpouring of Anguish — And Encouragement

IN THE PREVIOUS chapter, we read that the lost princess came to the place where the viceroy lay fast asleep and tried to wake him — to no avail. The viceroy had sunken so far into the dark pit of spiritual confusion that even a visit from the princess herself fails to inspire him. Anguished and despairing, she pours out her broken heart before his slumbering soul.

As in the meeting between the princess and the viceroy subsequent to his first failure, the princess does not mean to berate the viceroy with her words by accentuating the magnitude of his failure. In fact, her intention is quite the contrary. Having failed to waken the viceroy despite her best efforts, the princess realizes that his spiritual situation is extremely precarious. Her deeply intuitive wisdom grants her the understanding that the very last thing the viceroy needs is a talking to — he has already beat himself up more than enough. Indeed, this is what brought about his slumber of utter hopelessness in the first place. No, now is not the time to chastise the viceroy. Instead, the viceroy needs to be reminded of everything he has done right in the effort to free her. Her intention is to encourage the viceroy by reminding him how resolute he has been in desiring holiness and empathizing with his pain at having failed in the mission for which he sacrificed so very much.

Along the journey toward the Lost Princess of our lives there are times we fail to reach a certain goal despite our very best efforts. After days or weeks of working hard on our *shemiras einayim*, the *yetzer hara* blindsides us with a tremendous *nisayon*, catching us unprepared. Soon after taking it upon ourselves to speak only good about others, office politics trip us up and our streak comes to an end. In the midst of our efforts to erase anger from our lives, someone spills his coffee all over our freshly laundered shirt, sending us into a rage. While the natural, proper reaction in these situations is to be disappointed in ourselves and utilize this brokenheartedness to return with even greater commitment, there are times when the fall is so devastating that instead of serving a constructive purpose, the intensity of the disappointment leads to hopelessness and despair.

Here, Rebbe Nachman is teaching us an important lesson: In this case, a different response is called for: *Pride* over the resolve and tremendous effort we exhibited, and *compassion* for ourselves over the acute pain we are feeling.[1]

In the words of Rav Kook:

> When one feels so weighed down that one cannot even take the smallest step toward growth, it is necessary to rise up through the trait of holy pride. One must look at himself in an entirely positive way and find the good qualities inside all of his flaws.[2]

In another place:

> Just as regret in the heart of man is a positive thing, encouragement is also absolutely essential, so as to allow him to serve Hashem in Torah and *avodah* with a clear mind.[3]

---

1. It is also helpful to remember Chazal's teachings: "One who performs an *aveirah* and is ashamed because of it is forgiven for all his sins" (*Berachos* 12b), and "Better is a single pang of guilt in one's heart than many lashes" (*Berachos* 7a). Reb Tzadok HaKohen elaborates: "The anguish that one feels over the sins he committed are literally the suffering of Gehinnom for those sins..." (*Tzidkas HaTzaddik* 57; see also 153). See also *Orchos Tzaddikim Shaar HaCharatah*: "Regret... is a straight path with regard to the matter of *teshuvah*, for one who sins and regrets it, it is considered as if he did not sin," and *Chayei Moharan, Sippurim Chadashim* 91: "This that I threw down my head — if a person who had transgressed the entire Torah eight hundred times had thrown down his head with such bitterness, he would certainly have been granted forgiveness."

2. *Middos HaRAYaH,* "*Gaavah*" 26.

3. *Oros HaTeshuvah* 14:13.

By stressing how greatly she is depending on him to rescue her from the palace of evil and reiterating that he is her only hope, the princess intends to encourage the viceroy. She hopes that by letting him know how much she still believes in his ability to carry out his mission — if he will only allow himself to see beyond the failure of the past and look toward a brighter future — the viceroy will be strengthened to wake from his slumber and continue his journey.

This is one of the main lessons Rebbe Nachman intends to impart through the medium of this awesome tale: *the princess of holy passion never, ever gives up on any Jew.* Regardless of how far one has fallen or how numb he or she has become to a spiritual lifestyle, the princess of youthful vitality forever maintains a connection with the core of the Jewish soul, the place where he or she is entirely pure, perfectly good, and completely innocent. Indeed, even when the viceroy, the inner tzaddik, falls into spiritual slumber, the princess can intuit the deep center of holiness even further within — the *Nekudah Tovah* within the *Nekudah Tovah*,[4] the indestructible holiness at the core of the Jewish soul. In their holy words, the tzaddikim intend to teach our nation to pick up the frequency of her whispered messages. This story is Rebbe Nachman's way of opening our hearts to reality as seen from her elevated perspective.

✻ Garments of Light:
The Inner Dimension of the Torah

AFTER POURING OUT her heart in an impassioned soliloquy, the princess removes her headscarf and writes on it with her tears. The Breslover *mashpi'im* teach that these tear-soaked words

---

4. See *Liktuei Moharan* 282.

represent the teachings of *"Penimiyus HaTorah"* — the inner dimension of the Torah wherein God's presence can be readily experienced in the deepest manner.[5] What is the connection between a headscarf and the teachings of the tzaddikim wherein the awesome secrets of the Torah are disclosed in a manner accessible to each and every Jew?

As a portion of God on High, the Jewish soul has the unique capacity to bind itself to a world of spiritual illumination and fill the mighty headquarters of heart and mind with the most profound thoughts and feelings. Reb Nosson of Nemirov teaches that these spiritual lights are shining constantly. Founded upon its holy letters, creation's daily renewal is an embodiment of the *Chiddushei Torah* constantly being channeled into our world, brand-new vistas of the deepest and most delightful teachings of absolute truth.[6] But in order to access these life-giving streams of illumination, one must have the proper vessels. If one who has not

---

5. *Penimiyus HaTorah* may be defined as any works that relate to the deeper elements of our tradition and delve into the inner nature of the Torah's precepts, including, but not limited to, Hashem's creation of and relationship with the world, the human soul, *Shabbos Kodesh*, Eretz Yisrael, *Limud HaTorah*, *Tefillah*, the mitzvos, the deep symbolism underlying the various episodes in Tanach and the *aggados* of Chazal, etc. While, in its purest form, *penimiyus haTorah* is sourced in the *Zohar HaKadosh* and the writings of the Arizal, Ramak, and Rashash along with their various commentaries, due to the intricate, abstract, and difficult nature of these studies, tzaddikim of recent centuries have been rendering these concepts into terms that are far more accessible to us. Some examples of these works (most of which have been translated into English) are: the writings of the Maharal MiPrague, the writings of the Ramchal, the writings of the Leshem, *Sefer Nefesh HaChaim*, the writings of Rav Avraham Yitzchak HaKohen Kook, the writings of Rav Yitzchak Hutner, and, it goes without saying, the works of the Chassidic masters such as the Baal HaTanya, Reb Tzadok HaKohen, Rebbe Nachman and his students, the Sfas Emes, and the Nesivos Shalom which seem to most effectively set the heart of the student aflame with the depth, sweetness, and relevance of Hashem's Torah.

6. See *Tzidkas HaTzaddik* 217.

achieved the requisite purity attempts to tap this flow and delve into these great insights on his own, he may experience them as darkness.[7] Much like a person who walks directly into brilliant sunlight after spending months in a pitch-black cave, the light will damage his eyes instead of helping him to see. How, then, is it possible for a simple Jew to tap into this awesome light, our holy nation's inheritance?

This is the sacred task of the tzaddikim in each generation. Rebbe Nachman teaches that the entire focus of the true tzaddikim is to enable Jews to escape cycles of lowliness and sin by granting them access to the greatest and most elevated wisdom.[8] Acutely aware that only the greatest spiritual lights are powerful enough to illuminate the awesome darkness of our times, these merciful leaders seek to allow us to taste from this special realm of Torah where the awesome sweetness, relevance, and absolute truth of our tradition oozes from every corner and angle.[9] But how are they to deliver these earth-shattering ideas, vast as the ocean, into the puny, broken vessels of the nation entrusted to their care? This conundrum is the primary focus of their toil and represents their main accomplishment.

Reb Nosson explains that in order to allow even the lowliest Jew to safely access Torah secrets that stand at the very apex of the world, the tzaddikim create garments which allow the most powerful spiritual lights to filter through in a manner that will not cause damage to the yearning eyes of their simple followers.[10] The teachings, parables, stories, hand motions, facial expressions, and melodies of the great tzaddikim represent garments of different sizes, shapes, and functions that allow their students to

---

7. See *Sparks from Berditchov*, p. 121.
8. *Likutei Moharan Tinyana* 7.
9. *Likutei Moharan* 30.
10. *Likutei Moharan* 60:6. See also *Mei HaShiloach*, Vol. 1, *Chukas*, "*Vayikchu*."

catch a glimpse of a realm beyond. The tzaddikim are not the light itself, but the channel through which the light is revealed to their generation. These leaders are brilliant tailors; their *sefarim* are closets full of the most awesome garments — tapestries of illumination created by the intricate weaving together of verses, statements of Chazal, and teachings of the Kabbalah.[11] It is for this reason that the teachings of *penimiyus haTorah* are symbolized in our tale by a garment.

Rebbe Nachman specifically chose a *mitpachat*, a garment related to the head, to convey that these teachings grant the Jew a brand-new consciousness, an elevated way of processing the world around him and life within it. The headscarf upon which these words are written symbolizes the ability of these teachings to envelop our intellect with holy concepts and guard our mind from improper ideas.[12]

While the teachings of these tzaddikim appear to be written in black ink upon white parchment, Rebbe Nachman is teaching us that this is merely an illusion. In truth, every letter is written with the tears of the Shechinah, the essence of the collective Jewish soul which, while often lost and ignored, never despairs from being reinstated to her former glory and continuously pleads with the inner tzaddik to rescue her from captivity. From the yearning eyes of a national soul refined to the core in a two-thousand-year process of pain and wandering flow the sweetest waters of holy stubbornness, lucidity, and radical optimism.[13]

---

11. *Likutei Halachos, K'lei Begadim* 4. See also *Tiferes Shlomo, Vayikra*, "O"Y v'kamatz misham."

12. See *Shabbos* 77b: "The head covering of Torah scholars is called *sudara*, an acronym for "*sod yareh*," which is a reference to the verse: "The counsel of the Lord is with those who fear Him [*sod Hashem lirei'av*]" (*Tehillim* 25:14).

13. See *Likutei Moharan* 262, where Rebbe Nachman teaches that the novel Torah thoughts revealed by the tzaddikim are a result of their crying. In *Likutei Moharan* 250 the Rebbe teaches, based on a *gemara* in *Shabbos*, that tears are

Although previously inaccessible to the masses, at the very end of time, wondrous garments have been constructed to disclose the healing light of the Torah's soul — illuminating every letter and law with lofty light and relevance. The princess leaves this awesome tool alongside the slumbering figure of the viceroy, trusting that by studying the works of these merciful tzaddikim, he will find the inner strength to hear her voice, accept her message, and carry on with his mission.

❀ A Progression of Disclosure

AS IT IS clear to any student of Rebbe Nachman's works, the Rebbe was speaking directly to our generation, the final generation before the coming of Mashiach.[14] This focus upon the teachings of *penimiyus haTorah* and the central role they play in the redemption of the Lost Princess of youthful passion and soulful connection is another example of the far-reaching vision of this awesome tzaddik.

A brief survey of our nation's glorious past reveals that as history unfolds, this dimension of Torah study has been, and continues to be, progressively disclosed by the tzaddikim of each subsequent generation. Beginning with the publication of the *Zohar HaKadosh* in the thirteenth century, which allowed every Jew access to teachings which, while given to Moshe Rabbeinu on Har Sinai, had been hitherto concealed from the public eye, this process continued with the writings of the Arizal, Maharal, Ramchal, Rashash, and the Vilna Gaon, among others. Finally,

---

an extension of one's eyesight, and that portions of vision are drawn into the tears. Thus, the teachings of the tzaddikim are filled with their holy eyesight, their elevated perspective on the world.

14. See *Sichos HaRan* 207 and 208.

nearly three hundred years ago, the Baal Shem Tov, founder of the Chassidic movement, constructed a mighty archway into this dimension of Torah study by rendering Kabbalistic ideas into immediate psychological terms relating to the Jew's inner world and religious experience. This initial revelation was greatly expounded upon by the subsequent generations of Chassidic masters, especially by Rebbe Nachman of Breslov and the tzaddikim of the Lubavitcher dynasty, until our times, a period about which the venerable Leshem, Rav Shlomo Elyashiv writes:

> What was forbidden to investigate and expound upon just yesterday becomes permissible today. This is felt by every true scholar. Numerous matters whose awesome nature repelled one from even approaching in previous generations — behold, they are easily grasped today. This is because the gates of human understanding below have been opened up as a result of the steadily increasing flow of Divine revelations above.[15]

Rav Kook elaborates:

> Together with the tangible compulsion to expand the mind with the secrets of Torah comes the increase of ability and capacity to fulfill this obligation. Furthermore, it is not simply that the ability for the mind to grasp deep and hidden thoughts has increased. The ability to develop [this area of Torah] in a concrete manner, through classes and writing, with the mouth and the pen, has strengthened as well.[16]

The question begs: What is the reason for this development so clearly sanctioned by the Divine Master Plan? Why is it so important

---

15. *Leshem Shevo V'Achlamah, Sefer HaBiurim,* part 11, p. 22. See also *Tanya, Iggeres HaKodesh,* Chapter 26, and *Hachsharas HaAvreichim: Mevo HaShearim,* Chapter 3.
16. *Havu Ohr,* p. 36.

for our generation in particular to be exposed to the awesome secrets of Torah which, until relatively recently, had been so heavily concealed from public view? Why is it that the Jews of our generation feel an urgent need to dig deeper than their grandparents ever dreamed possible, to clarify the deepest issues of faith and peel back the layers of the Torah to discover its shining core?

⊛ The Search for Emotional Stimulation

AMONG THE PERSONAL writings of the Piaseczner Rebbe *Hy"d*, we find the following passage:

> The human soul relishes sensation; not only a pleasant feeling but simply the very experience of stimulation — even if that sensation comes from depression or crying. People will watch distressing scenes and listen to heartrending stories so that they might cry and experience emotional stimulation. Such is human nature and a need of the soul, just like all its other needs and natures. Therefore, one who is clever will fulfill this need with passionate prayer and Torah learning. The soul whose Divine service is without passionate feeling will have to find its stimulation elsewhere: It will either be driven to cheap, even forbidden, sensation, or it will become emotionally ill from lack of stimulation.[17]

More so than at any other time in history, the heart and mind of today's Jew is engulfed with negative passions stemming from the newfound, almost total accessibility of the transient pleasures this world has to offer. In order to combat this onslaught of impurity, Hashem has granted our generation equally newfound access to the deepest light of Torah; teachings of a deep, emotional, and exciting nature that allow for every detail of Torah to be placed in

---

17. *Tzav V'Ziruz* 9.

an all-encompassing system of lucidity, meaning, and emotional import. As we have discussed, negative passions often serve to indicate tremendous spiritual energy waiting to be channeled in the proper manner. This elevated awareness allows us to understand that beyond our generation's lusts, desires, and anxieties lies a collective soul that is crying out for depth and light, for broad expanses in Torah thought that can illuminate the impenetrable obscurity of our faith's myriad particularities. It is only when the passion and excitement afforded by the inner light of Torah is denied to our souls that we search elsewhere for the stimulation we so desperately crave.

Rebbe Nachman of Breslov taught:

It is not good to be old; even to be an old chassid or an old tzaddik. Being old is not a good thing, for one must constantly renew himself.[18]

When David HaMelech begged Hashem, *Al tashlicheini l'eis ziknah*, "Cast me not into old age!", he wasn't asking Hashem to spare him from physical aging. Rather, as Rebbe Nachman explains, David's cry embodies the terrible fear of the true servant of God that the flame of his youthful excitement in *avodas Hashem* may one day flicker and grow dim. Just as one can be physically old and yet young at heart with eyes still filled with the wonder and excitement of a small child, it is possible for the agile body of a young teen to house the weak heart, infirm mind, and impassive mentality of an old, lonely person whose broken dreams of the past and harsh reality of the present make life hardly worth living. This is what Rebbe Nachman meant when he echoed David's plea of "Cast me not into old age!" with the words "It is not good to be old." The tzaddik is teaching that it is of ultimate importance in our generation to address the problem of how to study and fulfill every detail of halachah with a lively spirit of excitement and the conscious awareness of Hashem's presence which serves as the

---

18. *Sichos HaRan* 51.

soul to this seemingly technical checklist, imbuing it with a sense of warmth, life, and spirit. If we are to preserve the chain of an age-old tradition that has survived the storms of history to be entrusted into the hands of the final generation by those marked with pale blue numbers, we need to discover a way to engage with Yiddishkeit on an emotional level, using Torah and mitzvos not as an end, but as the ultimate means toward our true goal of building a personal relationship with our Father in heaven. Only such a Judaism will make an impact on our children strong enough to prevent them from seeking this emotional fulfillment elsewhere, as the Piaseczner has taught us. Only involvement with Torah and mitzvos in which an all-important relationship with the Master of the world is at stake can enable them to stand strong in a world where their souls are constantly under the powerful draw and magnetism of physical delights and the false grace of secularism.

In addition to the emotional impact of the manner in which the deeper texts frame *avodas Hashem* as a relationship with the Master of the world, Rebbe Nachman taught that the very process of studying Torah of this nature is one that engenders passion and excitement. In the tzaddik's words:

> Attaining a fiery passion and enthusiasm for Hashem requires movement. This is something we can perceive with our senses; movement causes heat. If one shoots an arrow tipped with wax, the wax will melt because of the warmth generated by the arrow's movement. Similarly, when a person moves from place to place, his movement causes him to (grow warm and) sweat... This applies in a spiritual sense as well. When one's mind contemplates the greatness of Hashem and His holy Torah, passing quickly from thought to thought, this mental friction and the warmth it generates causes his heart to become enflamed toward Hashem.[19]

---

19. *Likutei Moharan* 156.

While it is possible for one who is fluent in the underlying laws that manifest throughout the Torah's legal system to attain this mental friction using the laws of the revealed portion of Torah, this kind of spiritual friction is most easily attained in the realm of *penimiyus haTorah.* It is there that the underlying spiritual system that binds all of Torah — both the stories in Tanach and its laws, both halachah and Aggadah — in a single bond of Divine unity is revealed. These theological constructs lend themselves to imagery that may be explored with the mind. Elsewhere, Rebbe Nachman writes:

> Know, that there are "rooms of Torah." If one merits, when he begins to originate novel Torah thoughts, he enters into these rooms and passes from room to room. For in each room there are many doors to other rooms, and from those rooms to different rooms, and he enters, exploring them all and collecting riches and tremendously valuable and dear treasures — fortunate is his portion![20]

Although Rebbe Nachman refers here to originating our own *chiddushim,* something not everyone merits to do, this exploration of the "rooms of Torah" is something that can be experienced by anyone who studies the *chiddushim* of our tzaddikim whose teachings treat the inner dimension of Torah.[21] In these teachings, one finds various bonds illustrating the connections between disparate Torah ideas which on the surface seem to share nothing in common, such as the seven days of Sukkos, the seven days of *sheva berachos,* mourning, Miriam's days of quarantine outside the camp, and the seven openings in the human face,[22] or the forty-nine gates of *teshuvah,* the forty-nine days of

---

20. *Likutei Moharan* 245.
21. See Reb Nosson's introduction to *Likutei Moharan.*
22. *Likutei Moharan* 21.

Sefirah, and the forty-nine letters in the names of the *shevatim*.[23] Each verse in the Torah carries so many hidden meanings hinted by the opening and closing letters of the words, ideas disclosed by way of splitting up the words in a given phrase differently than the way it is written in the Torah,[24] and messages that may be understood by using different *nekudos* than the ones used to convey the simple level of understanding.[25] The deeper *sefarim* demonstrate that each Torah concept contains various *"bechinos,"* spiritual aspects, each of which highlights its bond to so many other disparate Torah concepts and ideals.

> And this process specifically requires diverse imagery... When you wish to reveal your holy passions for a *chag* or *Shabbos Kodesh*, you must think strongly about the various *inyanim* related to that *chag* or to Shabbos. Merely thinking a single, simple thought such as "Shabbos is holy" will not work, because such a thought cannot be expanded and elaborated upon. Rather, you need to fill your mind with many different images and constructs and to think of them strongly.... Only in this manner will you succeed in revealing the emotions of your soul.[26]

When one enters this inner world of Torah and becomes familiar enough with even the more basic hints and links that form long chains of thought and spiritual imagery revealed by our tzaddikim, he is able to review them in his mind, moving rapidly through the various rooms in the grand palace of Torah. As his mind passes from one image to the next, the mental friction produces sparks of spiritual wonder and deep pleasure

---

23. *Likutei Moharan Tinyana* 73.
24. See introduction to *Ramban al haTorah*.
25. See *Shailos u'Teshuvos Ridvaz* Vol. 3, *siman* 643; *Degel Machaneh Ephraim, Vaeira, "Vaeira el Avraham,"* and *Bo, "Ul'chol B'nei Yisrael."*
26. *Hachsharas HaAvreichim*, pp. 36–37.

that quickly ignite the parched landscape of a slumbering soul, spreading warmth throughout his entire being and setting his heart aflame with passionate love and excitement toward our Father in heaven.

Hovering above the connections that crisscross the entirety of *Torah sheBichsav* and *Torah sheBe'al Peh* is the Infinite Light of Hashem Whose presence becomes tangible to the mind and soul when various pieces of the Torah's puzzle lock together: "the Torah is one with God";[27] "Although HaKadosh Baruch Hu is concealed from the eyes of the living, He is found in the heart and revealed in the mind";[28] "Those who have attained Godly wisdom (a reference to Kabbalah whose ideas are rendered accessible in the sefarim of *penimiyus*) are fortunate, for they fulfill this mitzvah [*emunah*] in the choicest manner."[29]

In the words of Rav Kook:

> The primary fulfillment of *"Torah Lishmah"* is accomplished though the study of those areas of Torah which are more spiritual in nature, for man is elevated by them. When it comes to the more practical matters, one must arrive at the understanding that they are all subsections and garments for the Godly light, upright and just. And among all particularities when taken as a whole can be found the Godly soul of the world's perfection; in life, matter, and spirit. Naturally, the light penetrates and descends into each and every detail.[30]

Coming face to face with truth of the Torah and the way each of its narratives, laws, and ideals combine to create a glorious

---

27. *Zohar*, Vol. 3, 73a.
28. *Orchos Tzaddikim, Shaar HaBushah.*
29. *Sefer HaChinuch*, Mitzvah 25.
30. *Oros HaTorah* 2:2.

tapestry of clarity into life's great questions and the general mission of the Jewish soul, our souls are wakened and warmed by the great light of the *"me'or she'Bah."*[31] The resultant excitement fortifies our personal relationship with Hashem and enables us to serve Him with passion and joy.

⊛ Quenching the Desperate Thirst of Our Generation

RAV AVRAHAM YITZCHAK HaKohen Kook understood the searching spirit of our generation perhaps better than any other leader in recent times and frequently used his golden pen to express his thoughts on this pressing issue — clearly, and in no uncertain terms. Throughout his glorious works, one finds encouragement toward engaging with the "all" of Torah, a push toward a national and personal engagement with the inner depth of our tradition which can alone satisfy the deepest yearnings of our generation.[32]

---

31. See *Degel Machaneh Ephraim, Lech Lecha, "V'lo yikarei shimcha."*

32. Before exploring Rav Kook's writings about the necessity of this kind of Torah study in our generation it is important to familiarize ourselves with the perspective of the tzaddikim on two reasons commonly offered by those who desist from this study. 1] One must **"fill his belly"** with Shas and *Poskim* before delving into the secrets of Torah: Rav Kook held that while it is certainly necessary for one to ground his study of *penimiyus haTorah* with Gemara and halachah (*Havu Ohr*, pp. 43–44), the requirement of holding off on studying deeper teachings until one has "filled his belly" with Shas and *Poskim* has lessened in our generation. In a letter, the Rav writes: "The matter has changed in two primary ways. The first is the necessity to make compromises and leniencies with regard to the conditions of preparation regarding which the *Rishonim* were so stringent, because the measure of 'filling one's belly with meat and wine (the foundational studies of Judaism)' requires much clarification.

While earlier generations were exceedingly stringent in this, the awesome *me-kubalim* took a more lenient stance, even then... In our generation, where the spiritual yearning has so significantly increased that we have established a foundation in saying that the greater portion of our generation's ills comes from this thirst which is yet unquenched, those whose innermost spirit moves them to act in the manner of those who have been lenient in this matter are not sorely mistaken, for they were men of great stature (*gedolei olam*)... The revelation of this wisdom in the final generations, lowly and corrupt, is for the purpose of providing a shield so that one may hold firm to our Father in heaven with a complete heart. Who will protect us if we do not study this awesome and deep wisdom? The hidden have now been transformed into revealed." (*Igros HaRAYaH* Vol. 2, p. 231) With regard to individuals who felt a special propensity toward these studies, Rav Kook took an even more lenient stance, stating that, "With regard to this rule that one who has not filled his belly with meat and wine may not tour the *Pardes* (the studies of *penimiyus haTorah*), it is possible to suggest that this only applies to one who is concerned to fulfill the basic obligation incumbent upon him. However, one who feels in his heart a desire and yearning to study these deep matters, to delve into Hashem's truth, this falls into the category of, 'A person only studies Torah in the place where his heart desires' for it seems that he has a special talent in this area of study... To such a person, these studies are certainly considered his 'meat and wine'" (*Oros HaTorah* 9:12). Other tzaddikim who understood the profound power of *penimiyus haTorah* to protect a person from heretical influence and other impure thoughts, such as the Bnei Yissaschar and Rav Yitzchak Eizik of Komarna, held that this requirement did not apply in our times at all. In addition, it is known from many of the tzaddikim that with regard to Kabbalistic concepts brought in the works of the Chassidic masters, no requirements apply at all. (See *Sifsei Chein*, p. 46.) **2] One who errs in these studies can corrupt the very foundations of our faith:** Rav Kook held that the possibility of spiritual damage resulting from abstaining from this area of Torah study is far greater than the possibility of this study corrupting our faith. In the tzaddik's words: "The portions of studies in faith (in comparison with studies in *mussar*) is even worse: due to the lack of study, the opinion was established that studies in faith involve a prohibition and an awesome danger, and that there is nothing better than for faith to be left alone, without development, without opening and sprouting... Therefore, we are required to uproot the iron beams, and to demonstrate to the world that there *is* a study of faith — there *is* what to study! But most of all, that there is no danger in this study, and that the most terrifying danger is only in the absence of studies in *emunah*." (*Oros HaKodesh*, Vol. 1, p. 89)

The following are selected quotes from the tzaddik's writings where this topic finds expression.

> The insolence of the generation preceding Mashiach's arrival stems from the fact that the world has been readied to the point that it demands the understanding of how all particularities are bound to the All. A part which is not bound to the expanse of the All will not be able to settle in one's mind. If the world would occupy themselves with the light of Torah in this manner, nurturing the soul until it is able to perceive the proper bond between the details with the spiritual rules, *teshuvah*, and the fixing of the world which will follow, would appear and come to actualization. But laziness has prevented this, and the inner light of Torah — which demands elevation and intense holiness — has not yet properly appeared in the world. When the demand for this standard of living and understanding how each detail is bound to the All arises at a time when the completion of a viable path toward this understanding has not yet come to be, this causes an awesome destruction. We must utilize the lofty antidote: The strengthening of our spiritual capacities until the manner in which one may come to understand the abiding bond between all matters of Torah's theological and practical elements with the most elevated All becomes simple to grasp by way of an explication which is founded upon the familiar emotions of the soul. Then, the spiritual life-force of action and theology will return and appear in the world and the general *teshuvah* will begin to give forth fruit.[33]

In another place:

> It is vital for the spiritual element of the Torah — in all its expansiveness, depth, and reach — to have a place in our *yeshivos*. Aggadah, Midrash (both revealed and hidden),

---

33. *Oros HaTeshuvah* 4:10.

the works of philosophy and Kabbalah, Mussar and theology, grammar, poetry, and song (penned, of course, by the *Chachmei Emes* and the *Chassidim HaRishonim*) are also part of the Torah's primary body. While it is impossible to grant these subjects as much time as we do to the study of halachah, Gemara, *poskim*, and the Rishonim and Achronim, it is completely unviable — particularly in our generation, and even more so in Eretz Yisrael, which demands a spiritual proliferation from her children in the very nature of the holiness that fills the air — to prevent these subjects from occupying a respectable place.[34]

In a third:

The most important thing is the need to gather as one to shine forth the Godly light in the world with wisdom, understanding, and knowledge, and to strengthen the *yeshivos* in the diaspora — and even more so in Eretz Yisrael — that matters pertaining to spirituality be studied there consistently, with a broad mind, pure and clear... Immediately after this banner is raised, the spirit of wickedness in the holy Land will be weakened and the Most High One will be praised... We need to shine forth the inner light, whether by means of increasing the study of Chassidus or any other secrets of Torah, both for the purpose of *avodah* or for study itself, so that the light of Godliness becomes revealed in the world and all rectifications become possible.[35]

Reb Tzadok HaKohen teaches that *yeridas hadoros*, the apparent lessening of spiritual stature from generation to generation, is only an external phenomenon. On a deeper level, the very opposite is true; as global society continues to sink to new moral lows, the souls Hashem sends down to the world to serve Him amidst

---

34. *Oros HaTorah*, "L'chizuk Divrei Torah" #4.
35. *Igros HaRAYaH*, Vol. 1, p.161.

the terrible filth are that much more precious, rooted in the loftiest places.[36] While they may appear simple, unassuming, and even unworthy, the shining souls at the end of time are thirsting for the deepest secrets of the Torah that will alone enable them to survive the ocean of heresy, immorality, and shallowness that threatens to drown them.

In the words of my Rebbe, Rav Moshe Weinberger *shlita*:

> Jews today must involve themselves in the study of the light of the Torah — i.e., its deeper meaning. This was not true in the past. Generally speaking, our grandfathers were not studying the writings of the Maharal or the Ramchal. They managed without *Sfas Emes, Tanya,* or *Nefesh HaChaim.* They saw no need to comprehend the entire picture. They believed with simple faith, which is a precious thing. But now, at the end of time, people are seeking to understand the principles of our religion... Because this search for the whole is growing so prevalent, *yeshivas* must devote serious amounts of time to presenting Jewish thought, the word for which, *hashkafah,* means "inclusive gaze." Many students have difficulty with Gemara because it presents a mass of details in which they get lost. Since this is a generation demanding to know how everything fits together, they turn away from it. But after they learn *hashkafah,* the Gemara takes on a completely different appearance and grows exciting.[37]

As parents and educators, we must ask ourselves: How many children who fail out of our schools and fall out of touch with Yiddishkeit do so not out of rebellion or theological crisis but simply because the greatness of their souls compels them to thirst for a level of Torah that is unavailable to them? With our own

---

36. See *Tzidkas HaTzaddik* 111.
37. *Song of Teshuvah,* Vol. 1, pp. 158–159.

eyes we see the manner in which so many of the teens we labeled angry, rebellious, and apathetic return to our communities a few years down the line with works of Chassidus, Midrash, Aggadah, and *sifrei* Ramchal, Breslov and Chabad tucked lovingly under their arm; the teachings for which their souls had been so desperately yearning all along.[38] How many years of anguished wandering might have been prevented had we recognized the spiritual source for the dissonance before they left, or were thrown out, from our homes and schools? Who can say how much pain might have been averted had we only broadened our definition of *limud haTorah* to include the entirety of our holy Torah given on Har Sinai instead of reserving validation and respect for a hyper-specific method of Torah study?

This certainly isn't to suggest that a focus on Aggadah and *penimiyus haTorah* should take precedence over the normative study of Gemara and halachah, only that it command at least as much respect as part and parcel of Hashem's Torah, no less holy or important than Talmudic and halachic discourse. Indeed, the founder of the yeshivah movement, Rav Chaim of Volozhin, writes in no uncertain terms:

> And even if he busies himself with words of Aggadah which hold no practical application to any law, he is also bound to the Speech of HaKadosh Baruch Hu, for the entirety of Torah, in general and in all of its particularity and nuance, was uttered by the mouth of Hashem to Moshe on Har Sinai... And therefore, the holiness of the entirety of Torah is absolutely equal, without any difference or change at all.[39]

---

38. This phenomenon has been documented in a number of publications, among them: "Rekindling the Flame," *Jewish Action*, Winter 2014, and "Meeting the Baal Shem Tov in 2018," *Mishpacha*, Issue #710. Further articles on this subject may be found at the Lost Princess Initiative website, LPITorah.org.

39. *Nefesh HaChaim* 4:6.

It goes without saying that, like in all areas of life, balance is the key.[40] In the lucid articulation of a great Jewish scholar:

> The Chumash is more than a system of laws; only a small portion of the Chumash deals with the law. The prophets, the Psalms, the Aggadic midrashim, are not part of halacha. Like body and soul, they are mutually dependent, and each is a dimension of its own... The collections of Aggadah that have been preserved contain an almost inexhaustible wealth of religious insight and feeling, for in the Aggadah the religious consciousness with all its motivations, difficulties, perplexities, and longings, came to immediate and imaginative expression...To maintain that the essence of Judaism consists

---

40. See *Bava Kama* 60a: "Rav Ami and Rav Asi sat before Rabbi Yitzchak Napcha. One Sage said to Rav Yitzchak: Let the master say words of halachah. The other Sage said to Rav Yitzchak: Let the master say words of Aggadah. Rabbi Yitzchak began to say words of Aggadah but one Sage did not let him. He began to say words of halachah but the other Sage did not let him. Rav Yitzchak said to them: I will relate a parable. This can be compared to a man who has two wives, one young and one old. The young wife pulls out his white hairs, so that her husband will appear younger. The old wife pulls out his black hairs so that he will appear older. And it turns out that he is bald from here and from there, i.e., completely bald, due to the actions of both of his wives. Rav Yitzchak continued and said to them: If so, I will say to you a matter that is appropriate to both of you, which contains both halachah and Aggadah." See also the Maharsha's introduction to his commentary on Shas, where he writes that he was mistaken in separating his commentary on the halachic sections from his commentary on the aggadic sections: "In truth, I now understand from this that the Sages of the Gemara made one work of halachah and Aggadah — for we have but one Torah, and both serve to explain *Toras Moshe*, and so many words of *mussar* and wisdom and instruction are to be found in the words of Aggadah, in accordance with *Toras Moshe*. Therefore, I was mistaken in this that I originally separated my work into two sections, with a separate section on *aggados*. It would have proper not to separate them, but rather to combine them; a woman and her sister." The relationship of the two elements in Torah and the importance of binding them together in our generation is discussed at length in *Oros HaKodesh* 1:1:18.

exclusively of halacha is as erroneous as to maintain that the essence of Judaism consists exclusively of Aggadah. The interrelationship of halacha and Aggadah is the very heart of Judaism. *Halacha without Aggadah is dead, Aggadah without halacha is wild*...There is no halacha without Aggadah, and no Aggadah without halacha. We must neither disparage the body nor sacrifice the spirit. The body is the discipline, the pattern, the law; the spirit is inner devotion, spontaneity, freedom. *The body without the spirit is a corpse; the spirit without the body is a ghost...*[41]

---

41. *God in Search of Man*, pp. 324–341. The debate regarding the importance of Aggadah vis-a-vis halachah has been conducted — in a wide range of various forms — in every era throughout our long and glorious history. Ultimately, both sides of this debate are sourced in a fundamental dichotomy that sits at the very core of creation; *tzimtzum* and *kav*, *memaleh* and *soveiv*, *chessed* and *din*, etc. (I have touched upon this dichotomy in my article "The Two Mountains of Judaism" which appeared in the April 2019 edition of Aish UK's *Perspectives* Magazine. With Hashem's help, I plan to treat this topic more fully in a future work.) Without delving too deeply into an expansive topic which is beyond the scope of this note, one of the most foundational manifestations of this dichotomy is expressed in the contrasting energies of *Har Sinai* and *Har HaBayis*, *Eretz Yisrael* and *Chutz La'Aretz*. This disparity ultimately led to a foundational disagreement between the sages of Talmud Bavli and Yerushalmi regarding the place of Aggadah in the life of a Jew. (It is important to note that while dichotomies can simplify things, the temptation to do so often leads to oversimplification. While there is certainly much evidence to the truth of this particular dichotomy, it must not be seen as an ironclad rule, as many exceptions abound.) The *sefer Torah Min HaShamayim* demonstrates that while the teachings of the Chachamim from Bavel (*Har Sinai, chutz la'aretz*) generally reflect an anti-Aggadah sentiment (see, for example, *Shir HaShirim Zuta* 26a; *Shir HaShirim Rabbah* 2:5; *Berachos* 8a; *Sotah* 35a), the teachings of the Yerushalmi Chachamim (*Har HaBayis, Eretz Yisrael*) embody their love for Aggadah and the esteem in which they held this area of Torah (see, for example, *Midrash Tehillim* 28:5; *Sanhedrin* 100a; *Chagigah* 14a; *Berachos* 33b; *Eiruvin* 18b). Indeed, a large bulk of the Aggadic tradition, including *Bereishis Rabbah, Vayikra Rabbah, Eichah Rabbasi, Midrash Tehillim*, and many of the Aggadic portions that appear in Talmud Bavli was produced in Yerushalayim.

(See *Shelah HaKadosh* to *Pesachim* 17a.) Rav Kook writes that whereas *chutz la'aretz* is bound up with action, Eretz Yisrael, which is bound up with speech, shares in the energy of the Beis HaMikdash, which is bound up with thought. While the Torah of *chutz la'aretz* is focused on practical details (halachah), the Torah of Eretz Yisrael is concerned with the spirit and holistic cognition of *machshavah*. (*Shemoneh Kevatzim*, 6:211. See also *Oros HaTorah*, Chapter 13.) Thus, we find that while Rav Yochanan Ben Nuri referred to halachah as "*gufei Torah*" and Aggadah to wine (*Sifrei, Haazinu* 317), something which is not constantly needed (*Yerushalmi Horayos*, 3:48), R' Dimi, who was from Yerushalayim, compared Aggadah to water (*Chagigah* 14a), something that is always needed. (See introduction to *sefer Menoras HaMeor*.) While Rava, an Amora from Bavel, held that David HaMelech was punished for referring to Torah as a "song" (*Sotah* 35a), Rav Yirmeyah Ben Elazar and Rav Bivi, who were Amora'im from Eretz Yisrael, saw no problem with referring to the Torah in this way (see *Eiruvin* 18b and *Yalkut Shemoni, Korach*, 856). Similarly, while a Midrash from Yerushalayim teaches that David praised Torah as "not being a burden, but a song" (*Midrash Tehillim* 119:41), Rava ruled that "the mitzvos were not given for our pleasure, but as a yoke on our necks" (*Rosh Hashanah* 28a, *Rashi*). R' Shimon ben Lakish, an Amora from Eretz Yisrael, ruled that mitzvos require intent (*Pesachim* 114b) while Rava ruled the opposite (*Rosh Hashanah* 28b). These and many other examples support the notion that *Har HaBayis-Eretz Yisrael* is in conceptual congruence with the study of Aggadah and a more emotional, poetic perspective on our tradition (indeed, the majority of our prayers and *piyyutim* were also born in Eretz Yisrael). In the words of Rav Kook: "Eretz Yisrael, which is the place of prophecy, maintains an influence of the prophetic energy in its mode of Torah study. Its way of understanding is clarified through a worldview rooted in depth and thus does not require lengthy explanations; "The air of Eretz Yisrael makes one wise." This is not the case with Talmud Bavli. Prophetic wisdom, which is the foundation for the wisdom of Aggadah, which is, in turn, the inner dimension of the Torah's roots, is far more active in Eretz Yisrael than in Bavel which is not fit for prophecy." (*Igros HaRAYaH*, Vol. 1, p.103).

Therefore, it is possible to suggest that the reestablishment of Torah Jewry in the Holy Land in the final generation before Mashiach's arrival as well as the yearning for mass physical return to Eretz Yisrael in our times is another expression of the national thirst for the teachings and consciousness of Aggadah and *penimiyus haTorah* which are spiritually congruent with this Land in whose energy they are sourced. In the final generation, preparing for Mashiach, the physical return to our Land must be mirrored by a scholastic return to Toras Eretz Yisrael, the perspective of Aggadah and *penimiyus haTorah*. (See Rav Kook's vivid description of this process in *Shemoneh Kevatzim* 2:313.)

Much like every category of the food pyramid is required for physical health, every area of Torah is required for spiritual health and vitality. Additionally, much like the required amount of a given category of food varies in different environmental and climatic circumstances, the levels of each area necessary for spiritual vitality changes with the spiritual climate of each generation. Rav Chaim Vital, the primary student of the Arizal, taught that while Chazal have certainly taught, *Talmud Torah k'neged kulam*, "Torah study is equal to all other mitzvos"[42] this was in reference to previous generations. In the last generation before the coming of Mashiach, the primary focus in our *avodas Hashem* must be fixed upon *tefillah*, prayer.

The act of supplication, *tefillah*, is in a larger sense, synonymous with faith. Torah study does not necessarily indicate faith in the Divine authorship of the Torah; many secular professors in academies the world over are involved in Talmudic scholarship as a purely intellectual exercise. *Tefillah*, on the other hand, is where we allow our soul to express her faith in the spiritual realm, to strengthen her bond with Hashem in a conscious manner. On the verse "And Moshe's hands were faithful (*emunah*)," Onkelos comments: "Moshe's hands were spread in prayer"[43] — prayer is the deepest expression of faith. Faith, in turn, is the deepest expression of our awareness of the spiritual reality that lies beyond the physical world, an awareness that is attained by learning about that reality; the details of the soul's parts and their functions, the details of the way Hashem creates and sustains the world by means of its three forerunners in the spiritual realm, the details regarding the manner in which Hashem reveals Himself to the world and the vision He has for His treasured nation and their mission throughout history. Involving oneself with studies of this

---

42. *Peah* 1:1.
43. *Shemos* 17:12.

nature, the teachings of *penimiyus haTorah*, strengthens one's faith in a way that few other things can. Indeed, when discussing the mitzvah of *emunah*, the *Chinuch* writes that the way to attain the highest degree of faith is by studying "*chochmas Elokus*," *penimiyus haTorah*.[44] "Know God and serve Him,"[45] David HaMelech taught his son; a Jew must first come to know the Being he intends to serve, if he is to serve Him properly.[46]

When it comes to understanding Yiddishkeit, there are two levels of question: "how" and "why." The question of "how" is less fundamental as it presupposes the answer to "why"; once one is on board with the answer to *why*, he can now ask *how* he is to perform what is necessary. The question of "how?" asks about the details of halachic observance, how one is to properly live a lifestyle of Torah and mitzvos. The question of "why" is far deeper. When we ask "why," we are inquiring about the deeper reasons behind the *halachos*, the spiritual concepts that underlie the foundations of our faith; the Aggadah beyond the halachah. In other words, whereas the question "how?" relates to the various details and particularities of which the "all" of Yiddishkeit is composed, the question "why?" relates to the "all" itself. The process of asking this level of question and exploring its answers is the way to attain vibrant faith and give life to our relationship with Hashem, the area of Jewish practice that needs the most support in our generation.

As we have learned, Rav Kook taught that our souls are no longer satisfied with mere bits and pieces of the truth, but rather yearn for the great "all" of Torah. He saw the youth's mass rejection of the Torah transmitted in the *yeshivos* of pre-war Europe as due not to rebellion but to desperation. In the eyes of "kids at

---

44. *Sefer HaChinuch*, Mitzvah 25.
45. *Divrei HaYamim* 28:9.
46. See *Tzidkas HaTzaddik* 2.

risk" and the "Footsteps" community, he saw not sparks of audacity but the holy thirst for the great fire of Judaism their souls were being denied in our institutions. In their vulgar language, biting cynicism, and apathetic sentiments he heard them begging to be taught the "whys" of religious life: "Why am I in this world?" "Why does my soul contain different elements and how do those functions differ from one another?" "Why is the human body in the form that it is?" "Why is Shabbos on the seventh day?"

Rav Yaakov Kamenetsky was once asked for his take on those who cite a feeling of being "choked" and restricted by *avodas Hashem* as the reason for abandoning the Torah lifestyle.

He answered with the following analogy. "When a little boy turns three years old, we make an *upsherin* and present him with his first pair of tzitzis. Children grow quickly, and after a year or so, we need to replace this *tallis katan* with a *beged* of a larger size. As the years pass and the boy grows bigger and bigger, his parents continue to update his *tallis katan* so it will fit his growing frame. Now imagine for a moment if that boy had never received a new *tallis katan* as he grew older and is still walking around as a fully grown man at age twenty, wearing the same pair of tzitzis he had received at his *upsherin*. Would it be any wonder to us that he feels as if his tzitzis are choking him?! They are far too small!"

The Rosh Yeshivah paused for a moment to let the image sink in before continuing. "The same is true regarding one's conception of Yiddishkeit. A child has an extremely limited conception of Hashem, *Shabbos Kodesh*, Yamim Tovim, and mitzvos. As he grows, his understanding of Yiddishkeit's theological principles need to expand and deepen in accordance with his ever-broadening experience and emotions. Unfortunately, this expansion often never takes place. Too many of our twenty-year-olds walk around with the same limited and immature conception of Hashem, Torah, and Yiddishkeit's perspective on life that they had at their *upsherin*. Their fully grown frame is outfitted with properly sized clothes, but their *tallis katan* hangs around their neck, tiny and limiting. Is it any wonder, then, that they feel choked by Yiddishkeit?"

The collective Jewish soul is yearning for a deeper answer. Somewhere deep down, we are yearning to get in touch with the questions our souls have been asking all our lives, to discuss them, analyze them, and bring them to life with the deepest answers offered by our tradition. When our shuls and schools do not guide us through a process of theological expansion by engaging — in a balanced way — with *penimiyus haTorah*, we feel as if we are choked by this limited conception and soon lose our connection. Getting in touch with the relevance of Jewish practice by receiving the deepest answers the Torah holds regarding every detail of the universe is the surest guarantee of spiritual rejuvenation and the ability to reclaim a passionate relationship with Hashem.

Another burning issue of our times is an abiding sense of despair, anxiety, and sadness which, as both a cause[47] and effect[48] of sin, leaves the Jew trapped in a miserable cycle of darkness and inner turmoil. Living life in the shadow of the Holocaust, in a society which appears to have become post-truth and post-civility, many lack the energy necessary to prevent oneself from falling into the abyss. The daily newsfeed is chock full of violence, hate, tragedy, destruction, pain, lies, and inanity. The world has gone to the dogs, and there seems to be nothing that can halt this downward spiral. In response, we have become numb and despondent, experiencing life through a veil of gloominess, apathy, and despair. But this, too, can be fixed! Rav Kook teaches that this attitude can be resolved and transformed through exposure to the Torah's inner light:

---

47. See *Sichos HaRan* 20 and *Likutei Moharan* 169.
48. See *Oros HaTeshuvah* 14:7.

We observe that when one looks at the world in a simple manner, stemming from the influence of the revealed perspective of Torah alone without the influence of *Toras Chessed* which flows forth from the source of a hidden, Godly understanding, *Middas HaDin* proliferates in great measure — hatred of creation and despair abound from all sides. There is no way to stand secure, immersed in holiness, in a generation in which boundaries have been so widely breached, without assistance from the sense for nuance granted by the revealed Torah along with the kindness and light of the concealed Torah. It is then that the energies of kindness mix with those of strict judgment to produce sweetness.[49]

In another place:

The idealistic nature of theoretical Kabbalah comes to expression in the "new Chassidus"[50] of the past few generations. The good is [seen as being] absolute and firm, and the evil is merely an illusion. Therefore, through clarity of the intellect and strengthening of the spirit, it is possible to turn everything to goodness. There is no room for sadness; joy and spiritual elevation must fill all.[51]

It is our soul that has dimmed, frightened into submission by

---

49. *Oros HaTorah* 10:16. See also *Pesikta d'Rav Kahana* 101b: *Panim sochakos l'Aggadah*, "One studies Aggadah with a happy face." Also, Aggadah is compared to wine (*Sifrei, Haazinu* 317) about which Chazal teach, "There is no joy without wine" (*Pesachim* 109a), and "There is no song without wine" (*Berachos* 35a).

50. Referring to the Chassidic movement founded by the Baal Shem Tov.

51. *Oros HaKodesh*, Vol. 1, p. 94. The radical optimism described here by Rav Kook is another aspect of the lost princess, the Shechinah. See *Berachos* 31b: "The Shechinah [*Malchus* — princess] is not to be found by you, for you have judged me harshly and have not judged me favorably." The tzaddikim who see the world through the tear-filled eyes of the Shechinah as conveyed in the teachings of *penimiyus haTorah* are forever judging their generation, and all of history, in a favorable manner, seeing everything as improving, rising, and growing ever closer to rectification and ultimate redemption.

the absurdity of a world gone insane. But there is a way to nurture the soul back to the healthy illumination of joy and completion. In the words of the Vilna Gaon:

> *Penimiyus haTorah* provides life-force to the interiority of the body — the soul... The *yetzer hara* is not able to sway those that occupy themselves with the study of *remez* and *sod*.[52]

The holy insolence of our generation finds expression in an inability to be satisfied with the simple *emunah* of our grandparents. We want more, we *need* more — not only the vague notion of a God who created the world, but the pulsating *hakarah*, recognition of His relationship with and imminent presence in our physical reality. Rav Shlomo Wolbe writes:

> One who is *makir*, recognizes his Creator, does so in his heart (*hakarah b'leiv*). His intellectual knowledge penetrates the emotions and encompasses all of the soul's powers, causing them to align with this *hakarah* and receive it willingly. At this point, it is no longer possible to rebel against Hashem.[53]

Chazal have revealed that it is indeed possible to attain this *hakarah* that our generation so deeply and desperately craves.

> The scholars of *derash* would say: Do you want to be *makir* the One Who spoke and brought the world into being? Study Aggadah![54] Through this, you will come to be *makir* HaKadosh Baruch Hu and bind yourself to His ways.[55]

---

52. *Even Sheleimah* 8:27.

53. *Alei Shur*, Vol. 2, Chapter 12.

54. See *Even Sheleimah* 8:26: "The *Aggados* which appear, *chas v'shalom*, as if they are meaningless, have all of the secrets concealed within them." See also *Gur Aryeh* to *Bereishis* 28:11.

55. *Sifrei, Eikev* 11:1. See also *Midrash Tehillim* 28:5: "'For they have not understood the works of Hashem' — this refers to Aggadah."

Discovering the Lost Princess of passion, excitement, and re-newal demands that we engage with the deeper elements of our holy tradition and absorb the elevated perspective on life expli-cated within.

In another place, Rav Wolbe writes:

> Creation is extremely deep. History is extremely deep. But it is possible to live in the world in a simple manner. We walk on the ground without thinking about all that is hid-den within its depths. We glance at the sky only to know whether to bring an umbrella — without experiencing the awesome loftiness of the heavens. We read in the newspaper about the statement of this president or that official or about events far or near without perceiving the deep *hashgachah* that works within the annals of history. It is even possible to live simply in Torah and mitzvos: wearing tzitzis, donning tefillin, keeping Shabbos, fulfilling our obligation in *tefil-lah* — without feeling the depth of the mitzvos at all. We believe with "simple faith," without any contemplation and without knowing which means enabled the great believers to reach "simple faith." But in truth: Why must we specifically strive to penetrate to the depths? Isn't it possible to be a good Jew and to live simply, to perform good deeds in a simple manner? Indeed, it is possible to remove oneself from the depth of all matters and remain a good Jew. However, *such a life is devoid of freshness and renewal.* Each day is like the last, everything is habit, all is rote. All discovery is a result of one's delving into the depths. Any true innovation in Torah thought is a product of one's delving into the depths. The only way one can renew himself is only if he encounters the depth he holds within. For it is only in the depths that one draws near to the apex of truth.[56]

---

56. *Alei Shur*, Vol. 2, introduction to the Second Gate.

✳ Illuminating the Details

ONE OF THE reasons that educators have been reluctant to include these deeper studies in the curriculum used in our institutions is the fear that studies of this nature will cause an abandonment of the more rigorous, practical studies that relate to the minutia of Torah law and how a Jew is to conduct himself religiously and behaviorally. While this concern is certainly valid if these studies are approached improperly, the vast majority of vocal advocates for an educational revolution make it absolutely clear that engagement with *penimiyus haTorah* should not, and indeed *must not*, supplant the other, foundational areas of Torah study such as Gemara and halachah. On the contrary, the encounter with the sweetness and truth of the Torah afforded by these illuminated teachings instills in the student the desire to engage in all areas of Torah study. Having encountered the great light of the "All," the student is able to perceive how that light filters down into each and every detail of Torah. No longer does one feel as though each halachah stands on its own, disconnected from the root of Torah. Rather, every *se'if katan* in *Mishnah Berurah* and each line in Tosafos is understood, in context of the mighty spiritual principles at the very root of our tradition, as containing the awesome light of the All.[57]

Rav Kook writes:

> When one studies the revealed portions of the Torah, one sees how the lofty light descends in the most awesome manner until it settles so beautifully in the world of action. His heart expands because of the preciousness and the strength of this life-force which, sourced in the Holy of Holies, flows down through the sanctified channel of the Jewish luminescence, to all the nations. He knows with certainty that this light, which is constricted into words and letters, *minhagim*,

---

57. See *Oros HaTorah* 2:2, 3:3,9; 4:4. See also *Sichos HaRan* 108: "Know, that studying *Zohar* grants one the desire to study all other areas of our holy Torah."

actions, laws, analyzations, and concepts, meets with that great light which transcends all of these and is cleansed within it and there they delight in each other, together. The light of the Life-giver of All Worlds is filled with illumination and tremendous delight from this constant meeting, the result of Torah *lishmah* which makes peace in the upper realms as well as the lower realms.[58]

In another place:

And so it is with the Torah. Her lofty general principles — those universal concepts, paths of elevated righteousness and spiritual wisdoms, reveal a complete world of greatness, of all-inclusive laws which are like stars in the sky. But specifically from amidst this elevation one must comprehend that just as there is found an enormous treasure in the great principles, so there is to be found in the piles and piles of novel rulings and formations founded upon each and every crown [of the letters], in every single detail of the Torah — the exacting boundaries and expanses which, resulting from each and every branch, continuously fragment into leaves and shoots, endlessly. Then, even if one is greatly inclined toward the enlargement of consciousness in the expansive universal principles, it will be pleasurable for him to study Torah for its sake in the exactness of its particularities, and he will succeed in the binding together of a "great thing" and a "small thing": "A great thing — the workings of the chariot. A small thing — the disputes of Abayei and Rava."[59,60]

In *Shivchei HaRAYaH* we read:

A man once said to Rav Kook, "My son is not motivated to study Torah." Rav Kook replied, "When I was young, I was

---

58. *Oros HaTorah* 2:3.
59. *Sukkah* 28a.
60. *Oros HaTorah* 3:8.

also not excited to study halachah. My heart was drawn after Aggadah. However, by studying Aggadah, I came to study halachah. I suggest you teach your son Aggadah. As a result, he will also come to study halachah.[61]

In a desperate attempt to shake the viceroy from his spiritual and emotional coma, the princess grants the viceroy a garment with words of tears — the teachings of *penimiyus haTorah* that grant every Jew access to the deep, broad, beautiful, exciting, true, and radically optimistic lessons of our holy tradition. Having gifted the viceroy with her headscarf of elevated consciousness, the princess feels confident in the viceroy's chances of attaining his objective — so confident, that she goes back to the chariot on her own, without any coercion on the part of the troops. She knows full well that the time for her redemption has not yet arrived — there is still much for the viceroy to accomplish. But if he will hold tightly to the scarf of tears, clinging to the deepest depths of the Torah with all of his might, he will find the strength to finish the task he set out to accomplish so many years ago.

⊛ A Necessary Constriction

IN THE PREVIOUS sections, we learned that the tzaddikim compose garments with their teachings and stories that allow us to access the greatest spiritual lights without being damaged. This counterintuitive model, in which covering something allows for its ultimate revelation, is one example of a Kabbalistic rule which states, "The concealment is the revelation."[62] This rule refers to the idea that oftentimes, in order for a tremendous revelation to be accessed and received in the proper manner, it first needs to

---

61. *Shivchei HaRAYaH*, p. 180.

62. See *Sefer Zohar HaRakia* 2b and *Tikkunei Zohar* 70, 127b. For a fuller treatment of this concept, see *Sunlight of Redemption*, pp. 115–119.

undergo some form of contraction, constriction, and conceal-ment. If the revelation is not tempered by a proper screen, it will be damaging to those who are to receive it.[63]

In his current spiritual state, the viceroy lacks the vessels to properly process a visit by the princess herself. On a deeper level, the lack of influence her words seem to have on the viceroy are not despite their great power but specifically because of it — her words are far too intense for him to handle. In his current state of spiritual slumber, a direct communication from the princess can do more harm than good. Recognizing this, the princess writes a message in tears on a garment which creates the necessary con-striction for her words,[64] rendering them in a manner accessible to the viceroy. This is why it is only *after* the princess leaves that the viceroy wakes up.

Here, Rebbe Nachman is teaching us an important lesson. When we attempt to wake a fellow Jew from a state of spiritual numbness, it is important to keep in mind that he may simply lack the vessels for intense levels of spirituality. Even if we give *mussar* in the sweetest way or drag him from one tzaddik's *tisch* to the next, it is possible that the effect will be minimal, because in his current state, he may be unable to process the enormity of that light. Therefore, instead of these intense experiences, simply reading something inspirational in a book or having a heart to heart talk about the purpose of life can have a far greater effect, because these activities suit the size of his vessels.

The same thing applies to attempts at self-awakening when we

---

63. The tzaddikim teach that in truth, the Plague of Darkness in Mitzrayim was, in fact, a revelation of the greatest spiritual light. However, since the Egyptians did not have the proper vessels, it overwhelmed them, and they ex-perienced it as darkness. (See *Sparks from Berditchov*, pp. 121–125.)

64. *Sefer Yetzirah* begins by disclosing three terms which are fundamental to Jewish thought, *Sippur*, *Sefer*, and *Sofer*; Story, Book, and Author. The level of "Book" (the headscarf) is one level removed from "Author" (the princess).

enter spiritual hibernation. At such a time, it is similarly important to properly assess our vessels in order to proceed in a manner
that will be beneficial to our current state. Rebbe Nachman refers
to this as *Baki b'Shov*, "The Expertise of Returning."[65]

Living in a highly institutionalized religious environment, it
becomes easy to fall into the trap of thinking that true *avodas
Hashem* has a definite appearance and if one cannot meet this
standard he is "out of the game," "burnt out," and must wait until
he can pull himself back into the arena of serving the Master
of the world. In truth, however, this is a tremendous mistake.
There is no such thing as "falling out" of serving Hashem. *Avodas
Hashem* encompasses all of life; every stage, every mood, good
day and bad day alike. The question is not *"Can I serve Hashem
in this situation,"* but *"How can I serve Hashem in this situation?"*[66]
This is what it means to be a *"Baki b'Shov,"* an expert in knowing
how to remain connected to Hashem even while sitting in midst
of the thickest spiritual darkness with a mind that is numb and
a heart that is frozen shut. Instead of foolishly using our clipped
wings to attempt to reach the loftiest plateaus and serve Hashem
"like everybody else," an endeavor surely doomed to failure, one
who is wise and cares not about his ego or impressing others but
solely about the honor of Hashem will find a way to serve Hashem
that is fitting for his current spiritual situation.[67] While it may
appear counterintuitive, when it comes to this realm of *avodas
Hashem*, less is often more.

---

65. See *Likutei Moharan* 6.

66. See *Likutei Moharan* 33.

67. For an early illustration of this idea, see *Berachos* 28a, where the Gemara
relates that when R' Zeira grew weak from his studies, he would sit by the
entrance to the *beis midrash* so he could rise when the scholars would pass
by and receive reward. For R' Zeira, it wasn't "study Torah like everyone else
or bust." Rather, each moment had its particular *avodah*; even in a weakened
state, he was able to find a way to serve Hashem.

LESSONS FOR LIFE

✱ The natural, healthy reaction to a spiritual setback is disappointment and brokenheartedness that will lead to a stronger resolve and heightened commitment. However, there are times when the devastating nature of the fall necessitates a different approach. In such a case, one must focus only on the positive, encouraging himself with whatever he can so as to ensure that he doesn't give up entirely.

✱ One of the most useful tools along the journey toward reawakening a sense of wonder, passion, and excitement in our lives is the great universe of *"penimiyus haTorah."* The teachings of the tzaddikim who revealed the Torah's inner light have the ability to transform the way we see ourselves, the world around us, and our relationship with the King of kings. The soul of our generation intensely thirsts for these teachings. In their absence, we begin to look elsewhere to satisfy the deep sense of lack that remains.

✱ It is important to remain ever aware of our spiritual vessels to ensure they do not become overwhelmed by an overpowering degree of intensity. Oftentimes, a constriction of the Divine illumination is required if it is to light up our lives.

PART III

DAWN

כִּי־עִמְּךָ מְקוֹר חַיִּים
בְּאוֹרְךָ נִרְאֶה־אוֹר

With You is the fountain of life,
in Your Light we will see light.

TEHILLIM 36:10

CHAPTER 16

Failure of Gold,
Setback of Pearls

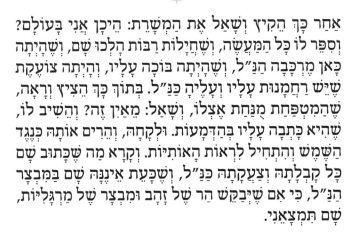

אַחַר כָּךְ הֵקִיץ וְשָׁאַל אֶת הַמְשָׁרֵת: הֵיכָן אֲנִי בָּעוֹלָם?
וְסִפֵּר לוֹ כָּל הַמַּעֲשֶׂה, וְשֶׁחֲיָלוֹת רַבּוֹת הָלְכוּ שָׁם, וְשֶׁהָיְתָה
כָּאן מֶרְכָּבָה הַנַּ"ל, וְשֶׁהָיְתָה בּוֹכָה עָלָיו, וְהָיְתָה צוֹעֶקֶת
שֶׁיֵּשׁ רַחֲמָנוּת עָלָיו וְעָלֶיהָ כַּנַּ"ל. בְּתוֹךְ כָּךְ הֵצִיץ וְרָאָה,
שֶׁהַמִּטְפַּחַת מֻנַּחַת אֶצְלוֹ, וְשָׁאַל: מֵאַיִן זֶה? וְהֵשִׁיב לוֹ,
שֶׁהִיא כָּתְבָה עָלָיו בְּהַדְּמָעוֹת. וּלְקָחָהּ, וְהֵרִים אוֹתָהּ כְּנֶגֶד
הַשֶּׁמֶשׁ וְהִתְחִיל לִרְאוֹת הָאוֹתִיּוֹת. וְקָרָא מַה שֶּׁכָּתוּב שָׁם
כָּל קַבְלָתָהּ וְצַעֲקָתָהּ כַּנַּ"ל, וְשֶׁכָּעֵת אֵינֶנָּה שָׁם בַּמִּבְצָר
הַנַּ"ל, כִּי אִם שֶׁיְּבַקֵּשׁ הַר שֶׁל זָהָב וּמִבְצָר שֶׁל מַרְגָּלִיּוֹת,
שָׁם תִּמְצָאֵנִי.

After this, the viceroy awoke and asked his servant, "Where in the world am I?" The servant told him (the viceroy) the entire story about the many soldiers that had passed, the chariot, the princess, and her great crying and grief. Suddenly he looked and noticed the headscarf next to him. "Where is this from?" he asked. The servant answered that the princess had written on it with her tears. The

> viceroy took the scarf and held it up to the sun. He
> began to see letters. (He read that) at this time, she
> is no longer in the previous palace. "Rather, you will
> need to search for a mountain of gold and a palace
> of pearls, and there you will find me."

❋ From a Simple Scarf to a Meaningful Message

THE OVERWHELMING PRESENCE of the princess has departed, but her anguish lingers. Her cries echo still, rousing the viceroy from his tortured sleep. Immediately upon awakening, the question rushes forth from the deepest depth of his being, shattering the dark shells of his apathy: "Where in the world am I?"

The servant begins to fill him in on all that has occurred, describing the frightening soldiers and the way the princess had descended to his sleeping body and cried over his miserable failures with a broken heart. As he is speaking, the viceroy suddenly notices the headscarf left behind by the princess. In order to read her tear-washed message, he holds it up to the sun.

If the viceroy does not hold the scarf to the sun, he will never be able to see the words written by the princess with her tears. All he will see is a plain old headscarf bearing no message or relevance to his situation. It is only when he holds it up to the sun's brilliant light that the letters become visible; a simple scarf is instantly transformed into something infinitely more valuable — a message from the subject of his most powerful yearning. What does this sun symbolize, and how does it enable the inner tzaddik to discover the life-giving teachings of *penimiyus haTorah*?

The Breslover *mashpi'im* explain that the only way for one to experience the inner light of Torah in the teachings of the tzaddikim is by having faith in their awesome power. If we approach these teachings as mere intellectual treats with little practical relevance to our lives, it is possible to miss out on the essence entirely and gain very little from them, if anything at all.

This very tale, a garment for the most awesome spiritual illumination, is itself a prime example. How easy is it to view Rebbe Nachman's story *The Lost Princess* simply as an interesting, if tragic, fairytale? So many will read the tzaddik's words and immediately write them off as shallow, meaningless, and holding no relevance to modern-day Jews centuries removed from kings and princesses, viceroys and servants. But the moment one approaches our story with the intent to mine its depths through close analyzation, what wondrous meaning and guidance for *avodas Hashem* he can perceive! The only way to properly study the works of the tzaddikim is to approach them with the intention of finding ourselves in their words, to realize that every word of their teachings is applicable to our lives, in our modern age.

Rebbe Nachman teaches:

> When a person looks into and studies from a *sefer*, and in every place he studies he finds himself — taking personally the moral instruction and from every place recognizing his own lack of importance and baseness, no matter from which book he studies — this is a sign that he desires to fulfill God's will. And this is [the meaning of]: "Then I said, 'Behold, I have come with the scroll of the Book which is written about me.'"[1] This is a sign that, "To fulfill Your will, my God, do I desire."[2]

In the opening lesson of his magnum opus, *Likutei Moharan*, Rebbe Nachman teaches that the sun symbolizes the greatest

---

1. *Tehillim* 40:8.
2. *Likutei Moharan* 121.

revelation of Divine wisdom.[3] Therefore, the viceroy's holding the scarf up to the sun symbolizes his deep faith that the teachings of the tzaddikim contain the deepest, most exalted revelation of Hashem's Mind. The moment he allows himself to stand upon this sturdy premise and begins to seriously explore the sayings, teachings, and stories of the tzaddikim with faith in the depth they intend to reveal, the viceroy is able to see the princess's tears and read her personal message to him as an individual, begging him to reveal Hashem's presence in the world with passionate *avodah*. If, lacking faith in the relevance of these messages to his particular journey, the viceroy does not hold the scarf up to the sun, he will fail to discover the awesome treasures held within. Instead of becoming the single most important treasure in his life, the scarf will remain just that — a simple, meaningless scarf.

✳ An Elevated Perspective

WHEN WE APPROACH the words of the tzaddikim with *emunas chachamim*, we allow them to guide us through the maze of *avodas Hashem* by clarifying the shifting goals of life's various ages and stages.[4] But first, before making us aware of the work we have yet to accomplish, the tzaddikim grant us deep encouragement and strengthen our spirit by stressing how much we have already accomplished and how far we have come.

As we have learned from Rav Kook in the previous chapter, those tzaddikim whose souls are bound with the world of *penimiyus haTorah* see the world and all that fills it as constantly ascending; everything is rising, history is reaching a glorious culmination, existence is always correcting itself, and each Jew

---

3. See *Sunlight of Redemption*, p. 108.
4. See *Mesillas Yesharim*, Chapter 1.

is approaching his or her rectification.[5] While confronted with the harsh realities of a cold, dark world that seem to directly contradict such an optimistic sentiment, some are quick to deride this worldview as naïveté and even a form of escapism, this couldn't be further from the truth. These tzaddikim aren't optimistic *despite* reality, they are optimistic *because of* reality — the elevated perspective of reality to which they are privy by means of their engagement with the deepest secrets of creation.[6] Their commitment to the inner dimension of our Torah allows them to perceive the inner dimension of a world which was created with its holy letters. Black ink becomes black fire, white parchment becomes white fire;[7] the world is bursting with energy of holiness, constantly rising toward its Source. Torah personalities are personas, dreams are stories and stories are teachings; a concept

---

5. See *Shemoneh Kevatzim* 2:162.

6. See Rav Kook, *Kevatzim M'Ksav Yad Kodsho 2, Pinkas* 5:145, and *Oros HaTeshuvah* 16:12. See also my article *A Matter of Perspective: Understanding the Advocacy of Rav Levi Yitzchak of Berditchov* — http://lpitorah.org/a-matter-of-perspective-understanding-the-advocacy-of-rav-levi-yitzchak-of-berditchov/. This distinction between the bliss of ignorance and the bliss of an elevated perspective is connected with Chazal's requirement to drink on Purim *"Ad d'lo yada,"* until one is able to say *"Baruch Haman."* This does not mean that a Jew should become inebriated on Purim to the point of mindless folly. Chazal expressed this requirement not with the words *"ad d'eino yada,"* but *"ad d'lo yada"* — not sub-knowledge but super-knowledge. The intention is that a Jew should drink on Purim in a manner of holiness until he rises above the constraints of an outlook that remains very much structurally intact so we may look upon it and respect it, and yet treasure the feeling of seeing it all from an entirely elevated perspective. It's a feeling of rising above the system of intellect (which we yet perceive to be absolute *emes*) and shaking with the laughter of *"vatischak l'yom acharon."* The tzaddikim lived on the level of *"ad d'lo yada"* all year round, seeing life from an elevated perspective of super-knowledge that enabled them to see the *"baruch,"* the hidden blessing, even in *"Haman"* — all manners of difficulty, pain, and lowliness.

7. See *Zohar*, Vol. 3, 132a: the black text written upon the white parchment of the Torah scroll is black fire atop white fire.

behind every structure, meaning at the core of each detail, all parts are bound to the unfathomable soul of existence which rises constantly toward embrace with the spiritual realm beyond our physical reality. It is this elevated manner of approaching life that compels these tzaddikim to provide gentle guidance founded upon respect for the individual's journey and the notion that progress doesn't always look the way we expect it to appear — all is not as it seems.

My Rebbe, Rav Weinberger *shlita*, is fond of telling the following story about the Rebbe Rashab of Lubavitch, which brings out this point in a beautiful way.

Two chassidim from Odessa, a city in southern Ukraine, came to visit their Rebbe. In his private meeting with the first chassid, the Rebbe asked how things were with Odessa's Jews. The man answered that although things were difficult, there were *baruch Hashem* many shuls filled with much learning and davening, as well as an assortment of *gemach*s to help people in need. The Rebbe seemed very happy with this and gave the man a donation of ten rubles, a large sum. Quite pleased, the man left the room and showed his friend the donation. His friend asked what he had told the Rebbe, and he recounted what he had told the Rebbe regarding the shuls, davening, learning, and *gemach*s. His friend was very surprised. In truth, things in Odessa were very bad! Such good things were hardly a prominent part of life for the people living there. It was clear to him that if the first man got such a sizeable donation for telling the Rebbe a misleading narrative, he would get an even bigger donation for telling the unvarnished truth.

The second man met with the Rebbe Rashab. As was his way, in the course of conversation, the Rebbe asked how things were for the Jews in Odessa. The man then laid the full story on the Rebbe. The city streets echoed with bitter disputes between Jews of different factions. Torah observance was almost non-existent. Physical life was also difficult and life in the city needed drastic improvement. When the chassid finished his tirade, the Rebbe thanked him and gave him one ruble, a relatively insignificant donation.

Surprised, the man asked why he had gotten such a small sum when he had merely told the truth about Odessa, while his friend had in fact exaggerated the significance of the good things happening there.

The Rebbe answered, "Do you think that I did not already know the situation of the Jews in Odessa? I have been involved in their welfare for a long time. The truth is that there are two Odessas: '*Odessa Illa'ah*,' Higher Odessa, and '*Odessa Tata'ah*,' Lower Odessa. Higher Odessa has shuls, learning, davening, and *gemachs*. Those things are happening in Odessa right now. But there is also a lower Odessa. That city is indeed full of *machlokes*, non-observance, and bitterness. I did not ask about the state of the community in Odessa to find out what was happening there. Rather, I asked you about the state of the Jews in Odessa only to discover which Odessa you were living in — '*Odessa Illa'ah*' or '*Odessa Tata'ah*,' Higher Odessa or Lower Odessa. In his optimistic answer, your friend revealed that he was living in the part of Odessa where good things were happening. He therefore saw the city through the eyes of one living in Higher Odessa. You, however, resolved to tell me the 'truth.' This revealed that you are immersed in the negativity and *machlokes* of Lower Odessa."

The message written by the princess with her tears is rooted in the worldview of the "Upper Odessa." Sticking to the strategy she has maintained since their initial reunion, the princess begins her message with encouragement — informing the viceroy that despite his failure to complete her redemption and bring her back to her father, his efforts over these decades on her behalf have succeeded in freeing her from her original captivity. True, she has been moved elsewhere, she is still very much imprisoned and her situation is yet dire, but it seems that her transfer to this new palace represents a significant improvement. From the princess's words, it appears as though the viceroy no longer needs to abide by any specific conditions in order to free her. While he has taken one step back, his devotions over the course of the year have propelled him two steps forward. Now, he must simply muster enough faith in her words to search for this fantastical palace of pearls on a golden mountain until he finds her. If he can do that, he will be able to free her and bring her home.[8]

✳ Bringing the Ultimate Honor to Hashem

AFTER POINTING OUT the improvement to her situation for the purpose of encouraging the viceroy, the princess reveals the final objective: *"You will now need to search for a mountain of gold and a palace of pearls, and there you will find me."* In order to understand the depth of these words, we must begin with a short introduction.

In Chapter Thirteen, we explained that every growth process necessitates setbacks and failures. We explored the manner in which those setbacks and failures may retrospectively be utilized for the greater good of the process — we learn from our mistakes and adapt to changing circumstances to enable ourselves to grow smarter, stronger, and more adept at managing our situation. However, while this perspective allows us to perceive the value in the lessons flourishing on the banks of error, the process is comparable to mining gold from a muddy mountain: The *gold* is shining and valuable, but the *mountain* is dark and dirty — the lesson learned is indeed precious, but the failure itself remains unfortunate.

The tzaddikim teach that while this perspective is certainly

---

8. The *sefer Shaarei Orah* (Second Gate) explains that the word *"Har"* is deeply associated with the *Sefirah* of *Yesod*. This is an indicator that the viceroy is engaged in a process of *teshuvah* — rediscovering and returning to his deepest essence.

true, there is a deeper way of viewing challenges and failures from the retrospective security of *teshuvah*.

One of the deep truths of life is that *avodas Hashem* is not a *goal*. Rather, *avodas Hashem* is a *process*, a long and remarkable progression of revealing Hashem's honor in the world and expressing the depth of our commitment to His service. There are many ways in which a Jewish person brings honor to Hashem. Chief among them are halachah observance, overcoming base desires, Torah study, prayer, *emunah*, acts of *chessed*, and the personal refinement, nobility, and integrity which are a byproduct of true engagement with the spirit of Yiddishkeit. But in addition to these elevated paths of righteousness, the tzaddikim whisper that there is another way, a path to the side, a wondrous and mysterious form of honoring the Master of the world particularly prevalent in our lowly generation where "there is no righteous person in the land who does only right and never sins."[9]

Chazal teach that when Yisro forsook all the idols in the world and drew himself close to the Jewish faith, the Name of Hashem was glorified in the greatest possible manner. Rebbe Nachman of Breslov explains that since Yisro's approach to the realm of holiness required him to pull away from the profound darkness of his past as an idol-worshiper, his journey revealed the greatest extent of the Torah's power, bringing Hashem the ultimate honor.[10] In the same way, Chazal teach, "In the place where a *baal teshuvah* stands, even a perfect tzaddik cannot stand."[11] When a Jew who has sinned overcomes all obstacles and the seductive comfort of despair to do *teshuvah* and return to *avodas Hashem*, his journey brings great honor to the Master of the world. In fact, according

---

9. *Koheles* 7:20.
10. *Likutei Moharan* 10.
11. *Berachos* 34b.

to the *Zohar HaKadosh*, this Jew's powerful, sincere yearning, and his courageous return to *avodas Hashem* — which reveals a level of commitment to Yiddishkeit and refusal to live in a world absent of Hashem's presence — gives Hashem the *ultimate* honor.[12] Every time we experience a setback in our *avodah* and — presented with the choice to despair or continue the fight — we choose life, strengthening our resolve to continue the journey, we are bringing incredible honor to Hashem and revealing our intense love for Him.

The following, remarkable teaching goes a long way to explain why it is so very precious to Hashem when a Jew gathers his strength to embark on the path of *teshuvah* after performing a sin.

> Rebbe Nachman said: When the *yetzer hara* seduces a person to perform a sin *chas v'shalom*, his primary focus is not on the sin alone, but rather on the depression and discouragement the Jew will feel after the sin, for through this bitterness, he will fall into many more sins and go from bad to worse. Therefore, a person must be very careful not to fall into despair, no matter what![13]

The implication of this important teaching is that, in a certain way, the effort required to get back up after a sin instead of sinking into despair is greater than the effort necessary to withstand the temptations of sin in the first place, as this frustrates the *primary* intention of the *yetzer hara*. From the *yetzer hara*'s perspective, the sin is only a means to the end of despair — it is *after* the sin that the *yetzer hara*'s troops begin their mighty assault in earnest.

In the words of Reb Nosson:

---

12. *Zohar, Terumah* 128b. See also *Sfas Emes, Toldos,* "*U'bechinas.*"
13. *Siach Sarfei Kodesh*, Vol. 5, p. 49.

There is no greater excuse (to forsake Yiddishkeit entirely) than that which results from the *yetzer hara*'s strategy of discouragement — this that he demonstrates to the Jew, time and time again, that he has no hope. For he himself has seen with his own eyes how he has attempted to return to Hashem after having failed only to fail once again, each person in accordance with his failure, and this has happened innumerable times. Therefore, he absolves himself from again seeking to return to Hashem. But in truth, all of these thoughts and assumptions are acts of the *yetzer hara* so as to provide him with an excuse to separate from Hashem and follow his desires, *chas v'shalom*. For, as Rebbe Nachman yelled in a great voice which never ceased, "There is no despair in the world at all!"... *This is the primary test of a person*, that he encourage himself in all of his descents, no matter what happens to him, to constantly begin anew, forgetting everything that has happened to him in the past, and considering it as if he was born today.[14]

The ability for a Jew to remember that a momentary lapse of service doesn't represent his innermost essence and that it is the *ruach shtus* within him that has prevented him from thinking straight — as Chazal teach, "At the moment of engagement with the *yetzer hara*, one does not remember the *yetzer tov*,"[15] and "Our will is to do Your will, but the yeast in the dough prevents us"[16] — truly reflects the extent of his courage. We are defined not by the fall[17] but by the struggle that ensues in the moments *after* the fall. It is then that our commitment to *avodas Hashem* is

---

14. *Likutei Halachos, Hilchos Pesach*, 9:21. See also *Derashos Chasam Sofer* 4:13.

15. *Nedarim* 34b.

16. *Berachos* 17a.

17. Although avoiding sin in the first place is certainly a more preferable method of expressing this commitment, as Chazal state, "Who is mighty? He who conquers his *yetzer hara*" (*Avos* 4:1). See *Toras Menachem* 5744, Vol. 3, p. 1630.

truly put to the test: will we use the guilt, shame, and brokenness as an excuse to throw it all away, or is Yiddishkeit so dear to our broken heart that, come what may, we are somehow able to muster the strength to walk the paths of *teshuvah*?

⊛ Radical Encouragement

IN *MISHNEH TORAH*, the Rambam introduces a famous and confounding paradox regarding the concept of free will. This paradox involves the utter incompatibility of two truths, both of which are central to our faith. These truths are: A] Man's free will (*bechirah*), and B] Hashem's absolute knowledge of everything that will happen (*yedi'ah*). The paradox is simple: If Hashem knows what we are going to do before we do it, how, then, do we have free will? Surely it is impossible to act in a way which contradicts Hashem's knowledge! If Hashem knows that we are going to perform a mitzvah, how can we choose not to do so? More importantly, if Hashem knows that we are destined to sin, is it then possible to choose a different path?

While others submit to the impossibility of reconciliation[18] or attempt to resolve this paradox by limiting the extent of God's foreknowledge and leaving man's free choice completely unchallenged,[19] preserving the full extent of God's foreknowledge and

---

18. [The following four footnotes are based on the presentation of various approaches to this paradox in *Illuminating Jewish Thought*, a remarkable compendium by Rabbi Netanel Weiderblank (Maggid Books).] This seems to be the approach of **Rabbeinu Bachya** (*Chovas HaLevavos, Shaar Avodas Elokim* 8) who teaches that while there is a resolution to this issue, Hashem limited our intellect so that we cannot possibly grasp it.

19. This position is taken by the **Ralbag** (*Milchamos Hashem* 3:6) who holds that Hashem has limited His knowledge so that He knows only the choices available to a person but not the choice the person will make, and the **Shelah**

limiting the free choice of man,[20] or unraveling the paradox altogether,[21] the Rambam chooses a different path. After stressing that man has absolute free-choice and is not in any way compelled to act in a manner he has not chosen, the Rambam writes that God's foreknowledge of our actions is also a concrete, while albeit incomprehensible, reality. In this vein, the Mishnah states: "Everything is foreseen, yet freedom of choice is granted"[22] — both truths function at once. Although everything is foreseen in the fullest extent of the word and thus predetermined, this does not negate our experience of free will and the ability to freely create our destiny. Validating both truths and stressing that, as our experience demonstrates, they do not negate one another, the Rambam preserves the paradox. Still — as the Rambam makes quite clear — because Hashem's knowledge of the future does not negate our freedom of choice, it has little

---

HaKadosh (*Toldos Adam, Beis HaBechirah*, p. 289) who similarly limits Hashem's knowledge to natural progressions based on current circumstances.

20. This appears to be the (radical) approach of R' Chasdai Crescas, a student of the Ran, who posits that human actions are taken based on absolute conditions known and caused by Hashem. Because Hashem knows the causes, He knows the effects that must necessarily follow.

21. This approach is taken (with varying shades of nuance) by *Tosafos Yom Tov, Midrash Shmuel* (to *Avos* 3:21) and *Shiurei Daas* (2:8) who point out that, because Hashem is outside of time, the concepts of "before" and "after" do not apply. Therefore, there is truly no contradiction between foreknowledge and free choice. (This solution is challenged by the *Ohr Sameiach* [*Hilchos Teshuvah*, Chapter 5] who wonders whether this truly solves the problem), the **Maharal** (*Derech Chaim* 3:15) who teaches that God indeed sees everything, yet in such a way that does not impact free choice — like the knowledge of one who looks out the window and sees his friend approaching does not impact the approach of his friend, as well as **R' Saadya Gaon** (*Emunos V'Deios* 4:4) and the **Rivash** (*Shu"t HaRivash* 118) who hold that God's foreknowledge of our choice does not cause that choice but He rather knows what we will choose freely.

22. *Avos* 3:19.

practical effect on our day to day lives. Because our reality is one in which free choice is granted, there is certainly place for a system of reward and punishment; we are charged with making the proper choices and following the will of Hashem as revealed in His holy Torah.

Seizing on the preservation of Hashem's foreknowledge in the words of the Rambam,[23] Reb Tzadok HaKohen of Lublin makes a series of important statements on the matter, some quite radical.

The first step Reb Tzadok takes in expounding upon this Rambam is to clarify the manner in which both truths can function at once.[24] He states that it is all a matter of perspective. From Hashem's perspective, everything is foretold.[25] Hashem knows everything that is going to happen and, indeed, everything must play out in accordance with that predetermination. However, from our perspective, everything is left up to our own choice. In our condition of independent consciousness, we experience the absolute freedom to make decisions and shape our destiny in accordance with the choices we make.[26]

Having assigned these contradictory truths to separate experiences of reality, Reb Tzadok then treats an unspoken question: Is it ever possible for a Jew to peek behind the curtain and attain

---

23. See *Pri Tzaddik*, Yisro #3.

24. Although conceptually similar to the Rambam, Reb Tzadok differs in that while the Rambam maintains that there is a logical compatibility here we cannot fathom, Reb Tzadok's approach seems to deny the need for logical compatibility. (See *Illuminating Jewish Thought*, p. 99.)

25. The Arizal (quoted here by Reb Tzadok) assigns this perspective to the spiritual world of *Atzilus*, the world of Emanation, which is nearest (*"eitzel"*) to God (*Arbah Meos Shekel Kesef* 91b).

26. See a similar formulation from Rav Hutner (*Pachad Yitzchak, Igros U'Michtavim* 9), who writes that although there are indeed sins which are beyond one's freedom of choice (*"l'maalah min habechirah"* — see Rashi to *Yoma* 20a), one must do *teshuvah* for all sins. See, too, Rav Dessler's position in *Michtav M'Eliyahu*, Vol. 3, p. 262.

the Divine realization that the sins he committed were in fact predetermined and part of God's will which is perfectly good? Although, as we have said, this truth does not challenge our *bechirah*, does there ever come a time when we can make use of this awesome knowledge, seeing our negative decisions as having been part of the Master Plan?

In the previous section, we learned that the primary test of a Jew begins after one fails to control his desires and commits a sin. Because it is after the sin that the *yetzer hara* truly begins his work, when a Jew gathers his strength to return to the proper path instead of taking the easier route and giving in to the comfort of despair, this brings Hashem the greatest possible honor. While Rebbe Nachman does not say so explicitly, this model of "the post-sin test," where the transgression is seen not as a failure in and of itself but rather as the premise for a *nisayon*, could provide the theoretical groundwork for an understanding of how a sin could possibly be understood as having been the will of Hashem. If the primary honor a Jew can bring to Hashem is by returning to His service after a devastating failure — which the *yetzer hara* intends to use for the purpose of casting him into hopelessness and despair — it becomes possible to understand how a sin may be seen as part of a process leading to a greater good.[27]

While other tzaddikim refrained from discussing these awesome ideas openly for fear of their views being abused and misused, Reb Tzadok HaKohen of Lublin, following in the lead of his Rebbe, the Mei HaShiloach, wrote explicitly about this process for the sake of granting Jews the courage never to forsake their journey toward closeness with Hashem. These are his holy words:

---

27. See *Likutei Halachos, Areiv* 3:4, where Reb Nosson discusses the concept of "*yeridah l'tzorech aliyah*."

The essence of *teshuvah* is the point when Hashem enlightens one's eyes, and [he realizes that] his sins have been transformed into merits — meaning, he recognizes and understands that all of his sins were also the will of Hashem.

Both [*yedi'ah* and *bechirah*] are true; each in their own place. In the place of *bechirah*, there is no room for *yedi'ah*. And in the place of *yedi'ah*, there is truly no place for *bechirah*. When one attains this awesome light, all of his sins return as not having departed from Hashem's knowledge, which is one with His will.[28]

Here, Reb Tzadok is teaching that after one has done complete *teshuvah* for his sins[29] and merited to bring the ultimate honor

---

28. *Tzidkas HaTzaddik* 40. See also 100, 139, and 156; and *Pri Tzaddik*, Vol. 4, *L'Rosh Chodesh Menachem Av*, pp. 236–237.

29. Which is the point when "his heart burns toward Hashem like a fire until it burns and destroys all the impurities and evil in his heart, and he becomes completely '*Kodesh LaShem*'" (*Divrei Sofrim* 38). See *Likutei Moharan* 156, and *Kedushas Levi, Emor, "U'bas Kohen"* for earlier sources that discuss this process. "Of course, internalizing this message is not easy; if a person truly believes that nothing exists besides God (*ein od milvado*), he never would sin (at least in the normal sense). This realization, therefore, goes beyond *teshuvah mi-yirah* (repentance out of fear), which 'merely' requires sincere acknowledgment of wrongdoing, regretting the sin, and honestly resolving to do better in the future. *Teshuvah mei-ahavah* demands recognizing that everything comes from God. Achieving this is an extraordinary accomplishment for a sinner. Sinning generally is a demonstration of independence from God. Thus, the submission implied by recognizing one's absolute dependence upon God reflects an absolute transformation. This personal revolution allows a person's sins to be transformed at will to align with his newfound negation... To reach the level of *teshuvah mei-ahavah*, one must achieve a high degree of self-abnegation and apply it consistently throughout his life (*Illuminating Jewish Thought*, p. 96). See, however, *Pri Tzaddik, Kedushas Shabbos*, fourth discourse, "*V'zehu tefillas haminchah*" — although this seeming exception may be qualified by Reb Tzadok's teaching in *Pri Tzaddik, Ki Savo, "Isah b'Likutei Torah mei'haArizal*," where it is explained that someone who ascribes all of his good deeds to Hashem as well may make use of this concept post-sin as a means of retrospective encouragement.

to Hashem in his return, it is indeed possible to peek behind the barrier which stands between our perspective and that of Hashem in order to attain the awareness of *yedi'ah*, the knowledge that his sin was, in fact, pre-ordained.[30] This is truly a radical idea and requires much clarification.

Let's begin with what Reb Tzadok is *not* saying. Reb Tzadok is neither saying that it is ever permissible to act based on the awareness of the truth of *yedi'ah* nor that one may simply "choose" to retrospectively view an action as having been in accordance with the will of Hashem. In these sentences Reb Tzadok makes it quite clear that he feels just as strongly as the Rambam regarding the truth of our free-will.[31] "In the place of *bechirah*,

---

30. Perhaps it is possible to suggest that this idea is hinted at in *Shabbos* 89b. The Gemara states: "...It says: "If your sins be like scarlet [*ka'shanim*], they will become white like snow" (*Yeshayahu* 1:18). Why does the verse use the plural form: *Ka'shanim*? It should have used the singular form: *Ka'shani*! Rav Yitzchak said that HaKadosh Baruch Hu said to the Jewish people: Even if your sins are as numerous as those years [*ka'shanim*] that have proceeded continuously [*seduros u'ba'os*] from the six days of Creation until now, they will become white like snow." Perhaps we may read the Gemara as follows: *"Im yiheyu chata'eichem kashanim hallalu seduros u'ba'os m'sheishes yemei bereishis v'ad achshav"* — not "even if," but it is specifically if one arrives at the realization that his sins had been arranged and preordained from the six days of creation [in many places, we find the "six days of creation" mentioned in the context of something having been prepared from that time] then one can be sure that *"k'sheleg yalbinu,"* they are white like snow and he is forgiven. (The astute student will recognize that this idea finds further expression in the Gemara's second interpretation as well, where Hashem says, "Since you made yourselves dependent on Me, 'If your sins be like scarlet, they will become white like snow.'")

31. Although, in the Morning Blessings we refer to Hashem as *"Hameichin mitzadei gaver,"* the One Who arranges all of our steps, we also thank Hashem *"shelo asani aved,"* that we are not enslaved by any external forces. The *yedi'ah* of Hashem is absolute, but we are still granted with the freedom to choose. Another hint to this may be found in the verse, "By the directive of Hashem they traveled and by the directive of Hashem they rested — by the word of Hashem, in the hands of Moshe" (*Bamidbar* 9:23). While a Jew's spiritual

there is no room for yedi'ah" — outside of this hyper-particular situation in which a person attains the most complete levels of *teshuvah*, it is never possible to excuse our negative choices with claims of predeterminism.[32] Because we live in the realm of *bechirah* and experience the absolute freedom to make our own decisions, it is impossible to attain this deep awareness before the act.[33] This would be tantamount to living a lie, a path that can only lead to spiritual atrophy, never to growth, as the Mishnah teaches, "One who says 'I will sin and then do *teshuvah'* is not afforded the opportunity to return."[34] In this world, we live with the reality of *bechirah*, the ability to make our own decisions, and this — from our perspective — is not an illusion but rather the concrete truth, the foundation for the entire Torah which serves as the premise for any measure of spiritual growth and accomplishment. Indeed, the realization that a human being ever has the freedom to change his spiritual position and freely choose a life of Torah and mitzvos was one of the first lessons the viceroy learned along his journey — and it served as the primary catalyst for his *teshuvah*. Had the viceroy not realized the liberating implication of his freedom to choose a better life and change his ways,

---

resting is dictated by the word of Hashem, it is always *"b'yad Moshe"* — from our perspective, it is always our own responsibility.

32. See *Sefer HaZichronos*, mitzvah 3.

33. See *Tzidkas HaTzaddik* 43.

34. *Yoma* 8:9. See also *Tzidkas HaTzaddik* 174; *Mei HaShiloach*, Vol. 1, *Korach*, "*Vayikach Korach* 2"; and *Even Shleimah* 4:4, where the Gra illustrates the misuse of this idea.

In his *sefer Illuminating Jewish Thought* (p. 8), Rabbi Netanel Weiderblank writes: "Psychological studies show that people who believe they have free will tend to act with a greater sense of moral responsibility than fatalists and determinists who deny their ability to control their destiny... Moreover, as Dr. Eddy Nahmias writes, 'Simply exposing people to scientific claims that free will is an illusion can lead them to misbehave, for instance, cheating more or helping people less.'"

he would never have reached the elevated level he now enjoys! Therefore, it is important to clarify that Reb Tzadok's radical idea is intended solely for the sake of encouragement, to provide the recovering Jew with the knowledge that if he *chooses* correctly from this point onward, it is possible that one day in the future he will attain the awesome awareness that validates the entire journey, both the triumphs as well as the failures.[35]

This idea comes to expression in the writings of another *"Kohen Gadol,"* Rav Avraham Yitzchak HaKohen Kook. In *Oros HaTeshuvah*, the tzaddik writes:

> One of the foundations of *teshuvah*, in the mind of a person, is the recognition of his culpability for his actions which is an extension of one's faith in his ability to choose freely. This is the content of the *vidui* (confession) composition which is so bound with the mitzvah of *teshuvah* — a person admits that there is nothing and nobody else to blame for his sins and their effects, but himself alone. With this, he clarifies for himself the freedom of his will and the extent of his influence over the ways of his life and actions.

---

35. In the words of Rabbi David Bashevkin: "Religious life has both a floor and a ceiling. The ceiling is built upon the ideals and values we reach towards, which we may never attain. The floor, however, is the framework and perspective from which we deal with failure and those still mired in sin. Much of religious life is spent vacillating somewhere in the middle. The more radical deterministic elements of Izbica-Lublin can provide cushions and comfort on the floor of Judaism without altering the ceiling. Sometimes, when religious life feels closer to the floor, there may be a feeling that Godliness and spiritual meaning are unattainable. It is here that Izbician theology is most instructive, reminding us that 'Wherever a Jew may fall, he falls into the lap of God.' Applying a deterministic theology as a retrospective means of making spiritual sense of religious failure can be done without insisting on a deterministic perspective that undermines the ideals we are working towards... Failure and sin may indeed both be intractable parts of religious life, but the theological means with which we soften our 'floor' don't have to become the theological ends with which we secure our 'ceiling.'" (*Sin•a•gogue*, p. 48)

This allows him to clear a path to return to Hashem, to renew his life with proper order which, drawing from the source of wisdom, he perceives as representing his success — a path bound with the holy light of the Torah which revives the soul.

In these words, Rav Kook stresses the concrete truth of *bechirah*, and the tremendous role that accepting responsibility for our actions and freely choosing a better future must play in the *teshuvah* process. The recognition that we are not bound by the cycles of sin that saturate our past and can begin to choose to live an elevated life freely, at any moment, is a major source of encouragement and serves as a catalyst for our return to Hashem. The tzaddik continues:

After one attains clear knowledge (the question regarding two incompatible truths functioning simultaneously is only paradoxical from *our* perspective, in accordance with our limited intellectual capacity, and doesn't relate at all to the principles of the Creator of all, the Master of all principles, the Cause of all causes, the Source of wisdom and Constructer of understanding Blessed be He), we are able to understand that there is place for both the awareness of man's ability to choose and his free choice, in addition to his *inability to choose* and his *lack of free choice*. This matter draws from all streams within creation. However, all the while that one has not returned from his sin and has not established the paths of his *teshuvah*, he is yet found under the burden of his choice and his culpability for all of his actions and all the negative effects which are his responsibility. However, after the radiance of *teshuvah*, all of the shortcomings in his life as well as the actions which, from our perspective, appear to be negative and have caused bitter consequences, are immediately retrospectively given over to the influence of the Most High. They are all arranged outside of his freedom of choice and become part of the influence of the elevated governance, the power of the Most High, which [is referred to in the verse], "You have caused all of our actions."[36, 37]

In this remarkable paragraph, Rav Kook stresses that the truths of *yedi'ah* and *bechirah* both present a crucial form of encouragement.

The truth of *bechirah* provides a *future-oriented* encouragement by granting every person the ability to choose to live in a proper manner, regardless of how badly one has sinned in the past. However, this truth also gives rise to a discouraging thought. After choosing to embark on the paths of *teshuvah* and correcting his ways, one may come to feel that a natural corollary of the very freedom of choice that has allowed him to do *teshuvah* is a debilitating sense of guilt stemming from the awareness that he alone, having chosen those actions with his free will, is responsible for burden of his sins — a burden too heavy for him to bear.

At this point, having achieved a secure plateau of growth and rectification, the truth of *yedi'ah* provides a retrospective, *past-oriented* encouragement, bringing one to the awareness that this entire process was part of the Master Plan and that it couldn't have happened any other way: "In the place where a *baal teshuvah* stands, even a perfect tzaddik cannot stand."[38,39]

---

36. *Yeshayahu* 26:12. See *Divrei Sofrim* 38 where Reb Tzadok brings this verse in the same context.

37. *Oros HaTeshuvah* 16:1.

38. *Berachos* 34b. See *Takanas HaShavin* 5 and *Pri Tzaddik*, Acharei Mos 6, where Reb Tzadok uses this statement from Chazal to provide a slightly different approach as to the reason a person's sin may have been the true *ratzon Hashem*.

39. The astute student will recognize that theoretically, in the same manner as the truth of *bechirah* provides a reason for discouragement in addition to its encouragement by accentuating one's culpability in his sin, the past-oriented encouragement provided by the truth of *yedi'ah* is accompanied by a discouraging idea as well — the notion that one's good deeds were similarly

✳ The Golden Mountain

AFTER THIS IMPORTANT introduction, we are now able to understand the depth of the princess's communication to the viceroy.
In her message of tears, the princess tells the viceroy that she
may be found in a palace of pearls atop a mountain of gold. The
Breslover *mashpi'im* unravel the riddle in the most wondrous
way.

Earlier on in this book, we have described the potential benefit of an error as embodied in the lesson this error will ultimately yield; pure gold mined from the dark bowels of a muddy
mountain. Here, the princess tells the viceroy of a far greater
awareness; the ability to do *teshuvah* to the point where one can
enter the realm of *yedi'ah*, seeing how the entire journey was
in accordance with the deepest will of Hashem. After reaching
the plateau of ultimate success at the end of his mission, it is
possible for the viceroy to attain the deep realization that in
persevering throughout this difficult journey, yearning for the
princess with an intensity that allowed him to defy despair even
after challenge and *failure*, he has not merely mined gold from
a dull and dirty mountain, learning lessons for the future from
the shameful and unfortunate failings of the past. Rather, after complete *teshuvah*, he will come to the awesome awareness
that the mountain is *itself* made of gold; the winding path of his

---

predetermined and that he will therefore receive no credit for performing
them. Further on, Rav Kook addresses this point and teaches that it isn't true.
Even after one rightfully and truthfully attains the awareness of *yedi'ah* and
the clarity that his sins were part of Hashem's Master Plan, his good deeds
remain the product of his own will. In fact, Rav Kook writes that the more illumination one receives from this hidden realm of *yedi'ah* which weakens the
bond between his freedom to choose and the sins he committed, the *stronger*
his bond grows to the good deeds he performed — the more they are credited
to himself alone. See *Berachos* 32b for a possible precedent for this idea.

journey — including the terrible darkness he has experienced along the way — is shining brilliantly from one end of the world to the other.[40]

This is the deep, hidden message the princess is relaying here to the viceroy, the inner point of righteousness who has courageously continued his journey despite suffering setback after setback. She is telling him that in addition to realizing the value of the lessons learned from these errors, he will one day merit to attain the realization that those setbacks themselves were inherently valuable, that every stumble backward which resulted in a firm step forward is inherently precious, and that freeing the Lost Princess of youth is every bit as much about the journey as it is the destination.

---

40. It is fascinating to note that the first time the word *zahav*, gold, appears in the Torah, it is labeled "*tov*," good: *V'zahav ha'eretz hahi tov*, "And the gold of that land was good" (*Bereishis* 2:12). The *Torah Temimah* (12:30) quotes *Tosafos* as saying that the goodness of this gold refers to the fact that even when one scours it, none of the gold gets lost. Perhaps it is possible to suggest that the mountain of gold, which is called "*tov*," is the parallel in holiness to the place of "*lo tov*," where the princess was first taken. The awareness embodied by this golden mountain is hinted to in the words of *Tosafos* — even when it is scoured, nothing is lost; all of the darkness experienced by the viceroy on his journey was for the sake of his own cleansing and rectification. Thus, he is able to see in retrospect that "nothing was lost" — the mountain itself is composed of the gold of "*tov*." It is possible to suggest that these two retrospective realizations are hinted to in *Berachos* (5a) in the two opinions with regard to what happened to Rav Huna's wine. (The Gemara relates an episode where 400 barrels of Rav Huna's wine turned to vinegar. Once he accepted upon himself to fix his error of withholding grapevines from his sharecropper, something happened to the sour wine.) One opinion says that it turned back into wine — this is a reference to the idea of being able to learn from our mistakes, to extract the lessons and grow. The second opinion says the vinegar did not undergo a transformation, but vinegar prices rose to the price of wine — this refers to the idea that the sin itself "*naaseh lo k'zechus*," becomes seen as something essentially valuable. See also *Likutei Moharan* 22:11.

❋ The Palace of Pearls

THE PALACE OF pearls adorning this golden mountain is another symbolization of this lesson. It is a well-known fact that pearls are formed when a foreign entity, often a parasite, enters the shell of a mollusk such as an oyster or a clam and begins to irritate its flesh. When this happens, the oyster secretes nacre, a composite material made of calcium and protein, which coats the parasite to protect itself from harm. Over a period of time, as layer upon layer of nacre is applied, a pearl is formed.

Natural pearls are one of the most precious of all gems — considered to be even more valuable than diamonds. They are generally worn by the wealthiest class of a given society, and even then, only on special occasions. Their lustrous sheen sets them apart from all other precious minerals and assures that they are ever in style.

As we have learned, the splendor we now see before our eyes in a shining pearl is the result not of a beautiful, smooth process, but of an anomaly, a foreign parasite whose irritating presence caused the pearl-forming process to begin. However, from a retrospective awareness, we are able to look back at this unfortunate occurrence and see it as having been a truly wonderful thing, the factor that enabled this oyster to stand out from all the rest and bring awesome splendor into the world.

Seen in this way, the palace of pearls embodies the same lesson as the mountain of gold: after all of the pain, confusion, and descents experienced along the path toward spiritual fulfillment, a person can attain the retrospective realization that sees the darkness he experienced in his past illuminated by the awesome light of a present he never could have attained without the long and difficult journey.

When the viceroy can reach this awesome level of *teshuvah* and achieve the secret awareness of the golden mountain and the palace of pearls, it is there that he shall find the lost princess and redeem her at long last.

LESSONS FOR LIFE

❋ In order for the teachings of *penimiyus haTorah* to illuminate our lives, we must approach them with faith in their relevance as well as the awesome stature of the tzaddikim who revealed these teachings in their *sefarim*.

❋ The tzaddikim of *penimiyus* who always manage to find the good in society, history, circumstances, and other people are not naïve. Rather, they are connected to an elevated perspective on reality which sees things as they truly are instead of the way they appear on the surface.

❋ The *yetzer hara*'s primary intention in causing a Jew to sin is to utilize the sin as a means to drag the sinner into the depths of hopelessness and despair so that many more sins, and perhaps complete disengagement with Yiddishkeit, will follow.

❋ When a Jew refuses to give in to the seductive comfort of despair, overcoming all obstacles and returning to *avodas Hashem* after a spiritual failure, he expresses the ultimate extent of his desire and brings awesome honor to Hashem.

❋ In this world, we experience *bechirah*, absolute free choice, and are therefore responsible for the decisions we make. However, after complete *teshuvah*, it is possible for one to attain the awesome awareness that his sin was also *ratzon Hashem* — predetermined for the purpose of challenging him to battle the inclination toward despair and rise once more to the paths of *avodas Hashem*, bringing about the greatest *kevod Shamayim*.

CHAPTER 17

An Other-Worldly Awareness

וְהִשְׁאִיר אֶת הַמְשָׁרֵת וְהִנִּיחוֹ, וְהָלַךְ לְבַדּוֹ לְבַקְשָׁהּ. וְהָלַךְ כַּמָּה שָׁנִים לְבַקְשָׁהּ, וְיָשֵׁב עַצְמוֹ שֶׁבְּוַדַּאי בַּיִּשּׁוּב לֹא נִמְצָא הַר שֶׁל זָהָב וּמִבְצָר שֶׁל מַרְגָּלִיּוֹת, כִּי הוּא בָּקִי בְּמַפַּת הָעוֹלָם, וְעַל כֵּן אֵלֶךְ אֶל הַמִּדְבָּרִיּוֹת. וְהָלַךְ לְבַקְשָׁהּ בַּמִּדְבָּרִיּוֹת כַּמָּה וְכַמָּה שָׁנִים. אַחַר כָּךְ רָאָה אָדָם גָּדוֹל מְאֹד שֶׁאֵינוֹ [בְּגֶדֶר] אֱנוֹשִׁי כְּלָל שֶׁיִּהְיֶה אָדָם גָּדוֹל כָּל כָּךְ, וְנָשָׂא אִילָן גָּדוֹל, שֶׁבַּיִּשּׁוּב אֵינוֹ נִמְצָא אִילָן גָּדוֹל כָּזֶה. וְאוֹתוֹ הָאִישׁ שָׁאַל אוֹתוֹ: מִי אַתָּה? וְאָמַר לוֹ: אֲנִי אָדָם. וְתָמַהּ, וְאָמַר שֶׁזֶּה כָּל כָּךְ זְמַן שֶׁאֲנִי בְּהַמִּדְבָּר וְלֹא רָאִיתִי מֵעוֹלָם בְּכָאן אָדָם.

He left his servant behind and went to search for her, alone. His search for her lasted many years. Eventually, he came to the realization that this mountain of gold and palace of pearls certainly does not exist in the settled parts of the world, for he was an expert in all the maps of the world. (He said:) "I will go to the deserts," and he went to search for her in the deserts for many years. After this, he saw a tremendously large person, who didn't seem to be human at all because of his enormous size. He carried

300

a huge tree — no tree in the settled world was as large as this tree. The giant asked him: "Who are you?" He responded, "I am a human." The giant was astounded, and he said, "It has been so long since I have been in this desert, and I have never seen a human here!"

The Servant Departs

WHEN WE FIRST encountered the viceroy's servant toward the beginning of our tale, we learned that he represents intellectual integrity that forever remains bound to the mighty truths of our tradition. After his devastating failures and descent into spiritual hibernation, the viceroy relied on his trusty servant to remain unaffected by the emotional turmoil that so demolished his sense of purpose to ensure that, after bouncing back from this dark place of despair, the seeds of memory, aspiration, and commitment could be replanted for the sake of nurturing a future excursion.

But much has happened since the viceroy first set out, wide-eyed and confident, from the king's palace to seek the lost princess of youthful passion and vitality. Over many decades of a search marked by both triumph and catastrophe, he has learned powerful lessons that have completely transformed his perspective on living. He is wiser now, more mature. The many ups and downs he experienced along the way, while devastating and painful, have taught him more than he could possibly have learned any other way. Radical truths have effected a revolution in his essence — truths like the ideas that a lull can sometimes signify entry to a new phase of spiritual growth; failures are a necessary part of the growth process; personal prayer is the key to spiritual success; yearning is intrinsically valuable; freedom of choice sits at the core of human stability; and when the going gets tough, it is in an indicator that one is very close to his goal. Having done *teshuvah* for his sins and taken lessons from them for the future, he is not the same viceroy of decades past. This journey has changed his life forever.

At this point in his mission, the viceroy has subdued his natural inclination to react to sin by falling into an immobilizing state of anguish and despair. Although there is no guarantee the *yetzer hara* won't get the best of him in the future ("Do not trust yourself until the day you die" is another one of the many lessons he has learned) he now knows better than to immediately retreat into spiritual hibernation.[1] The snake may yet strike, its razor-sharp fangs sinking into his skin and drawing two points of blood, but the *venom* is gone. No longer will he fall prey to the diabolic strategy of his archnemesis who seeks to magnify a single misdeed in the hope that the Jew will be discouraged from returning and apathetically do far more damage than the small dent he had originally made. Therefore, as he begins to set out on the final stage of his noble mission, the viceroy no longer requires the services of his servant and leaves him behind. Now he stands all alone with the expansive sky above his head, endless ground beneath his feet, the gift of a promise in hand, and an undetermined amount of time to further integrate the lessons he has learned.

Rebbe Nachman relates: *He left his servant behind and went to search for her, alone.* The fact that the Rebbe stresses both the viceroy's parting from his servant in addition to his being left alone, indicates that both elements are meaningful in and of themselves.

As we have discussed, leaving the servant behind reflects the confidence, maturity, and experience the viceroy feels at this point

---

1. See *Likutei Halachos, Netillas Yadayim L'Seudah* 6:55.

along his journey. But there is also something particularly significant in his being left alone. A veteran rider of life's thrilling roller coaster that has all its occupants throwing up their hands and screaming — some of them with laughter and others with pain, sometimes with pleasure and other times with sorrow,[2] the viceroy has reached a point of serenity where he feels safe on his own, with nothing to distract him from the inner world of the spirit. Having battled his inner demons and discovered major points of vulnerability by exposing their true intentions, he treads the threshold of a new stage alone, with the confidant optimism of a warrior. He has made peace with himself; his ugly errors are illuminated with the brilliant light of the lessons at their core. Now he is ready to search for the fantastical place the princess had written about and the awesome awareness it represents — the palace of pearls atop a mountain of gold.

✳ An Illogical Mode of Progression

REFRESHED AND REJUVENATED, the viceroy sets out to find the palace the princess had described. He walks not for days, weeks, or months, but for *years, "many years,"* before finally coming to the realization that he is simply searching in the wrong place. The Hebrew words Rebbe Nachman uses to express the viceroy's realization are *meyasheiv atzmo,* "he settled himself." As we have learned above, this term is a reference to *hisbodedus.* Setting aside time for personal prayer can enable the recovering Jew to realize that oftentimes, instead of indicating failure, his inability to find that which he is searching for simply indicates that he is searching in the wrong place! Utilizing this tremendous tool of direct dialogue with the Master of the world, the viceroy settles

---

2. See *Yeshayahu* 65:14.

his mind and achieves great clarity into his situation, the sudden awareness that the place he is searching for is not on the map. The Breslover *mashpi'im* reveal the deeper meaning behind this development.

In the previous chapter, we learned that the "mountain of gold and palace of pearls" symbolizes a lofty retrospective awareness — a point when the viceroy can arrive at the elevated realization that the struggles, challenges, and even the mistakes he made along his journey were in fact part of the process of growth and that, in a deep and hidden way, they actually aided him in coming closer to freeing the lost princess by allowing him to bring honor to Hashem in his return. *"Zedonos naasos lo k'zechuyos"* — he can reach the level where it becomes clear to him that his sins have been transformed into merits.[3] Having already begun to hear an echo of this truth resonating within the concrete change in his personality and the ultimate extent of holy desire which, like fine wine oozing from trampled grapes, his failures have forced him to express, the viceroy has an epiphany. In a moment of sudden inspiration, he realizes that while it is certainly possible to be grasped in this world by a sensitive, receptive soul, this consciousness truly does not belong to our reality at all.

As we have discussed in the previous chapter, this gentle, retrospective awareness may only be grasped by a person who understands that — from our perspective — freedom of choice is an absolute truth. It is only one who takes full responsibility for his actions and bears the burden of guilt for the years it takes to rectify his misdeeds in a future filled with positive choices who can merit this awareness at the proper time and in the proper manner. One who enters the realm of *yedi'ah* without the requisite anchoring in the truth of *bechirah* causes a tremendous breach which will likely have an incredibly detrimental effect on

---

3. *Yoma* 86b.

his *avodas Hashem, chas v'shalom.*[4] The foundational premise of our holy Torah is the experience of *bechirah*. That is our truth, and the absolute reality of our perspective.

The viceroy trusts implicitly in the princess's promise — transmitted through the words of the tzaddikim in their teachings of *penimiyus haTorah* — that there is a single shining moment in life, forever within the grasp of even the most ordinary individual, during which looking back over a difficult phase or even the entirety of a lifetime is accompanied by a deep serenity founded in the certain realization that every challenge moved him closer to his goal in the most hidden, mysterious way. But it is equally clear to him that such a moment is qualitatively different from a moment spent brushing one's teeth, browsing the web, or driving to work. The very nature of this all-important moment is *otherworldly*. It is eternity expressed in time, a single moment that transcends itself to kiss the great expanse, a glimpse of our reality as seen from a standpoint beyond its own constraints.[5] This peek behind the iron barrier of our experience — a glimpse into the realm of *"yedi'ah"* wherein Hashem knows every action be-

---

4. See *Mei HaShiloach*, Vol. 1, *Korach*, *"Vayikach Korach."* See also *Pri Tzaddik, Shelach* #6 regarding the sin of the *Mekosheish Eitzim* (*Bamidbar* 15:32–36): "The *Mekosheish* thought that perhaps the will of Hashem is for one to sin and then do *teshuvah* afterward to produce the aspect of *tov me'od*, 'very good,' thus bringing one to an even higher level... But he erred in this, for this model is only *b'dieved*, ex post facto — if one corrupted his way and subsequently does *teshuvah*, then it will be clarified in the future... and his sins will be turned into merits. But certainly *l'chatchilah*, before the event, God forbid that a person should think like this! It is forbidden to rely on this. About this our Sages taught, 'One who says, "I will sin and repent" is not afforded the opportunity to repent.'"

5. Indeed, as discussed earlier, this level of *teshuvah* carries one to the level of the *Kisei HaKavod* which is bound with the world of *Binah* and the number eight which transcends the sevenness of nature as reflected in the realm of time.

fore we perform it and everything, *everything*, is part of Hashem's Master Plan, is a lightning bolt from the loftiest spiritual realms which grants one the momentary insight that "*Hakol b'yedei Shamayim*" — including "*yiras Shamayim*,"[6] and that had one thing gone differently in his life — *had one less mistake been made* — he would not be where he stands today.[7] Because it is not from our reality, the very nature of this gentle understanding, this lofty "aha" moment, demands that it be attained from a perspective spanning all of life's journey, a place where it becomes gradually possible to see things with the 20/20 vision of hindsight.[8] Paradoxically, then, unlike other concepts that are grasped by actively engaging with them, this revelation can only be attained by turning away from it, by living life with simplicity, in the consciousness of *bechirah* that allows us to make the right decision in the heat of the moment — only allowing this lofty light from the realm of *yedi'ah* to settle in on its own at the proper time.

When Rebbe Nachman writes about the viceroy's realization that the golden mountain doesn't exist on the map of the world,

---

6. See *Mei HaShiloach*, Vol. 1, *Vayeira*, "*Vatichacheish Sarah*" where the Ishbitzer discusses this idea and ends with the words: "And understand this, for it is exceedingly deep." See also *Likutei Tefillos* 116, where Reb Nosson writes, "And You have given over *bechirah* into the hands of man as if it is not in Your hand, as our Sages say, 'Everything is in the hands of heaven, except fear of heaven.' But even so, the truth is that even *bechirah* is in Your hands, for everything is from You, and You give life to all." See also *Avodas Yisrael, Shelach*, "*V'atah yigdal*," and *Balak*, "*Vayashes*."

7. See *Likutei Moharan Tinyana* 82, a lesson founded upon the mystical intentions of Elul, the month of *teshuvah*, where Rebbe Nachman discusses the concept of "*K'Seder*" and "*Shelo k'Seder*," and teaches that the ultimate goal is to demonstrate the manner in which all that appears to be "*Shelo k'Seder*" is truly the deepest expression of "*K'seder*." This lesson is deeply bound with our tale, as the concepts of male (*viceroy*) and female (*princess*) are discussed as well.

8. See *Pri Tzaddik, Kedushas Shabbos* 4.

he is referring to his understanding that this lofty moment of retrospective clarity cannot be understood with a this-wordly consciousness that necessitates the possibility to perform an action that is indeed opposed to the will of Hashem. It is only when a lofty light shines upon him from behind the mighty curtain of the awesome *tzimtzum*-constriction which grants the illusory reality of man's independent will, that he may experience an other-wordly reality where the whole story was guided by Hashem from beginning to end, and where the mountain is *itself* golden. It is only from this retrospective standpoint that he can attain the shining clarity that the entire journey — with its dizzying highs as well as its devastating lows — formed one giant torch of *kevod Shamayim.*

Rebbe Nachman tells us that the viceroy "was an expert in the maps of the world." He was intimately familiar with the standard growth process, the iron-clad rules of a geographical journey where only *forward* movement brings one from point A to point B — steps in the opposite direction will never effect advancement. At this stage, after going through this seemingly irrational process of falling only to rise to an even higher plane, he has begun to taste the reality of heaven's super-rational perspective, the "other-wordly" method of growth, which can only be attained in retrospect. After years of rooting himself in the absolute reality of free-choice, the viceroy arrives at the realization that this special kind of journey isn't to be found on the "regular maps of the world" where forward movement alone is productive. Thus, he continues his searching elsewhere, in a realm Rebbe Nachman labels a "desert."

A place of parched ground, wild beasts, and little growth or life, it seems logical that it is in the desert, seemingly devoid of "standard growth," that the viceroy might find the golden mountain and pearl castle, the headquarters for "non-standard growth," learning lessons from failures and mistakes. As he walks in this arena, elevated beyond the lowliness of this world, the viceroy

encounters the most incredible sight, a human being of unbeliev-
ably gigantic proportions.

⊛ *Malchus:* Light and Dark, Full and Empty

BEFORE EXPLORING THE identity of this giant, it is important to
focus upon a deep point that sheds greater light on this critical
topic and provides further clarity into the viceroy's journey and
his ultimate destination.

In the opening chapters of this book, we described the manner in which the princess of our story embodies the *Sefirah* of
Malchus. As part of that discussion, we surveyed a few aspects
of *Malchus* such as its feminine, inward, and emotional nature,
for the purpose of illustrating just what it is that a Jew loses when
the princess of his life, marriage, ambitions, and *avodas Hashem*
becomes concealed. In addition to these facets, there is another
deep and important element of *Malchus* that requires exploration
to allow for a complete understanding of the princess.

The tzaddikim explain that as the receptive vessel for the various energies of the upper *Sefiros, Malchus* adopts the nature of
the energies flowing down into it. Because the *Sefiros* above her
derive from both *Chessed*/Kindness and *Din*/Judgment, *Malchus*
consists of a dual nature; at times it is shining with the fullness of
blessing, life, joy, and all measures of goodness, while, at others,
it is dull, devoid of light, and fraught with severity and judgment.
Likened to the moon by the *Zohar HaKadosh*,[9] *Malchus* is dynamic; she ebbs and flows in a cyclical progression; full at times
and empty at others, sometimes illuminating the night with a soft
glow of contentment and other times fading behind the clouds
into darkness and obscurity.[10] The tzaddikim teach that *Malchus*

---

9. *Zohar, Vayechi* 238a. See *Sunlight of Redemption*, pp. 120–125.

10. As the collective soul of the Jewish nation, *Knesses Yisrael*, is related to

is referred to by the word *"Nesher,"* which signifies both the positive implication of **Osher**, wealth, as well as the negative imagery of *"Ilan nosher peirosav,"* fruits that have become detached from the tree. In addition, *Malchus* is an aspect of both *"Mikveh hamayim,"* a stream in which flows all manner of goodness and blessing, and *"Yabashah,"* dry, parched earth.[11]

The tzaddikim teach that each of the Seven Shepherds, Avraham, Yitzchak, Yaakov, Moshe, Aharon, Yosef, and David, served as chariots for one of the lower seven *Sefiros*. Avraham Avinu, for example, was the *Ish HaChessed*, constantly seeking to perform limitless kindness with everyone around him. Yitzchak embodied *Gevurah*, allowing himself to be tied down on the altar by the Akeidah. And so it is with the rest; Yaakov is bound with *Tiferes*, Moshe with *Netzach*, Aharon with *Hod* and Yosef HaTzaddik with *Yesod*. Finally, the *Sefirah* of *Malchus* is embodied by David HaMelech, the paradigm of kingship.

As the chariot for the *middah* of *Malchus*, the energy of the lost princess, the persona of David HaMelech reflects all facets of her energy. In a lifetime marked by tremendous grandeur and success as well as devastating hardship, David came to embody the pulsating heart of the Jewish nation. His vulnerable expressions in

---

the *Sefirah* of *Malchus*, we count our days by the moon. Collectively, we are a nation of "Moon-people" with a long history marked by golden eras as well as devastating persecution and bitter tragedy. Adam sins, and, gathered at the foot of Sinai to receive the Torah, Klal Yisrael rectifies this sin. The disaster of the Golden Calf brings death back into the world, and they lose the awesome levels they had attained. Entering the land of their inheritance, Klal Yisrael build the Beis HaMikdash. Eventually, it is destroyed. After a seventy-year exile, they return with great joy again. Eventually, the Second Temple is destroyed as well, and they return to exile... Our holy nation counts time by a moon whose cycle of brightening and dimming encompasses the twenty-eight times mentioned by Shlomo HaMelech — fourteen times of positivity, and fourteen times of trouble. (See *Likutei Halachos, Birchos HaPeiros* 5:15.)

11. See *Shaarei Orah*, First Gate.

Tehillim represent the rawest illustration of both a Jew's rejoicing in spiritual success as well as the desperate yearning of a distant sinner — the moon in its journey from fullness to emptiness and back again.

On his level, David sins[12] or at least appears to sin,[13] with Bas Sheva, and carries the pieces of his broken heart back to the Master of the world in melodies of hope and desperation. He is at times a king[14] and at others an outcast,[15] at times a chassid[16] and at others a wrongdoer,[17] at times a fearsome warrior[18] and at others a kind-hearted musician.[19] Like the *Sefirah* of *Malchus*, David's stormy soul ebbs and flows, rises and falls, brightens and dims.[20]

⊛ The Mysterious Nature of *Malchus Beis David*

THERE IS AN important statement from Chazal that addresses David's "failures" and, thereby, the descents of *Malchus*, with an extremely illuminated perspective.

---

12. See *Yoma* 22b and *Avodah Zarah* 4b.

13. See *Shabbos* 56a.

14. *Shmuel II* 5:3.

15. *Shmuel I* 23:14.

16. *Tehillim* 86:2.

17. *Tehillim* 51:3.

18. *Shmuel II* 5:25.

19. *Shmuel I* 17:23.

20. See *Shaarei Orah*, Third Gate, where the verses "And he was ruddy with beautiful eyes" (*Shmuel I* 17:12) and "And David performed justice (*mishpat*) and righteousness (*tzedakah*)" (*Shmuel II* 8:16) as similarly referring to the *chessed/din* dichotomy held within David's soul, the human chariot for the *Sefirah* of *Malchus*.

These are their holy words:

> It was not fitting for David to have performed the act (with Bas Sheva).... Why, then did he do it? So that we are able to tell an individual who sins, "Seek out the individual" (referring to David HaMelech, the individual who serves as the quintessential model for *teshuvah*.)[21]

Rashi comments on this Gemara, saying: *"Gezeiras haMelech haysah,"* David's sinful act was a Divine edict from the King of kings. These words are explosive in implication! According to this interpretation, our Sages are teaching us that David HaMelech's spiritual misstep was specifically orchestrated by the Master of the world as part of a greater plan in which this error led to tremendous positivity for both David as an individual as well as all future generations of sinners who would be able to follow in the footsteps of David's *teshuvah*. *"Gezeiras haMelech haysah"* — somehow, in some mysterious way, this was how things were supposed to unfold — it couldn't have happened any other way!

But in truth, this phenomenon reaches past David's individual act to touch the very conception of his heritage. While perhaps its ultimate embodiment, David HaMelech represents a single link in a long and glorious chain stretching from Yehudah all the way until Mashiach, as the verse states, "The scepter will not part from Yehudah... until Shiloh (Mashiach)[22] arrives."[23] Although this awesome lineage was marked by tzaddikim of the highest caliber, it is well-known that many of the links in the ancestral chain of *Malchus Beis David* came into being through questionable unions. With Yehudah and Tamar on one side of the family tree,[24] Lot and his daughters on the

---

21. *Avodah Zarah* 4b–5a.
22. See *Rashi* to *Bereishis* 49:10.
23. *Bereishis* 49:10.
24. See *Rus* 4:18–22.

other,[25] and David and Bas Sheva in the middle,[26] the final redeemer who will lead the world to its ultimate rectification embodies centuries of dubious if not outright sinful behavior. Chazal
accentuate this point when they teach that whereas Shaul's reign
did not last, David's monarchy would continue until the end of
time, because "One appoints a leader over a community only if he
has a box full of creeping creatures trailing behind him." Rashi
explains that while Shaul's lineage was impeccable, David's was
questionable, and this is what lent such strength to his kingdom.[27]

The question begs: What lesson does Hashem hope to convey
with this counterintuitive arrangement?

In the teachings of the Chassidic masters, Mashiach is portrayed as a figure who will reveal the true goodness in each and
every Jew, ushering in a realm of teshuvah-filled retrospective
clarity during which the world will be filled with knowledge (yedi'ah) of God like water covers the sea.[28] In order to aid this campaign, Hashem arranged that Mashiach's very existence should
serve as evidence to the notion that, in truth, all of human history
is foretold and that an abiding seed of goodness is thus present
even in spiritual uncertainty -— though it may take a lifetime, or
many lifetimes, to finally bear fruit. The story of our nation and
the ultimate redemption of existence is the story of teshuvah, a
long tale of falling and again rising to greater heights that will

---

25. Rus, David's maternal ancestor, was a descendant of Moav who was born
out of the union of Lot and his daughter, an act which, although performed
with noble intention, is still called a "sin." (See Horayos 10b–11a.) The dubious
relationship between Boaz and Rus is itself another link in this chain.

26. Although Bas Sheva was a single woman as her husband had been rightfully killed for rebelling against the king, David was still rebuked for this act.
(See Shmuel II, Chapter 12.)

27. Yoma 22b.

28. See, for example, Machshavos Charutz 8 and Mei HaShiloach, Vol. 2, Behaalosecha, "Im yihyeh."

culminate with the arrival of Mashiach.[29] Therefore, the figure who is going to bring the world to its final, eternal rectification must embody the spirit of *Malchus Beis David*, the kingdom of *teshuvah* — a living testament to the concept of *"Gezeiras haMelech"* — the eternal truth that Hashem's unfathomable Will encompasses all.[30]

The tzaddikim teach that in accordance with the concept of *Sof maaseh b'machshavah techilah*, "the final deed is etched in the earliest thought,"[31] the final *Sefirah* of *Malchus* is bound with the uppermost realm of *Kesser*. This means that from an elevated retrospective standpoint, our reality (the level of *Malchus*) and everything that occurs within it, is inundated with the ultimate Will (the level of *Kesser*) of Hashem. The tzaddikim interpret the verse *Eishes chayil ateres baalah*, "Woman of valor, crown of her husband"[32] in the same vein: After the evolvement and eventual conclusion of action within *Malchus* — the feminine aspect of *"Eishes"* — we will come to the realization that it was bound with *"Ateres baalah,"* the *Kesser*-crown of her husband, representing the deepest will of Hashem. It is in the embodiment of *Malchus*, marked by the humble realization of one's emptiness and impassioned prayer[33] that one cracks through the veneer of *"bechirah"* which is founded upon an egotistical sense of independent existence, breaking into the realm of *"yedi'ah,"* the realization that nothing truly happens outside of Hashem's deepest will.

This nature of *Malchus Beis David* is the other core element of

---

29. See *Likutei Sichos*, Vol. 11, *Shemos* #2.

30. See *Mei HaShiloach, Vayeishev*, *"Vayeishev Yaakov."*

31. See *Kesubos* 8a.

32. *Mishlei* 31:10.

33. As David HaMelech sings, *"V'Ani tefillah"* (*Tehillim* 109:4); when one lives a life of *Malchus D'Kedusha*, his very identity (**Ani**) becomes defined by his nullification to Hashem (**Ayin** — *Kesser*); the entirety of his being bespeaks the humility of prayer. (See *Mevo L'Chassidus Ul'Darkah shel Chabad*, p.88.)

the lost princess; she rises and falls, she ebbs and flows. The verse states "*Seven* times shall the tzaddik fall and again rise."[34] Perhaps we may suggest that by linking the process of falling and rising with the number seven, Shlomo HaMelech is hinting to the seventh *Sefirah* of *Malchus*, the spiritual legacy of his very own lineage.[35]

On a very deep level, this constant cycle serves as the reason for the princess's passion, vibrancy, and wonder. Constantly on the move, forever "running and returning,"[36] the princess always has an end for which to create the means. Her perpetual oscillation between having and not having, "reaching and not reaching,"[37] leaves her with endless goals for which to strive and vast distances to cross. Certain of her ultimate success, the princess yearns powerfully for her goal and does everything in her power to bring her holy desires to actualization. Nothing can stop her, not even the apparent rejection of Hashem Himself. Firmly rooted in the realm of *Bechirah*, she takes her freedom of choice very seriously, realizing her ever-present ability to begin making the correct decisions and bearing full responsibility for her missteps along the way. Indeed, on occasion she falls short of her lofty aspirations and fails to live up to her highest ideals. However, armed with the awareness of a retrospective clarity that may be attained at a future point if she utilizes her freedom of choice in the present moment to again pick herself up and rectify her mistake, she proceeds confidently, with an eye on the prize. *The princess never gives up hope!* No matter how empty she feels, or how utterly devoid of light she may be, nothing can stop the moon's determined

---

34. *Mishlei* 24:16.
35. The name of the woman with whom David erred, "Bas Sheva," also hints to *Malchus*; the word *Bas* means daughter, a reference to the feminine nature of *Malchus*, and *Sheva*, seven, refers to the final of the lower seven *Sefiros* (see *Shaarei Orah*, first chapter).
36. See *Yechezkel* 1:3.
37. *Zohar, Noach* 65a.

orb from beginning the journey toward fullness anew; heralding a fresh **chodesh**, month, built on the ever-present spirit of *hischadshus*, renewal.[38]

In light of this description, we are now able to understand why it is so devastating when the princess becomes convinced by her father's show of anger and falls into a state of despair. When she reacts in this manner, the princess is rebelling against her very nature. For a brief moment, she is forgetting her most essential characteristic. When she is subsequently taken away, and, with the old month fading into the past, the moon despairs of beginning its hopeful journey toward fullness once again, it seems as if all is lost.

In Chapter Nine, we explained the viceroy's strategy of freeing the lost princess of passion and excitement as extraction via emulation. There, we described how the viceroy's longing for the princess as per her bidding was an active component of redeeming her. Being as desire sits at the core of the princess's essential energy, when the viceroy engages in yearning of holiness, he is slowly but surely extracting the spirit of the princess from captivity by bringing her back into his own life.

At this point in the tale, having discovered a second facet of *Malchus*, it becomes clear that if the viceroy is to extract the princess of youththful passion and connection by way of emulation, he, too, will need to experience the frenzied ups and downs of her cyclical journey. Like the moon, he will need to experience

---

38. Just as *Malchus* contains the dialectic energies of fullness and emptiness, *chassadim* and *gevuros*, so does Shabbos — as a culmination of the six days of the week — contain within itself the six polarities of *kasher* and *pasul*, *assur* and *mutar*, *tamei* and *tahor*. However, although its very essence pulsates with dichotomic tension from its this-wordly influence, the tzaddikim teach that the holiness of Shabbos is *"Kvi'ah v'kayma"* (*Beitzah* 17a; *Yerushalmi Megillah* 1:4) — an other-worldly spirit of perfection bestowed upon it by the Master of the world that encompasses all deficiency. See *Likutei Halachos, Hilchos Shabbos* 7.

successes and failures, rising and falling, running and returning — learning how to strive toward a goal with all his heart and
soul. Waking up from spiritual hibernation after twice failing to
heed the princess's conditions and yet refusing to become discouraged, hitting the road once more with renewed passion, the
viceroy is emulating the princess in the deepest way. With each
fall and subsequent rise, he slowly transfers her holy spirit of passion and yearning into his heart and frees her, in the process,
from the bonds of the error she committed so many decades ago.
At this point in the tale, after years of weathering the various
storms of his treacherous journey and rectifying his errors, the
viceroy begins to approach the awesome awareness that, like the
failings of *Malchus Beis David*, his slip-ups and missteps were
part and parcel of a glorious process that has brought tremendous
honor to Hashem. With each step he takes, the viceroy grows
more excited, more passionate, and more committed. Merely
hearing about the mountain of gold has set his heart aflame; he is
almost there; he can feel it; he knows it to be true!

Closer than ever to reaching the grand culmination of this
difficult, yet life-changing journey, the viceroy proceeds in the
desert, yearning for the mountain of gold, the stability that will
confirm everything he holds in his heart.

But he is getting ahead of himself. The journey is not over just
yet.

✴ *Mashiach Ben David* and *Mashiach Ben Yosef*

AS THE VICEROY walks in the desert on a quest for the golden
mountain, he encounters a giant. This is the first of three giants
with whom the inner-tzaddik will interact on his journey. As we
shall see, these three giants are brothers, and each of them carries
a gigantic tree. What do these giants represent?

The Breslover *mashpi'im* teach that the giants are symbols for two concepts, each of which serve to teach us a particular lesson. In the coming chapters, we will use elements of both interpretations to discover the practical meaning in this segment of the story.

In the current chapter, we will be utilizing the first of the two interpretations of the giants. The first interpretation sees the giants as representing awesome tzaddikim who have attained spiritual perfection by way of a path that looked very different than that of the viceroy. In fact, the path of these tzaddikim runs exactly contrary to his path. While the viceroy's journey of failure and *teshuvah* is bound with the mysterious nature of Mashiach ben David, these tzaddikim are imbued with the spirit of Mashiach ben Yosef. What is the nature of this unique figure?

In contradistinction to the archetype of David HaMelech, a figure who falls to temptation and eventually comes to represent the quintessential *baal teshuvah*, Yosef is the perfect tzaddik, the one who does *not* fall in the heat of the moment. In every situation, he remains bound to Hashem's will as expressed in the Torah, successfully subduing his drives at a young age and living a lofty life of piety. These giants have never sunken to the depths, never truly tasted the tormented darkness of the human condition. Instead, they serve as angelic examples, eternal monuments of holiness and purity. This is reflected in the trees they carry on their shoulders. These trees symbolize the Torah which is called *Eitz Chaim*, "the Tree of Life"[39] — the giants carry the Torah with them wherever they go. They are scholars of awesome stature, rational, logical thinkers whose insight into the folly of material pursuit allows them to quash their passions and avoid the seductions of this-worldly pleasure. Residing in the desert, a realm of spiritual ruin, all lower forces are under their dominion. Indeed, Rebbe Nachman tells us that they "didn't seem to be human at

---

39. *Mishlei* 3:18.

all"; like angels, they transcend and lord over even the densest expressions of physicality.

In a fascinating Gemara filled with remarkable statements, Chazal teach that Hashem's honor is proliferated by way of giant and viceroy alike — both the kind of Jews whose personalities align with the *avodah* of Yosef haTzaddik, as well as those Jews whose *avodah* aligns with the eternal striving of *Malchus Beis David*. These are their holy words:

> Rav Chanin bar Bizna said in the name of Rav Shimon Chasida: **Yosef**, who sanctified the name of Heaven *in private*, merited that one letter from the name of HaKadosh Baruch Hu, was added to his name.[40] **Yehudah**, who sanctified the name of Heaven *in public*, merited that his entire name is called by the name of HaKadosh Baruch Hu.[41,42]

Caught in an intense struggle with his desire for the seductive wife of Potiphar, Yosef passes the test and runs out of the house without tasting sin. This brings honor to Hashem in private, and one letter from Hashem's Name is added onto his own. Faced with proof of his questionable union with Tamar, his daughter-in-law, Yehudah utters the words *Tzadkah mi'meni*, "She is more righteous than me,"[43] remorsefully accepting responsibility for his action and doing *teshuvah*. This brings honor to Hashem in public, and his name is seen as including all letters of Hashem's Name.

From here we see that both the paths of Mashiach ben Yosef as well as Mashiach ben David (of which Yosef and Yehudah serve

---

40. The *pasuk* states: "He appointed it as a testimony in Yosef [*b'yehosef*], when he went forth over the land of Egypt" (*Tehillim* 81:6). In this verse the name Yosef is written with an additional letter *hei*, a letter which is part of the *Shem Havayah*.

41. The name Yehudah contains all four letters of the *Shem Havayah*.

42. *Sotah* 10b.

43. *Bereishis* 28:26.

as the archetype) bring honor to Hashem — one in private and the other in public — and both are precious and necessary in the grand Master Plan of creation.[44]

There are two wondrous points that cry out to us from this Gemara: 1) While Yosef's concealed act of honoring Hashem earned him one letter of Hashem's name, Yehudah's public honoring of Hashem earned him all four. 2) While after Yosef's heroic act of passing the test, a letter was *added* on to his name, Yehudah's public *teshuvah* seems not to have changed anything — his name had always been Yehudah, long before he did *teshuvah*, and even long before the entire episode with Tamar!

In order to answer these questions, let us read a few lines further in the Gemara.

> [Yehudah said:] *Tzadkah mi'meni*, "She is more righteous than I." [The word *"mi'meni"* can also be understood as "from me." Therefore, in this verse, Yehudah seems to be admitting that he is the father. The Gemara asks:] From where did he know [that it was in fact from him that Tamar was pregnant? The Gemara answers:] A Divine Voice went forth and said: *Mi'meni yatzu kevushim*, "From Me (*Mi'meni*) these hidden matters emerged."[45]

---

44. While a full exposition on this topic is beyond the scope of this work, it is important to recognize that the source for these two models is rooted in the respective mothers of these two tzaddikim, Rachel and Leah. In Kabbalistic literature, Rachel, a woman of remarkably beautiful appearance, is related to the *"Alma D'Isgalya,"* the known, understandable working of creation, while Leah, a somber woman of unpleasant appearance, is related to the *"Alma D'Iskasya,"* the hidden, incomprehensible workings of creation. Thus, the spiritual progression of Yosef, the son of Rachel, concurs with the progression of our physical world: the beautiful forward movement from Point A to Point B. On the other hand, the less-attractive spiritual progression of Yehudah, the son of Leah, is far more difficult for the human mind to comprehend and is one of the great mysteries of creation. See *Mei HaShiloach*, Vol. 2, *Tetzaveh*, *"V'samta."*

45. *Sotah* 10b. See also *Makkos* 23b.

In the previous chapter, we learned that the primary foundation of *teshuvah* is the realization of one's free-choice and the
complete acceptance of responsibility for one's actions. After
expressing remorse and arriving at place of *tikkun*-rectification,
one can then merit a retrospective clarity that illuminates his
past with the knowledge that, in truth, the entire process aligned
with the true will of Hashem — bringing Him tremendous honor
and allowing us to reach our greatest potential. It is this idea that
forms the backbone of this Gemara. Chazal are whispering to us
that in the very moment Yehudah utters the word *Mi'meni* in an
effort to accept full responsibility for his actions and bear the burden of his error, a thin, still Voice can be heard uttering that very
same word — Hashem saying *"Mi'meni yatzu kevushim"* — The
deepest truth is that this was all part of My Master Plan. Rashi
comments here using the very same words he writes about David
HaMelech's sin with Bas Sheva: *"Gezeiras HaMelech."* This was
a Divine decree brought about for the purpose of bringing about
the ultimate *kevod Shomayim*.[46]

With this we can explain the reason why, while Yosef's heroic
act caused an additional letter to be added to his name, Yehudah's
reward doesn't seem to reflect anything new. Perhaps we may
suggest that the revelation of the latent holiness in Yehudah's
name that had been hidden in plain sight for many decades is
a reflection of the fact that the act was predetermined from the
outset. While the *kevod Shamayim* brought about by Yosef's action earned him a brand-new letter, Yehudah's *teshuvah*, which

---

46. Perhaps it is possible to suggest that this model is also reflected in the
connection drawn by Chazal between the verse, "And Yaakov was left alone"
(*Bereishis* 32:24), and the verse, "And Hashem will be elevated, alone, on that
day" (*Yeshayahu* 2:11). The more a Jew realizes that he is "alone," that he has
full and complete *bechirah* (*Tzadkah mi'meni*), the more it will eventually
come to be revealed that Hashem is "alone": everything was from Hashem
alone (*Mi'meni yatzah kevushim*).

brought about the awareness that the entire process was part of Hashem's Master Plan, allowed for the revelation that — while only being revealed now — the reward of Yehudah's *teshuvah* was present even before he ever sinned. Everything proceeded exactly according to the dictation of the *Gezeiras haMelech*.[47] While Yehudah's *teshuvah* is credited to him alone and he does indeed receive his reward, that reward was prepared at his birth by Hashem Who had waited for the time of his sin and subsequent rectification in order to formally activate the power of its presence.

Chazal teach, "In the place where the *baal teshuvah* stands, even perfect tzaddikim cannot stand." This teaching aligns with the fact that Yosef received one letter of Hashem's name while Yehudah received four. As we have learned, Yehudah's *teshuvah* brings about a public recognition of Hashem's greatness. Therefore, as the *baal teshuvah*, his stature exceeds that of Yosef — it is from him that the redeemer of the world will ultimately descend.

It emerges that there are two paths of spiritual progression, and that neither negate the other. Both are necessary to allow the honor of Hashem to come to its full expression in the world; the private expression brought about by Mashiach ben Yosef's holy perfection, and the public expression brought about by Mashiach ben David's brokenhearted *teshuvah*. In our interpretation of Rebbe Nachman's remarkable tale, these paths are embodied by the viceroy and the first giant he encounters on his journey through the desert.

As the viceroy walks on his path, filled with the spirit of Mashiach Ben David, he encounters a mighty giant, the spirit of Mashiach Ben Yosef. Stunned by the greatness of the figure before

---

47. See *Berachos* 7b, "*Shma ka'garim*"; a person's name is given with *ruach hakodesh* of what will occur in the future.

whom he stands, the viceroy is unsure what to do. After a moment of hesitation, he overcomes his initial fear and approaches this colossal being. Somewhere in the world, a little boy is reading a *pasuk* in a sweet sing-song voice: *Vayigash eilav Yehudah*, "And Yehudah approached Yosef..."[48]

⚜ The First Giant: Master of the Beasts

THE GIANT SPEAKS first, his words rumbling in the viceroy's ears. "Who are you?" he asks. This question is expansive: "What are you all about? What is the essential characteristic of your identity?"

In previous phases of his journey, during which the viceroy needed to access the holiness at his core for the purpose of encouraging himself to carry on, he might have answered this question with an elevated discourse on the holiness of the Jewish soul. However, at this point, having made peace with his past mistakes and sufficiently fortified his self-esteem, the viceroy offers a different answer: "I am a human." In the Hebrew version of our tale, the words used by the viceroy are *"Ani adam."*

In a famous teaching, the Shelah HaKadosh writes that the word *"Adam"* carries two opposing connotations which relate to the contrasting polarities of the human condition. On the one hand, *"Adam"* derives from the word *Adamah*, connoting earthiness and physicality. On the other, *"Adam"* derives from the phrase *"Adameh l'Elyon,"*[49] a reference to man's ability to walk in the lofty ways of Hashem. While these may seem to be contradictory ideas, it is in only when both aspects are present that the essence of the human experience emerges in all of its struggle and

---

48. *Bereishis* 44:18.
49. *Yeshayahu* 14:14.

glory. This is the experience of what it means to be human, what it means to be a Jew — constant fluctuation between attraction to the basest drives in creation, *"Adamah"* and striving for the pinnacle of spiritual greatness, *"Adameh l'Elyon."*[50]

When the viceroy answers the giant with the words *Ani adam*, he means to say, "I am a human being in the fullest sense of the word. On a long and arduous journey of ups and downs, marked by frequent attraction to earthiness and rare glimpses of heaven, my desire for holiness has allowed me to overcome many hurdles and obstacles of different shapes and sizes. Although I harbor no delusions of perfection, I try as hard as I can to serve Hashem and hope to one day fix all of the brokenness in my life."

When the giant hears the viceroy's words which so perfectly mirror his puny appearance, he is absolutely astonished. On an external level, the viceroy looks mightily pathetic in this unique setting. A tiny, fragile human being walking among fearsome giants with no scholarly accomplishments or visible spiritual grandeur to show for himself, he is quite out of place. After a moment of shocked silence, the giant finds his tongue. *"It has been so long since I have been in this desert and I have never seen a human here!"* The place where the pair stand represents an advanced level of spiritual development where only those whose sacrifice and super-human effort transformed them into spiritual giants can walk unfazed by the wild animals and lifeless terrain — the negative traits and the spiritual rot found in this place over which they rule with ease. As far as this tzaddik knows, here it is sink or swim — in order to survive in the desert, one needs to have become a giant, a person who has attained easily demonstrable greatness in Torah and *avodah*! How did this *"Adam,"* this human being still caught in the grand tension and struggle of this-worldliness, make it to this advanced stage of spiritual consciousness?

---

50. *Shelah*, Vol. 1, *Toldas Adam*, p. 3.

Ironically, the viceroy has no idea where it is that he is standing. He doesn't consider himself to be anything special; on the contrary, he frequently experiences broken-heartedness over his perceived lack of success and the fact that he has yet to complete his mission. The viceroy doesn't understand why the giant is astonished — not because he consciously knows that his journey represents a hidden, alternate route to spiritual greatness paved with bricks of yearning and repentance, but because he is completely unaware of what he has achieved. This humility, simplicity, and wariness encapsulates the viceroy's true greatness. The *baal teshuvah* constantly feels as if he is only just beginning, proceeding with a simple sweetness and a sense of modesty. Not knowing where he is or the reason for the giant's great wonderment, this human among giants begins to tell his tale.

LESSONS FOR LIFE

❋ The two methods of progression in spiritual growth, exemplified by Yosef and Yehudah, are equally valid and both bring a special kind of honor to Hashem.

❋ At a certain stage in his spiritual recovery, a Jew reaches a place where he feels comfortable admitting to his being an "*Adam*," a human being caught in the struggles of this world and doing everything in his power to rise above.

CHAPTER 18

A Giant Obstacle

וְסִפֵּר לוֹ כָּל הַמַּעֲשֶׂה הַנַּ״ל, וְשֶׁהוּא מְבַקֵּשׁ הַר שֶׁל זָהָב וּמִבְצָר שֶׁל מַרְגָּלִיּוֹת. אָמַר לוֹ: בְּוַדַּאי אֵינוֹ בַּנִּמְצָא כְּלָל, וְדָחָה אוֹתוֹ וְאָמַר לוֹ שֶׁהֱשִׂיאוּ אֶת דַּעְתּוֹ בִּדְבַר שְׁטוּת, כִּי בְּוַדַּאי אֵינוֹ נִמְצָא כְּלָל. וְהִתְחִיל לִבְכּוֹת מְאֹד [הַיְנוּ הַשֵּׁנִי לַמַּלְכוּת בָּכָה מְאֹד, וְאָמַר] כִּי בְּוַדַּאי בְּהֶכְרֵחַ הוּא נִמְצָא בְּאֵיזֶה מָקוֹם. וְהוּא דָחָה אוֹתוֹ, [הַיְנוּ הָאָדָם הַמְשֻׁנֶּה שֶׁפָּגַע דָּחָה אוֹתוֹ בִּדְבָרָיו וְאָמַר] כִּי בְּוַדַּאי דָּבָר שְׁטוּת אָמְרוּ לְפָנָיו. וְהוּא אָמַר [הַיְנוּ הַשֵּׁנִי לַמַּלְכוּת], שֶׁבְּוַדַּאי יֵשׁ.

The viceroy told him the whole story, and about how he was searching for a mountain of gold and a palace of pearls. The giant responded, "Certainly, this place doesn't exist." He repressed him, telling him that his mind had been led astray by folly, for it was clear that no such place existed. The viceroy began to cry very much, for he was certain that the place existed. The giant repressed him again, saying, "It is certainly folly!" And the viceroy said, "It certainly exists."

⊛ Sun-People and Moon-People

IN THE PREVIOUS chapter, we mentioned that in the writings of the Breslover *mashpi'im*, we find two mutually exclusive, interpretations of the three giants.

Previously, we discussed the first interpretation; the perfect tzaddik who embodies the spirit of Mashiach Ben Yosef and cannot understand how it is that the viceroy, still caught in the tension of the human struggle, has attained such a lofty level of closeness with Hashem.

In this chapter, we shall explore the second interpretation of the three giants. This interpretation will allow us to understand the awesome obstacle the giants represent and their mighty attempt to discourage the viceroy from continuing his journey.

Reb Shlomo Carlebach often taught that there are two kinds of people in the world. In his inimitable fashion, he referred to them as "sun-people" and "moon-people."

Sun-people are shallow, vain, and drawn after externalities. With no grand aspirations for their personal development, they live lives free of inner struggle and failure. They do not feel as if their existence is uncertain, precariously positioned under the threatening shadow of Sinai. Their lives are not marked by the endless searching of a stormy soul for the deeper meaning of existence.

On a religious level, such people are perfectly satisfied with the level of their *avodas Hashem*, feeling no sense of lack or compulsion toward growth. Like the sun, they are unchanging, always shining the same.

Moon-people, on the other hand, are just the opposite. In touch with the loss of the princess in their lives, these Jews feel compelled to embark on a soul-journey, an epic search for the inner-dimension of Yiddishkeit; constantly wondering how they might fill the Vacant Space that sits at the essence of their being. Such Jews are attracted to the depth of life, the grand expanses of thought which give rise to mighty principles that illuminate all streams of creation.[1] In the words of Rav Kook:

> These people never have any rest. They are always in a state of drama: either they are ascending to the sublime heights of heaven or they are descending into the bitter depths of disaster. These people need to concentrate on spiritual growth every day. Such people, when they have discovered ways of life that suit them, will ascend higher and higher. On the other hand, if they neglect their personal paths, they will most likely collapse and descend lower and lower.[2]

Constantly aspiring toward greater vistas of religious life, these Jews are always rising and falling.[3] Like the moon, their

---

1. See Appendix F, R' Hillel Zeitlin's essay: "Berel the Chassid."
2. *Oros HaKodesh* Vol. 3, pp. 126–127 (*The Spiritual Revolution of Rav Kook*, p. 19).
3. See *Shabbos* 156a: "One who was born under the influence of the moon will be a man who suffers pains: who builds and destroys, destroys and builds."
   In Chapter 2, we described the princess as being related to a spirit of contentment. How does this fit with the stormy nature of the Moon-Person? Our tzaddikim teach, *Tachlis hayedi'ah asher lo neida*, "The pinnacle of knowledge is to know that one does not know" (*Bechinas Olam* 13:33). This expression does not intend to champion ignorance. Rather, the intention is for one to constantly ascend in levels of wisdom so that one discovers that there is far more to know then he ever imagined. At this point, one both knows, and does not know. One may celebrate the knowledge he has amassed and yet, at the very same time, desperately strive for greater heights. Perhaps we may use this idea to resolve the contrasting natures of contentment and striving which are both features of the princess's spirit. On one level, a Jew who is engaged with the princess is absolutely content, having "reached" and attained a perception of the inner meaning of life. On the other, his realization that he has "not yet reached" compels him to continue striving toward ever greater perceptions. The Mittler Rebbe of Chabad (1773–1827) captures this anxious-contentment in the following description: "One whose heart is constantly worried stands on a very high level, for the source of his angst is not the desire to obtain something [of the physical world], but rather because the inner core of his heart is

light grows stronger and then dims once more as they travel the
daunting hills of their struggle.[4]

Although it may seem useful to split all of humanity into these
broad categories, the reality is a bit more complicated. While
such people certainly do exist, it is rare to find a person who
perfectly fits the definition of the sun-person or moon-person,
respectively. More accurately, the human being is a composite

---

bound with the Infinite One to the point that all other desires are completely
worthless to him. This is the reason his heart is constantly worried: "When
will I finally merit to perceive the face of the Living King, the Light of the Infinite One?" When this mighty worry nullifies one's personal life entirely, to
the point that nothing can stand before the true light of his inner life and the
joy of the bond between soul and eternity, one has already reached the level
of a life of joy and eternal pleasure which flows forth from cleaving to the
essence of the Infinite One." (*Mevo l'Chassidus Ul'Darkah shel Chabad*, pp.
30–31)

4. In addition to the hints toward the two approaches to life presented in
the contrasting natures of the sun and the moon, the segments of the day
during which they reign, day and night, are saturated with these energies as
well. Historically, the daytime has been the kingdom of quantitative pursuit;
a time for business meetings and production, factory chimneys belching out
thick clouds of smoke and streets teeming with a human race in frantic pursuit
of this-wordly gain. The reason for this is simple — before the invention of the
lightbulb, it was only possible to properly see physical objects during the day.
Therefore, as long as the sun shone in the sky, the world was filled with an involvement with tools and instruments that could be seen with physical eyes.
The nighttime, however — the reign of the moon — is a time for introspective,
contemplation, and the fortification of qualitative pursuits. At night, the farm-
er leaves his plow in the darkened field and joins his family around the dinner
table, appreciating their company. In the moonlight, the tzaddik sits alone in
the privacy of his home, crying bitter tears over the destruction of the Beis Ha-
Mikdash at *Tikkun Chatzos*. The nighttime is when humanity leaves the world
of things and enters the silent space of the spirit, ripe for religious engagement
and qualitative pursuits. Indeed, Rebbe Nachman teaches that the primary
time for *hisbodedus* and nullification of the ego is not during the day, the reign
of the sun, but rather at night, when the air is no longer filled with the spirit of
shallowness and physicality. (See *Likutei Moharan* 52.)

of both elements; part moon, part sun; part soul, part body; part angel, part beast. The person to whom we refer here as a sun-person also contains an inner drive toward depth and growth. The great existential question mark burns within him just the same. However, it does not merit expression because the sun-element within him constantly silences the inner moon-element, covering it over with thoughts, words, and actions of vanity and transience. On the other side of the coin, the moon-person contains the sun-element within him as well! He, too, is not "deep" all the time; he also feels a drive toward shallow pursuits. However, he does not allow this element to define him. Instead of masking his soul with deceptive stability and sophistication, he allows his vulnerability to shine forth and illuminate his life with its soft, gentle, glow.[5]

If all people contain both elements in their inner makeup, why do some engage with their inner moon-person and allow him to assume their public identity while others so violently push him away and conceal him behind so many barriers? While it is obviously futile for us to attempt to provide a definitive answer to a question that demands a level of insight into the human soul to which we are not privy,[6] there are a few answers

---

5. It goes without saying that this discussion about the sun-people and the moon-people mirrors our overview of the six sons and the princess in Chapter 2. While the sun-people are comfortable living with the six sons in the absence of the princess, the moon-people see finding and recovering the lost princess as their primary mission.

6. It is important to remember the words of Rav Kook: "One can never really know the true essence of a person — not one's own, and certainly not that of another person; not of an individual and certainly not of a people. We are circling around the center of knowing. We are forced to estimate and guess, to look for direction from external action. But even these are mostly hidden from us... Based on these little pieces of information, we try to talk about a unique personality type and soul." (*Oros HaKodesh*, Vol. 3, p. 119, cited in *The Spiritual Revolution of Rav Kook*, pp. 22–23.)

we can attempt to offer that concur with human logic and experience.

The first, more speculative reason we may suggest is that it is simply a matter of nature. While some people are more sensitive by nature and have a greater propensity toward depth in thought and feeling, others lack this inclination and feel more at home in the world of "doing" than that of "thinking" and "feeling."

But there is a second reason that is far more probable and seems closer to the truth. This reason is *discomfort* and *despair*. More often than not, the sun-people have engaged, at one point or another, with the moon-element within. Perhaps sparked by a stint in therapy, a death in the family, an inspirational *shiur*, or an empowering seminar, they genuinely attempted to allow the moon-person within to emerge and elevate their lives. But alas, overwhelmed by the sensation of vulnerability and introspection, or frustrated after not seeing the immediate results they had come to expect from their sun-pursuits, these people give up. With time, they return to their former lifestyle with a greater vengeance, feeling silly for having ever believed they could attain spiritual connection and vowing never to attempt to engage the inner moon-person again. Fearful of the impact deep introspection may have on their lives, they abandon the silence of "time" and return to the din of "space." Here, surrounded by the distractions of this fleeting life, they feel comfortable and secure. Never again shall they meditate, never again shall they attempt to delve into the deeper elements of the Torah. Burned, scarred, they scurry back to the comfort of the daily grind, surrounding themselves with everything they need to maintain the status quo of their shallow and illusory happiness.

In the words of Rav Moshe Weinberger:

> A Rabbi who gives conventional speeches, focusing on current political or social events in light of the *parshah*, will not be the object of scorn. But if a rabbi tries to shake people

to the essence of their souls, many of them will grow uncomfortable. They do not mind if someone skillfully demonstrates how two disparate verses fit together, but they get nervous if a rabbi tries to put their lives together.[7]

It goes without saying that due to their unfortunate experience, the sun-people have a negative, if not belligerent attitude toward the moon-people. From their perspective, there is no need for spiritual seeking; life is straightforward — you do what you need to do and that's basically it. They can't grasp why some people always feel a lack in their lives and *avodas Hashem* or why others insist on seeing life as a "personal journey" or some kind of "search." Lacking sensitivity to the depth of a moon-person's struggle (or, more accurately, threatened by the reminder that there is more to life than the one they currently lead), the sun-people generally respond in two ways — either by mocking the moon-people and their search, or by growing angry and insisting that the search is futile; that the kind of life the moon-people are looking for simply doesn't exist.

This is the second interpretation of the giant: the quintessential sun-person, oblivious to life's depth and threatened by the notion that it is indeed possible for one to discover a sense of meaning and true joy. The giant is that family member, mentor, business associate, or childhood friend in front of whom we feel uncomfortable engaging in our search for the Lost Princess. He represents the great intellectuals: the scientists, philosophers, mathematicians, doctors, and historians who have unanimously come to the authoritative conclusion that the human soul is a myth and that there is no more to life than can be tested, comprehended, and calculated.

On a far more focused and painful level, the giant takes the form of a great Torah scholar who engages with Yiddishkeit on a

---

7. *Song of Teshuvah*, p. 75.

purely intellectual level, lacking a sense for the spirit of our holy tradition and the imperative role the Lost Princess of *emunah*, prayer, *hisbodedus, yiras Shamayim, simchah*, simplicity, sweetness, humility, yearning, and broken-heartedness must play in a Jew's relationship with the Master of the world.[8] Despite a vast knowledge of the holy texts represented in the giant trees they carry on their proud shoulders, these so-called "teachers" maintain an incredibly shallow relationship with Yiddishkeit.[9] While the trees they carry are indeed impressive and grand, they are unfortunately no longer connected to the ground of the *neshamah* and her desire for true closeness with her Source. Their Torah is uprooted from the source of living waters — "If one does not merit, it becomes a deadly poison."[10] Making use of every opportunity to mock, berate, belittle, condemn, and delegitimize the moon-people and their tear-soaked journey of deep sincerity, these giants insist that there is no more to Judaism than the purely intellectualized study of Gemara and rote conformance to the minutia of halachah. Their sardonic expressions of pride and arrogance shatters the viceroy's already broken heart into millions of pieces.[11]

---

8. One opinion in the Gemara (*Chullin* 91a) states that the Angel of Edom which wrestled with Yaakov Avinu appeared in the guise of a Torah scholar. In light of our exploration of the *Yaakov/Eisav paradigm* presented in *Sunlight of Redemption*, we understand Eisav as representing the quintessential sun-person, focusing only on the external elements of life.

9. See *Mishnas HaMaggid M'Zlotchov*, p. 284.

10. *Yoma* 72b.

11. While it is tempting to merge the two interpretations of the giant, aligning the perfect tzaddik who embodies the spirit of *Mashiach Ben Yosef* with the quintessential sun-person who engages with our holy tradition in a shallow way, doing so is both inappropriate and inaccurate. While they may seem to share certain similarities, such as their distance from struggle and failure, it is purely coincidental. In truth, while not in the same manner as the repentant sinner filled with the spirit of *Mashiach Ben David*, it is clear that the giant

Rebbe Nachman writes that human beings can represent the greatest possible obstacle on the path to true closeness with Hashem. While the *yetzer hara* comes from one specific level of the spiritual realm, the human being contains elements from millions of spiritual levels spanning the entirety of existence. Therefore, man's power is certainly far stronger than that of any damaging angel.[12] A snide comment here, a scornful glance there, the sun-person causes us to rethink the entire journey. In the words of Reb Nosson:

> All the backward ideas which pervert the truth, particularly those which cause people to become discouraged from their improper actions to the point that they become even further from Hashem, are caused by "blemished teachings." The *yetzer hara* uses these teachings to make it appear to a person as if it is no longer possible to draw near to Hashem. All similar ideas that enter the heart of a Jew are drawn from the "fallen Torah." Indeed, it is necessary to daven very much to Hashem to be saved from this.[13]

The *mishnah* in *Avos* states:

> One whose wisdom exceeds his good deeds, to what is he similar? To a tree whose branches are many and whose roots are few; the wind will come and uproot it and turn it over.

---

tzaddik described in the previous chapter is intimately familiar with spiritual struggle — on his level, in addition to all of the qualities of the lost princess listed above. To ascribe a negative connotation to such a tzaddik by comparing his path with the shallowness, incapability of understanding depth, and vanity of the sun-person is disrespectful and out of touch with reality. This kind of tzaddik is not "worse," *chas v'shalom*. He is simply different. The fact that our tradition includes both a *Mashiach Ben David* and a *Mashiach Ben Yosef* demonstrates the mutual validity of the paths they represent.

12. See *Sichos HaRan* 80 and 81.

13. *Likutei Halachos, Birchas Hamazon* 5:4.

> As it is said: "And he will be like a lonely tree in a wasteland
> that will not see when good comes. It will dwell on parched
> soil in the desert, on a salted land, uninhabited."[14,15]

As they walk along on the "parched soil in the desert," these giants carry uprooted trees with many branches but pitifully few roots. Having engaged with Yiddishkeit on a purely intellectual level which derides a heartfelt, emotional involvement with our tradition, the giants are far more concerned with "wisdom" than "good deeds." Experts on every theological trend in Jewish thought, they remain effected by none.[16] They are unable to draw the Torah they study down into their hearts and souls; they may study all of *Shas* and *Shulchan Aruch*, but, never holding their holy pages up to the sunlight of faith, these texts teach them nothing at all.

With everything in their head and nothing in their hearts, these giants represent the greatest challenge the viceroy has yet encountered on his journey.

❋ "This Place Doesn't Exist!"

GRATEFUL FOR THE chance to unburden himself, the viceroy recounts his journey before the giant. He leaves nothing out, baring his soul unabashedly. With great excitement, he finally reaches the glorious conclusion, telling the giant about the mountain of gold and the palace of pearls.

But to his great shock, instead of empathy or encouragement, the giant responds with a curt refusal to validate the viceroy's

---

14. *Yirmiyahu* 17:6.

15. *Avos* 3:22.

16. See *Alei Shur*, Vol. 2, Introduction to Second Gate: "There is a big difference between *knowledge of depth* and a *life of depth*." See also Second Gate, Chapter 1.

journey. With a sense of annoyance, the giant flatly denies the existence of everything the viceroy has been so desperately seeking for so many years. The sun-person is convinced that the moon-person is wasting his time. Rather than enmity, there is a certain level of care that underlies his protest; he is genuinely concerned over the moon-person's making what he perceives to be a tremendous mistake. "Why can't you conform to the system like everyone else?" he asks, in a tone of consternation. "Why are you always running after tzaddikim, performing *segulos*, and attempting to delve into the Torah's inner light? Don't you realize that you are wasting your time? Have your failures not taught you that you will never find what you are looking for? Have mercy on yourself and listen well to what I am telling you — the place you are looking for simply doesn't exist! It is impossible to experience Gan Eden in this world, to live life with a sense of childlike wonder, excitement, and passion. Grow up, get real, and realize that there is no princess! She is a figment of your imagination!"

The viceroy knows the princess well; he has spoken with her no less than three times over a lifetime consumed with his search for her. But to this giant, it is all one big waste of time. To him, it is all make-believe — there is no princess, and nothing was lost that needs to be found. There is no depth to life — what you see is what you get, and that's the end of the story.

❋ An Extreme Response

ALTHOUGH THE VICEROY has struggled against obstacles before, none elicit the level of emotion he exhibits here, in response to the giant's dismissal of a decades-long mission for which he has sacrificed everything. Overwhelmed by these words that cut straight to his core, he burst into tears.

At this point, the viceroy is at the end. A lifetime spent searching for the lost princess -— the key to his essence — his repeated failures to succeed in this precious mission, and his unwavering determination, culminates in this moment. We can envision the viceroy dropping to his knees before this relative, friend, rebbe, or mentor that denies his life's mission and breaking down into tears — not of frustration or despair, but of absolute clarity into the very core of his being; an expression of his overwhelming certainty in the existence of the mountain of gold and the palace of pearls and his iron will to free the lost princess despite the great difficulty involved. As he weeps, the viceroy gives himself strength that no matter how difficult the obstacles may seem, he must never give up on what he knows in his heart of hearts to be unequivocally true.

The entirety of his shaken identity reverberates with the sentiment expressed in Theodore Roosevelt's famous declaration:

> It is not the critic who counts; not the man who points out how the strong man stumbles, or where the doer of deeds could have done them better. The credit belongs to the man who is actually in the arena, whose face is marred by dust and sweat and blood; who strives valiantly; who errs, who comes short again and again, because there is no effort without error and shortcoming; but who does actually strive to do the deeds; who knows great enthusiasms, the great devotions; who spends himself in a worthy cause; who at the best knows in the end the triumph of high achievement, and who at the worst, if he fails, at least fails while daring greatly, so that his place shall never be with those cold and timid souls who neither know victory nor defeat.[17]

Seeing the tears of the viceroy, the giant thinks they are tears of regret. Surely, this is the first time anyone had the courage to set him straight, and the viceroy is now coming around to see

---

17. "Citizenship in a Republic," an address delivered on April 23, 1910 in Paris, France.

the folly of his error. He smiles, mentally patting himself on the back for another job well done. But he is sorely mistaken. As a sun-person, the giant is out of touch with a deeper kind of crying; the war cry of a Jew who is deeply in tune with his innermost core, encompassing the holy-stubbornness, unrelenting courage, and refusal to give up that bursts like a powerful geyser from the essence of his being.[18] This mighty conviction is captured magnificently in the tear-drenched words of Reb Nosson's prayer:

> Hashem, God of truth, assist me, save me, strengthen me, and truly fortify me in Your service. Grant me the merit of drawing close to those who fear You and to the wholesome ones who walk in the ways of truth. Let no person in the world, neither stranger nor acquaintance, have the power to prevent me from the path of truth in any way. Strengthen my conviction and faith constantly, and let me see myself as being alone in the world, as the verse states, "Avraham was one." Enable me not to see and not to hear anyone who seeks to prevent, withhold, scoff, ridicule, or confuse me. May no person be able to confuse me from the straight path of truth — even those who are greater and more righteous than me. Instead, may I merit to go in a way of simplicity, in accordance with what I have been taught from my youth by the words of our holy and true sages. Let me be accustomed to say, "I don't know what is right for every person in the world. All I know is what is right for me, in accordance with my level as I have been taught by the choicest of the true tzaddikim, who represent the point of truth in all worlds."[19]

---

18. It is important to stress that the viceroy is neither rude nor disrespectful in his response. He does not try to argue or prove his position, an endeavor that would be both inappropriate as well as useless. Rather, he reaches inward to consult the point of certainty at the core of his being and stands resolute.
19. *Likutei Tefillos* 149.

When a Jew gets in touch with the singular mission he was sent to accomplish, the essence of his personal journey in *Olam HaZeh*, nothing can deter him from pursuing it.[20] The viceroy knows, with every fiber of his being, that he must continue his search for the lost princess. And although he might accept the giant's advice on any other matter, nothing he may say to dissuade the viceroy from continuing to search for the lost princess can prevent him from doing so. He has met the lost princess and he has spoken to her. He has given everything up for this mission because he knows that this is his personal duty to the king whom he loves so very much. This absolute clarity affords him the holy brazenness to look up through his tears at the impressive frame of the sun-person and, with every ounce of strength he can muster in his puny form, continue to insist that there is indeed a princess and that, no matter how fantastical it may sound, she is waiting for him to free her from a pearl palace atop a golden mountain.

LESSONS FOR LIFE

⊛ There are two kinds of people in the world: "sun-people" and "moon-people." While sun-people live shallow lives of distraction from the great existential questions of being and the meaning of life, moon-people are compelled to search for depth hidden beyond the surface of this world, the Lost Princess of their lives.

---

20. The Ishbitzer goes so far as to say that when one has discovered this mission, he is permitted to give up his life for it — an extreme measure of reverence that is traditionally extended to three actions, murder, idol worship, and adultery. See *Mei HaShiloach*, Vol. 2, *Shoftim*, "*Ki yikarei*."

⊛ The derisive attitude of sun-people toward the efforts of moon-people represents the single most difficult obstacle toward the searching Jew's spiritual growth. There is nothing that challenges a moon-person's conviction more than being mocked, scorned, and ridiculed by others, especially by those who appear to be great Torah scholars who deny the validity of his journey.

⊛ When a Jew gets in touch with his personal mission in this world, nothing can shake him from it. Come what may, he will find the strength to hold on to what he knows to be true.

CHAPTER 19

Helpful Challenges

אָמַר לוֹ [הָאָדָם הַמְשֻׁנֶּה לְהַשֵּׁנִי לַמַּלְכוּת]: לְדַעְתִּי הִיא שְׁטוּת. אַךְ מֵחֲמַת שֶׁאַתָּה מִתְעַקֵּשׁ, הִנֵּה אֲנִי מְמֻנֶּה עַל כָּל הַחַיּוֹת, אֶעֱשֶׂה לְמַעַנְךָ וְאֶקְרָא לְכָל הַחַיּוֹת, כִּי הֵם רָצִים אֶת כָּל הָעוֹלָם, אוּלַי תֵּדַע אַחַת מֵהֶם מֵהַר וּמִבְצָר, כַּנַּ"ל. וְקָרָא אֶת כֻּלָּם מִקָּטָן וְעַד גָּדוֹל, כָּל מִינֵי הַחַיּוֹת, וְשָׁאַל אוֹתָם, וְכֻלָּם הֵשִׁיבוּ שֶׁלֹּא רָאוּ. וְאָמַר לוֹ: רְאֵה שֶׁשְּׁטוּת סִפַּרְתָּ לְפָנֶיךָ! אִם תִּשְׁמַע, שׁוּב לַאֲחוֹרֶיךָ, כִּי בְּוַדַּאי לֹא תִמְצָא, כִּי אֵינֶנּוּ בָּעוֹלָם. וְהוּא הִפְצִיר מְאֹד, וְאָמַר שֶׁבְּהֶכְרֵחַ הוּא נִמְצָא בְּוַדַּאי. אָמַר לוֹ [הָאָדָם הַמְשֻׁנֶּה לְהַשֵּׁנִי לַמַּלְכוּת]: הִנֵּה בַּמִּדְבָּר נִמְצָא שָׁם אָחִי, וְהוּא מְמֻנֶּה עַל כָּל הָעוֹפוֹת, וְאוּלַי יוֹדְעִים הֵם, מֵחֲמַת שֶׁהֵם פּוֹרְחִים בָּאֲוִיר בְּגָבוֹהַּ, אוּלַי רָאוּ הַר וּמִבְצָר הַנַּ"ל. וְתֵלֵךְ אֵלָיו וְתֹאמַר לוֹ, שֶׁאֲנִי שְׁלַחְתִּי אוֹתְךָ אֵלָיו. וְהָלַךְ כַּמָּה וְכַמָּה שָׁנִים לְבַקְּשׁוֹ, וּמָצָא שׁוּב אָדָם גָּדוֹל מְאֹד כַּנַּ"ל, וְנָשָׂא גַּם כֵּן אִילָן גָּדוֹל כַּנַּ"ל. וְשָׁאַל אוֹתוֹ גַּם כֵּן כַּנַּ"ל, וְהֵשִׁיב לוֹ כָּל הַמַּעֲשֶׂה וְשֶׁאָחִיו שְׁלָחוֹ אֵלָיו. וְהוּא דָּחָה אוֹתוֹ גַּם כֵּן, כִּי בְּוַדַּאי אֵינוֹ בַּנִּמְצָא, וְהוּא הִפְצִיר אוֹתוֹ גַּם כֵּן, וְאָמַר לוֹ [הָאָדָם הַזֶּה לְהַשֵּׁנִי לַמַּלְכוּת]. הִנֵּה אֲנִי מְמֻנֶּה עַל כָּל הָעוֹפוֹת, אֶקְרָא אוֹתָם, אוּלַי יוֹדְעִים הֵם. וְקָרָא כָּל הָעוֹפוֹת, וְשָׁאַל אֶת כֻּלָּם מִקָּטָן וְעַד גָּדוֹל, וְהֵשִׁיבוּ, שֶׁאֵינָם יוֹדְעִים מֵהַר וּמִבְצָר הַנַּ"ל. אָמַר לוֹ: הֲלֹא אַתָּה רוֹאֶה שֶׁבְּוַדַּאי אֵינֶנּוּ בָּעוֹלָם. אִם תִּשְׁמַע לִי, שׁוּב לַאֲחוֹרֶיךָ, כִּי בְּוַדַּאי אֵינֶנּוּ! וְהוּא [הַיְנוּ הַשֵּׁנִי לַמַּלְכוּת] הִפְצִיר אוֹתוֹ וְאָמַר שֶׁבְּוַדַּאי יֶשְׁנוֹ בָּעוֹלָם.

He said to him (the giant to the viceroy), "In my opinion, it is folly. But because you are adamant about it — I am appointed over all of the wild animals. I will do you a favor and call these animals, for they run all over the world. Perhaps one of them will know about the mountain and palace of which you speak. He called to all of them from the smallest to the largest, all kinds of wild animals, and he asked them. All of them answered that they hadn't seen such a place. "You see?" said the giant. "You have been told foolishness. If you will listen to me, turn back! For you will certainly not find it, for it is certainly not in the world." The viceroy adamantly insisted, saying that it must certainly exist. He said to him (the giant to the viceroy), "Further in the desert you will find my brother. He is in charge of all the birds. Perhaps they will know something, since they fly up high in the air, maybe they saw the mountain of gold and the palace of pearls. Go to him and tell him that I sent you."

The viceroy searched for him for many years, until he again encountered a giant like the previous one. He, too, carried a great tree. The giant asked him all that the first one had. The viceroy told him his whole story and how the giant's brother had sent him here. This giant began pushing him away as well, telling him that it certainly didn't exist, but the viceroy remained adamant. He said to him (the giant to the viceroy,) "I am appointed over all of the birds. I will call them, perhaps they know." He called all the birds, and asked them all, from the smallest to the biggest. They answered that they did not know of this mountain or palace. "Now you can see for yourself that it doesn't exist in the world. If you will listen to me, turn around and go back, for it doesn't exist!" But the viceroy adamantly insisted, saying that it certainly did exist.

❋ Teardrops on a Heart of Stone

IN THE PREVIOUS chapter, we learned about moon-people, Jews whose lives are consumed with a search for depth and true serenity and the challenge they face from sun-people who mock their spiritual striving and attempt to convince them out of their search. The viceroy represents the ultimate moon-person, a Jew on a fateful mission to discover the ever-elusive lost princess of passion and youthful wonder in relationships and his *avodas Hashem*. As he searches for her in the deserts of the world, he encounters the ultimate sun-person in the form of a giant, a religious or secular authority who maintains a purely intellectual approach to living. This giant denies the validity of his mission and tries to convince him that the place he seeks doesn't exist and that it is all a waste of time.

But the viceroy can't be swayed. Strengthened by years of courage in the terrifying face of failure, the inner tzaddik contains the holy brazenness necessary to stand his ground and continue to insist that what he searches for is not only real, it is eminently attainable.

As we have discussed in a few places, *"Azus D'Kedusha,"* holy stubbornness, is an extremely valuable trait. The viceroy has displayed *Azus D'Kedusha* consistently throughout his search for the lost princess, beginning when he courageously walked right past the armed guards at the gate of the beautiful and orderly palace of evil. Consider this: Had the viceroy lacked this imperative trait, his search would have ended there — he would still be sitting outside those gates, all these years later! However, because he understood, and continues to understand, his holy mission as being of absolute importance, he feels that he has nothing to lose. To the viceroy, a life lived in the absence of the lost princess is not much of a life at all. Therefore, he consistently displays tremendous courage in the face of obstacles and finds the strength to continue his search no matter what; beginning again even after the most devastating falls and pressing onward in the face of the fiercest adversity.

Here we find another example of how this trait of holy stubbornness enables the viceroy to move ever closer to his goal. When, faced with the giant's discouraging skepticism, he refuses to be fazed — clinging to his conviction that the path he treads is valid and true, something amazing happens. The giant offers his service to the viceroy!

Unnerved by the viceroy's tears and expression of stubbornness, the giant begins to lose his confidence. This is his first time seeing anyone cry over an ideal. That a religious matter should elicit such a deeply emotional response is an absolute novelty in his eyes. Something stirs in the giant's heart, an age-old chord reverberates from a time dead and gone, a time where he, too, had tasted the sweetness of the *neshamah*. Terrified by these strange feelings, the giant quickly escapes back into the fortress of his intellectual sophistication. Snapping out of the momentary lapse of his arrogance, he clears his throat, straightens his posture, and fixes his tie. "*L'daati*," he says, "to my knowledge, it doesn't exist." But the viceroy's tears, like the water dripping on Rabbi Akiva's rock, have created a crack in the edifice of the giant's haughty assumptions. Although he is not ready to admit that the viceroy might be on to something, he agrees to do something to help this sweet Jew with a fire in his soul. The giant now seeks to *assist* the viceroy in his search, not despite the viceroy's stubbornness, but *"because you are adamant about it"* — as a direct result of his refusal to be swayed. The deep desperation and yearning that finds expression in a Jew's refusal to give up on his mission makes an impression on even the detracting forces, causing them to come to his aid.

✳ To Reveal the Soul

IN THE OPENING chapters of his remarkable work, *Hachsharas HaAvreichim*, the Piaseczner Rebbe delves into the manner in which the human soul expresses itself using the five senses. He explains that the soul, as a unified being, contains the abilities to hear, see, taste, smell, and feel within its indivisibility, as one. When the soul reveals itself in the physicality of the human ear, it has the ability to hear the sounds of this world. When it reveals itself in the physicality of the human eye, it has the ability to see physical objects, and so on. On its own, the soul is a seeing, hearing, smelling, tasting, and feeling being — all at once. Filling the physical vessels of ears, eyes, nostrils, hands, and mouth enables its capacities to come to expression.

But it goes one step deeper. Even while revealed within the human ear, were there to be no sound, the soul's capacity of hearing would never come to expression.[1] The same with sight — theoretically, if there were nothing to see, even while filling a working pair of human eyes, we would never know that the soul has this special ability.[2]

This introduction allows us to discover an unbelievable truth. While perhaps the most fundamental and commonly utilized, the

---

1. See *Avodas Yisrael, Bo,* "*HaChodesh*."
2. *Hachsharas HaAvreichim,* Chapter 2. For a reference to this concept in Chazal, see *Berachos* 31b.

senses of hearing, sight, taste, smell, and touch represent only the very basic capacities of the soul, that service its other, far deeper, abilities. The soul has the ability to love, to cry, to feel lonely, to be joyous. Within its perfect unity, the soul contains a great many powerful abilities as one. But perhaps the greatest capacity of the soul is its ability to overcome the most difficult challenges with faith and conviction. The ability to be *"maavir al middoseinu,"* to overcome our base inclinations and act in accordance with our higher ideals is uniquely human and represents the pinnacle of our greatness. However, much like the other senses require an external stimulant for activation, so does this one: Just like a sound allows for the activation of the soul's ability to hear, so do the unique challenges, struggles, and difficulties each of us experience in our lives allow our soul's greatest abilities to merit expression. Based on the Gemara that states, *Ein Hakadosh Baruch Hu ba b'trunia im briyosav,* "Hashem does not intent to torment His creations,"[3] the tzaddikim teach that Hashem gives each person challenges that are precisely commensurate with that person's ability to deal with them.[4] This means that each and every difficult situation we go through is for the purpose of revealing the expansive power of our soul. If it weren't for sounds, we would never know that the soul could hear. If it weren't for challenges, we would never know that the soul could persevere. Commenting on the verse, "I will make for him a helper, opposite him,"[5] the Ishbitzer comments: "For this is the Will of God — that one's help should come from that which is positioned against him."[6] This is the way of the world; challenges are for our ultimate betterment, to allow us to reveal the extent of our soul's incredible power.

---

3. *Avodah Zarah* 3a.
4. *Likutei Moharan Tinyana* 66.
5. *Bereishis* 2:18.
6. *Mei HaShiloach*, Vol. 1, *Bereishis*, *"E'eseh lo."*

On a deeper level, then, although the giant seems like he seeks to prevent the viceroy from continuing his journey, he is truly there to aid the viceroy. In *penimiyus*, all challenges are given to us by the Master of the world to compel us toward a true relationship with Him and guide us toward the fulfillment of our potential.

When the animals under the giant's authority have nothing to report; the challenge deepens. Indeed, the most difficult challenges are those that seem to lift you up, only to slam you to the ground once more. After the viceroy's hopes have been raised by the giant's kind gesture which came about as a result of his holy obstinance, the disappointment is all the greater when the giant uses the animals' report, the concurrence of all the other sun-people to the giant's conviction, to buttress his discouragement. Still — although the struggle is great and the forces of doubt seem just about ready to storm the fortress of his certainty — the viceroy holds fast to his convictions, refusing to bend. This time, his *Azus D'Kedusha* leads to a truly useful development.

✳ The Second Giant — Master of the Birds

IN REFERRING THE viceroy to his brother who is in charge of all the birds of the world, the first giant assists him in a substantial way. On the surface, however, it does not appear to be very helpful at all.

The Breslover *mashpi'im* write that the second giant, master of the birds, is a more subtle iteration of the sun-person; one who has a measure of familiarity with the world of the spirit. While the first giant was associated with animals, representing base and shallow physicality, this giant is associated with birds, a lighter, more ostensibly spiritual person. Perhaps this *talmid chacham* is familiar with works of *hashkafah*, the writings of the Ramchal, Maharal, Rav Dessler, and Rav Hutner. However, even these studies remain purely intellectual treats — he does not seek to apply any of these illuminating teachings to his day-to-day life.[7]

Because of his familiarity with these teachings, the second giant's discouragement is even more devastating than that of the first. When the gigantic flock composed of all the word's birds flying among a million quotes from *Derech Hashem* and the *Kuzari* is utilized by the giant to further deny the existence of this golden mountain and pearl palace, the challenge seems almost too great to bear. However, as the saying goes, "He who has a why to live for can overcome almost any how" — having bound his soul with the ultimate "why," his goal of freeing the lost princess with whom his soul is so intimately bound, the viceroy is able to overcome any "how," surviving the harrowing hurdles along the final phase of his journey. Once the viceroy's position has been fortified to this point, nothing and no one can move him. If he has learned

---

7. A great Jewish thinker drew a mighty distinction between speculative/conceptual study and situational/religious study. The **speculative** approach focuses on the *known*, dealing with the problem of the world's *cause* and concerning itself with questions *about* Hashem. The **situational** approach focuses on the *unknown*, dealing with the problem of what the world *stands for* and exploring questions *from* Hashem perpetually addressed to each and every Jew. To the **conceptual** thinker, the world is an *enigma*, and demands *study* to clarify doubt and *assuage one's sense of curiosity*. To the **religious** thinker, the world is an active *challenge*, demanding *wisdom* to adequately discharge our obligation in fostering a *sense of awe*. While the **speculative** approach is *stagnant*, founded upon the stable plains of *arrogance*, the **situational** approach is *dynamic*, ever riding the waves of a deep *humility*. While the second giant may be engaged in the deeper texts of our tradition, delving into the "why" underlying the pragmatic realm of the "how," it is in a manner of speculative/conceptual study. He does not see his own life as being at stake in his inquiry, the thinker stands outside the arena of his thought, a stranger to the world in which the ideas he ponders function as truth. As such, they cannot affect his behavior or enable him to encounter his soul. See Rabbeinu Yonah's fascinating comment on *Avos* 4:1: A wise person who is not emotionally connected to wisdom is a fool.

just one thing throughout this journey it is that remaining firmly committed to his holy mission in the face of obstacles will in the end enable him to proceed. He has already grown accustomed to the strange conditions of this "side path" to God. With the lost princess at stake, he is ready to ride out any storm, no matter what it may take.

LESSONS FOR LIFE

❋ When, faced with mighty obstacles on the path to closeness with the Master of the world, we respond with holy stubbornness, the challenges themselves come to our aid — pointing us to the next hint along this glorious scavenger hunt.

❋ Just as the existence of sounds and sights allows our soul's ability to hear and see to come to expression, so do life's difficulties and the challenges we face allow for the expression of our true greatness in overcoming these hurdles.

CHAPTER 20

Breakthrough

אָמַר לוֹ [הָאָדָם הַב׳ הַזֶּה לְהַשֵּׁנִי לַמַּלְכוּת] לֵהָלָן בַּמִּדְבָּר נִמְצָא שָׁם אָחִי שֶׁמְּמֻנֶּה עַל כָּל הָרוּחוֹת, וְהֵם רָצִים כָּל הָעוֹלָם, אוּלַי יוֹדְעִים הֵם. וְהָלַךְ כַּמָּה וְכַמָּה שָׁנִים לְבַקֵּשׁ, וּמָצָא אָדָם גָּדוֹל גַּם כֵּן כַּנַּ״ל, וְנָשָׂא גַם כֵּן אִילָן גָּדוֹל כַּנַּ״ל. וְשָׁאַל אוֹתוֹ גַם כֵּן כַּנַּ״ל, וְהֵשִׁיב לוֹ כָּל הַמַּעֲשֶׂה כַּנַּ״ל. וְדָחָה אוֹתוֹ גַם כֵּן, וְהוּא הִפְצִיר אוֹתוֹ גַם כֵּן, וְאָמַר לוֹ [הָאָדָם הַשְּׁלִישִׁי הַזֶּה לְהַשֵּׁנִי לַמַּלְכוּת] שֶׁלְּמַעֲנוּ יִקְרָא שֶׁיָּבוֹאוּ כָּל הָרוּחוֹת, וְיִשְׁאַל אוֹתָם. וְקָרָא אוֹתָם, וּבָאוּ כָּל הָרוּחוֹת, וְשָׁאַל אֶת כֻּלָּם, וְלֹא יָדְעוּ שׁוּם אֶחָד מֵהֶם מַהֵר וּמִבְצָר הַנַּ״ל. וְאָמַר לוֹ [הָאָדָם הַשְּׁלִישִׁי לְהַשֵּׁנִי לַמַּלְכוּת]: הֲלֹא אַתָּה רוֹאֶה שֶׁשְּׁטוּת סִפְּרוּ לְפָנֶיךָ! וְהִתְחִיל לִבְכּוֹת מְאֹד, וְאָמַר: אֲנִי יוֹדֵעַ שֶׁיֶּשְׁנוֹ בְּוַדַּאי.

בְּתוֹךְ כָּךְ רָאָה שֶׁבָּא עוֹד רוּחַ אֶחָד, וְכָעַס עָלָיו הַמְּמֻנֶּה הַנַּ״ל: מַדּוּעַ נִתְאַחַרְתָּ לָבוֹא? הֲלֹא גָזַרְתִּי שֶׁיָּבוֹאוּ כָּל הָרוּחוֹת, וְלָמָּה לֹא בָּאתָ עִמָּהֶם? הֵשִׁיב לוֹ שֶׁנִּתְעַכַּבְתִּי מֵחֲמַת שֶׁהָיִיתִי צָרִיךְ לָשֵׂאת בַּת מַלְכָּה אֶל הַר שֶׁל זָהָב וּמִבְצָר שֶׁל מַרְגָּלִיּוֹת. וְשָׂמַח מְאֹד.

The giant said to the viceroy, "Further on in the desert, you will find my brother. He is appointed over all of the winds that travel throughout the world. Maybe they know something." The viceroy

349

walked for many, many years until he found another giant, carrying a tree like the others. The giant asked him who he was, and the viceroy told him the whole story. Like the others, this giant tried to discourage him, but the viceroy stood his ground. The third giant said to the viceroy that he would call all of the winds of the world on his behalf and ask them. He called them, and they came. He asked them all, and they said they had never seen such a mountain or palace. The giant said: "Now you surely see that you have been led along by folly." And the viceroy began to cry very greatly, saying, "I know with certainty that it exists."

In the middle of this conversation, they saw that another wind had come. The giant grew very angry, saying, "Why did you come so late? I decreed that all of the winds should come, why did you not come together with them?" The wind answered, "I was held up because I needed to carry a princess to a mountain of gold and a palace of pearls." And he was very joyous.

⊛ The Third Giant — Master of the Winds

STILL TAPPING HIS seemingly endless reservoir of holy stubbornness, the viceroy ignores the second giant's words of discouragement, refusing to give up. As had happened the first time, when the giant saw that the viceroy refused to give up, he offered to try and help him by referring him to the third and final brother — the master of the winds.

Just as the second giant, appointed over the birds, represents a scholar who is more in tune with spiritual works, thus representing a greater obstacle to the viceroy who is searching for something these giants can't seem to understand — the third and final giant, who is appointed over all the winds, represents an even more spiritually inclined figure. The spiritual connotation of *ruach*, wind (literally "spirit"), tells us that this giant is connected to the deepest depths of the Torah's mystical thought, fluent in the teachings of the *Zohar*, Arizal, Ramak, Rashash, Gra, and works of Chassidus. Still, having never sufficiently applied those teachings to his own day-to-day experience and gotten in touch with the simple faith and humble joy these deep works ultimately intend to foster, he finds it impossible to believe that a lowly *adam* who is yet stuck in the tension between *"Adam min ha'adamah,"* dross and lowly physicality, and *"Adamah l'Elyon,"* the greatest spiritual calling, can access the Lost Princess of passion and true *deveikus* with Hashem. Although this giant has some level of insight into the context of the viceroy's lifelong search, his opposition represents the greatest obstacle of them all: He knows what the viceroy is after and *still* thinks his search is futile. He does not deny the premise of the search, but rather repudiates the viceroy's chances of success. When a relative, friend, rebbi, or mentor who is a master over the winds, fluent in the studies of *"ruach"* that treat the inner spirit of life and *avodas Hashem*, pushes one away with discouraging and disapproving words, the Jew's convictions are tested in the most extreme manner possible.

❄ Climax

STUNNED BY THE enormity of this obstacle, the viceroy stumbles backward, in a daze. His head spins. The entire journey dances before his eyes. A thousand voices echo in his mind, all speaking at once. He can make out vague sentences from among the din: "This is the place of no good", "Do you recognize me?", "Choose for yourself a place", "Look how beautiful those apples are!", "Where in the world am I?", "I have been captive here for so long...", "Where in the world am I?!"

The panoramic echo chamber fades, giving rise to booming voices punctuated by the cries of a great multitude of animals and birds: "Certainly this place doesn't exist", "You have been led along by folly", "It is certainly not in the world." A million lions roar. "Turn back!" The cry of two million hawks fills his ears. "Turn back, turn back!"

The noises fade and scenes from the decades of his journey begin to ripple through his consciousness. In waves, the various pictures enter and glimmer for a moment before fading away. Deserts, fields, and forests, the great ballroom, the accursed apple in hand, waking from his slumber, facing the princess, the river of wine, holding a tear-soaked headscarf to the sun, hordes of animals, endless flocks of birds; the images go by faster and faster.

Emotions begin to flash by in rapid succession: confidence, surprise, resolve, yearning, devastation, hope, stubbornness, sadness, triumph, apathy, joy. The feelings spin like a top until suddenly beginning to shrink smaller and smaller, consolidating to the center point in the deep blackness of his mind. When they are finally compacted into an infinitesimal kernel of pulsating essence, the spot erupts in an explosion of color and a river flows out — a river of holy desire. Flowing with great strength, the river overflows the banks of his psyche, sweeping up the voices and the sounds, the visions and the emotions which all melt into the roiling flow of passionate fury. Above the frothing river, the face of the princess appears, begging, beseeching, strengthening.

This is all he has left. Desire, endless desire. And desire is all he needs.

"And the viceroy began to cry very greatly, saying, "I know with certainty that it exists." The pressure that has been steadily building throughout the chapters of this epic tale reaches its climax in

these lines. Our hero has been faced with obstacle after failure after difficulty, learning valuable lessons from each and refusing to let anything hold him back from reaching the goal he set out to attain, a lifetime ago. Instead of weakening his resolve, each setback served only to strengthen his desire and fortify his unbearable yearning to see the lost princess at home again with her father, the king, who loves her more than anything in the world. But all the obstacles he has experienced pale in comparison to the discouraging words of the three giants. Just like the most frequent, intense, and painful contractions occur just before birth, the viceroy has undergone an intense series of obstacles that put his resolve to the ultimate test. Three well-intentioned mentors who seek to set the viceroy on a path that is not his to take become mighty "birth pangs" in the dark, cold desert night, moments before the warm sun of salvation rises once more.[1] Out of words and at the end of his strength, the viceroy bursts into tears. The *Zohar HaKadosh* teaches:

> When the Jewish nation is in exile, it is said that all the gates are locked, for the Shechinah — which is *Malchus* — is outside of the palace... and there is no way for prayers to ascend. However, the gates of tears are not locked. But no one can open these gates [of tears] except for the master of tears, as it is written: "And she opened it [the ark] and saw within it the child, behold a little boy was crying"[2] — [which means that] the palace will be opened in merit of this crying... This is the significance of the verse: "They will come with crying"[3] — in merit of their weeping, Klal Yisrael will be gathered from the exile.[4]

---

1. See *Even Sheleimah* 11:5.

2. *Shemos* 2:6.

3. *Yirmeyahu* 31:8.

4. *Tikkunei Zohar* 11. See also *Berachos* 32a: "Even though the gates of prayer may be locked, the gates of tears are never locked." The *Shaarei Orah* (Second

At the breaking point, nullified before the awesome yearning that has grown in tandem with the obstacles he has faced
throughout these long and bitter years, the viceroy whispers
hoarsely, through his tears, that he *knows* the golden mountain
and pearl palace exist. These tears of holy stubbornness and commitment to *avodas Hashem* open all gates. When a Jew reaches
the level where a challenge to his Yiddishkeit moves him to tears,
there is nothing that can stand in his way. For the first time,
the viceroy utters the words *Ani yodei'a*, "I *know* it exists." This
demonstrates that the obstacles he has faced and the desire they
enabled him to express in order to overcome them have finally
propelled him to a place of the most unshakable certainty — *absolute knowledge* that the lost princess is yet within his reach.

The Breslover *mashpi'im* teach that the words *"Ani yodei'a
she'yeish bevadai"* share the same opening letters as the phrase
"Ein shum yi'ush ba'olam," the iconic battle cry of Rebbe Nachman
of Breslov, the tzaddik who implanted in the hearts of all future
generations that "there is no despair in the world at all."[5] This
similarity is significant. In expressing certainty in the face of
the mightiest challenge, the viceroy embodies the idea of eternal
hope and the inner flame that continues to flicker no matter how
mightily the dissenting forces attempt to blow it out.

These opening letters, *aleph, shin, yud, beis*, which serve as
the core for Rebbe Nachman's awesome expression of hope, spell
the word *"Ashiv."* Remarkably, this word makes an appearance in
an awesome verse that conveys this very message.

Yirmeyahu HaNavi mourns over the Beis HaMikdash: "I said,
'My strength and hope have perished before Hashem.'"[6] But in

---

Gate) teaches that the "Gates of Tears" are related to the *Sefirah* of *Yesod* —
they have a particular relationship with the viceroy.

5. See *Likutei Moharan Tinyana* 78.

6. *Eichah* 3:18.

midst of this encounter with hopelessness, the prophet strengthens himself, saying: "But with this I respond to my heart (*"Ashiv el libi"*), therefore I do have hope: the kindness of Hashem never ends, His mercy will never be used up."[7]

With these words, Yirmeyahu is going through the process experienced by the viceroy in the encounter with the third giant. Falling into the abyss of despair, Yirmeyahu is able to catch himself just in time: *Ashiv el libi* — "I *do* have hope." *"Ein shum yi'ush ba'olam!"* *"Ani yodei'a she'yeish bevadai!"* "The night will pass, and the darkness will give way to the blessing of a brand-new day. There is no despair in the world at all, the golden mountain certainly exists! Nothing in the world can ever convince me otherwise!"

This expression of certainty demonstrates that the viceroy has rectified the spiritual chill of Amalek, the aspect of *"Asher karcha baderech"* which this story, told along that very same *derech*, aims to combat. We have mentioned that the word *Amalek* shares the same numerical value with the word *safek*, doubt. The inner force of Amalek aims to cool the fiery passion of a Jew by casting him into a place of doubt and confusion. When a Jew's convictions are weakened and he or she feels as if *avodas Hashem* is no longer worth fighting for, all excitement dies. Unsure if Hashem is still interested in his service after so many years of sin, he finds it far more difficult to pray with feeling and connection. Doubtful that her adherence to *tzni'us* makes a difference in the larger scheme of things, she is flippant in her adherence to those *halachos*. The attitude of s*afek*, Amaleki doubt, is perhaps the strongest indicator that one has lost touch with the princess of youth.

At this point in his mission of redeeming the lost princess via emulative extraction, the viceroy has succeeded in pushing the troops of Amalek out of his life. His life is filled with the deepest sense of meaning, his actions saturated with yearning and holy

---

7. *Eichah* 3:21–22.

desire. It is here that the viceroy deals the final blow to this spiritual archenemy, banishing the frostiness of Amalek once and for all. By using the words *Ani yode'a she'yeish* **bevadai**, "I know *for certain* that it exists," the viceroy annihilates the spirit of Amalek which is founded upon **safek**, doubt and spiritual *uncertainty*.

Having reached this place of awesome inner strength and broken through all of the gates with his tears of yearning, the viceroy is ready, at long last, for true salvation.

❧

✳ The Tardy Wind

JUST LIKE THE night grows darkest just before the dawn, the salvation of Hashem comes at the very last minute, when all hope seems lost. Just after the viceroy's intense expression of holy desire and eternal commitment to his mission, a new wind appears to join the gathering. This wind is the key to the viceroy's salvation. It specifically needed to be late, arriving only after all the other winds had already taken yet another mighty hammer to his beliefs, because this tardiness allowed for the viceroy to express the absolute extent of his conviction. When the viceroy demonstrates that he is able to hold tightly to his holy desire even when it seems as if the whole world is against him, it is then salvation begin to sprout.

Yeshuas Hashem k'heref ayin, "The salvation of Hashem comes in the blink of an eye."[8] In the midst of the viceroy's excruciating inner storm, the tears yet coursing down his face, everything changes, and his deep soul knowledge is validated at long last. In a single moment, "*Venahafoch hu*"[9] — the whole world is transformed. Finally, after so many years of bouncing between doubt and faith, fighting to stay committed to his soul's certainty in the

---

8. *Midrash Lekach Tov, Esther* 4:17.
9. *Esther* 9:1.

face of the greatest failures and discouragement, he is completely and utterly vindicated.

"I was held up because I needed to carry a princess to a mountain of gold and a palace of pearls." We can only begin to imagine the joy the viceroy felt when the wind uttered those words. We can only dream about how brightly his universe must have been illuminated as any lingering vestige of doubt and fear was washed away. It was a truly glorious moment, saturated with a spirit of ultimate triumph.

The verse states: *V'ruach Elokim merachefes al p'nei hamayim*, "The spirit of *Elokim* was hovering above the face of the waters."[10] The Midrash[11] explains that the spirit (*ruach*) referred to in this verse is the spirit of Mashiach ben David, about whom the verse states, "And the spirit (*ruach*) of Hashem shall rest upon him — a spirit of wisdom and understanding, a spirit of counsel and heroism, a spirit of knowledge and fear of Hashem."[12] This means that on a very deep level, the spirit of Mashiach who is to bring the world to its ultimate rectification was present even before Adam's eating from the *Eitz HaDaas*, the primordial sin from which all subsequent sins originate.[13] Prepared from the outset and present in every generation, the spirit of Mashiach ben David comes to finish the story, to demonstrate how the tale of the Jewish nation is that of the ultimate *baal teshuvah* who reaches a place of retrospective clarity wherein all sins are transformed to merits, and how all of history was "His Story," pre-ordained by the Master of the world.[14] It is this *ruach*-wind which arrives to validate the

---

10. *Bereishis* 1:2.

11. *Bereishis Rabbah* 2:5.

12. *Yeshayahu* 11:2.

13. See *Oros HaTeshuvah* 6:2.

14. This spirit of Mashiach shares a deep bond with the nature of the princess, as it is saturated with the passion of youth. See *Shabbos* 119b: "'Do not touch my anointed ones (*meshichai*)' — these are the schoolchildren." See also *The Scroll of Secrets*, pp.128–134.

viceroy's journey. It arrives late, an aspect of the Thirteenth principle of faith, in which we declare our abiding faith in the arrival of Mashiach: *"And even if he tarries,* even so, I await him each day, that he may come."* Just like the spirit of Mashiach hovering over the face of the waters at the outset of creation, this wind had been present long before the princess had been lost, prepared for this magnificent moment where the streams of struggle empty into the endless ocean of ultimate meaning.

But on a focused level, this mysterious *"ruach"* contains an implication that is far more relevant to the individual's spiritual journey.

The Gemara in *Makkos* presents an attempt by certain Biblical figures to whittle down the 613 mitzvos to their most basic foundations so as to simplify Yiddishkeit for the later generations. David got the mitzvos down to eleven, Yeshayah to six, Michah to three, and Yeshayah to two. Finally, Chavakuk revealed a single, absolute foundation of Torah for the generation before Mashiach's arrival. *Ba Chavakuk v'he'emidan al achas: 'V'tzaddik b'emunaso yichyeh,'* "Chavakuk came and established them on a single foundation: 'And the righteous person shall live by his faith.'"[15,16]

On a simple level, the pillar to which Chavakuk was referring is *emunah,* faith, which the supporting verse teaches is the very life-force of the righteous person. But there is an alternative approach as well. In the back of *sefer Tzror HaChaim,* penned by my ancestor, the famed *gaon* and tzaddik Rav Shmuel Shmelke Klein (1804–1875), Rav and Rosh Yeshivah in the Hungarian cities of Balkany, Chuszt, and Selish, appears a novel interpretation of Chavakuk's foundational pillar. My Zeide taught that the Gemara should be read in the following manner: ***Ba Chavakuk***

---

15. *Chavakuk* 2:4.
16. *Makkos* 24a.

v'he'emidan al achas: V'Tzaddik, "Chavakuk came and established them upon a single foundation: *The tzaddik.*" *B'emunaso*, "through our faith in him," *yichyeh*, "we will find life." Using his prophetic foresight to peer into the darkness of the final generation, Chavakuk handed us the golden key: bind yourself to the tzaddikim and you will forever maintain your connection to the Source of life.

Throughout *Likutei Moharan*, Rebbe Nachman draws a connection between the tzaddik and *ruach*, spirit.[17] In the context of Yehoshua's appointment as leader of the Jewish nation, the Torah refers to him as *"Ish asher ruach bo."*[18] Rebbe Nachman sees this as the model for all future tzaddikim as well. In a remarkable teaching,[19] the Rebbe uses the analogy of a coal to reveal a fundamental expression of this connection. Soon after it is lit, a burning coal glows red with heat. With time, however, although it is still burning hot, a layer of grey ash will begin to grow until the spark is completely covered over. In order to ensure that the coal will continue to burn at full strength, one needs to simply blow off the layer of ash and the inner spark will be revealed once more.

Rebbe Nachman teaches that the Jewish heart is like a burning coal, ever on fire with the love of Hashem and the mission of revealing His light in the world. However, with time, a layer of ash begins to settle over this flaming heart, covering it over and making it appear as if we have lost our spark. But *"ani yisheinah v'libi eir"*[20]; although on the outside it may look as if all hope is lost and our sense for spirituality and desire for *teshuvah* extinguished, all that is needed is a little bit of wind, some holy *"ruach,"* that can blow off this external layer and reveal the truth of our essential

---

17. See, for example, *Likutei Moharan* 8, 10, and 66.
18. *Bamidbar* 27:18.
19. *Likutei Moharan Tinyana* 9.
20. *Shir HaShirim* 5:2.

goodness and deep-seated yearning for closeness with our Source. This *"ruach,"* says Rebbe Nachman, is the tzaddik. Through his Torah teachings, guidance, advice, encouragement, and shining example, the tzaddik lovingly blows the ashes off of the Jewish heart, stripping away the external garments to reveal the essence of life and the exalted holiness of the Jew's core identity. This is the pillar of our salvation: *"V'tzaddik,"* Hashem has granted us tzaddikim who felt our pain, who understood the darkness of the final generation. *"B'emunaso,"* when we will have faith in this tzaddik and study his teachings with intent to apply his advice, *"yichyeh,"* we will discover a path toward a life bursting with passion, strength, joy, and everlasting vitality. This mighty connection will grant us the ability to adopt a perspective which sees all of our lacks as fulfilled beyond our wildest dreams.[21]

In the beginning of *Chayei Moharan*, Reb Nosson records an announcement once made by Rebbe Nachman before a group of his chassidim, "When you travel away from here and they ask you what you accomplished, answer them, *'Ruach.'"*[22] Based on these sources, it seems obvious to suggest that the *ruach*-wind that appears at the very end of our tale to carry the viceroy to his ultimate salvation is a reference to the tzaddik who revealed this story, Rebbe Nachman himself. Famously, this exalted tzaddik stated that his fire would burn until the Mashiach's arrival and that after him there would be no more novel souls sent down to this world. Chazal teach that Hashem sends the remedy before the sickness. Preceding the final generation of Jews who would need to persevere in the most spiritually hostile societal atmosphere in history, Hashem sent the soul of Rebbe Nachman of Breslov into the world to grant us a taste of *Olam HaBa* in this world, in order to give us life and carry us until the arrival of

---

21. See *Likutei Moharan* 8.
22. *Chayei Moharan* 4.

Mashiach and the national and personal discovery of the Lost Princess. Rebbe Nachman is the *ruach*, the tzaddik foreseen by Chavakuk who — as the singular pillar of the entire Torah ("the Tzaddik is the foundation of the world"[23]) — would breath life to the final generation, blowing the foreign ashes of negativity and despair off the flaming Jewish soul with his constant reminders about simplicity, joy, the possibility of hope, our essential holiness, and Hashem's constant accessibility.

❋ The Giant Rejoices

INTERESTINGLY ENOUGH, WHEN Rebbe Nachman writes *V'samach meod*, "And he was very joyous," he doesn't specify who it was that was joyous. On a simple level, it is logical to assume that these words are referring to the viceroy. He has finally attained the excitement and simple joy of living he had been seeking all along, the spirit of the lost princess burns within him in a mighty bonfire of holy desire.

But the ambiguity of the sentence allows for a deeper understanding. Perhaps these words refer both to the viceroy *and* the third giant. As one who is in tune with the realm of spirit and the consuming search of the moon-people, the giant is overjoyed to learn that a passionate and intimate relationship with Hashem is truly attainable and that it is possible to live a life of innocence, wonder, sweetness, and simplicity. The master of spirit is committed to the truth in a manner which allows him to overlook the affront to his dignity in having been proven wrong and rejoice in the implication of the tardy wind's declaration. As we shall learn in the next chapter, the giant commands this wind to carry the viceroy to the palace of pearls atop the mountain of gold.

---

23. *Mishlei* 10:25.

Relieved that such an elevated perspective is indeed attainable, and that there is more to life and the Torah and *avodas Hashem* with which he was previously familiar, he sends a part of himself along to accompany the viceroy on the remainder of his journey.

❋ The Journey Is the Destination

"I WAS HELD up because I needed to carry a princess to a mountain of gold and a palace of pearls." Taking a moment to think about the words of the tardy wind, a glaring question presents itself. As we have read, it has been many, many years since the princess left her headscarf at the side of a slumbering viceroy detailing her new location. Rebbe Nachman wrote that it took years for the viceroy to find each of the three giants. This means that decades had passed since the princess departed to the final place of her captivity. Doesn't it seem strange, then, that the princess would only be arriving at the mountain of gold and the palace of pearls now, so many decades after writing her future whereabouts on the scarf and taking leave of the slumbering viceroy?

As we have discussed, a major part of the viceroy's journey toward freeing the princess is the yearning that continues to form and solidify with each subsequent failure and obstacle. His strategy is extraction via emulation; the stronger he yearns for her, nurturing her passionate spirit within his heart and soul, the more of her he is freeing. Indeed, this is the deep secret of our tale: The journey *is* the destination — the search for the Lost Princess of passion and youth in *avodas Hashem* itself awakens her passionate fire, deep yearning, and youthful wonder within, enabling one to build an intimate connection with Hashem. Seeking the depth of life, we have already begun to find it. Yearning for purpose and meaning, they have already begun to illuminate our experience. Struggling toward redemption from shallowness and apathy creates a healthy tension and desire that brings our inner universe to life. This is why our tale is titled "The Lost Princess" and not "The Princess Who Was Found" — the primary focus is on *the search*, the spotlight is fixed upon the journey itself.

In a classic teaching, Reb Nosson writes:

> If one searches, one will certainly find. Even during the time when one has not yet found, even so, by way of the toil and the search one has already found plenty. For no toil or quest is ever wasted, and one certainly discovers much in every word or prayer and every effort, for "a positive desire is never lost."
>
> This is the explanation of our Sages' teaching, "If one says 'I have toiled and I have found,' believe him." It seems difficult to understand why we must merely believe him? Shouldn't it be possible to simply see if he has found or not? The answer can be understood in light of our discussion. For in truth, as we have learned, even if one does not yet see what he has found and it appears to him as if he hasn't found anything at all and that he is still just as far away from Hashem as he was at the outset, even so it is necessary to believe with perfect faith that he has indeed found, by virtue of the search itself. Therefore, when our Sages teach, "If one says, 'I have toiled and I have found,' believe him," the word "believe" is used specifically, for one must believe that searching always produces discovery. Even if one is unable to see what it is that he has found.[24]

In his seminal work, *Man's Search for Meaning*, Dr. Viktor E. Frankl opines that struggle and tension are vital elements of mental health and emotional vibrancy. He writes:

> To be sure, man's search for meaning may arouse inner tension rather than inner equilibrium. However, precisely such tension is an indispensable prerequisite of mental health. There is nothing in the world, I venture to say, that would

---

24. *Likutei Halachos, Birchas HaPeiros* 5:1.

> so effectively help one to survive even the worst conditions as the knowledge that there is meaning in one's life. There is much wisdom in the words of Nietzsche: "He who has a why to live for can bear almost any how." ... I consider it a dangerous misconception of mental hygiene to assume that what man needs in the first place is equilibrium or, as it is called in biology, "homeostasis," i.e., a tensionless state. What man actually needs is not a tensionless state but rather the striving and struggling for a worthwhile goal, a freely chosen task. What he needs is not the discharge of tension at any cost but the call of a potential meaning waiting to be fulfilled by him.[25]

When man sets his eyes on an object of his desire, his struggle for a *future* attainment brings his *present* to life.[26] The earthiness of his days is imbued with the living spirit of purpose and meaning, all in accordance with the content of his pursuit.[27]

However, Dr. Frankl wasn't the first to discuss this awesome truth. Nearly 150 years earlier, Rebbe Nachman of Breslov discussed this deep idea with his chassidim. In his magnum opus, Rebbe Nachman teaches that yearning and longing toward an objective grant life to the struggle in which they are expressed. Rebbe Nachman supports this idea with a verse in *Tehillim*: "*Nichsifah v'gam kalsah nafshi.*"[28] On a simple level, these words are translated as "My soul longs and yearns." But the tzaddik teaches that they may also be read in the following, wondrous, manner:

---

25. *Man's Search for Meaning*, pp. 104–105.

26. See *Mussar Avicha* 1:8.

27. It is possible to suggest that Chazal hint to this idea as well in their teaching that, "Tzaddikim have no rest (*menuchah*) in this world, and not in the next" (*Berachos* 64a), and, "Tzaddikim are called alive even in their death" (*Berachos* 18a). Perhaps it is because the tzaddikim are constantly striving, struggling, and yearning toward greater levels of *avodas Hashem* that their entire being is pulsating with life, both in this world and the next.

28. *Tehillim* 84:3.

Nichsifah v'gam kalsah — When one longs and yearns for a personal relationship with the Master of the world, *nafshi* — this fills his service with life-force and vitality, a living spirit that animates his thoughts, words, and actions of holiness.[29]

Rebbe Nachman finds another support for this idea in the words in *Shir HaShirim*: *nekudos hakesef*, "sequins of silver."[30] In *lashon hakodesh*, *nekudos*-vowels are to letters what the soul is to the human body. Bereft of a soul, the human body remains inanimate and powerless. Similarly, without *nekudos*, the letters remain lifeless; we are unable to enunciate or read them.[31] The word *hakesef*, "silver," is related to the word *kisufim*, "longing." Bearing these two ideas in mind, the phrase *nekudas hakesef*, "sequins of silver," may be seen as suggesting that *nekudos* — the animating life-force of the soul, *hakesef* — is produced by means of the Jew's yearning to grow close to Hashem by serving Him with the deepest devotion.[32]

This important teaching from Rebbe Nachman introduces the idea that, on a certain level, yearning for and struggling toward a spiritual goal is *itself* the primary source of vitality.[33] Over the decades of his search, the viceroy's life has been entirely transformed. From the moment he began this momentous mission of epic proportion, his existence has been energized by a powerful sense of purpose and meaning. Committed to his lofty

---

29. We often find that the word *"nefesh"* itself is interpreted as "desire." See, for example, *Bereishis* 23:8, *"Im yeish es nafshichem."*

30. *Shir HaShirim* 1:11.

31. See *Nefesh HaChaim* 2:16.

32. *Likutei Moharan* 31. See also *Mei HaShiloach*, Vol. 1, *Bereishis*, *"Zeh Sefer*," and Vol. 2, *Vayishlach*, *"Vayishlach Yaakov"*; *Pri Tzaddik*, *Va'eschanan* #13; *Parparaos L'Chochmah* 20:10; and *Likutei Halachos*, *Netillas Yadayim L'Seudah* 6:106.

33. See also *Likutei Moharan* 24:1: the only way to attain the infinite light is by pursuing it endlessly.

aspirations, the viceroy has never lived more authentically. Every moment is precious, pulsating with the glorious tension of a life well lived. As he grows closer to the lost princess, her spirit continues to fill his heart, causing a great sense of yearning, desire, joy, excitement, and passion to proliferate within. Sensitive to the Divine beauty reflected by the world around him, his natural surroundings take on ultimate significance.[34] Indeed, he now realizes that, in a certain way, searching is finding, and *the journey is the destination*; *Yismach leiv **mevakshei** Hashem*, "Joyous is the heart of those who *seek* Hashem."[35]

This profound awareness grants the answer to our question. The princess has only just arrived at the place where she is to be rescued and brought back home because, having stood his ground against an inconceivably daunting obstacle, the viceroy has only just now revealed the pinnacle of his yearning. Only when — faced with the most difficult obstacles of all — the viceroy demonstrated the ultimate extent of his fortitude, faith, yearning, and resolve to get in touch with a passionate relationship with Hashem, was the princess finally able to proceed to the place where she could be rescued. The level of his desire and her accessibility to him are absolutely commensurate. Paradoxically, then, while it seems as if the viceroy is searching for the lost princess, the lost princess is, in fact, searching for *him!* This is very deep.[36]

---

34. See *Liktuei Moharan* 52.

35. In his wonderful *sefer The Depth of Our Connection*, (pp. 48–49), my friend R' Binyamin Kaufman writes that according to a Midrash, the wooden box of the *Aron* centered between two gold boxes on either side represents the struggle of life situated between the purity of youth and spiritual greatness. Fascinatingly, this wooden box is part of the *Aron* situated in the holiest place on earth, Kodesh HaKodashim, and used to support the *luchos!* The message here is that the wooden box of spiritual challenge is not secondary. It itself is part and parcel of the ultimate destination.

36. At this stage, it is possible to suggest that, in a very deep way, the princess's error in perceiving Hashem's show of anger as representative of His true

LESSONS FOR LIFE

❋ The moment in which, facing an awesome obstacle, a Jew's yearning for closeness with Hashem and refusal to give up moves him to tears, the gates of his salvation swing open.

❋ When a Jew falls into a state of confusion and doubts the foundational truths of his relationship with Hashem, a spirit of cool apathy blows over his life, extinguishing all passion and excitement for spiritual pursuit. Regaining certainty and absolute commitment, he is able to battle this emotional lethargy and embrace life with vitality.

❋ When one strives to attain meaning, fulfillment, and the depth of life, the very journey toward these goals already fills him with their gifts. The journey *is* the destination.

---

feelings was also orchestrated by the Master of the world. Perhaps this story, while seemingly about the lost princess, is truly about the *viceroy*; her being taken was pre-ordained so that the viceroy would have to search, and, in the process, attain the deepest destination. When we first introduced the viceroy, we explained that he represents the *Sefirah* of *Yesod*, the level of Yosef HaTzaddik. Perhaps the king arranged for the abduction of the lost princess in order to allow the viceroy, who embodies the perfection of Mashiach ben Yosef, to experience the deep emotion and vibrant vitality of Mashiach ben David, the repentant spirit of the *baal teshuvah*. This is exceedingly profound and requires further exploration.

CHAPTER 21

The (Endless) End!

וְשָׁאַל הַמְמֻנֶּה אֶת הָרוּחַ: מַה יָּקָר שָׁם? [הַיְנוּ אֵיזֶה דְּבָרִים
הֵם שָׁם בְּיֹקֶר וּבַחֲשִׁיבוּת.] וְאָמַר לוֹ, שֶׁכָּל הַדְּבָרִים הֵם
שָׁם בְּיֹקֶר גָּדוֹל. וְאָמַר הַמְמֻנֶּה עַל הָרוּחוֹת לְהַשֵּׁנִי
לַמַּלְכוּת: בַּאֲשֶׁר שֶׁזֶּה זְמַן גָּדוֹל כָּל כָּךְ שֶׁאַתָּה מְבַקְשָׁהּ,
וְכַמָּה יְגִיעוֹת שֶׁהָיוּ לְךָ, וְאוּלַי יִהְיֶה לְךָ עַתָּה מְנִיעָה
מֵחֲמַת מָמוֹן. עַל כֵּן אֲנִי נוֹתֵן לְךָ כְּלִי, כְּשֶׁתּוֹשִׁיט יָדְךָ
לְתוֹכָהּ, תְּקַבֵּל מִשָּׁם מָעוֹת. וְגָזַר עַל הָרוּחַ הַנַּ"ל, שֶׁיּוֹלִיךְ
אוֹתוֹ לְשָׁם. וּבָא הָרוּחַ סְעָרָה וְנָשָׂא אוֹתוֹ לְשָׁם, וְהֵבִיא
אוֹתוֹ אֶל שַׁעַר. וְהָיוּ עוֹמְדִים שָׁם חֲיָלוֹת, שֶׁלֹּא הִנִּיחוּ
לִכְנֹס אֶל הָעִיר, וְהוֹשִׁיט יָדוֹ אֶל הַכְּלִי, וְלָקַח מָעוֹת,
וְשִׁחֵד אוֹתָם, וְנִכְנַס לְתוֹךְ הָעִיר, וְהָיְתָה עִיר נָאָה. וְהָלַךְ
אֶל גְּבִיר וְשָׂכַר לוֹ מְזוֹנוֹת, כִּי צָרִיךְ לִשְׁהוֹת שָׁם, כִּי צָרִיךְ
לָשׂוּם שֵׂכֶל וְחָכְמָה לְהוֹצִיאָהּ.
וְאֵיךְ שֶׁהוֹצִיאָהּ, לֹא סִפֵּר. וּבַסּוֹף הוֹצִיאָהּ.

The giant asked the wind, "What is precious there?" (Meaning, which items are valuable there and held in esteem?) The wind responded, "Everything there is tremendously valuable and expensive." The one appointed over the winds said to the viceroy: "Because you have been searching for her for such a great amount of time and you had so many struggles, it is possible that you will now have a further obstacle because of money. Therefore, I will give you a vessel. Whenever you reach inside, you will take money from there." The giant commanded the wind to bring the viceroy to this place. The storm wind came and carried him there, bringing him to the gate. There were troops there who did not let him enter the city. He reached his hand into the vessel and took out money. He bribed them and entered the city. It was a beautiful city. He went to a wealthy man and rented food and board, for he would need to stay a while. He would need to devote much thought and contemplation to free her.

(Reb Nosson writes:) The manner in which he freed her was not told. But in the end, he freed her.

A World of Absolute Value

THE *RUACH*-WIND TELLS the third giant that in the city atop the golden mountain, *"everything is tremendously valuable and expensive."* The Breslover *mashpi'm* reveal multiple, concurring interpretations of this statement.

1] As we have discussed at length in the Chapters Sixteen and Seventeen, the mountain of gold represents the awareness that the struggle toward a goal, with all of its challenges and failures, is part and parcel of the goal itself. Here, the viceroy reaches a level of retrospective clarity that grants him a deep appreciation for each step of the journey, an appreciation expressed so wonderfully in the words of a great Jewish thinker:

> In our own lives the voice of God speaks slowly, a syllable at
> a time. Reaching the peak of our years, dispelling some of
> our intimate illusions, and learning how to spell the meaning
> of life-experiences backwards, some of us discover how the
> scattered syllables form a single phrase.[1]

Rebbe Nachman teaches that in this transcendent city of retrospective clarity, *everything* is valuable — even those things which seem to have been negative and harmful; it was all for the purpose of enabling the viceroy to reach the peak of his potential and to bring the ultimate honor to Hashem.

2] In the world of the six sons, everything is cheap. Relationships are shallow, words are meaningless, and experiences detached from the essence of one's life. Nature, of interest because of its beauty at best and its ability to be harnessed for human ends at worst — is never seen as a hint to the transcendent Designer of our universe calling for awe, wonder, and humility. As one writer put it, "Nature as a toolbox is a world that does not point beyond itself." Moments slip by with nary a thought as to their endless value and great opportunities are dismissed with the simple wave of a hand. When we fall into the mindset of the six sons, instead of waking up each day into a world of brilliant meaning and glorious prospect, and living life with excitement, passion, and joy, life becomes a dull, passive process. Nothing holds any value, nothing is precious. Each day is just like the last, and, as the old song goes, "nothing really matters."

In contradistinction to this sorry experience, in the city atop the golden mountain pulsating with the holy energy of the lost princess, everything is valuable. A person who is in touch with the Lost Princess of life approaches the world with wide-eyed wonder and radical amazement. To him, every experience is an *event* bursting with meaning, every circumstance carries Divine

---

1. *Between God and Man*, p. 72.

messages intended solely for him, and each relationship is deep, genuine, and precious. "He knows that there are laws that regulate the course of natural processes; he is aware of the regularity and pattern of things. However, such knowledge fails to mitigate his sense of perpetual surprise at the fact that there are facts at all... no routine of the social, physical, or physiological order must dull our sense of surprise at the fact that there *is* a social, a physical, or a physiological order."[2] Such a person sees life as the greatest gift, each moment is a key to eternal bliss. In the place of the Lost Princess, *everything* is tremendously valuable.[3]

3] When it is applied to *avodas Hashem*, the mentality of the six sons sees grand acts of devotion or awesome levels of sacrifice as alone sanctioning joy or fulfillment. Small expressions of love or awe that are easily accomplished are overlooked and unrewarded. The six sons of *avodas Hashem* look exclusively toward great goals shining with an aura of grandeur. Wearing tzitzis, lighting Shabbos candles, donning tefillin, dressing modestly, making *berachos* with *kavanah* — these are all seen as too easy, simple, and basic to elicit gratitude, holy pride, and abiding joy.

In addition to looking toward those very same goals and aiming for greatness, the mentality of the princess values each and every step of the journey, taking the deepest pleasure in every encounter with Hashem, no matter how slight it may appear. Every word of *tefillah* is shining from one end of the world to

---

2. *Between Man and God*, pp. 41, 43.

3. See also ibid., p. 52: "The meaning of awe is to realize that life takes place under wide horizons, horizons that range beyond the span of an individual life or even the life of a nation, a generation, or an era. Awe enables us to perceive in the world intimations of the Divine, to sense in small things the beginning of infinite significance, to sense the ultimate in the common and the simple; to feel in the rush of the passing the stillness of the eternal." And p. 54: "It is the *extremely precious*, morally, intellectually or spiritually, that we revere."

the other, each *berachah* made with *kavanah* is bursting with meaning.[4] The smallest whisper of holy desire is reason enough to dance for two thousand years. The Baal Shem Tov and his students came to the world to teach us this secret: a Jew only ever has the present moment, and each moment is an embodiment of eternity. Therefore, the joy expressed in a moment of engagement with holiness is an eternal joy, an ultimate sense of fulfillment. The Jew whose service of Hashem is imbued with the spirit of the princess never feels hurried — he doesn't feel the need to rush out of *tefillah* to engage in Torah study — each moment of his *avodah* stands alone, each step of the journey carries a preciousness which remains independent of the goal.

In the words of Rav Kook:

> For some individuals, there is a great divide between the goal and the journey. Having decided on a certain goal, one feels as if the entire detailed journey is some heavy burden. He feels frustrated and tries to hurry everything. Deep inside his soul, he feels discomfort and pain... Such a goal-oriented mental state begins to affect one's physical movements, until one starts to take rushed steps. All of his steps are simply an effort to remove the frustrating requirement of the journey.
>
> A wise person understands that each and every step has the profound effect of bringing one to a greater level of perfection. This person knows that the very journey of reaching

---

4. My father *shlita* once shared a beautiful understanding of why, at *Matan Torah*, each word uttered by Hashem caused the members of the Jewish nation to die, requiring them to be brought back to life. By causing their souls to leave them after hearing each and every word of Torah, Hashem was teaching them a profound lesson: it is worth being born and living an entire lifetime for the singular purpose of hearing just one word of our holy Torah. This is the spirit of the princess embodied in the city atop the golden mountain where "everything is precious."

perfection should be valued and treasured. One who thinks this way will find constant satisfaction and peace of mind in each and every step. This is the meaning of "In all of your ways, know Him."[5,6]

This is a third level of insight into Rebbe Nachman's teaching that in the city atop the mountain of gold, everything is precious. Saturated with the presence of the princess, every experience of holiness is valuable, no matter how slight. An awesome peace of

---

5. *Mishlei* 3:6.

6. *Ein AYaH, Berachos* 2, p. 33. See also *Oros HaTeshuvah* 6:7, where Rav Kook uses this idea to explain Chazal's teaching that, originally, the tree tasted like the fruit it produced. The tzaddik explains that the tree represents the steps along the path toward the ultimate goal which shines with the light of fulfillment — the sweetness of the fruit. In a rectified world, the tree tastes like the fruit itself. This means that we are able to take as much pleasure in the steps toward the goal than in the attainment of the goal itself. Every mitzvah along the path toward personal fulfillment, no matter how slight, is sweet and delicious. As the first deviation from the will of Hashem, the distinction in taste between tree and fruit can be seen as a precursor to the sin of Adam and Chava. Indeed, their punishment mirrors this model as well — while the birth of a child is an incredibly joyous occasion, Chava must suffer the pains of pregnancy. Although reaping one's crop is accompanied by deep satisfaction and pleasure, Adam must take great pains to battle the weeds and ensure the crop grows properly. These effects similarly represent the bitterness of a process despite the great joy of the goal, the anguish of the journey despite the awesome preciousness of the destination. When one reaches this elevated plateau of retrospective clarity, the mountain of gold, he is able to recognize that the "Garments of Skin" with which he is enclothed are truly "Garments of Light" — the challenges and failures along the way served not to conceal his success but to reveal it, to help him reach the loftiest heights. (See *Bereishis Rabbah* 20:12.) The *Zohar HaKadosh* teaches that the concept of the esrog is bound with the final *hei* of the *Shem Havayah*, which is related to the *Sefirah* of *Malchus*. How fascinating it is, then, that the esrog tree is the only species of plant in which the tree tastes like the fruit! *Malchus* is bound to the concept of the golden mountain and the esrog; she represents the awareness that the journey toward the goal is just as important as the actual goal itself, "*Sof ma'aseh b'machshavah techilah*."

mind rests over the inhabitants of this place who are able to serve Hashem with confidence and eternal joy, conscious of the awesome import of even the simplest expressions of their love and commitment toward Hashem and His Torah.

✳ The Vessel of *Bitachon*

WHEN THE MASTER of the winds hears that everything is very expensive in this place, he gives the viceroy a special vessel from which he will be able to draw as much money as he needs. Although he originally represented the greatest obstacle the viceroy had ever encountered along his journey, this giant who has a connection to *ruach*, the world of spiritual depth, becomes his ultimate aid. While the viceroy's path to *avodas Hashem* is one with which he unfamiliar, the moment the giant recognizes its validity and truth, he is ready to assist the viceroy in any way he can.

Perhaps this is another reason this giant is appointed over the *ruchos*, the winds of the world. Referring to Yehoshua Bin Nun, the Torah states: *Ish asher ruach bo*, "He is a man of spirit."[7] Commenting on this verse, Rashi writes: *Sheyuchal l'haloch k'neged rucho shel kol echad v'echad*, "He knows how to relate to the varied dispositions of each and every individual." With this kind gesture, the giant appointed over the winds, the *"memuneh al ha-ruchos,"* demonstrates that he is truly an *"Ish asher ruach bo"* — ultimately driven not by his own considerations and feelings but rather by his love for the Master of the world and the desire for every Jew to serve Him, each in a manner appropriate to his or her unique character.

What is the nature of this remarkable vessel from which

---

7. *Bamidbar* 27:18.

endless funds may constantly be drawn? The Breslover *mashpi'im* offer the most amazing insight.

In *Likutei Moharan*, Rebbe Nachman teaches that because Hashem is above the constraints of time, the future solution to a person's current problems already exist in the present as well. However, in order to draw the salvation from the future to the present, a vessel is needed. That vessel is *bitachon*, a deep and abiding trust in Hashem's ability to provide the solution to all of our difficulties.[8]

A corollary of trusting that Hashem will provide one with financial stability, health, and all means of goodness is the trust that whatever one presently has is exactly what he needs in this moment. *Bitachon* does not only mean to trust in a better future, it also means to believe in the glory latent in a difficult present. When a Jew puts *bitachon* into practice, he may have only a little bit in quantitative terms, but qualitatively he feels as if he has everything. Chazal teach us: *Eizehu ashir, hasameach b'chelko*, "Who is wealthy, he who is happy with his portion." Trusting that he has just what he needs to serve Hashem, this Jew lives a life of endless wealth and ultimate pleasure.[9]

The trait of *bitachon* was imbedded into the Jewish psyche by our forefather, Yaakov Avinu. When Yaakov offers Eisav his tribute, Eisav demurs, saying, *Yeish li rav*, "I have very much."[10] Two verses later, Yaakov insists that Eisav accept the tribute, saying, *Yeish li kol*, "I have everything."[11] The difference between these two statements, "I have very much," and "I have everything," is greater than the distance between heaven and earth.

In *Sunlight of Redemption*, we explored Eisav's attraction to

---

8. See also *Sparks from Berditchov*, pp. 33–34.

9. See *Mei HaShiloach*, Vol. 1, *Noach*, "*V'atem shirtzu*."

10. *Bereishis* 33:9.

11. *Bereishis* 33:11.

superficiality and abhorrence for a perspective of *emunah* that sees the world as a spiritually meaningful place. Seeing physicality as detached from the spiritual life-force permeating all of creation, Eisav experiences only the tangible, limited element of existence devoid of essence and other-worldly spirit. Therefore, Eisav proclaims *"Yeish li rav"* — I have many animals, property, and slaves, but I am constantly in pursuit of the physical satisfaction that seems ever to elude me.

Yaakov's statement is a different world entirely. Founded upon the deepest application of *bitachon*, a true embodiment of *"sameiach b'chelko,"* Yaakov Avinu answers, *"Yeish li kol"* — I may have far less animals, property, and slaves than you do, but I have *everything*. I am utterly satisfied with my life and feel no need to seek anything I do not have. I trust that whatever Hashem has given me in accordance with my *hishtadlus* is exactly what I need in order to live a life of true contentment, gratitude, and joy, and I feel no lack in my life at all.[12]

---

12. See *Sifsei Tzaddikim, Bechukosai, "V'im mach,"* and *Degel Machaneh Ephraim, Eikev, "Eretz Asher."* While Eisav's worldview is connected to noise and speech, Yaakov's *middah* of *bitachon* and *histapkus* is bound to the concept of silence. The lives of sun people, whose days are filled with the pursuit of material gain, is filled with a vast noise that pulls them away from the "thin, still voice" (see *Melachim I* 19:12) of the *neshamah*. If they feel that something is lacking, they protest angrily, vociferously voicing their indignant frustration. However, a moon person, one who feels most at home in the calm hours of the nighttime, accepts his circumstances joyfully, with silence. Bound to the *Sefirah* of **Chochmah** whose vitality fills the *Sefirah* of *Malchus* — the lost princess (see *Sunlight of Redemption*, p. 122) — he lives a life of a silent inwardness: *"Seyag l'chochmah, shetikah"*(*Avos* 3:3). Thus, we find that when faced with the immense tragedy of the loss of his precious children, Aharon reacts with silence: *"Vayidom Aharon"* (*Vayikra* 10:3). Similarly, when Moshe challenges Hashem regarding Rabbi Akiva's brutal murder, Hashem advises him to stay silent: *"Shtok! Kach alah b'machshavah"* (*Menachos* 29b). On a simple level, these words are translated as, "Be silent, so it arose in the Mind." On a deeper level, however, perhaps it is possible to suggest that Hashem is telling Moshe that by entering into the silence of *bitachon*,

In the words of Rebbe Chaim of Chernovitz:

> The tzaddik is content with all the good he has and lacks nothing. He rejoices with his good, for he has everything, as Dovid HaMelech said, "For those who fear Him do not lack," meaning that those who fear Hashem lack nothing at all, for the good they have is enough for them and they are not compelled to attain more of this-worldly things. This is the true blessing from the Creator, that when He bestows His blessing upon a person, it is wrapped in another blessing — that he be satisfied and joyous with what he has attained and not constantly desire more and more. For if he does desire more, this would mean that his blessing is not complete, for he still lacks and his soul yearns and must worry about amassing more. What kind of blessing is this? This is why, commenting on the verse, "And I will pour down My blessings upon you," our Sages said, "Until your lips wear out from saying, 'enough,'" for this is the true blessing with which a person can be blessed — that the blessing he receives should be enough for him and that he not feel compelled to pursue more... Therefore, Yaakov said, "*Yeish li kol*," meaning, "In my eyes, whatever I have contains everything. I don't feel any lack that compels me to notice more."
>
> However, the goodness of the wicked is the exact opposite. For the more they have, the more they truly lack — "If one has one hundred, he desires two hundred." Therefore,

---

"*kach, alah b'machshavah*" — *this is the way* one is able to enter into a deeper level of existence and live life in tune with the all-encompassing spirituality infusing the physical world. Indeed, it is because the sun represents distracting noise and excessive speech that in order to halt its movement, Yehoshua — who is bound with the concept of the moon (see *Bava Basra* 75a) — utters the words: *Shemesh b'Giv'on dom*, "Let the sun in *Giv'on* be silent" (*Yehoshua* 10:12). In contrast with the energy of Rachel, the "*Alma d'Isgalya*," the energy of Leah/Mashiach Ben David, the "*Alma D'Iskasya*," is bound with the concept of silence and acceptance. (See *Likutei Amarim Tanya*, Chapter 26.)

"the more property, the more worry," for the more he has, the more he worries... This is why Eisav said, *"Yeish li rav,"* and did not say, "I have everything" like Yaakov who lacked nothing. Rather, he said, "I have a lot, but I want far more."[13]

As the children of Avraham and Yitzchak, Eisav and Yishmael may be seen as the dregs of the *Middos* of *Chessed* and *Gevurah*, respectively. Rooted in the extremes, these two figures constantly seek that which is outside of themselves — Yishmael is attracted to adultery, a corruption of *middas haChessed*, and Eisav is attracted to murder, a corruption of *middas haGevurah*. These affinities imply a constant feeling of lack, which compels a human being to breach the boundary of another's life for the sake of his own personal gratification. Always looking to the world outside themselves for joy, contentment, and satisfaction, Eisav and Yishmael can only ever look in a single direction at once and are thus constantly haunted by the anxiety of lack deriving from their inability to grasp all of this-worldliness. Tormented by the mere *"cheilek"* of life with which their souls are wed, unable to attain the "All" of existence, they are hounded by jealousy, desire, and honor, which — as our Sages teach — remove a person from the world, that is, prevent them from living healthy lives.[14] No matter how much they are able to grasp, no matter the abundance referred to in the statement *"yeish li rav,"* they suffer from a constant sense of lack and incompleteness: "A person doesn't die with even half of his desires fulfilled"[15]; "A person who loves money is never satisfied by money"[16]; "The more property, the more worry"[17]; "There is a small limb in man — the more one

---

13. *Be'er Mayim Chaim, Lech Lecha*, 13:6.
14. *Avos* 4:28.
15. *Avos* 1:14.
16. *Koheles* 5:10.
17. *Avos* 2:7.

satisfies it, the hungrier it is."[18] Therefore, Eisav and Yishmael frantically pursue bigger, better, nicer, grander, faster toys, always seeking to be *mosif*, to add to their growing collection of things. However, lacking an essential, spiritual, foundation, the beautiful body of their lives is without a soul, and an unbearable measure of anguish fills the vacuum.

In contrast, Yaakov Avinu, the chariot for the *middah* of *Tiferes*, is rooted not in the extremities of life, but in the center point. This is an expression of his lifestyle — instead of looking outside of himself for fulfillment and satisfaction, Yaakov calmly looks toward the treasure chest he holds deep within his soul.[19] Although physical eyes, opened to the world outside, can only take in a **cheilek**, a

---

18. *Sukkah* 52b.

19. Indeed, Yaakov Avinu is an *"Ish tam, yosheiv ohalim"* (*Bereishis* 25:27) — he sits inside his tent, an aspect of binding himself to the energy of *penimiyus* and inwardness, much like Yehoshua, the aspect of the moon (see *Bava Basra* 75a) about whom the *pasuk* states, "And Yehoshua Bin Nun did not leave from the tent" (*Shemos* 33:11). See *Likutei Moharan* 6 where Rebbe Nachman expounds on this connection and binds the aspect of Yaakov and Yehoshua to the concept of silence in the face of challenges. There are many more wondrous and deep ideas that emerge from this connection, but they are beyond the scope of the current work. In contrast to the seventy nations who derive from the two extremes of Eisav and Yishmael (thirty-five are associated with each side, see *Shaarei Orah*, Fifth Gate), the seventy members of Yaakov Avinu's household from whom the entire Jewish nation derives, are rooted in this center point. Their land, Eretz Yisrael, is the center of the world. (*Midrash Tanchuma, Kedoshim* 10.) When our holy nation veered from the inner point of life and began to turn toward the extremes of external gratification, this manifested in our exile from the center point, Eretz Yisrael, into the lands of the seventy nations which are positioned to the right and the left of the center. Based on this idea, perhaps we may suggest another interpretation of our Sages' teaching that when Klal Yisrael strayed from the proper way, the *keruvim* would turn their backs on each other (*Bava Basra* 99a). Perhaps, in addition to representing our disconnection from Hashem, this turning away mirrors the nation's shift of focus on the center point to the external extremes of Eisav and Yishmael.

broken shard of our transient world, spiritual eyes opened to one's inner universe, looking to the core of being, can perceive the All of life, the *"cheilek Elokah mimaal"* within.[20] Encountering the Godly portion at the center of his being, Yaakov Avinu experiences the completeness reflected in the microcosmic projection he holds in his essence. Instead of feeling pained by his inability to grasp all the physical pleasure this world has to offer, Yaakov is *"sameach b'chelko,"* rejoicing in the awesome spiritual treasure which imbues his physical constriction with ultimate meaning — the spirit of *Olam HaBa*[21] — that satisfies him in the deepest way.[22]

---

20. See *Mei HaShiloach*, Vol. 1, *Lech Lecha*, *"Vayomer,"* where the holy Ishbitzer teaches that in the early days of his spiritual discovery, Avraham Avinu looked around at all the lack, worry, and anxiety involved in the world's materialistic pursuits and wondered, "Is this all there is to life? If every desire fulfilled begets a greater lack, where is the essence of living?" It was in response to this deep query that Hashem commanded Avraham: *"Lech lecha,"* which can be translated as, "Go to yourself." With these two words, Hashem was telling Avraham that the only way to find true contentment is to close our eyes to the world outside and go within, to the core of our being.

21. See *Likutei Halachos, Betzi'as HaPas* 2.

22. Perhaps it is possible to suggest that this very realization enabled Yosef HaTzaddik to overcome the *nisayon* of *Eishes Potiphar*. Chazal teach that at the height of his struggle with the yetzer hara, Yosef saw "his father's likeness" in the window. This gave him the strength to cast off his garment and emerge victorious. The commentators struggle to understand exactly what it means that Yosef saw his father's likeness in the window. Why did Yaakov appear specifically in a window? Why not on the floor or on the ceiling? The Ben Ish Chai offers an astounding explanation. Chazal teach us that Yosef and Yaakov looked exactly alike. Therefore, when Chazal teach that Yosef saw his likeness in the window, they are referring to his catching a glimpse of *his own reflection* in the windowpane. While fascinating, this explanation gives rise to two more questions: Why, then, did Chazal refer to the reflection as "his father's likeness," and how did this enable him to overcome his desires? Based on what we have learned about Yaakov's worldview, it becomes increasingly clear. In contradistinction to Eisav and Yishmael, Yaakov Avinu looks inside himself for joy, contentment, and satisfaction. He realizes that nothing external can ever

In the words of Reb Nosson:

This alone is considered "wealth," for certainly one who has many riches, much property, and many vessels of gold and silver and yet has no satisfaction from his wealth and, on the contrary, finds that all his days are full of anger, anxiety, sickness, and confrontation on account of his many desires — for he is bewildered, frantically seeking to amass more and more riches and is extremely jealous of those who

---

truly satisfy him, that it is only a perpetual encounter with the Master of the world through *emunah* and *bitachon* that can enable him to live a life of true joy and fulfillment. Caught in the *kelipah* of Yishmael, the desire for adultery, Yosef HaTzaddik catches a reflection of his own image. This reminds him that it is futile to look *beyond himself* for happiness, everything he is looking for is already present *within!* This transformative concept is indeed "the likeness of his father," Yaakov Avinu, for this is the message he lived and passed on to the *shevatim*, from whom every member of our holy nation derives. (See a different interpretation of this episode in *Sunlight of Redemption*, pp. 109–110. The discerning reader will realize that, in truth, they are two sides of the same coin.)

The concept of *bitachon* is one that is fundamental to the holiday of Sukkos, which commemorates the huts built by the Jewish nation in the desert after their exodus from Egypt. About this period of time, Hashem speaks through the prophet: "So says Hashem: I remember the *kindness of your youth*, your love as a bride, when you followed Me into the desert, into an unsown land." Sukkos celebrates the princess of *youth*, the *bitachon* of our following Hashem into the desert with complete trust in the face of an uncertain future. Thus, it was about the *simchas beis hashoeivah* on Sukkos that Hillel issued his strange and uncharacteristic proclamation, *Im ani kan, hakol kan*, "If I am here, then everyone is here." Arrogance being the very antithesis of Hillel's nature, it is clear that there is a deeper meaning to this statement than appears on the surface. Perhaps, in this statement, Hillel is pithily summarizing the very essence of the message Sukkos holds: *Im ani kan*: If the inner "I," the essential point of inner contentment is engaged in one's life, then *hakol kan*, one is able to tap into the *"kol"* of Yaakov Avinu's statement: *"Yeish li kol."* Living with *bitachon* in Hashem and the satisfaction with the glory that is to be found within the essential nature of one's personality enables the Jew to tap into the great "all" of existence: a feeling of utter and perfect contentment.

are wealthier than him, aside from all of the innumerable other stresses and pains he experiences every day and even every hour — this is certainly not considered "wealth" at all. Certainly, the primary wealth and sustenance is when Hashem's blessing settles in one's endeavors, an aspect of the verse, "The blessing of Hashem will bring riches, and there will be no depression added to it."[23] This is a person who merits to be *sameach b'chelko*, resolute in his *bitachon* that Hashem provides whatever is necessary for his sustenance in the proper time...[24]

The simplicity and faith expressed in Yaakov Avinu's small, but powerful statement of *"yeish li kol"* is a frequently raised topic in Rebbe Nachman's writings and a particularly major theme in his stories. In the ninth story in *Sippurei Maasios*, the tale of the *Chacham v'Tam*, The Sophisticate and the Simpleton, Rebbe Nachman describes the difference in the quality of the experiences of these contrasting characters.

About the **Chacham**, a brilliant and accomplished man of endless ambition and exaggerated self-worth, the tzaddik writes:

Afterward he (the sophisticate) concluded, "Even though I have this trade in hand, nonetheless I do not have enough with this. Today, this is an important [profession], but maybe at another time some other thing will be considered important." So he went ahead and placed himself with a gem cutter. On account of his cleverness he acquired this

---

23. *Mishlei* 10:22.

24. *Likutei Halachos, Netillas Yadim L'Seudah* 6:85. Reb Shlomo Carlebach relates that although R' Shayale of Kerestir was extremely poor, his rebbe, the Tsanzer Rav, would refer to him as, "My Rothschild," a reference to Baron Edmund de Rothschild, a banker world renowned for his enormous wealth. When asked what he meant by this unlikely comparison, the Tsanzer Rav would reply, "Baron Rothschild has whatever he needs, and my Shayele also has whatever he needs."

skill in a short time as well — in a quarter year. Then he decided, "Even though I have two trades in hand, who knows, perhaps neither of these will remain important. It would be better for me to learn a craft that will always be important." Probing with his insight and philosophy, he determined to learn medicine, which is always needed and always esteemed. Now, the way of learning medicine is to first learn Latin, the language and its writing, as well as the wisdoms of sophistry. This too, on account of his brilliant mind, he mastered in a short time — a quarter year — and he became a big doctor, a philosopher, and expert in all fields of wisdom. After all this, the world began to seem, in his eyes, as nothing. For due to his genius, and since he was such a great craftsman and so wise and such a doctor, every person in the world was like nothing to him. He calmed himself down and decided to find purpose [in his life] and take a wife. He thought to himself: "If I marry here, who will know what has become of me? Let me rather go back home, so that people will see what has become of me. I left as a young boy and now I have come to such greatness." And he picked up and traveled home, experiencing great afflictions on the way. For on account of his sophistication he didn't have anything in common with people about which to converse. [He was so worldly and refined that] he found no lodging up to his standards and so, he felt constantly afflicted.

After describing the various stresses and difficulties experienced by the *Chacham*, a figure who says *"Yeish li rav,"* yet constantly experiences the anxiety of lack, Rebbe Nachman portrays the life of the *Tam*, one who lives with simplicity and *bitachon*, the melody of *"Yeish li kol"* ever on his lips.

[The simple man's] customary behavior was to be always very joyful. He was constantly full of happiness. And he had all the foods, all the drinks, and all the clothing. He would say to his wife, "My wife, give me to eat;" and she would give him a piece of bread and he would eat. Then he would say, "Give me the sauce with buckwheat groats," and she would cut off another slice of bread for him and he would eat. And he would praise it and say, "How very good and nice is this sauce!" Similarly, he would order himself served meat and other delicacies, and for each dish, she would give him a slice of bread from which he would have great pleasure and give great praise. "How well prepared this is!" as if he had actually eaten that very dish. For he would really and truly feel, in the bread that he ate, the taste of all the foods he wanted on account of his great simplicity and his immense joy. Similarly, he would say, "My wife, give me a drink of beer." She would give him water and he would praise, "How nice is this beer!" [Then he would summon,] "Give me mead." She gave him water and he would praise it the same way. "Give me wine" or other drink; she gave him more water and he would delight in and praise the drink as if he really drank [wine, etc.] So too with clothing. He and his wife shared one *peltz* [an unfinished piece of fur used as a coat]. He would say, "My wife, give me the *peltz*," when he needed to go to the market. She would give him the *peltz*. When he needed a *tulep* [a fancy overcoat with fine fur on the inside which rolls over onto the collar] to go out socially, he would say, "My wife, give me the *tulep*," and she would give him the *peltz*. He would take great delight in it and praise, "What a beautiful *tulep* this is!" When he needed a *kaftan* [a long suit coat] for instance, to go to shul, he would summon and say, "My wife, give me the *kaftan*," and she would give him the *peltz*. He would praise and say, "How nice and beautiful is this *kaftan*!" And so too when he needed to don a *yupa* [a long silk robe worn for formal occasions] she would also give him the *peltz*, and he would also give praise and delight: "How beautiful and nice is this *yupa*!" And the like. Thus, he was full only of joy and delight constantly.

The ability to have only bread, water, and an unseemly *peltz* coat and yet live like a king who lacks nothing in the world is the unique lot of a person who lives with true *bitachon*. When a person lives with simple faith to the point that he can genuinely say, *"yeish li kol,"* this is the best life there is. No matter how miserable his lot, he is able to remain joyous, excited, and grateful for what he has.[25]

The third giant gives the viceroy a vessel (*kli*) that contains an endless supply of money. *"Whenever you reach inside, you will*

---

25. For a possible source to the contrary outlooks of the *Chacham* and the *Tam*, see *Berachos* 58a: Ben Zoma would say: A good guest, what does he say? "[See] how much effort the host expended on my behalf, how much meat the host brought before me. [Look at] how much wine he brought before me and how many loaves he brought before me. All the effort that he expended, he expended only for me!" However, a bad guest, what does he say? "What effort did the host expend? I ate only one piece of bread, I ate only one piece of meat, and I drank only one cup of wine..."

Although it is easy to confuse the two, the bliss associated with the *Tam's* *"temimius"* is the absolute contrast of the bliss associated with an ignorant disconnection from reality. Rebbe Nachman teaches, *Gam b'temimius, assur lihyos shoteh*, "While simplicity is important, it is forbidden to be an imbecile" (*Sichos HaRan* 51). *Temimus* doesn't mean that one should live life like an ignorant fool, with a subperspective which may indeed produce a fraudulent and dangerous bliss. Rather, *"Gam b'temimus"*; Rebbe Nachman intends for our engagement with *temimus* to be *additive* in nature, to lift us *above* the apparent reality of that which we are truly aware, not to drag us below it. Therefore, *"Assur lihyos shoteh,"* it is forbidden to be a fool in the name of "simplicity."

The bliss that is a result of Rebbe Nachman's simplicity may be seen as synonymous with the requirement of drinking *"Ad d'lo yada"* on Purim (see footnote 6 on page 279); an elevated perspective which transcends (yet does not negate) wisdom: not *sheker* and not *emes*, but *"emes l'amito."* In a different place, Rebbe Nachman writes: *Hachochmah hagedolah sheb'chol hachochmos: l'vli lihyos chacham klal!*, "The greatest wisdom of all wisdoms is not to be wise at all!" (*Likutei Moharan Tinyana* 44). This is true *temimus*. *"Hachochmah hagedolah"* — This is true *ad d'lo yada*: **Tachlis hayedi'ah asher lo neida**, "The pinnacle of knowledge is to know that one does not know." The *Tam* is not an idiot. He is not a fool who lives in a way that is out of touch with reality and reaps bliss that is the sorry reward of his miserable ignorance. In truth, *the Tam is the greatest chacham of all*, for he is engaged in a simplicity that is not sub-rational but super-rational, an elevated perspective on life that fills his days with joy and the deepest contentment.

take money from there." The Breslover *mashpi'im* teach that this vessel is the vessel of *bitachon*. Indeed, the opening letters of the words "*Yeish li kol,*" spell **kli**. Like a money pouch that never runs out, *bitachon* is an endless source of meaning, joy, and pleasure.[26] Whenever we stick our hand into the vessel of *bitachon*, we feel as if "*yeish li kol,*" we lack nothing at all.[27] Immediately, one feels the fulfillment of the verse *yitein lecha kil'vavecha* — "May He grant you your heart's desire,"[28] the opening letters of which also spell "*kli*" — the vessel of *bitachon*. This is the giant's gift to the viceroy. As a fearsome obstacle transformed into the greatest assistance, the third giant fortifies the viceroy's *bitachon*, his faith that everything is in the hands of Hashem.

⊛ Atop the Golden Mountain

REBBE NACHMAN RELATES that the giant commanded the wind to carry the viceroy to the mountain of gold. Here, the wind is referred to as a *ruach se'arah*, a mighty storm wind. In the deeper works, this term always refers to the forces of evil and impurity.[29] This is another manifestation of the manner in which evil assists the searching Jew who remains stubborn in the face of the obstacles along the journey and refuses to give up.

---

26. The viceroy experiences this level of *bitachon* atop the golden mountain. Interestingly enough, in his commentary on the Torah, Rebbe Ephraim of Sudylkov draws a connection between a life of *bitachon* and the concept of gold. (See *Degel Machaneh Ephraim, Devarim, "O"y bein Paran."*)

27. The *mekubalim* (see, for example, *Shaarei Orah*, Second Gate) explain that the word *kol* is deeply associated with the *Sefirah* of *Yesod*. This is another indicator that the viceroy has done *teshuvah* in the deepest sense of the word, rediscovering and returning to his deepest essence.

28. *Tehillim* 20:6.

29. See, for example, *Likutei Moharan* 8.

The indifferent soldiers at the gates of the beautiful and orderly palace of evil where the princess was originally held did nothing to stop the viceroy from entering, representing the mere illusion of an obstacle. Here, however, the guards do indeed move to prevent him from entering the city. This is in accordance with what we learned in Chapter Six — it is only the realm of impurity which is easily accessible. As the headquarters of true holiness, the golden mountain is far more difficult to access.

After using his *bitachon* to overcome the obstacle represented by the guards, the viceroy heads to a *gvir*, a wealthy man, to buy some food and rent a place to stay where he would be able to contemplate how to finally free the Lost Princess of youthful passion. The Breslover *mashpi'im* teach that this wealthy person hints to Yaakov Avinu, about whom the verse states, *Hevei gvir l'achecha*, "May you be a wealthy man, over your brothers."[30] In discussing Yaakov's declaration *"Yeish li kol,"* we learned that even though Yaakov may have had less than his brother in a quantitative sense, his attitude of *sameach b'chelko* rendered him the true *ashir*. Rebbe Nachman teaches that in order to fortify his *bitachon*, the viceroy goes to a *gvir* — he strengthens himself by holding on to the *middah* of Yaakov Avinu, who became a *"gvir l'echav"* through his utter satisfaction with whatever Hashem had given him.

Rebbe Nachman relates that the viceroy buys food from the wealthy man and rents a place to rest so that he may think about how to proceed. Earlier in the story, the viceroy had first abandoned his horse and then his servant. These elements respectively represent his physical concerns and the powers of intellect. Here, Rebbe Nachman teaches that these two elements rejoin him at this stage (food and rest, thought and contemplation.) Having spent many years penetrating into his essence in the deepest way, the viceroy is ready to emerge from this place of intense

---

30. *Bereishis* 27:29.

introspection and complete his mission as an *adam hashaleim*, a complete person with all aspects of his humanity sanctified in a life of perpetual embrace with the Master of the world.

✳ The Journey Is Still in Progress

THE VICEROY HAS arrived, at long last, in this elusive place of retrospective clarity. From this vantage point he is able to look back over the turbulent decades' journey and see how every single step — both the progress and the failures, was necessary to bring him to this point. The city is heartbreakingly beautiful, a taste of *Gan Eden* in this world.

Reb Nosson concludes his recording of this glorious tale in a peculiar way — by not concluding. *"The manner in which he freed her was not told. But in the end, he freed her."* In one manner of interpretation, the tale of the Lost Princess is a microcosm of history in its entirety — from the creation of the world until the coming of Mashiach. Since freeing the princess symbolizes Mashiach's arrival and the rectification of the world, Rebbe Nachman did not disclose the details of how she is freed.[31]

On a more personal level, and in line with the path we have taken in this book, it is possible to say that the ending has not yet taken place — our journey toward the Lost Princess is still very much in progress. Although the Rebbe promises that if we learn from the viceroy and emulate the princess by way of holy desire, stubbornness, and absolute commitment to the goal of a passionate relationship with our Father in heaven, we will undoubtably free her in the end, it is impossible to tell exactly how and in what manner this occurs. The ending is for each of us to tell, in the

---

31. See Reb Nosson's second interpretation to *Sippurei Maasios* and *Alim L'Terufah* 2.

ever-unfolding story of our brief foray on this remarkable planet. May Hashem bless us to utilize the awesome wisdom packed into this remarkable story to search for and simultaneously discover the Lost Princess of our lives. *Bon voyage!*

LESSONS FOR LIFE

⊛ When a Jew's life is saturated with the spirit of the princess, every element of his experience is of absolute importance. His world is illuminated with the light of ultimate significance and true value.

⊛ In the consciousness of the six sons, only impressive acts of holiness are reason for satisfaction and joy. To a Jew in touch with the spirit of the princess, everything is valuable — even the tiniest holy act, word, thought, or expression of desire is a fountain of the deepest and truest joy that touches the core of his being.

⊛ The trait of *bitachon* is like a money pouch from which one may draw endless funds. A person who has true *bitachon* founded on simple faith may have little in terms of quantity, but the quality of the way he experiences what he has is absolutely unimaginable.

AFTERWORD

"*WHILE ON A journey, I told a story. Whoever heard it had a thought of teshuvah.*" With these words this book began, and to these words we return having reached the end of the tale — only to discover that the journey yet continues. But although the viceroy's mission is still underway and plans for our own spiritual excursion perhaps still in the making, we have indeed heard the story, and who among us can claim not to have been stirred? A flowing fountain of the deepest encouragement and the starkest portrayal of the love affair with Hashem that our *avodas Hashem* can truly be, it is impossible not to be moved by the tale of *The Lost Princess*. Encompassing all spiritual levels and stressing the necessity for one to discover his or her unique entranceway to closeness with the Master of the world, this story grants the broken Jewish heart permission to return to the essence of its individual holiness.

Throughout our interpretation of this story, we focused on the individual and the necessity for one to foster a sense of wonder, passion, simplicity, sweetness, and yearning in his or her personal life and engagement with Torah and mitzvos. While this journey is indeed best suited to the individual, it is my passionate conviction that the general goal is one which, if adopted on a communal and institutional level as well, could solve some of the major issues plaguing Orthodoxy in the modern age.

It is no secret that we are living in extraordinary times. Over the last decade, largely thanks to unprecedented technological advancements, we have witnessed enormous change in the way we behave, interact, and process information. On a communal level, a certain degree of openness and self-examination has caused boundaries to shift, old stigmas to lift, and new norms to rise to the fore. These developments have had an exceedingly positive impact on our communal establishments and educational institutions. Just a few decades after the near decimation of our holy nation in the Holocaust, the Torah world is flourishing in a manner that can only be described as miraculous. Our *yeshivos* and *kollelim* are literally bursting at the seams. Shuls are filled with *mispallelim* at all hours of the day and night. More Torah is being taught and learned today than perhaps at any other time throughout our glorious history. Boasting phenomenal *chessed* organizations, *gemachim* for everything under the sun, business expos, Yom Tov getaways, Shabbos lamps, high quality magazines, entertainment for all ages, kosher cruises, music of every genre to fit all tastes, and every delicacy imaginable certified with the best *hechsheirim*, it is easier and more enjoyable to live life as a *frum* Jew today than ever before. We truly are a remarkable generation.

However, along with the blessing of spiritual and physical plenty, we are also witness to the unique challenges of our times. In direct proportion with the opulent standards we have established for how a wedding, Yom Tov, wardrobe, or home is expected to appear, a general feeling of dissonance with the soul of our holy tradition has come to be felt throughout the spectrum of religious life. In addition to the financial woes our newfound cultural norms have brought upon many who feel compelled to conform despite their utter inability to do so, a deeper, more spiritual angst hovers over our lives — we are desperate for meaning, thirsty for the essence of our religion that seems to have been swallowed up by the society we have built. We have lost touch with the yearning so central to the soul of our holy nation, the longing for redemption; the feeling that we are on a long and arduous journey and that, contrary to what our deep comfort and external stability may suggest, we are yet distant from our ultimate destination.

In this book, we have discussed each Jew's individual search for the mountain of gold and its centrality to an experience of truly joyous, connected, and passionate living. Perhaps it is time for our community as a whole to embark on a search for the princess of emotion, passion, excitement, wonder, and simplicity that seems to have been lost on the astounding journey from our infancy on the shores of the *goldene medinah* to the sophisticated and grand structures of our collective maturity. Perhaps it is time for us to arise from the dust of our spiritual obscurity and commit to reengaging with the inner spirit of Yiddishkeit, to bring Hashem and the blessing of God-consciousness back into our shuls, homes, and *yeshivos*, and to center our Torah study and halachah observance around our desperate yearning for a relationship with our Father in heaven. Perhaps it is time that we place more of an emphasis on the deliciousness of *tefillah* than the carving station at the Kiddush, the beauty of the chuppah than the magnificence of the orchestra, and the wonder of the Haggadah than the grandeur of the resort. Perhaps it is time for our schools to incorporate intensive studies of *emunah* and the inner light of our holy Torah so as to grant our children a deep and expansive understanding of Hashem that can illuminate all areas of Yiddishkeit with the brilliant light of meaning. Perhaps this is the generation that will establish institutions whose halls are filled with the spirit of the princess of Yiddishkeit, where special focus will be placed on *emunah, tefillah,* simplicity, wonder, inwardness, *yiras Shamayim,* sweetness, *bitachon,* personal prayer, *kavanah,* holy desire, silence, and the inner light and awesome depth of our holy Torah. There certainly is a demand!

All structures are in place, the earth has been painstakingly gathered and formed into the glorious image of a shining nation of princes and priests. It is time for us to allow the life-giving spirit of Hashem's closeness and presence enter our nostrils and activate our true potential for health, joy, fulfillment, confidence, clarity, and true greatness, enabling us to finally serve as a light unto the majority of our brethren who are yet disconnected from Torah and mitzvos, and beyond — to the entire world. I firmly believe that this revolutionary transformation, which is already well underway, will reinvigorate our communities with a renewed sense of focus and pave the path for Mashiach Ben David along with the spirit of *teshuvah* that will imbue our dark and dismal earth with the shining glory of heaven.

I would like to close with words Rav Kook wrote more than 100 years ago, in 1913. They are more relevant now than ever before.

> We must not ignore the basic medicine that is capable of healing everything; it is only because we have abandoned it that our downfall has come about. It is the thing my poor and bitter soul has become accustomed to speak about and repeat hundreds and thousands of times: *"We have abandoned the soul of the Torah."* This is the great cry that contains in it the power of generations upon generations, from the days of the prophets to the ancient sages, from the greatest *Rishonim* to the wisest *Achronim*.
>
> For too long, the most talented among our people have focused almost exclusively on the practical aspects of the Torah, and even then, only on specific sections of it. Yet the emotional, philosophical, and all higher spiritual wisdom — where the secrets of redemption and salvation are hidden — we have totally abandoned. In fact, if a person came and complained about this great deficiency to the leaders of the Jewish people, he would be considered arrogant and absurd. The great voices of the philosophers of God, of the most exalted Chassidim, of the purest Kabbalists, who came with the secrets of God, the holy visions of courage, who waited and anticipated redemption, are like a lonely voice calling out in a desert wasteland. For too long, we have delayed dealing with this issue. Consequently, atheism has slowly risen before us in its thick, disgraceful, dark filth. It snatches up thousands of souls from our people each year. Yet, despite

this, in our own camp of Torah and faith, we find only darkness, not clearly defined goals... It is specifically at such moments of crisis and danger that we need to take the greatest
of all medicines. Yes, we must be radical in our approach.
Any form of compromise will not solve the issue. Faith has
been lost, and it is continuing to fade away because we have
abandoned the Torah and there is no one to interpret it and
search out its secrets.

At the present moment, Orthodox Judaism is fighting a
defensive and foolish war that attempts to argue that the
outside world is destroying itself and that all of its values
and beliefs will simply be destroyed along with it. But the
fact that secular Jews are more likely to fall apart than us is
not an actual consolation or comfort. Truly, the suffering of
the masses is not even half a consolation, but rather a double
agony. Pointing fingers at the sickness of our people will not
bring strength and life, since this attitude is pessimistic by
nature. Why do we need to walk such a winding path when
we could instead walk the open and straight road that stands
before us?

What we must do is reestablish the spiritual understanding of the entire Torah. Indeed, any person whose heart is
filled with courage, whose pen is filled with strength and
whose soul is filled with the spirit of God is being called to
march out onto the streets and cry out loud, "Let there be
light!"[1]

Friends, the decision is ours to make. The Lost Princess of our
communal spirituality is weeping, held captive in the palace of
the no-good one. Will we have the courage to finally seek her out,
for our sake and for the sake of our children?

---

1. *Igros HaRAYaH*, Vol. 2, p.123 (*The Spiritual Revolution of Rav Kook*, pp.
34–36).

APPENDICES

APPENDIX A

A Closer Look

IN THE PREFACE to this book, we learned that although it is permissible and indeed praiseworthy to discover guidance, advice, and encouragement from within Rebbe Nachman's thirteen tales,[1] this is not their primary purpose. Rather, the tzaddik revealed these stories with the intention of delivering the deepest and most unfathomable secrets of the Torah directly to our souls, something which, without the medium of these tales, would be utterly impossible. The true meaning of these stories transcends human comprehension. We have absolutely no knowledge of their inner meaning and can only begin to scratch the surface of Rebbe Nachman's true intention.[2]

Reb Nosson relates:

> Regarding the tales that he told, Rebbe Nachman said that that it would be better not to reveal any hint as to what the stories reference, because when the matter remains hidden,

---

1. See *Alim L'Terufah* 2.
2. In his first introduction to *Sippurei Maasios*, Reb Nosson writes, "One whose heart is complete, and who is an expert in all of the holy books — particularly the *Zohar HaKadosh* and the writings of the Arizal — is able to understand and to know a few small hints in a few of the stories if he focuses his heart and mind on them well." This should allow us insight into just how deep and exalted these stories truly are.

> it is better able to accomplish within the listener what it
> must. However, it is necessary, at times, to reveal some slight
> hint, so that one should be aware that they contain hidden
> things.[3]

It is for the purpose of making the reader aware of the awe-some secrets concealed within the story of the lost princess that the Breslover *mashpi'im* revealed a few hints, here and there, in order to demonstrate how one may find allusions to the characters and events of the tale in our holy Torah. In this appendix, a portion of those ideas are brought in a concise manner. I am confident that based on these introductory doorways of thought, the reader will be able to discover further references and interpretations of this awesome tale.

1. "On the way (derech) I told a story.... A thought of teshuvah."

In *Likutei Moharan* 6, Rebbe Nachman explains the deeper meaning of the Arizal's mystical intentions for the month of Elul which are based upon the verse, *Hanosein bayam derech*, "He Who placed a way in the sea."[4] Rebbe Nachman writes that the Hebrew word דרך is numerically equivalent to two times the word בקי, expert. This is because if one is to walk the path of *teshuvah*, he must attain two distinct expertise. The first expertise is necessary for a time of spiritual elevation. At such a time, one must be an expert in never becoming satisfied with his current level of growth and forever seeking greater spiritual vistas. This ability is referred to as *Baki b'Ratzo*, "Expert in Running." The second expertise is necessary for a time of spiritual descent. Here, one must be an expert in strengthening himself so that he does not fall into despair, continuing to serve Hashem in accordance with his current spiritual state. This ability is referred to as *Baki b'Shov*,

---

3. *Sichos HaRan* 151.
4. *Yeshayahu* 43:16.

"Expert in Returning." When a person has attained both kinds of expertise, he constantly walks the paths of *teshuvah*, seeing each circumstance as an opportunity for growth and closeness with Hashem. *The Story of The Lost Princess* is centered around these two paths of *teshuvah*, with a particular focus on *"Baki B'Shov"* — filled with advice for how one may encourage himself in a time of struggle and failure. This is a deeper explanation of the *"path"* to which Rebbe Nachman refers and the thoughts of *"teshuvah"* this story will certainly awaken within the listener.

2. "He grew angry... threw the following words from his mouth."

This strange term, *"Nizrikah m'piv dibbur,"* is closely related to the wording used by Chazal in their teaching that one should not recite a *berachah* in a hurried manner, *V'lo yizrok berachah m'piv*, "And he should not throw the *berachah* from his mouth."[5] Perhaps we can suggest that the tzaddik used these specific words to further illustrate what the princess did wrong. As we learned, the reason for the king's frustration was that the princess began to lose appreciation for the great privilege of her closeness with him. Similarly, one of the reasons that one might say a hurried *berachah* is because he lacks appreciation for its greatness and thus fails to accord it the proper respect. In response, the king "throws" the words of his decree out of his mouth, mirroring her flippant approach toward the great gifts he has given her.

3. "May the no-good one take you."

A] As we discover in a later chapter, the six sons are embodied in the physical sun while the princess, the *Sefirah* of *Malchus*, is related to the concept of the moon. In an episode that mirrors this portion of our tale, the moon is cast away from Hashem, Who

---

5. *Berachos* 46a.

says, "Go and make yourself small."[6] An in-depth study of this teaching from Chazal will certainly open new doors of understanding into this difficult portion of our tale.

B] At the end of the tale we reach the deep awareness that this story is truly about the viceroy and his journey toward personal fulfillment. The term *"Lo tov"* appears toward the beginning of *Bereishis*, directly before the creation of Chava: **Lo tov** *heyos ha'adam levado,* "It is not good for man to be alone."[7] Perhaps it is possible to suggest that on a deeper level, the phrase "May the no-good one (*lo tov*) take you" is actually referring to the viceroy, as he is now bereft of the princess and very much alone. Indeed, commenting on the verse that directs man to seek out a wife, the aspect of *Malchus*, Rashi writes *"Ruach hakodesh omrah kein,"* this is the directive of the holy spirit.[8] Perhaps this may be seen as a reference to the wind (*ruach*) which ultimately validates the viceroy's journey and carries him to the golden mountain — the spirit of Mashiach that was present from the very beginning, hovering over the waters even before the sin as the premise for the entire journey.

4. "And he went to search for her here and there ('anah v'anah')."

The words *Anah v'anah*, which literally mean "here and there," hint to the two mentions of *Anah* in the verse "Where (*anah*) has your Beloved gone, loveliest among women, where (*anah*) has your Beloved turned?"[9] Commenting on this verse, the *Zohar* teaches that Hashem never abandons the Shechinah (a reference to the *Sefirah* of *Malchus*), and when she goes into exile, He is found with her.

---

6. *Chullin* 60a.
7. *Bereishis* 2:18.
8. *Bereishis* 2:24.
9. *Shir HaShirim* 6:1.

5. "Finally, while traveling through the desert, he saw a path to the side, and thought it over. ... 'Let me follow this path. Perhaps it will bring me to an inhabited area.'"

The verse in *Tehillim* states: "They wandered in a desert, in a wasteland, they found no inhabited area...and they screamed out to Hashem in their pain and He rescued them from their troubles. He showed them a direct path to reach an inhabited area."[10] These verses provide further support to the interpretation that sees the "path to the side" as hinting to the *avodah* of *hisbodedus*. Here, it is apparent that the way one can merit to leave the desert and enter an inhabited area is through "screaming out to Hashem." This personal prayer is itself the "direct path" that leads to salvation.

6. "With the soldiers."

The Hebrew word for soldier is *chayal*. Perhaps this line may also be seen as a reference to the verse that expresses the unfortunate mentality of this wicked Kingdom: "My own power and the might of my hands has attained this wealth (*chayil*) for me."[11] Rebbe Nachman tells us that the palace looks very beautiful "*im hachayalos*" — surrounded by wealth and saturated with an abundance of arrogance, the pinnacle of "*sheker hachein.*" This "*chayal*" is contrasted by the "*Eishes Chayil,*" a reference to the feminine energy of holy princess who is trapped inside.

7. "Many soldiers and musicians."

This place represents *Malchus D'Sitra Achra*, the impure parallel of the princess's holy energy. Because, as we have learned, the *Sefirah* of *Malchus* is connected to David HaMelech who was both a warrior and a musician, this wicked palace is filled with both soldiers and musicians.

---

10. *Tehillim* 107:4–7.

11. *Devarim* 8:17.

8. "Choose for yourself a place."

As we have learned, prayer is one of the primary expressions of the *Sefirah* of *Malchus*. Thus, it is possible to suggest that the idea that "establishing a place" is part of the process of freeing the lost princess is connected to Chazal's declaration: "Whoever *establishes a place* for his *tefillah*, his enemies fall before him."[12] Additionally, the entire story of *The Lost Princess* can be seen as being encapsulated in the concept of *"semichas geulah l'tefillah"* — granting redemption to our prayers (*Malchus*).[13] Perhaps this is the reason Rav Brona couldn't stop smiling after being *someich geulah l'tefillah*[14] — having redeemed the Lost Princess of youthful vibrancy, he was filled with the greatest joy. Parenthetically, we discussed how the viceroy's first failing was caused by straying after his eyes. When the Torah refers to a sin that is *"Ra b'Einei Hashem,"* affecting the Godliness of one's eyes,[15] it is referring to *pegam haBris*, an action that involves the waste of *Yesod's* awesome potential for procreation. However, Chazal teach that there is an action that is *"Tov b'einei Hashem"* — the *tikkun* of *Yesod*: *"Semichas geulah l'tefillah."*[16] The binding of *geulah* to *tefillah* represents the union of *mashpia* and *mekabel* and fixes the aspect of *pegam habris*, the viceroy's error.

9. "On the last day of the year you must not sleep."

The Breslover *mashpi'im* teach that this day refers to Erev Rosh Hashanah, the last day of the year. Chazal teach that the verse, *Dirshu Hashem b'himatzo*, "Seek Hashem when He may be

---

12. *Berachos* 7b.

13. Indeed, the *Shaarei Orah* (Second Gate) teaches that the concept of *"Geulah"* is deeply associated with the *Sefirah* of *Yesod*.

14. See *Berachos* 9b.

15. See *Bereishis* 39:10.

16. *Berachos* 9b.

found"[17] is referring to the day of Rosh Hashanah, the day when the princess may be rescued.[18] Rosh Hashanah is the time when Klal Yisrael accept the sovereignty of Hashem over the world, seeing all of nature as the ultimate *Malchus D'Kedushah*.[19] Wary of this opportunity, the *yetzer hara* does everything in its power to prevent this from happening. Indeed, Rosh Hashanah is also Rosh Chodesh, the day on which the moon is entirely hidden,[20] an aspect of *Malchus* becoming obscured and difficult to access — *"Ba'keseh l'yom chageinu."*[21] Because it is possible to fall asleep and miss the opportunity, Hashem commands us to blow shofar on this day, which the Rambam famously tells us is for the purpose of awakening all those who slumber, obsessed with the vanities of life.[22] Indeed, Chazal suggest that one refrain from sleeping on Rosh Hashanah.[23]

10. "Immediately after eating the apple, he fell into a deep sleep, and he slept for a very long time."

The only reason the viceroy falls asleep is because he doesn't realize that Hashem is still with him, loving him unconditionally even though he has sinned. In *Parshas Vayeitzei*, Yaakov Avinu

---

17. *Yeshayahu* 55:6.

18. *Rosh Hashanah* 18a.

19. Perhaps this idea provides a deeper insight into why Rebbe Nachman, whose sole mission in the world was to help the Jewish nation achieve this elevated consciousness and live lives of *geulah* and expanded consciousness, stressed his personal connection with Rosh Hashanah time and time agan and was adamant that his followers spend this *chag* together with him at his gravesite in Uman, Ukraine.

20. *Rosh Hashanah* 33b–34a.

21. *Tehillim* 81:4.

22. *Yad HaChazakah, Hilchos Teshuvah* 3:4.

23. *Darchei Moshe* to *Orach Chaim* 583.

says, "Indeed, Hashem is in this place (*makom*) and I didn't know." Rashi comments: "For if I had known I wouldn't have slept in such a holy place as this." If the viceroy would truly understand that Hashem is in his *makom*, and that there is a part of him that remains holy regardless of his actions, he would feel no need to fall into spiritual slumber.

11. "And he went and tasted from the river."

The viceroy's first error in eating the apple is a reflection of Adam HaRishon's sin in eating from the Tree of Good and Evil. The viceroy's second error in drinking from the wine is a reflection of Noach's sin of drinking wine and falling asleep.[24] Just like the tree from which Adam ate was a mixture of Good and Evil, so does wine embody these two powers: "If one merits, he becomes the leader, if one does not merit, he becomes poor."[25] Both the apple and wine are thus a reflection of *Malchus*, which also contains these two elements of fullness and emptiness, warrior and musician.

12. "He immediately fell asleep and slept for many years, a period of seventy years."

A] The Hebrew word for wine, יין, is numerically equivalent to 70.

B] The seventy years that the viceroy sleeps after drinking from the wine, an aspect of Noach's sin, reflect the seventy nations who derive from Noach.[26]

C] The seventy years for which the viceroy sleeps is deeply connected to the story of Purim. Chazal teach that the reason Achashveirosh threw his great party is because he thought the

---

24. *Bereshis* 9:20–21, see Rashi.
25. *Yoma* 76b.
26. See *Bereishis*, Chapter 10.

seventy years of the Jewish nation's exile had passed and they had still not been redeemed.[27] (Choni Ham'agel's seventy-year sleep was also related to the seventy years of exile.[28]) At the party, the Jewish nation partook of the food and drink (symbolized in the apple and wine — see *Torah Temimah* to *Bereishis* 3:6 where a parallel is drawn between the feast of Achashveirosh and Adam's eating from the Eitz HaDaas) which caused a harsh decree to come upon them. Esther's being taken to the palace of Achashveirosh represents the lost princess being held captive in the place of no-good. Mordechai HaTzaddik is referred to as *"Mishneh l'melech Achashveirosh,"* an aspect of the viceroy.

D] David HaMelech was always searching for the place of the Beis HaMikdash (*Har HaBayis*, the mountain of gold.) Recognizing the danger of falling asleep along the journey, he declared, "I will not give sleep to my eyes or slumber to my eyelids until I find a place for Hashem."[29] Indeed, the Gemara teaches that David HaMelech never slept more than sixty breaths at a time.[30] David passed this secret on to his son, Shlomo HaMelech, who taught, "Allow no sleep to your eyes, no slumber to your eyelids."[31] But alas, before building the Beis HaMikdash, Shlomo HaMelech married Bas Pharaoh, the parallel of the lost princess in the side of impurity. Chazal teach that this union caused the Beis HaMikdash to be destroyed, and that after marrying Bas Pharaoh, Shlomo HaMelech would sleep until the fourth hour of the day, far later than usual.[32]

---

27. *Megillah* 11a.
28. See *Taanis* 23a.
29. *Tehillim* 132:4–5.
30. *Sukkah* 26b.
31. *Mishlei* 6:4.
32. *Vayikra Rabbah* 12:5.

13. "She then took the scarf from her head and wrote on it with her tears. She placed it next to him."

As we have discussed, the foundation for the viceroy's failures was his inability to guard his eyes. Following the desires stirred by his vision led to his two major errors: eating from the apple, and drinking from the river. In response, the princess gives him a headscarf, a garment, which plays a major role in rectifying his mistake. Similarly, after the sin of Adam and Chava which — as we have seen — was founded on the eyes, Hashem granted them garments with which to cover themselves. Additionally, after the sin of *Meraglim*, in which the Spies used their vision to perceive Eretz Yisrael in an exceedingly negative manner, Klal Yisrael received a garment-related mitzvah, tzitzis.

14. "He left his servant behind and went to search for her."

This point in the story reflects the verse: "On the third day, Avraham lifted his eyes and saw the place (*hamakom*) from afar. And Avraham said to his servants: 'You stay here with the donkey.'"[33] This is the viceroy's "third day," his third attempt at beginning his journey toward the lost princess. At this point, the viceroy has "lifted his eyes" and attained an elevated perspective that enables him to perceive his *makom* even from afar — he is flourishing even in the courtyards of *avodas Hashem*. Thus, he is ready to leave his servant behind as he did his horse, and travel alone toward his destiny.

The verse continues, *Va'ani v'hanaar neilchah ad koh*, "And I and the lad will continue until there." In these words, it is possible to further discern two hints to our tale: The tzaddikim explain that the word *"Koh"* is a reference to the *Sefirah* of *Malchus*.[34] On a deeper level, then, the verse teaches us that when a person

---

33. *Bereishis* 22:4–5.
34. *Shaarei Orah*, First Gate.

reaches a point in his journey toward "*koh*," the Lost Princess of passion and holiness, where he leaves his servant and heads off alone, it is then an aspect of "*va'ani v'hanaar*" — the fire of youth has begun to flicker within, cultivated through the process of emulative extraction.

15. "You will need to search for a mountain of gold and a palace of pearls, and there you will find me."

A] Referring to the *Eishes Chayil*, an aspect of the lost princess (see #4 above) the verse states: "Her value far exceeds that of *peninim*."[35] Rashi to *Mishlei* 8:11 translates the word "*peninim*" as "pearls."

B] Chapter 28 in *Iyov* mentions a place where the dust is golden. The entire chapter holds many references to our tale.

C] Reb Nosson writes that Esther's being taken to the palace of Achashveirosh — a parallel to the lost princess's captivity in the place of no-good — could retrospectively be seen as positive. How? When the Jews were freed from the terrible decree, many non-Jews converted, thus freeing the sparks of holiness that would have otherwise remained trapped forever. This parallels the idea of the golden mountain and the palace of pearls, the realization that even one's failures were part of a process to bring honor to Hashem.[36]

16. "The storm wind came and carried him there, bringing him to the gate."

This is an aspect of the verse that states "I carried you on eagle's wings and brought you to Me."[37] The *Zohar HaKadosh* teaches

---

35. *Mishlei* 31:10.
36. See *Likutei Halachos, Birkas HaPeiros* 5:4.
37. *Shemos* 19:4.

that the "eagle" mentioned here is synonymous with *"ruach,"* wind.[38]

17. "There were troops there who did not let him enter the city. He reached his hand into the vessel and took out money. He bribed them and entered the city."

The Breslover *mashpi'im* teach that this is an aspect of Yom Kippur, the day upon which the sins of the Jewish nation are transformed into merits, the message embodied in the mountain of gold. *Binah*, the place of *teshuvah*, is also the place from which harsh judgments derive — they stand at the ready to prevent one who seeks to return with a full heart. The *Zohar HaKadosh* teaches that in order to "bribe" the Satan, we send the goat to *Azazel*.[39] This is hinted to by the viceroy's bribing the guards preventing him from entering the city.

---

38. *Likutei Moharan* 8.
39. *Zohar, Bamidbar* 203a, and *Pinchas* 248a.

Studies in
the Commentary

In this section, we briefly explore running themes which appear throughout the length of the story. This concise study is by no means exhaustive.

A] The Return to Our Innermost Essence

PERHAPS THE PRIMARY theme of the Lost Princess as interpreted in this work is the idea that it is possible to live a life of dissonance with one's essential nature. When this happens, cycles of sin and foreign thoughts set in, causing feelings of anxiety, inhibition, meaninglessness, apathy, despair, wariness, and a feeling of existential angst. Therefore, it is of utmost importance for one to discover his or her core identity, the inner child of innocence, faith, wonder, sensitivity, holiness, and untouchable perfection which always sits at the center point of the Jewish person's inner world. References to this discovery can be found throughout the story and commentary.

This idea appears in the very **first chapter** of the book, where we discuss the common loss of this youthful clarity along the journey from childhood to adulthood. There, we define *teshuvah* as "returning to oneself," beginning to live a life of personal authenticity.

In the **second chapter**, this essence to which we wish to return is revealed as being synonymous with the princess of simplicity, inwardness, sensitivity, wonder, passion, and vibrancy.

The next place we find this concept is in **Chapter Five**. There, we discuss the importance of discovering a unique and personal approach to *avodas Hashem* in the realms of Torah study and prayer. When one's service of Hashem is in congruence with the nature of his particular soul, his experience will be filled with energy and excitement.

This concept shows up again in **Chapter Seven**, in which discovering the viceroy lying in a corner of the palace leads the queen of the evil realm to remember her true identity as the lost princess.

In **Chapter Eight**, we explore the concept of "choosing a place." Here, we stress the necessity of committing oneself to an essential identity and aligning with a manner of living that matches one's nature. This provides a sense of stability and will enable one to withstand any obstacles, staying true to his ideals even in the face of challenge.

Finally, in **Chapter Eleven**, we point out that the viceroy's exclamation of anguish over his failure is worded in a manner that makes it clear to us that although he has erred and expresses disbelief over *where* he is, he never questions *who* he is. Sufficiently bound with the goodness and desire for closeness with Hashem that sits at the pinnacle of his existence (see **Chapter Nine**), he never loses sight of his true identity.

B] The Shallowness of the Six Sons

In contrast to the Jew's essential self, represented by the princess of holy desire, the six sons of shallowness and meaningless pursuits represent a foreign identity, the strangeness of dissonance from one's true nature — the innocent child within. References to this obsession with externality and shallowness abound throughout our tale and commentary as well.

We first meet the six sons in the **second chapter**. There, we characterize this group as a focus on materialism, hedonistic pursuits, arrogance, shallowness, externality, sophistication, and pettiness.

In **Chapter Six**, the viceroy discovers a palace that appears beautiful, orderly, and neat. Filled with delightful food and drink, and magnificent orchestras, this place seems wonderful indeed. However, we soon learn that this is the place of no-good, the headquarters of *Malchus D'Sitra Achra*. The beauty and magnificence of this palace is an illusion — it only appears this way on the surface. In truth, it is completely devoid of any depth, purpose, and meaning. This palace is the second manifestation of the six sons.

In **Chapter Ten**, on the final day of the year, the viceroy is assaulted by a mighty *yetzer hara* that convinces him to look at the fruits of the tree. This *yetzer hara* stems in the approach of the six sons. Although it is indeed permissible for him to look at the fruits, the spirit of the princess demands a level of intuition which would direct him to distance himself so that he won't come to sin.

The six sons appear again in **Chapter Eighteen**, this time in the form of the "sun-people," secular and religious leaders who approach their studies in a dry, intellectual manner and remain far from matters of faith and piety.

Finally, in **Chapter Twenty-one**, we learn about the lifestyle of Eisav and Yishmael in contrast to that of Yaakov Avinu. Instead of looking inward to the *cheilek Eloka mimaal* within where one is able to perceive the All of life and experience true joy, contentment, and abiding satisfaction, Eisav and Yishmael are always looking outside of themselves to find happiness. This results in a consuming obsession with amassing wealth and physical treasures which is ultimately unable to satisfy a deep sense of lack and emptiness. This perspective is yet another manifestation of the six sons.

C] Emulative Extraction

In Chapter Nine, we present an important foundation of our interpretation which states that the method used by the viceroy to free the princess is one of extraction via emulation, or emulative extraction. When the viceroy emulates the core energy of the princess, bringing her spirit into his life, he is actively redeeming her from her captivity. By analyzing the viceroy's actions, this approach allows us to discover new facets of the princess' identity.

The first facet of the princess emulated by the viceroy is embodied in his travels through the deserts of *avodas Hashem* in **Chapter Five**. The concept of the *"Midbar,"* which relates to a certain emptiness, inadequacy, and thus humility, is an aspect of the *Sefirah* of *Malchus* about which the *Zohar HaKadosh* teaches, "She has nothing of her own." Meaning, *Malchus* needs to come on to the other *Sefiros*, acting as the receptive vessel for the manifestation of the various energies of these upper Sefiros. When the viceroy experiences a deep feeling of lack in his initial *avodah*, he is embodying the *middah* of *Malchus* and the deep humility that it connotes.

The next aspect of *Malchus* emulated by the viceroy is the *avodah* of holy desire. In **Chapter Nine**, we learn that the authentic brokenheartedness of a Jew's holy yearning, impossible to measure and apparently useless, is a core element of the princess's identity. Separation from physicality and focus on the spiritual is another element of the princess emulated by the viceroy in this chapter.

In **Chapter Eleven**, we read that despite his devastating failure, the viceroy refuses to abandon his goal, instead retuning to the princess in an incredible display of holy stubbornness. Doing so, he emulates another facet of the princess — her passionate commitment to the goals of her spiritual development.

In **Chapter Fifteen**, we learn that the Shechinah is associated with judging others favorably. The positive, optimistic perspective of *penimiyus haTorah* is an embodiment of the spirit of the princess.

In **Chapter Sixteen**, we discuss those who return to Hashem after having tasted the most profound extremes of impurity, and how they rise to the loftiest levels. This is an aspect of *Malchus* that is referred to as "the stone that was despised by the builders" which "became the cornerstone."[1] Lowest in rank, *Malchus* exceeds all other levels in her import and the holiness that is able to be expressed solely through her unique function. *Malchus* is the concept of אני/Manifestation, which becomes transformed into אין/Nothingness, the most elevated spiritual functionality of *Kesser*. It is the concept of *tefillah* which, while mocked, stands at the absolute apex of the world.[2]

In **Chapter Seventeen**, we read about the relationship between *Malchus* and the moon, exploring its dual nature and cyclical manner of progression. In experiencing both "fullness" and "emptiness" along his journey of both triumph and failure, the viceroy emulates the spirit of the princess whose path of growth is replete with hills and valleys.

D] Perspectives on Failure

The Lost Princess is the portrait of a spiritual journey, a tale of failure and triumph. The board framework of the story and its backdrop of encouragement and ultimate success allows for the discovery of a few powerful insights into spiritual failure. Although we have discussed these concepts at length in our commentary, we present them here in summarized form.

1. **On the Threshold of Greatness**: The first perspective on failure is discussed in **Chapter Five**, in the context of the viceroy's re-entering the desert after already having

---

1. *Tehillim* 118:22.
2. *Berachos* 6b.

attained the elevated level of the forest. There, we described the necessity for a Jew to experience a lull in his or her *avodah* before advancing to the next spiritual level. Here, we aren't talking about a slip into sinful behavior, but rather a *yeridah* that involves the reawakening of old desires, and a general loss of desire for *avodas Hashem*. Rebbe Nachman teaches that this kind of failing indicates our standing on the threshold of great elevation.

2. **Learning from Our Mistakes:** The second perspective on failure is discussed in **Chapter Thirteen** in the context of the viceroy needing to find a new place. There, we explored the manner in which failure can help us reassess our position and take the requisite action to ensure that we will never make such a mistake again. This perspective sees the sin itself as inherently negative, with a redeeming quality in the positive lessons that may be learned from unfortunate transgression.

3. **Honoring Hashem:** The final perspective on failure is discussed in **Chapter Sixteen** in the context of the golden mountain. There, we explained that from the retrospective standpoint of perfect *teshuvah*, one can attain the realization that the sin itself was part of Hashem's Master Plan. Furthermore, it contained a positive quality in allowing him to express the ultimate extent of his commitment to Yiddishkeit by refusing to give in to the post-sin message of hopelessness and despair amplified by the yetzer hara.

Lessons for Life

CHAPTER 1

⊛ In our formative years, our transformation from children into adults is oftentimes accompanied by a loss of the innocence, excitement, wonder, passion, and joy that is so natural to youth.

⊛ The essence of *teshuvah* is the return to our essential self and the closeness with Hashem which sits at the core of our being. The ability to rediscover vibrancy in all areas of life is ever-present. It is never too late! There is no despair in the world at all!

CHAPTER 2

⊛ All of life is made up of two contrasting components; a quantifiable measure of external, shallow accomplishment and a qualitative and inward spirit of depth, purpose, meaning, and vibrancy.

⊛ While it is possible to maintain an *avodas Hashem* that consists of pure action alone, Rebbe Nachman teaches us that Hashem delights in the desire of the heart more than anything else. He relishes the spirit of faith, passion, excitement, and youthful wonder that so animates the halachic experience.

CHAPTER 3

❋ When one of the parties in even the closest of relationships ceases to appreciate the gift of their bond and begins taking the other's love for granted, it is incredibly painful and destructive.

❋ Gratitude preserves the excitement, passion, and desire we once felt toward something even after attaining it. When we stop being grateful for the gifts in our lives, we have lost touch with the deep feelings we have toward those gifts and they cease to inspire wonder and joy in our hearts.

❋ All apparent Heavenly distancing is only for the purpose of bringing us closer. While it may seem as if Hashem is driving us away, in truth He wants us to use this challenge as an opportunity to express how much He means to us by returning to His service.

❋ When we make the mistake of thinking that Hashem's apparent rejection is for real and run away from His fury, this devastating error leaves us susceptible to the evil forces.

CHAPTER 4

❋ Oftentimes, because it is our perception of heavenly wrath that drives us away from *avodas Hashem*, heaven-sent inspiration will not suffice to convince us of our error. Instead, we need to feel an awakening from within.

❋ Every Jewish person contains an inner point of perfect purity, a place which remains ever untouched by past misdeeds regardless of their severity. It is this *Nekudah Tovah* within which gives us no rest and relentlessly compels us to pursue a relationship with Hashem.

❋ Three elements create an emotional foundation conducive to spiritual searching: *intellectual, physical,* and *financial* wellbeing. Even though we have not yet been granted these three blessings, it is proper to set out on our spiritual journey in tandem with sincere prayer.

⊛ It is only possible to discuss the pain of failure when it is enveloped by a spirit of hope and ultimate triumph. When we must rebuke a child or a friend, it is imperative that we lay a foundation of comfort and support before focusing on the misdeed.

CHAPTER 5

⊛ *Avodas Hashem* contains various stages, including spiritual desolation, toil, and a success that presents a challenge of its own; the ability to hide from oneself and others behind the veneer of accomplishment.

⊛ As we proceed from one level of spiritual development to another, we must leave the highest stage of level one and enter the lowest stage of level two. Although this lull may be seen as a *yeridah*, a spiritual descent, it is, in fact, the surest sign of progress.

⊛ It is imperative for each Jewish person to search for his or her unique pathway in *avodas Hashem*. One way to accomplish this is by finding the areas of Torah that speak to our particular soul and allocate time to exploring them. Another is to discover the mitzvah, minhag, or *hanhagah* with which we feel most connected and focus our attention on that particular area of *avodas Hashem*.

⊛ The primary manner in which one can merit to build an intimate relationship with the Master of the world is by engaging in *hisbodedus*, personal prayer in one's own words. Setting aside time each day to speak candidly with the Creator of all solidifies our *emunah* and enables us bring Hashem into every detail of our lives.

CHAPTER 6

⊛ The worst kind of evil is that which appears, on the surface, to be moral, ethical, polite, and socially correct. Don't be fooled! Everything is not always as it appears!

⊛ While it may be possible for one who denies the active presence of Hashem in existence to attain glory and honor that accompany accomplishments he proudly claims to be his very own, the shame he will feel when the mask is removed and the true King is revealed will be commensurately overwhelming.

⊛ Although it takes many long years of effort and toil to attain elevated levels of holiness and purity, the *yetzer hara* is readily accessible to everyone, at all times.

⊛ Even a mundane meal can be considered a holy act if one eats with the proper intention. In a deep way, eating symbolizes the very essence of life, as it fills the desolate body with the great light of the soul.

CHAPTER 7

⊛ When energy and excitement toward matters of holiness gets lost, it reemerges under the disguise of the passion for physical pleasure and worldly pursuits. Although it may seem as if we lose our excitement for holiness due to a separate passion toward sin and negative traits, it is, in fact, the very same passion in disguise.

⊛ It is crucial that we recognize the holy potential of our passion from behind the guise of impurity. It is only when we affirm the essential goodness of these energies and see their redeemability that we can then channel them toward positive use once more. The same applies for others. Recognizing the holy energy hidden within decidedly unholy pursuits can enable our children, students, friends, and the Jewish nation as a whole to rediscover their essential selves and begin the journey toward spiritual redemption.

CHAPTER 8

❉ In order for the spiritual healing process to begin, we must believe, wholeheartedly, that Hashem yearns for our return and is pained over our distance from Him.

❉ A basic prerequisite for freeing the Lost Princess is the discovery of one's "place" in the world, a strong sense of identity and stability founded upon a resolve to change and grow.

❉ There are two elements that enable one to begin finding his place in the world — the awareness of Hashem's unconditional love, and belief in one's ability to succeed and the ever-present ability to make the right choices in life.

❉ It takes a full year for lasting spiritual transformation to take place.

CHAPTER 9

❉ Even if it does not merit actualization in acts of holiness, yearning for elevation and a relationship with the Master of the world is inherently valuable and precious in the eyes of Hashem.

❉ As the loftiest and most essential element of his being, nothing can prevent a Jew from desiring closeness with Hashem. Even when the desire is lacking, one can *desire to desire*, ad infinitum.

❉ When one devotes himself to fulfilling the directives of the Lost Princess — finding stability, yearning for her, removing himself from physicality etc. — he is emulating her nature, and, in the process, actively extracting her from the faithless kingdom.

⊛ The *yetzer hara* detests the completion of a holy endeavor. Just when a project is about to come to fruition, he launches a mighty attack in an effort to prevent it from happening.

CHAPTER 10

⊛ After one has experienced a measure of success in *avodas Hashem*, he may begin to grow proud, self-assured, and overly confident. Letting his guard down, he becomes vulnerable to the *yetzer hara*'s attacks once more.

⊛ When it is time for a Jew to wander onto the streets of the world, it is important for him to remain bound with his core identity and guard his eyes from exploring his surroundings lest he be drawn astray.

⊛ Even while a certain thing may be halachically permissible, Hashem has granted His holy nation the ability to access an inner intuition that dictates the proper standard. This intuition lends an additional level of sensitivity to a decision-making process, ensuring that one will stay aligned with the true spirit of our holy Torah.

CHAPTER 11

⊛ A purely intellectual engagement with Torah and *avodas Hashem* fails to engender the passion, wonder, desire, and qualitative spirit represented by the princess. It can, however, maintain one's general connection with Judaism in the event of a momentary lapse of commitment and the spiritual numbness that ensues.

❋ When a Jew cries out from the core of his being, expressing deep anguish over his spiritual failures and his distance from Hashem, this is the beginning of his salvation.

❋ It is important to remember that even when one falls into the foreign world of negative desires and sinful behavior, his essence remains pure and bound to the realm of holiness. *Where* one is does not define *who* one is.

❋ After a spiritual descent, a Jew must exhibit *Azus D'Kedusha*, holy stubbornness, summoning the courage necessary to stand up from that place and seek out ways to make things right.

CHAPTER 12

❋ The cry of our *neshamah* that echoes through our being after a devastating fall from our devotions, expressing pain over our failure to live up to her expectations, should not be interpreted as a cry of anger, anguish, and despair. Rather, her expression of just how much she is depending on us to redeem her is intended to reveal her staunch faith in our ability to succeed.

❋ *Avodas Hashem* is not all or nothing. Present failure does not erase past progress. Every step in the direction toward closeness with the Master of the world is valuable in and of itself and its positive effect survives any subsequent downfall.

CHAPTER 13

❋ When returning to *avodas Hashem* after a fall, it is important to begin anew from a post-fall perspective, built on the lessons that were learned and the perspective gained. Eventually, one will come to see all of his mistakes as having been steps along the path to success.

❋ Just as wine has the ability to induce physical slumber, if used improperly, it can bring a state of "spiritual sleep" upon the Jew, numbing his sensitivities and causing him to lose his perception of the spiritual realm.

❋ Having learned a lesson about his vulnerability after initial failure, the Jew can no longer be easily seduced by overt temptation. Instead, the *yetzer hara* lures him in with the fascinating permitted — that which appeals to our innocent curiosity and sense for novelty. Once caught in the trap, it is very difficult to pull away.

CHAPTER 14

❋ With the inner point of righteousness obscured by spiritual slumber, the *yetzer hara* attacks the intellect of a Jew, attempting to destroy his rational commitment to Torah and *avodas Hashem*. In this situation, one must exchange his intellectual understanding for simple faith; super-rational belief in God that is not contingent upon human reasoning.

❋ The evil forces cannot exist without drawing energy from the realms of holiness. Therefore, wherever a proliferation of spiritual darkness appears, one can rest assured that there is a large measure of holiness concealed within, waiting to be discovered and redeemed.

❋ When the motivating force of purity within a Jew is overcome with spiritual numbness and despair, it loses the ability to grasp its true essence — it ceases to recognize the holiness at its core. However, the passion of youth forever maintains the ability to penetrate beyond the surface, perceiving the true nature of the inner tzaddik's identity.

CHAPTER 15

⊛ The natural, healthy reaction to a spiritual setback is disappointment and brokenheartedness that will lead to a stronger resolve and heightened commitment. However, there are times when the devastating nature of the fall necessitates a different approach. In such a case, one must focus only on the positive, encouraging himself with whatever he can so as to ensure that he doesn't give up entirely.

⊛ One of the most useful tools along the journey toward reawakening a sense of wonder, passion, and excitement in our lives is the great universe of *"penimiyus haTorah."* The teachings of the tzaddikim who revealed the Torah's inner light have the ability to transform the way we see ourselves, the world around us, and our relationship with the King of kings. The soul of our generation intensely thirsts for these teachings. In their absence, we begin to look elsewhere to satisfy the deep sense of lack that remains.

⊛ It is important to remain ever aware of our spiritual vessels to ensure they do not become overwhelmed by an overpowering degree of intensity. Oftentimes, a constriction of the Divine illumination is required if it is to light up our lives.

CHAPTER 16

⊛ In order for the teachings of *penimiyus haTorah* to illuminate our lives, we must approach them with faith in their relevance as well as the awesome stature of the tzaddikim who revealed these teachings in their *sefarim*.

⊛ The tzaddikim of *penimiyus* who always manage to find the good in society, history, circumstances, and other people are not naïve. Rather, they are connected to an elevated perspective on reality which sees things as they truly are instead of the way they appear on the surface.

⊛ The *yetzer hara*'s primary intention in causing a Jew to sin is to utilize the sin as a means to drag the sinner into the depths of hopelessness and despair so that many more sins, and perhaps complete disengagement with Yiddishkeit, will follow.

⊛ When a Jew refuses to give in to the seductive comfort of despair, overcoming all obstacles and returning to *avodas Hashem* after a spiritual failure, he expresses the ultimate extent of his desire and brings awesome honor to Hashem.

⊛ In this world, we experience *bechirah*, absolute free choice, and are therefore responsible for the decisions we make. However, after complete *teshuvah*, it is possible for one to attain the awesome awareness that his sin was also *ratzon Hashem* — predetermined for the purpose of challenging him to battle the inclination toward despair and rise once more to the paths of *avodas Hashem*, bringing about the greatest *kevod Shamayim*.

CHAPTER 17

⊛ The two methods of progression in spiritual growth, exemplified by Yosef and Yehudah, are equally valid and both bring a special kind of honor to Hashem.

⊛ At a certain stage in his spiritual recovery, a Jew reaches a place where he feels comfortable admitting to his being an *"Adam,"* a human being caught in the struggles of this world and doing everything in his power to rise above.

CHAPTER 18

❋ There are two kinds of people in the world: "sun-people" and "moon-people." While sun-people live shallow lives of distraction from the great existential questions of being and the meaning of life, moon-people are compelled to search for depth hidden beyond the surface of this world, the Lost Princess of their lives.

❋ The derisive attitude of sun-people toward the efforts of moon-people represents the single most difficult obstacle toward the searching Jew's spiritual growth. There is nothing that challenges a moon-person's conviction more than being mocked, scorned, and ridiculed by others, especially by those who appear to be great Torah scholars who deny the validity of his journey.

❋ When a Jew gets in touch with his personal mission in this world, nothing can shake him from it. Come what may, he will find the strength to hold on to what he knows to be true.

CHAPTER 19

❋ When, faced with mighty obstacles on the path to closeness with the Master of the world, we respond with holy stubbornness, the challenges themselves come to our aid — pointing us to the next hint along this glorious scavenger hunt.

❋ Just as the existence of sounds and sights allows our soul's ability to hear and see to come to expression, so do life's difficulties and the challenges we face allow for the expression of our true greatness in overcoming these hurdles.

CHAPTER 20

❋ The moment in which, facing an awesome obstacle, a Jew's yearning for closeness with Hashem and refusal to give up moves him to tears, the gates of his salvation swing open.

❋ When a Jew falls into a state of confusion and doubts the foundational truths of his relationship with Hashem, a spirit of cool apathy blows over his life, extinguishing all passion and excitement for spiritual pursuit. Regaining certainty and absolute commitment, he is able to battle this emotional lethargy and embrace life with vitality.

❋ When one strives to attain meaning, fulfillment, and the depth of life, the very journey toward these goals already fills him with their gifts. The journey *is* the destination.

CHAPTER 21

❋ When a Jew's life is saturated with the spirit of the princess, every element of his experience is of absolute importance. His world is illuminated with the light of ultimate significance and true value.

❋ In the consciousness of the six sons, only impressive acts of holiness are reason for satisfaction and joy. To a Jew in touch with the spirit of the princess, everything is valuable — even the tiniest holy act, word, thought, or expression of desire is a fountain of the deepest and truest joy that touches the core of his being.

❋ The trait of *bitachon* is like a money pouch from which one may draw endless funds. A person who has true *bitachon* founded on simple faith may have little in terms of quantity, but the quality of the way he experiences what he has is absolutely unimaginable.

Likutei Moharan 60

*[This section is for advanced students, as in order to fully appreci-
ate the chiddushim, it requires familiarity with the sixtieth lesson
in Likutei Moharan, a lengthy and glorious revelation spanning
six-and-a-half pages of Hebrew text. Still, there is what to be
gained from studying this section even for those that are unfamiliar
with the lesson.]*

LIKUTEI MOHARAN 60 was revealed on Rosh Hashanah of the year
1806, less than two months after Rebbe Nachman first told the
story of *The Lost Princess* on 11 Av. This proximity of revelation,
in addition to clear allusions to the tale, point to the close bond
these teachings share. Throughout the generations, Breslover
mashpi'im have seen *Likutei Moharan* 60 as a sort of commentary
on The Lost Princess.

In this section, we briefly explore the manner in which segments of the lesson may be seen as referring to themes in our
story in accordance with our interpretation.

1] **60:1** — *The lesson opens with the idea that in order to attain
a lofty level of Torah wisdom, a phenomenal amount of wealth is
needed. This idea is bolstered by the fact that Moshe, who transmitted the entirety of Torah to our holy nation, was exceedingly
wealthy. The Rebbe quotes Chazal's teaching that Moshe's wealth
came from the "p'soles haluchos," the extraneous material that was
chiseled out of the luchos.*

"P'soles" carries a negative connotation, an implication of inferiority. Yet it is from there that Moshe received the great wealth necessary to achieve the deepest Torah wisdom. Perhaps we may suggest that the wisdom referred to here is the retrospective clarity of *teshuvah* associated with the world of *Binah*, *"Hisbonenus."* For such a level of understanding, great wealth is needed — a mountain of gold; wealth that comes from a place of apparent inferiority, the *p'soles* of the *luchos*. After one achieves this level of *hisbonenus*, retroactive clarity of *yedi'ah*, he realizes that the mountain itself is made of gold — the *"p'soles"* is itself what granted him his awesome wealth.

2] 60:2 — *The Rebbe explains that in order to achieve this level of wealth, one must constantly seek to ascend, to move past the constriction of a new beginning into the wide expanses of spiritual success.*

This hints to the difficulty experienced by the viceroy at the outset of his journey, the process of his proceeding from the level of desert to the level of field and ultimately to the level of forest. Later in the lesson (60:9), this progression from constriction to expansivity is linked to the symbol of the shofar which is narrow at the tip and grows progressively wider. This connects to the necessity of the viceroy to remain awake — as mentioned in Appendix A, the shofar is intended to wake us from our spiritual slumber.

3] 60:3 — *The Rebbe discusses the necessity to remove oneself from the "sheker hachein" of this world and attach to the "Ishah yiras Hashem" — the wonder and awe of inspired living.*

This segment relates to the shallowness of the six sons and the pettiness of their pursuits. Here, Rebbe Nachman is stressing the holiness of the feminine spirit of depth and the importance of engaging with this energy in one's life. In this segment, the feminine form, which — as Chazal teach — is narrow at the top and grows progressively wider, is linked to the concept of progressive growth embodied in the form of the shofar. This teaches that it is the feminine energy of depth, passion, and resolve that enables one to live a life of growth.

4] 60:4 — *The Rebbe introduces three modes of yirah/wonder connected to Chochmah, Binah, and Daas, and links them to the triumvirate of wealth.*

Throughout our story, we find a running theme of the number three. The viceroy makes three requests; a *horse*, a *servant*, and *money for expenses*. He travels through three spiritual topographies; *deserts*, *fields*, and *forests*. The headquarters of *Malchus D'Sitra Achra* is *beautiful*, *neat*, and *orderly*. The viceroy faces the princess three times; *in the palace*, after his *first fall*, after his *second fall*. He experiences three challenges: the *apple tree*, the *river of wine*, and the *giants*. There are three giants: the *Master of the Beasts*, the *Master of the Birds*, and the *Master of the Winds*. These sets of three correspond to the three modes of *yirah* and serve either to support or subvert the viceroy's attempt at attaining them.

5] 60:5 — *The Rebbe teaches that the revelation of yirah/wonder causes barren women to give birth. He mentions the birth of Yitzchak which took place on Rosh Hashanah in Sarah's old age.*

The concept of a barren woman having a child is the ultimate representation of the viceroy's ultimate success in redeeming the lost princess. A couple who is finding it difficult to conceive engages in the process of the viceroy (*Yesod/bris*) who strives valiantly to redeem the princess (*Malchus/mate*) despite many failed attempts. When a person achieves *yirah/*awe, the princess is redeemed, *Malchus* is free, and barren women can give birth. This is bound with the concept of Rosh Hashanah, for, as we have learned in Appendix A, Rosh Hashanah is the day when it is the easiest to redeem *Malchus* by accepting Hashem's sovereignty over the world and recognizing nature as a *Malchus D'Kedushah*.[1]

6] 60:6 — *Rebbe Nachman discusses different levels of spiritual slumber that derive from improper eating, and notes that one needs to waken by himself, aided by garments of holiness — deep Torah ideas concealed in stories. The Rebbe also mentions a kind of sleep in which one falls from all seventy faces of the Torah, requiring Stories from Ancient Times to wake him up.*

This is a clear reference to the viceroy's falling asleep after partaking of forbidden food and drink — particularly during his second failure, when he sleeps for seventy years and wakes up on his own, despite the princess's attempts to wake him. In addition, it describes the headscarf the princess writes on with her tears — connoting the concept of *penimiyus haTorah*, spiritual garments for the sake of disclosing the deepest wisdom — particularly the concept of *Maasios*, Stories from Ancient Times.

7] 60:8 — *The Rebbe mentions the relationship between the function of speech and the reproductive organ. He also discusses breaking the Sitra Achra's vessel of bitachon.*

Speech is a function of *Malchus*/princess, and reproduction is a function of *Yesod*/viceroy. One must seek to bring them together, to fill all bodily expressions with a purposeful spirit of meaning, awe, and wonder. The breaking of the *Sitra Achra*'s vessel of *bitachon* parallels the holy *kli* ("*yeish li kol*") of the viceroy's *bitachon*.

---

1. See also *Likutei Moharan Tinyana* 2.

Foundational Ideas
in Kabbalistic Thought:
An Introduction
to Chassidus

The following is a translated portion of an essay written by R' Hillel Zeitlin Hy"d (1871–1942), a great Chassidic thinker and writer of the pre-war era. This particular essay covers a wide range of foundational ideas in a relatively succinct and straightforward manner. The ideas discussed in this essay are absolutely fundamental to Chassidic thought. Comprehension of the material presented here will further clarify ideas referenced in The Story of Our Lives, *enabling the reader to attain a deeper understanding, as well as to begin laying the foundation for a lifetime of excursion into the works of penimiyus haTorah which are heavily founded on these basic concepts.*

This essay appears as Chapter Thirteen in R' Hillel's work on Chabad Chassidus, "Mevo L'Chassidus Ul'Darkah shel Chabad."

For the sake of further clarification of the difficult subject matter, I have added explanatory footnotes, which are marked "Ed." These notes, which are in no way exhaustive, draw heavily from R' Aryeh Kaplan's monumental introduction to Kabbalah, Innerspace.)

It goes without saying that the treatment of these deep ideas in this short essay is exceedingly basic and should be seen only as a primer for further exploration.

An Overview of The Ten *Sefiros*[1]

(*KESSER*-CROWN: "PRIOR TO the will of the King": it first arose in the primordial Divine will [the level of *"Kesser,"* the tip of the letter *"Yud"* (of the four-letter Name of Hashem, *Yud-Kei-Vav-Kei*)] — in its hiddenmost space, the aspect of *"Ayin,"* Nothingness, the hidden and wondrous pleasure of creation [*"Atik Yomin,"* the Ancient of Days] — to create the world.)[2]

---

1. The Ten *Sefiros*, or *Middos*-Traits, are the basic modes of Hashem's creative power. They constitute the inner structure and makeup of existence in all of its forms and the ways in which Hashem governs and interacts with creation. While nothing in the world takes place except through the medium of the *Sefiros*, it is important to stress that the *Sefiros are not Hashem* or Divine in any way. From Hashem's point of view, even the loftiest *Sefiros* are *"bli mah,"* lacking essential content. They are simply tools through which Hashem's unity comes to expression through the creative process. This section presents a basic overview of the Ten *Sefiros* as links in a chain of development from the loftiest point in the structure of creation (*Kesser*) all the way down to our physical reality (*Asiyah*).

I have placed the opening paragraph which introduces the *Sefirah* of *Kesser* in parenthesis because when the *Sefirah* of *Daas* is included in the accounting of the Ten *Sefiros*, as it is here, *Kesser* is not included, due to its hiddenness and utter ineffability as seen from our perspective. R' Hillel makes this point in a footnote later in the essay. If the Ten Utterances with which the world was created are related to the Ten *Sefiros* (see *Zohar* 2:14b), this explains the teaching of Chazal that the first Utterance, relating to *Kesser*, is concealed within the word *"Bereishis."* (*Bereishis Rabbah* 17:1). This is also why *teshuvah*, which utilizes the total mercy associated with the realm of *Kesser* to function, preceded the world. Indeed, as a "crown," *Kesser* sits on the head, not part of the body but rather presiding above it. As R' Hillel points out, unlike the other *Sefiros*, *Kesser* is related not to an actual letter of Hashem's name, but only to the crown, another representation of the qualitative difference between *Kesser* and the other *Sefiros*. Ed.

2. *Kesser* is the first link in the *Seder HaHishtalshelus*, the chain of development. It represents the deepest will to create, a will founded — as we shall see — in the desire to receive pleasure by bestowing goodness through self-revelation (*Ani*) which would eventually culminate in *Malchus*, the final

Chochmah-Wisdom: When this Nothingness was revealed, meaning, when this primordial Divine will descended from interiority to exteriority (from *"Atik Yomin,"* Ancient of Days,[3] to *"Arich Anpin,"* the Long Countenance[4]), *Kesser* emanated *"Chochmah."* In other words, the primordial thought — hidden, essential, and all-encompassing — was born. *Chochmah* is the hidden point — like a kind of formless material from which it is possible to create all vessels.[5]

Binah-Understanding: Afterward, *Chochmah* emanated *"Binah."* Meaning, the concealed, all-encompassing *Chochmah* expanded, spread out, became clarified, and particularized into countless details. The spring of life became an unending river, *("Rechovos haNahar"),* *"Shechintah Illa'ah,"* Leah. The spring of Divine *Chochmah* constantly gushes and the river flows, always widening

---

link in the chain. At the stage of *Kesser,* the interface between the Infinite *Ain Sof* (Creator) and creation is completely beyond our perception and thus referred to as *Ayin,* Nothingness. Here, every detail of being that will unfold in time and space exists in an undifferentiated state of potentiality. Ed.

3. This term is used in *sefer Daniel* (7:9). This level represents the interior, infinite aspect of *Kesser,* Hashem's desire and purpose for creation as it originates at a level beyond the mind's ability to grasp. Ed.

4. This term is related to the phrase *"Erech Apayim,"* which connotes mercy. This level represents the exterior, finite aspect of *Kesser* which involves a constricting of Hashem's perfect will so that we can have some conception of Him. (*Arich Anpin* represents the idea that creation is founded on mercy, on the desire to bestow goodness.) Ed.

5. The verse (*Iyov* 28:12) states, *"V'hachochmah mei'ayin timatzei."* The Kabbalists rendered this as, "And *Chochmah* emerges from the realm of *Ayin-Kesser."* The *Sefirah* of *Chochmah* relates to all basic axiomatic principles upon which creation is founded. It is related to holistic, creative, "right-brain" cognition — a burst of intellect, the creative potential associated with the male reproductive function. Related to the sense of vision (see *Avos* 2:1, *"Eizehu **chacham** ha'roeh etc."),* *Chochmah* is the ability to see the big picture in a single flash of clarity. Founded in established, super-logical realities, it is related to the *past.* Ed.

and spreading out. It is impossible to have a river without the spring that flows into it: *Chochmah* and *Binah* are therefore referred to as "*Trein rei'in d'lo misparshin* — Two friends that do not separate."[6]

Daas-Knowledge: Until this point, we are still dealing with Godliness as it envisions within itself everything that will be created — in other words, Godliness as it knows itself and only itself. In addition to explaining, widening, deepening and explicating the *Sefirah* of *Chochmah*, the *Sefirah* of *Binah* portrays everything. The *Sefirah* of *Chochmah*, the hidden point, lacks any portrayal. However, the *Sefirah* of *Binah* portrays all things from all worlds in an elevated, Divine portrayal, "He imagined in potentiality all things that would exist in actuality." But subjects are still missing from this Divine, global vision. The Divine thought is still occupied in self-vision. One level below *Binah*, the Godliness sees the subjects of the vision — the things that are outside of it. It sees things that are defined, concretized, and foundational, and its thought binds and connects with them. This *Sefirah* is the *Sefirah* of "*Daas*."

"*Daas* implies connection," say the Chassidim. That is, *Daas* is the recognition, the clarity. When we attain a clear picture of

---

6. If *Chochmah* is related to the past, *Binah* is related to the future. This spiritual function develops the potential of *Chochmah* much like a womb stores and develops the past in order to give birth to the future. *Binah* is the ability to be "*meivin davar mitoch davar*," the cognitive ability to explicate the axioms behind our thinking and derive additional information from the data received. *Binah* is related to logical, linear "left-brain" cognition, the feminine quality of breaking down big concepts into small parts and analyzing each part on its own. It is thus related to the sense of hearing ("*V'sein b'libeinu binah l'havin ul'haskil, lishmo'a...*") which can only process individual sounds ("*trei koli lo mishtama'i*"). However, because all logic is founded upon axiomatic principles, *Binah* is the river that flows from the spring of *Chochmah*, carrying its waters to heretofore unknown vistas. Without the spring, there could be no river. *Chochmah* and *Binah* (male and female energies) are thus bound together. Ed.

a given subject, we say that we "know" the subject in question. In Godliness, the *Sefirah* of *Daas* represents the Godly thought as it sees all things in eternity as subjects, picturing them with a clear portrayal, seeing all thing clearly as they stand prepared to be created.

The will of *HaMakom*, both on the level of its interiority — *"Atik,"* and the level of its exteriority — *"Arich,"* and His primordial thought (in its three revelations: the concealed *Chochmah*, the expansive *Binah*, and the clear *Daas*), preceded everything. When the final *Sefirah* of these "mental" *Sefiros*, *Sefiras HaDaas*, was revealed and the "Primordial Three" were emanated, the actual creation began, the "Seven Days of Building," the seven "traits."[7]

Chessed-Kindness: The first trait to be revealed is the *Chessed*-Kindness of God. (*Olam chessed yibaneh*, "The world is built with *Chessed*.") The deepest depths of the Godly will, just like the deepest depths of the will of every creator, is the pleasure associated with the creation. What pleasure is associated with creation in accordance with His essential nature? The desire to bestow, to display goodness, to give life. Creation and the act of creation — behold, they are one. When it is the desire of the Creator to bestow and there is no one upon whom to bestow, He creates creation; the Creator creates for Himself a creation and invests it with all of His love.

---

7. *Daas* is the interface between the blueprint of creation in the state of potential and the actualization of that vision. It represents the sum of the relationship between *Chochmah*, super-creative, axiomatic thought, and *Binah*, explication and definition of that thought to produce a plan of action that is possible to be implemented. *Daas* is the thought-process looking outward, prepared to interact with the emotions for the sake of actualizing the blueprint conceived and envisioned in the steps above it. It is on the level of *Daas* that we are able to perceive of Hashem as *mudah, yodeah, yedi'ah*, the Known, the Knower, and the Knowing. At this level of finitude and limitation, He is prepared to interact with the creation that is to be created. Ed.

Here, there is room for further contemplation. The purpose of the world, according to the *Zohar*, is *b'gin d'ishtemod'an leih*, "for the sake of making Himself known." Meaning, in order for all hidden and concealed Godly powers — closed and shut within themselves, unknown and unrevealed as if sunk in a deep slumber — to leave their awesome hiding place, from the realm of "Nothing" to the revealed "Something." And all this would be to facilitate the creation of the upper and lower worlds, which would recognize the powers of Godliness, and so that the slumber would come to wakefulness and all the clarity associated with it would be revealed.

This thought of the *Zohar* is as deep as the void. It grasps the ultimate goal of the world's craftsmanship, allowing us to know why the Infinite One caused all to emerge from the realm of "Nothingness." However, we still stand in wonder: What would be missing if everything would remain in the Godly Nothingness? Could it be that the Infinite One, "the completion of everything," would be missing something without the knowledge, gratitude, and recognition of created beings?

The Chassidim explain this thought with additional words taken from the Arizal and other *gedolei Yisrael*: "Creation is founded upon the desire of the Good to do good." "The purpose of creation was so that God could bestow goodness in accordance with His Goodness, the very pinnacle of good." "The collectivity of any causal governance until its completion as well as the collectivity of all that exists make up one matter and one order which was established by the Emanator, may His Name be blessed: the ultimate goal is goodness, perfect with all means of perfection. The condition of this order is represented by all creations and the laws of their behavior." So writes the explicator of the Arizal, the Ramchal.[8]

---

8. *K'lach Pischei Chochmah* 7, 12.

Wisdom will come easily to the wise — this very matter and this very order in the *Middos*-traits is the *Sefirah* of *Chessed*. In addition, it itself is the hidden pleasure within the Godly will. (In the order of the *Sefiros*, *Kesser*; in the order of the worlds, *Adam Kadmon*). The Creator wanted not only to reveal His power and goodness, but He wanted His creatures to experience all of the Divine Goodness. He thus emanated the first emanation.[9]

Gevurah-Judgment: However, "the Infinite One wanted to bestow goodness in a way that was perfect with all means of perfection, so that there should not even be any embarrassment on the part of its recipients. He envisioned revealing His complete unity in actuality in a way that no obstacle or lack would be found before Him. Therefore, He instituted a functionality that He governs through which all evil — the space originally given for evil to carry out its will — would return to good. Ultimately, all corruption will be rectified, and all evil will actually return to good. The unity, which is the pleasure of souls itself, will then be revealed."[10]

In other words: The Creator desired that His creation should experience not only goodness, kindness, and benevolence, but also a sense of freedom, of standing in their own dominion, the grand illusion of the worlds — as if they themselves, with their positive actions, were "creating" this goodness. The Creator wanted His creations to see themselves not "as material in the hands of the Craftsman," but rather as craftsmen themselves. The Source of good wanted that all things that would emerge and branch off

---

9. As the first of the seven lower traits associated with creation itself, *Chessed* mirrors the motivating force for creation found in the first of the upper *Sefiros*, *Kesser* — the pleasure associated with the creative act. This *Sefirah* reveals that the pleasure Hashem derives from Creation is by revealing Himself to His creations, thus giving them His greatest giftEd.

10. *K'lach Pischei Chochmah* 4.

from Him to see themselves as a "source" and a "giver," not simply as one who receives everything through kindness and benevolence.

It was for this purpose that a boundary was set for *Chessed* which would have otherwise proceeded and extended infinitely, and judgment was fashioned, punishment and reward, the possibility of evil; the Divine light as if closed up within itself. Concealment was fashioned; the boundary, a shield, and case for the Divine light of the sun. In the emanation of the worlds, we refer to this process as the *tzimtzum*, constriction, and in the emanation of the *Sefiros* we refer to it as "*Gevurah*." (*Shemesh u'magein Hashem Elokim*, "God, Hashem is a sun and a shield." Hashem's four-letter name, "*Havayah*," corresponds to *Chessed*, while "*Elokim*" denotes *Gevurah*, *tzimtzum*. Therefore, the name *Elokim* is to the name *Havayah* as a shield is to the sun — withholding its light and allowing for the illusion of separation from the Divine Source of existence.)

In this manner did *Chessed* originally emerge and extend limitlessly, and afterward, its opposite was produced, *Gevurah* which constricts and conceals.[11]

Tiferes-Beauty: From the blending of these opposites, a third trait emerged: *Tiferes*. *Tiferes* is harmony, the collectivity of both *Chessed* and *Gevurah*, a color that is formed from the blending of other colors, a sound produced from the blending of opposing voices, the trait that balances between the boundlessly extending *Chessed*, boundless goodness, and boundless *Gevurah*, judgment.

---

11. *Gevurah* and the limitation it implies represents the concealment of Hashem's presence in His creation for the purpose of freewill. If the Name Hashem, which is associated with *Chessed*, is related to the blinding illumination of the sun, the Name *Elokim*, which is associated with *Gevurah*, is a shield which shuts out that sunlight. See *Shaar HaYichud V'HaEmunah* Chapters 4–6. Ed.

In general, *Tiferes* is the truthful measurement of everything. Indeed, it is the trait of mercy and truth.[12]

The *Dorshei Reshumos* have said: *Chessed* is Avraham. (The benevolence of Avraham, his goodness, his kindness — *"Chessed l'Avraham"*); *Gevurah* is Yitzchak (*"Pachad Yitzchak"*). *Tiferes* is Yaakov (the choicest of the Avos, *"Titein emes l'Yaakov"*). "The Avos themselves are the chariot" — this is because their souls, *Chessed*, *Gevurah*, and *Tiferes*, are Godly traits, the revelation of Godly powers.[13]

Netzach-**Endurance:** *Netzach*, *Hod*, and *Yesod*, the three traits that come after *Chessed*, *Gevurah*, and *Tiferes* are the completion of all the *Sefiros*. When the Godly will, thought, and traits arrive at application, at the resolve to act, this produces *Netzach*. *Netzach* is victory, strength, might, and the application of will.

Hod-**Submission:** When the Godly desire, thought, and traits arrive at the sight and perception that everything has been done well, meaning that what was necessary to be done has indeed been accomplished, this produces *Hod*. *Hod* is beauty, revealed. According to the allusions of the Chassidim, *Hod* derives from the word *"Hodaah,"* thanks; it is Godly power thanking itself, as it were.

Yesod-**Foundation:** *Yesod* is the end of everything, the arrival of Godly power at experientiality and reality. However, this is not

---

12. *Tiferes* is to *Chessed* and *Gevurah* in the *Middos* what *Daas* is to *Chochmah* and *Binah* in the *Mochin*. It represents the balanced product of these two extremes; neither unrestrained kindness nor total restraint, but rather justice, mercy, and truth — kindness when appropriate and in the proper proportions. Ed.

13. The Avos may be seen as having represented three different colored panes of stained glass through which Hashem's light flowed to the world, revealing the three traits which underlie all of creation — *Chessed*, *Gevurah*, and *Tiferes*. Ed.

yet the revealed reality that may be seen with physical eyes, but rather the alternate, spiritual, universal reality.[14]

Malchus-**Kingship:** *Malchus*, the final *Sefirah*, is everything and nothing, nothing and everything. *Malchus* is the final revelation of all Godly powers, a revelation to Man who recognizes it as such. Man can perceive the Godly desires and Godly thoughts as they are revealed in creation and sense that even they are not all; in addition to these Godly powers there are concealed and hidden matters, that which is without name, without allusion, not even in the tip of the letter *"Yud"* (of the four-letter Name of Hashem, *Yud-Kei-Vav-Kei*). Indeed, this is not simply beyond the innermost capacity of man's thought but even beyond any thought in the world of *Atzilus*; that thought, that light, against which "even *Adam Kadmon*, which is a delicate and brilliant light, is dark."

Man perceives the order of Godly powers and feels, with a feeling closed and sealed, that which is Hidden of all things hidden. (This is knowledge only of its existence, not the knowledge of its nature.) How? By way of the trait of *Malchus*, the revealed power of creation, by way of the expression, the portrait, the vision, the actualization of the revealed.

---

14. *Yesod* represents the culmination of the creative process, the sixth day on which man, the pinnacle of creation, is formed. Everything stands at the ready, waiting to be revealed through the consciousness of man who will experience it all, fulfilling the purpose of existence. The second triad (extreme right, extreme left, and balance in the center) of *Netzach-Hod-Yesod* parallels the first triad of *Chessed-Gevurah-Tiferes*. Thus, the six days of creation, which are aligned with the first six of the seven lower Sefiros, mirror each other: On the first day (*Chessed*), light was created; on the third day (*Netzach*), the luminaries were created. On the second day (*Gevurah*), Hashem divided the waters; on the fourth day (*Hod*), fish were created. On the third day (*Tiferes*), Hashem revealed the dry land; on the sixth day (*Yesod*), the occupant of that land, man, was created. Ed.

Malchus is "the final deed, first in thought." *Kesser Elyon ihu kesser Malchus v'aleha itmar: Maggid m'reishis acharis,* "The elevated *Kesser* is the crown of kingship, concerning which is said, "He tells the end from the beginning." As if to say, the end of the *Sefiros* is bound up with their beginning. The final revelation, *Malchus,* is at the same time an even deeper beginning, for the interiority of *Kesser* is the pleasure associated with creation. This pleasure is the desire for the revelation of powers. When this pleasure is hidden in its abode, this is *Kesser.* When it comes to its final, external revelation, it is *Malchus.* The perception of the Godly presence is His "desire to rule." And when the Godliness sees the final deed which is first in thought, behold we have before us the crown of kingship, *Kesser Malchus.*"

Because *Malchus* is the revelation of the hidden Thought, it is also called "saying," "speech," and "word," just as the speech of a person reveals his hidden thoughts. And because she is revealed to humankind and via her we see and feel everything, she is the Shechinah of men (*Shechinta Tata'ah, Rachel*). Because she only comes to reveal that which is above her and is only the recipient of bounty, but not the giver (because whatever she reveals is not herself, but only her hidden and concealed Source), she is called *aspaklarya d'lo ne'hara* — a clouded window; *sihara d'leis lah migarmei klum* — the moon which has no light of her own; and *ulemta shapirta d'leis lei aynin,* a beautiful maiden who has no eyes.[15]

---

15. The last of the *Sefiros, Malchus* is the actualization of the primary purpose of creation rooted in *Kesser* and subsequently formulated and developed in the *Mochin* (*Chochmah, Binah*) and the *Middos* (*Chessed, Gevurah, Tiferes, Netzach, Hod, Yesod*). Thus, *Malchus,* which is last in action, is rooted in the very first thought. *Malchus* represents the speech of Hashem; it is through creation that He is able to communicate with us if we are wise enough to seek His presence and recognize His sovereignty. When a person approaches *Malchus* as the actualization of *Kesser,* the most elevated level in creation, one can

Allusion to the *Sefiros* in the *Shem Havayah*

WE THUS HAVE, before us, the ten *Sefiros*[16] that are reliant on Godliness like a flame to a coal. Their source is in *Stima d'chol stimin*, "Sealed of all sealed," and the governance of the world is through them and their permutations (each particular *Sefirah* contains within it all the others; each contains Ten *Sefiros*) and the permutations of those permutations (i.e., all of the aspects and levels of the *Sefiros* in their development from world to world and their revelation). The permutated permutations and particularized details of the *Sefiros* are themselves names of Hashem: the combinations of the powers in all worlds and the permutated letters in the Torah. However, they are collectively hinted to in the four letters of the *Shem Havayah*: **Yud** — The sealed and constricted point, *Chochmah*; **Hei** — Expansion, river, *Binah*; **Vav** — the **six** *Middos, Chessed, Gevurah, Tiferes, Netzach, Hod,* and *Yesod* (hinted to with the acronym *"CHaGaS NeHI"*), the letter *vav* also contains the form of both a point and a line, a flow deriving from a source, drawing from above to below; the final **Hei** — the final expansion, *Malchus*.[17]

---

utilize the human experience as a doorway into the loftiest levels of God-consciousness and spiritual revelation. Ed.

16. Even though, when *Kesser* is included, we have eleven, the *Sefiros* are indeed ten because *Kesser* is often not counted among the Sefiros due to its position above them. Other times, *Daas* is not counted among the accounting of the *Sefiros* because it is merely the revelation and actualization of *Chochmah* and *Binah*.

17. The Kabbalists teach that the four letters of the *Shem Havayah* which, as we have seen, contain the Ten *Sefiros*, also represent the process of giving charity, the true purpose of creation. According to this teaching, the first letter, *Yud*, small and simple, can be likened to a coin. The second letter, *Hei*, which is numerically equal to five, represents the hand (five fingers) that gives the coin. The third letter, *Vav*, which has the form of an arm, denotes reaching out and giving. Finally, the fourth letter, the final *Hei*, is the hand of the recipient of this

Manifestation of the Ten *Sefiros* in Soul and Body

THE TEN *SEFIROS* also manifest in the soul as ten personality traits bound to the ten Godly powers in the collective worlds which, dependent on God, are in His hand like an axe in the hand of a woodchopper. It is because these personality traits align with the collective powers of the worlds that we refer to the *Sefiros* by the names of these personality traits. Because the most perceivable revelation of the spirit is the physical body (according to Kabbalah, the body is merely a garment for the soul), and that which is more readily perceived is also that which is most easily understood, we may also refer to the *Sefiros* with terms taken from the human anatomy, in the following manner:

Chochmah — brain; *Binah* — heart; *Chessed* — right hand; *Gevurah* — left hand, *Tiferes* — torso; *Netzach* and *Hod* — the two thighs, *Yesod* — "end of the body, the mark of the holy covenant (*bris kodesh*)"; *Malchus* — the mouth (revelation, speech, utterance), "she is called Torah *sheBe'al Peh*." And when *Malchus* is bound to the *Sefirah* from which she receives, we refer to her as the "crown upon the *bris*."

Partzufim[18]

ACCORDING TO THE deep insight of the Arizal, if the body is, in fact, a garment for the soul, it must be that whatever is found

---

coin. The greatest good that Hashem gives is existence itself. The *Yud* thus represents the gift of existence itself (*Chochmah*, the coin). The first *Hei* (*Binah*) represents Hashem's hand which holds the existence He wishes to give us. The *Vav* (Six *Sefiros* from *Chessed* — *Yesod*) represents Hashem's arm reaching out to give us existence. Finally, the last *Hei* (*Malchus*) represents our hand which receives existence. Ed.

18. We have mentioned above that the *Sefiros* may be arranged into five groups: 1] *Kesser* — apex of *Yud*, 2] *Chochmah* — *Yud* itself, 3] *Binah* — initial

in the body is also found in the soul, only in a spiritual sense. If so, aside from the ten primary powers of the spirit, each *Sefirah* contains particular details of the organs; 248 spiritual limbs and 365 spiritual sinews, that is, 613 streams in all. And now that we have learned that the powers of the worlds are arranged in alignment with the soul of a person, it follows that there exists in every world, in every *Sefirah*, and in every trait the entire countenance of Man; that is, 613 channels, delicate and spiritual.

Based on this, the Arizal arranged the *Sefiros* in the order of *Partzufim* — archetypal personas. For example, the *Sefirah* of *Chochmah* is not simply a given expression in the soul or the worlds, but is rather a complete countenance, an entire structure complete with elevated limbs, entirely spiritual, which are arranged in the form of the human body.

This is the order of the *Partzufim*:

The first *Partzuf* is **Arich Anpin** (or simply *Arich* for short), "Long Face"; the primary collectivity, the externality of the Divine will (as opposed to its interiority, which is *Atik*); **Kesser** with all of the Godly powers included and hidden within it. (*Kesser* is called

---

Hei, 4] Six *Sefiros* from *Chessed* through *Yesod* — *Vav* 5] *Malchus* — final *Hei.* In an earlier iteration involved in the creation of the Ten *Sefiros* referred to as *Olam HaNekudim,* the *Sefiros* existed as ten distinct entities which could not interact with each other, neither giving nor receiving. When Hashem's light filled these primitive spiritual vessels, they were overwhelmed and shattered in what is known as *Sheviras HaKeilim,* "The Shattering of the Vessels." When the *Sefiros* were rebuilt in a stage referred to as *Olam HaBerudim* or *Olam Ha-Tikkun,* they were created as archetypal personas, parallels to the human experience of developmental relationships referred to as "*Partzufim.*" In this state, the *Sefiros* were built in the image of humankind which includes both male and female, giving and receiving. They could then earn what they were receiving by giving as well as receiving. Only in this way were they able to endure. The *Sefiros* as *Partzufim* embody the dynamic process involved in Hashem's unfolding plan for creation. They are constantly interacting with each other in different ways to execute this plan. Ed.

"*TaRaCH amudei ohr,*" 620 pillars of light; 613 mitzvos and 7 rabbinic commandments.)

The second *Partzuf* is **Abba**, "Father." That is, "the father of the world," elevated *Chochmah*, the giver, together with all forces included in it.

The third *Partzuf* is **Ima**, "Mother." That is, *Binah*, the elevated expansion, the *Sefirah* which is explicated to reveal all the details of her properties.

The fourth *Partzuf* is **Zei'er Anpin**, "Small Face," that is, the collective of Godly traits. This includes all six traits: *Chessed, Gevurah, Tiferes, Netzach, Hod,* and *Yesod.* Because the construction of the world is founded upon these six traits (the six days of creation, the six directions), their collectivity mirrors the very first collectivity, *Kesser.* "*Zei'er Anpin*" aligns with "*Arich Anpin*" — a miniature world aligned with a full-sized world.

The fifth *Partzuf* is **Nukva d'Zei'er**, "Female Mate of *Zei'er Anpin.*" She is the trait of *Malchus* which receives from all the traits above her and from that which is above the traits — of herself, she has nothing at all. Therefore, she only has an elevation when she cleaves to that which sustains her, "*Zei'er Anpin,*" the upper *Middos.*

L'sheim Yichud Kudsha B'rich Hu u'Shechintei

AT THE TIME that "*Zei'er Anpin*" and "*Nukva d'Zei'er*" are completely unified — when the external revelation of the worlds is bound with its inner, Godly Source — there occurs a unification between *Malchus* and her Beloved (referred to as the unification between *Malchus* and *Zei'er* or the "*Yichud Kudsha B'rich Hu u'Shechintei*" — in Kabbalah, the term "*Kudsha Brich Hu*" is an aspect of *Zei'er Anpin*).

Because all of the traits draw from the Godly mental forces, there occurs, at the time of the Shechinah's unification, the unification of all Godly powers hinted to in the mystery of the unification between *"Yud-Hei"* and *"Vav-Hei."* That is, the unification of *Chochmah* and *Binah*, or *Abba* and *Ima* (which are hinted to in the letters ***"Yud-Hei"***) with *Zei'er Anpin* and its *Nukva* (which are hinted to in the letters ***"Vav-Hei"***). How does this unification take place? *Al yedei hahu tamir v'ne'elam* — "By way of that which is hidden and concealed," by way of the *Ayin*, the Godly Wonder, which sustains them.[19]

But *Malchus* is not always unified with her Beloved. There is an aspect in which the external revelation of the spiritual worlds is perceived as an independent existence, a separate being detached from any Godly Source; for that was the purpose of the *tzimtzum*-constriction and *Sheviras HaKeilim* which came only to make this separation possible (so that man, with his thoughts, words, and actions, could reunite the separated). The primary exile of the Shechinah was thus produced through the natural development of creation. After this, the *Shechinah-Malchus* was continually banished in exile after exile: through the sin of the *Eitz HaDaas*, through the sins of each person, and the sins of Am Yisrael as a whole. She is in exile at all times — in every detail, in every action big or small; in every distancing of nature, the external revelation of the spiritual worlds, from its hidden Source.

And when the Shechinah is distant from Her Beloved, she gives life to all forms of *Kelipos* (negative forces) and fears — to all evil in both natural and moral realms. Man and all living beings are then entangled in the complex web of incorrect premises and all natural difficulties which give room for the wicked to swallow up the righteous, "like fish trapped in an evil net and birds held in a cage, trapped by humans."

---

19. This is the true explanation of that which is said before every mitzvah: *L'sheim yichud Kudsha B'rich Hu U'Shechintei, l'yachada sheim Yud-Kei b'Vav-Kei, b'yechuda shlim al y'dei hahu tamir v'ne'elam...,* "For the sake of the unification between Kudsha Brich Hu and Shechintei, to unify 'Yud-Kei' with 'Vav-Kei,' by means of that which is hidden and concealed...."

Therefore, there is no other recourse for one who seeks to be free of the wicked net of the overpowering external influence but to return *Malchus* to Her Beloved, which is to return the external revelation and the confused mass of disparate premises to the Godly traits — by way of thought, speech, and actions of holiness and purity.

At the time Godly revelation appears, that illusion we call "nature" is immediately nullified, and man takes refuge in God, his Rock and Redeemer Who lifts him up and elevates him above all happenstance and assumed causes.

A Letter from Berel the Chassid

R' Hillel Zeitlin

The following is a translation of an essay written by R' Hillel Zeitlin Hy"d (1871–1942), a unique figure in the Yiddish literary community of pre-war Poland. Raised in a Chabad family, R' Hillel was recognized as a child genius and an elevated soul at a very young age. After a years-long foray into the secular world of the "Haskalah," R' Hillel forsook that lifestyle and returned to religious observance and Torah study, which he wrote about extensively and intensely engaged with until his murder in the Warsaw ghetto by the hands of the accursed Nazis, wrapped in his tallis and tefillin and holding a copy of the Zohar HaKadosh. Hashem yinkom damo.

In this highly autobiographical piece, R' Hillel captures the struggle, joy, loneliness, and inner drama of "an elevated soul." The reader will notice many subtle references to major themes discussed in our commentary on The Lost Princess.

DO YOU KNOW who I am? I am Berel the Chassid. Sometimes dark like the blackness of night, sometimes shining like the light of day. Sometimes descending and buried in the ground, and sometimes lifted beyond; soul hovering in the upper realms, heart becomes light, eyes shining, feet carrying themselves. I sing the

Rebbe's *niggun* then, I burst into a little dance, entirely filled with happiness and rejoicing.

I am often lost among barren paths and desolate deserts, searching for a way nearby that will lead to the Mashiach. It always appears to me as if it is here, here, I can see it! Here, I have found it!

I can perceive from afar something which appears to be a small flame. It is likely that this is the light of Mashiach. I quicken my pace and draw close, only to find a piece of rotten wood, the trick of a scoffer.

I walk and I walk, I search and I seek, but I do not find a path or a way. I have grown old upon my footsteps, tired and sick, broken and shattered.

In this moment a desire arises within me to forsake this journey entirely. What is this eternal search?

The One Who sits in heaven laughs. Is God is mocking us? Relishing it all, in His hidden places?

He is hidden, but we desire to find Him. We are obligated to reveal Him.

And so I continue to roam, wandering wherever my eyes lead me.

In my searching and wandering I am oftentimes trapped by mountains of darkness, I become acquainted with all forces of impurity, defiled by all kinds of impure desires and sins.

All kinds of *Kelipos* (impure forces) call to me: "Come to us! Come with us! All the treasures of heaven and earth are found in our hands! We will give you everything, and the crown of the Satan shall nod to you."

But in that very moment, I suddenly hear the *Bas Kol* cry out, "Return, my wayward children!"

It is the *Bas Kol* which emerges day after day, calling for *teshuvah*. Has anybody ever heard it? Not a single person. If nobody hears it, why then does it emerge?

This *Bas Kol* manifests in the thoughts of *teshuvah* which give no rest even to the greatest sinner.

It is only that man makes it as if he doesn't hear, as if he doesn't know. He magnifies his sin and sinks further into the forty-nine gates of impurity solely to banish the thoughts of *teshuvah*, to quiet the voice.

But my ears hear this *Bas Kol* very well. My heart feels these thoughts of *teshuvah* in all of their intensity. No attempt at banishing them will help, no attempt at quieting them will work.

I am hereby notifying all scoffers: Leave me. Leave! You have not yet found the address you seek. I have no connection with you.

And so I once more take up the walking stick in my hand, sling my sack over my shoulder, and proceed to seek out different ways.

In this moment it is clear to me that I am obligated to search. This is the reason the Creator fashioned His world, so that man would constantly search but never find.

The craft of searching is a unique endeavor. Man never finds; he searches eternally. And the more he searches, the more he is able to stand with courage against all kinds of difficult trials, the more he succeeds in these tests, the more he rises and is strengthened, the more he becomes transformed into a better and more refined person.

Without question, one will fall quite frequently. Yes, at times one will even break one's bones. No amount of effort or wisdom can change this, because this is the way it needs to be. If you want to rise higher and higher, on and on, you are going to need to also fall from time to time.

The opponents to the Chassidic way, those who follow the path of *Mussar*, say that I am not balanced. Even our own men call me "the failure." Of course, both groups are fools.

It's one thing to hear from the opponents, about whom much has already been said. Yes, it has already been known for some time that these men cry only when whipped and laugh only when tickled... How could they possibly understand a person who laughs and cries, experiences ecstasy and sadness, searches for something but doesn't find, constantly rolls around, never finding peace? These people understand only one thing: sit next to the fireplace, bind yourself to the Gemara day and night, gather mitzvos upon mitzvos, more and more mitzvos, gather a tremendously large bundle and you will be able to trade it all in for a choice cut of the *Leviyasan* in the World to Come.

For all intents and purposes, they are what they call in your language "Capitalists." The only difference is that the capitalists gather this-worldy capital while these gather the capital of the World to Come.

But even our own men, those who are expected to know and understand — even they have failed to comprehend this.

Sure, they have learned that "descent is for the purpose of ascent." They even know what is written in the *sefarim hakedoshim* that the tzaddik himself must frequently descend from his elevated level. But they don't truly understand the definition of "descent."

They think that "descent" means to fall from the chair to the floor, that "ascent" means to climb up to the roof. However, the truth of the matter is that "descent" means to fall from the highest mountaintop to the very bottom of the deepest pit and yet, if there is still some lifeforce left in you, to try to dig and proceed, to rise even higher.

But they are not able to understand things like this. Indeed, our men are *yarei Shamayim*, but with limited vision.

How does the song go?

> *Mother sent us to gather walnuts*
> *To gather walnuts.*
> *Oh, how high are the walnuts!*
> *Oh, how short are the children!*
> *They do not reach.*
> *They do not reach.*

Yes, elevated visions are not fit for their immature minds. They understand everything in a constricted way: a small *aveirah*, a small mitzvah; a small act of mischief and then immediately "*Hashiveinu!*", the return. One, two, three and they are finished!

They will not be able to attain *Mochin D'Gadlus*, expanded consciousness. They are able to understand neither big *aveiros* nor big mitzvos, they do not understand how it is possible to be within the *Kelipos* and yet to remain alive.

All of this is beyond their understanding. You can argue with them day and night in the hope that they will attain broad visions, but you will accomplish nothing. It appears that for this, one needs to have been born with an elevated soul.

But very few elevated souls descend to our world. Generally, immature souls descend; impoverished, scared, mediocre. Go try speaking to them about lofty worlds!

It is possible that they will, at times, understand that hidden worlds exist, but they will never understand their makeup, their inner nature.

They can even be great Kabbalists, but they will only be experts in the names of the worlds alone. Even if they recognize all of those places, they will never truly decode the composition of those worlds. This is comparable to a person who sits in Warsaw and knows that there exists a city called Paris. Even if he will learn the names of all the Parisian streets and attractions from books, this does nothing to change the reality that he has never been there. They speak about elevated worlds, hidden worlds, but they were never there. What, then, is the big wonder when they don't understand what "descent" means, what "ascent" means, what is the nature of this eternal search after the *nekudas ha'emes*, the kernel of truth?

And so I have left them all behind, both the warm Chassidim as well as their cold detractors, and I have embarked to wander across the expanse of the globe.

THE LOST PRINCESS
PRINCIPLES

In an effort to distinguish this work from the vast corpus of inspirational literature often superficially perused and quickly forgotten, a comprehensive webinar course, "The Lost Princess Principles for Inspired Living," has been created to accompany the present volume. This course presents a complete program for guided group exploration, allowing for maximum comprehension and lasting internalization of this book's foundational concepts.

The twenty-five Lost Princess Principles that sit at the core of this program are deeply transformative and liberating truths containing the fundamental messages of *The Story of Our Lives*, distilled from its sixty-six Life Lessons. Meeting virtually twice a week via Zoom for the seven weeks of the program to work through the study guide together with R' Yaakov Klein, the members of the LPP course explore these principles together in great depth. Personal reflection, exploration of original Hebrew sources, guided exercises, and focused discussion with fellow journeyers along the narrow bridge of Olam HaZeh enable the lessons of The Lost Princess to settle into the reader's heart and manifest in the reality of his or her day-to-day life. The LPP course provides a breathtaking wealth of guidance, encouragement, clarity, and deep Torah wisdom enabling us to live freer, healthier, and more passionate lives.

If you are interested in joining a group of like-minded Jews on a search for the soul of our tradition, please register online at LPITorah.org today!

LOST
PRINCESS
INITIATIVE

Rediscovering the Soul
of Our Tradition

Searching for the Lost Princess of Connection

In the early 1800s, Rebbe Nachman of Breslov began telling his legendary stories with a uniquely beautiful tale, "The Lost Princess." The tzaddik's tale tells of the long and glorious journey of a viceroy who devotes his life to locating a princess abducted from her father's palace and returning her home. The Breslover *mashpi'im* explain that the princess represents the soul, faith, passion, inwardness, and wonder of youth that have become lost over time in the murkiness of the modern experience. The viceroy represents the souls of our generation, wandering through the post-modern darkness on a mission to reclaim the passion of youth.

As individuals and as a community, we have set our eyes on a life that is filled with wonder, illumination, and excitement. We long for an *avodas Hashem* that is bursting with a tangible feeling of closeness with our Creator. Yes, we are all searching for the princess, the soul of life. Founded on twenty-five core principles derived from *The Story of Our Lives*, the **Lost Princess Initiative** seeks to provide a compass for this essential search, using the life-changing teachings of our greatest tzaddikim to guide us toward our goal.

A Little History

By all estimations, our generation is experiencing the final era before the coming of Mashiach. This special time is known as *ikvisa d'meshicha*, "the heels of Mashiach," as those with discerning ears can already begin to hear the approaching footsteps of the final redemption. However, the words *"ikvisa d'meshicha"* hold a secondary implication as well. Like the heel, the souls of our generation are particularly susceptible to spiritual numbness and emotional detachment. The awesome potential for spiritual elevation in our time is matched by a deluge of impurity, lowliness, and despair. But there is yet a ray of hope, shining through the darkness of our times. In His overwhelming mercy and love, Hashem sent the remedy before the disease set in.

In the early 1700s, Hashem brought an exalted soul into the world to illuminate the darkness of broken and battered European Jewry. This soul was Rebbe Yisrael Baal Shem Tov, "the light of the seven days of creation." Following many years of intense Torah study and prayer, the holy Baal Shem Tov began to reveal deep and liberating Torah teachings he had received from the upper realms, eventually founding the Chassidic movement whose various tzaddikim and dynasties would revolutionize European Jewry in the coming decades. Two generations later, a great-grandson of the Baal Shem Tov, Rebbe Nachman of Breslov, continued the work of his forebear by re-establishing the spiritual foundations of Chassidus that had become obscured by the garments of institutionalization. It was the teachings of these exalted masters that would support a spiritually exhausted Jewish nation as they took the last few steps toward the finish line of history. It was the consciousness these tzaddikim yearned to foster that would prepare *Am Yisrael* for the final redemption.

Just a few short years ago, the term "Chassidus" was a fairly uncommon expression. There were certainly "Chassidim," and various "Chassidic courts," but Chassidus as a philosophy, as a comprehensive path toward closeness with Hashem, had not yet risen to the forefront of our consciousness as a community. Today, all of this has changed. Looking past the externalities of a heavily institutionalized movement to tap the eternal spirit of the masters and teachings that sit at its core, many thousands of Jews from all walks of life have begun to taste from the bubbling spring of the holy Baal Shem Tov. Across the entire spectrum of Orthodoxy, there is a deep thirst for the teachings of Chassidus and the life-giving waters of clarity, depth, beauty, and relevance that flow forth from the foundational works of the early masters.

R' Yaakov Klein founded the Lost Princess Initiative in May, 2020 for the purpose of encouraging this national discovery of Hashem's remedy to our generation's ills. Through its various projects, this broad initiative aims to foster a Yiddishkeit that is deep, passionate, sincere, joyous, inspirational, positive, vibrant, profound, individualistic, broad-minded, healthy, and eminently relevant. LPI brings the leading lights of this silent revolution under a single banner, consolidating talent, vision, and energy for the purpose of amplifying the communal voice that is continually crying out for a deeper way of engaging with our tradition. With Rebbe Nachman's tale as our guide, we pray that the dawn of Mashiach will continue to spread its healing rays over our community and that the study of Chassidus and *penimiyus haTorah* facilitated by LPI will bring both personal and general redemption for our holy nation.

Our Projects

⊛ Engaging Chassidic content disseminated via social media channels

⊛ Rich online resources for further Chassidic exploration and study

⊛ Lost Princess Principles webinar course

⊛ Lost Princess Publishing

* Lost Princess *Minyanim*
* "My Journey to the Princess" Documentation Project
* *Hachanah* Events
* Inspirational merchandise

Our Vision

At LPI, we believe that engagement with the inner light of Torah will transform the consciousness of our generation and solve many of today's difficulties, symptoms of having lost touch with the princess of deep, soulful, and inspired living. We envision a positive Yiddishkeit experience filled with the consciousness of Hashem's love and centered around fortifying our essential relationship with Him through the Torah and its diverse array of contact points with the Divine.

Our Mission

LPI is an educational platform dedicated to increasing awareness of and engagement with the study of Chassidus and *penimiyus ha-Torah* via a variety of mediums. Our mission is to spread a message of depth, soulfulness, God-consciousness, hope, and unity to Jews of all ages via premium in-print publications, engaging social media content and campaigns, and inspirational live events featuring our *mashpi'im* and musicians.

For more, please visit LPITorah.org!

לעיילוי נשמות

הורינו מורינו

ר׳ **יחזקאל** בן ר׳ **יצחק אהרן**

ר׳ **חנניה** בן ר׳ **דוד**

ר׳ **דניאל** בן ר׳ **יונה**

מרת **איטה מרים** בת ר׳ **דוד הכהן**

ר׳ **נח אברהם** בן החבר **חיים יהודה הכהן**

מרת **חיה לאה** בת ר׳ **משה**

הרב **משה** בן ר׳ **שלמה יעקב**

אחינו

רחמים יעקב שמעון בן **חנה**

דבורה דינה בת ר׳ **דניאל**

מרת **שרה גיטל** בת ר׳ **צבי**

רב **מרדכי מנחם מנדל** בן רב **דוד אריה**

מרת **אלטא חוה העניששא** בת ר׳ **יעקב צבי**

נכדינו

אלישע ברוך טוביה בן ר׳ **אורי מנחם** יבלחט״א

The inner essence of

Reb Shlomo Zalman Cheshin *z"l*

was a lighthouse shining through the dark
of night to all the troubled souls
lost in the stormy seas of life.

He was the quintessential *"Ner l'echad, ner l'elef"*;
his own candle shined for hundreds, if not
thousands of souls with the perfect
messages at the most crucial times:
"You are amazing"; "Hashem loves you";
"Let not your past overwhelm you —
look forward, not backward."

With the sheer power of his confidence and
simchas hachayim, Reb Shlomo opened the windows
of your heart and mind so that Hashem's light could
shine into your soul. Like a lifeguard pulling the
weakened swimmer to shore, he let you hold on
to him until your strength returned and you
were able to stand on your own.

This book, too, is a
product of his heart, mind, and soul.
Our lives were deeply touched by Reb Shlomo's
warmth and friendship. And for that,
we are forever grateful.

משפחת ברוך וצירל קליין

Dedicated in memory of

Isaac *ben* **Abraham**

Dan Feinstein

Dedicated as a merit for the
speedy *refuah sheleimah*
of *kol cholei Yisrael.*

Pessi and Moishe Wieder
and family

Dedicated in loving memory
of our grandparents

Diane (Devorah Kenya)

and

Jim (Yaakov Tuvia) Kauders *z"l*

Who exemplified love, determination,
integrity, and selflessness.
The light of their souls inspired
all of us and will always radiate.

With love,

Moishe and Avital Gottesman

DEDICATION ON CHAI ELUL 5780

The first Rebbe Nachman story I read was "The Rabbi and the Only Son." I think that for many people who discover Rebbe Nachman, this story describes a need and an experience that resonates deeply. Now that I have been blessed to be a father, I hope to assist my children in finding their path to Hashem and to Tzadikim. I want to thank R' Yaakov Klein for working so hard to bring us all closer to finding the Lost Princess, each one for ourselves, in our way. May Hashem help all children keep looking for themselves and for the Tzadik.

In honor of my boys

Aharon Yechezkel Ben Xenia Devorah

and Hillel Elimelech Ben Xenia Devorah

Please Hashem, don't let me get in their way.

Zev Alexander